AUTHORITATIVE GUIDE
—— TO SELF-HELP RESOURCES ——
IN MENTAL HEALTH

THE CLINICIAN'S TOOLBOX™
A Guilford Series

EDWARD L. ZUCKERMAN, Series Editor

Authoritative Guide to Self-Help Resources in Mental Health

John C. Norcross, PhD
John W. Santrock, PhD
Linda F. Campbell, PhD
Thomas P. Smith, PsyD
Robert Sommer, PhD
Edward L. Zuckerman, PhD

THE GUILFORD PRESS
New York   London

© 2000 The Guilford Press; revisions © 2001
A Division of Guilford Publications, Inc.
72 Spring Street, New York, NY 10012
www.guilford.com

Printed in the United States of America

This book is printed on acid-free paper.

Last digit is print number: 9 8 7 6 5 4 3 2

Library of Congress Cataloging-in-Publication Data is available from the Publisher.

ISBN 1-57230-506-1 (cloth); ISBN 1-57230-580-0 (pbk.)

John C. Norcross, PhD, is a professor and former chair of psychology at the University of Scranton and a clinical psychologist in part-time practice. Author of more than 150 scholarly publications, he has cowritten or edited 12 books, including the *Insider's Guide to Graduate Programs in Clinical and Counseling Psychology*, the *Psychologists' Desk Reference*, and *Systems of Psychotherapy: A Transtheoretical Analysis*. He has served as president of the American Psychological Association's Division of Psychotherapy and on the editorial boards of a dozen journals. Dr. Norcross has received many awards for his professional contributions, including being named the Pennsylvania Professor of the Year by the Carnegie Foundation and being elected as a Distinguished Practitioner in the National Academies of Practice.

John W. Santrock, PhD, taught at the University of Charleston and the University of Georgia before joining the psychology department at the University of Texas at Dallas, where he is a professor and former department chair. He was recently a member of the editorial board of *Developmental Psychology*. Dr. Santrock has authored multiple textbooks, including *Psychology*, *Life-Span Development*, *Child Development*, *Children*, *Adolescence*, and *Human Adjustment*, and is the coauthor of *Your Guide to College Success*.

Linda F. Campbell, PhD, is an associate professor and director of the training clinic in the Department of Counseling and Human Development at the University of Georgia. She is coauthor of several books and scholarly publications, editor of *The Psychotherapy Bulletin* (a publication of the American Psychological Association's Division of Psychotherapy), and member of several editorial boards. Dr. Campbell is chair of the Georgia Psychological Association Ethics Committee and Council Representative to the American Psychological Association. She has received several awards for service to her state association and for excellence in teaching from the University of Georgia.

Thomas P. Smith, PsyD, is a licensed psychologist in the Counseling Center at the University of Scranton. As a clinician for more than 20 years, he has practiced in both outpatient and inpatient psychiatric settings. An adjunct faculty member, he has taught graduate psychology and counseling courses for both the University of Scranton and Marywood University. He has also chaired a county task force on juvenile violence in schools and has cowritten a chapter on enhancing adherence in the *Psychologists' Desk*

Reference. He recently completed his PsyD requirements in clinical psychology from the Philadelphia College of Osteopathic Medicine.

Robert Sommer, PhD, is a professor and former chair of psychology at the University of California, Davis. Author of 11 books and numerous articles, he has done research on autobiographies of mental health clients for almost four decades. He is president of the American Psychological Association's Division of Population and Environmental Psychology. Dr. Sommer received a Fulbright Fellowship to Estonia, a Career Research Award from the Environmental Design Research Association, a Research Award from the California Alliance for the Mentally Ill, the Kurt Lewin Award, and an honorary doctorate from Tallinn Pedagogical University.

Edward L. Zuckerman, PhD, was in full-time independent practice of clinical psychology for almost 20 years and taught psychology courses at the University of Pittsburgh and Carnegie Mellon University for a total of 25 years. Dr. Zuckerman is currently a consultant to Social Security Disability Determination Division and editor of The Clinician's Toolbox series for The Guilford Press. He is the author of the *Clinician's Thesaurus*, a guidebook for writing reports, and *The Paper Office*, a manual for improving ethical and legal practices.

ACKNOWLEDGMENTS

This massive project required the generous contributions of a number of people over the years. First, we especially acknowledge the 2,500-plus clinical and counseling psychologists who took the time from their busy schedules to complete the lengthy questionnaires associated with our five national studies. Second, we publicly thank Dr. John W. Santrock for collegially sharing the data and wisdom gleaned from his pioneering work, *The Authoritative Guide to Self-Help Books*. We are delighted that he is coauthoring this volume with us. Third, we genuinely appreciate the diligent assistance of five research assistants at the University of Scranton who shepherded the three latest national studies through their entire development—from gathering prodigious lists of books and movies, through creating the questionnaires, to stuffing and mailing 6,000 questionnaires, inputting all the returns, and conducting the data analyses. Heidi Bechtoldt, Laurie Wyckoff, Melyssa Pokrywa, Mary Santarelli, and Bill Alarcon survived and thrived throughout the 9-month ordeal.

We each would also like to acknowledge the individuals and organizations who assisted us personally. John Norcross appreciates the continuing financial support of the University of Scranton, specifically the Department of Psychology and the Undergraduate Research Stipend Program. John Santrock is grateful to the many students who tracked down books, references, and reviews and to Bert Moore, Dean of the School of Human Development, University of Texas at Dallas, who generously supported the first national study. Linda Campbell expresses her appreciation to her husband, Alan, and to her mother for their support. She is also grateful to Betty Tanner and Tracy Talmadge for their assistance in accessing materials for this book and to her departmental colleagues who pursue and value scholarship. Tom Smith appreciates the expert library guidance of Joseph Fennewald and the word processing marvels of Sandra Toy. Bob Sommer credits Sheila Layton for helping him collect information on many autobiographies.

Last but not least, a rousing thanks to the good folks at The Guilford Press. Seymour Weingarten, Editor-in-Chief, and Kitty Moore, Executive Editor, continually expressed confidence in the project and translated their enthusiasm into concrete suggestions that improved the final product.

CONTENTS

AUTHORITATIVE GUIDE
——— TO SELF-HELP RESOURCES ———
IN MENTAL HEALTH

CHAPTER 1

Introduction to Self-Help in Mental Health

You have probably heard about or read one or more of the following self-help books:

Feeling Good by David Burns
What Color Is Your Parachute? by Robert Bolles
Dianetics by L. Ron Hubbard
Infants and Mothers by T. Berry Brazelton
The Courage to Heal by Ellen Bass and Laura Davis
Ageless Body, Timeless Mind by Deepak Chopra
The Dance of Anger by Harriet Lerner
When Bad Things Happen to Good People by Harold Kushner
Reclaiming the Inner Child by Jeremiah Adams
Your Perfect Right by Robert Alberti and Michael Emmons
The Silent Passage by Gail Sheehy
Men Are from Mars, Women Are from Venus by John Gray
Listening to Prozac by Peter D. Kramer
Winning through Intimidation by Robert Ringer
You Just Don't Understand by Deborah Tannen
Don't Sweat the Small Stuff . . . and It's All Small Stuff by Richard Carlson
How to Win Friends and Influence People by Dale Carnegie
The Power of Positive Thinking by Norman Vincent Peale
The Battered Woman by Lenore Walker
Emotional Intelligence by Daniel Goleman
Dr. Atkins' New Diet Revolution by Robert C. Atkins
The 7 Habits of Highly Effective People by Steven Covey

You have probably also seen several of the following movies on family relationships and mental health topics:

The Color Purple
The Prince of Tides
Cat on a Hot Tin Roof
Days of Wine and Roses
The War of the Roses
As Good as It Gets
9½ Weeks
Good Will Hunting
Ordinary People
What about Bob?
Rain Man
When Harry Met Sally
Field of Dreams
Shine
Dead Poets Society
The Piano

Each of these books has been at or near the top of national best-seller lists, and each of the movies has been seen by millions of people. Are they good self-help books and movies? That is, do they provide accurate information? Do they help individuals cope effectively with problems? The consensus of mental health experts in the United States is that one-third of these self-help books and movies are *not* effective self-help resources; even though they were best-sellers and top-grossing films, most mental health experts view them negatively. The other two-thirds of the books and movies on this list are excellent self-help materials. In this book, we tell which are the good ones, which are the bad ones, and why.

SELF-HELP RESOURCES

Self-help materials have become an indispensable source of psychological advice for millions of Americans. Whether we want to improve our marital lives, control our anger, gain self-fulfillment, overcome depression, become better parents, lose weight, solve sexual problems, cope with stress, recover from addictions, or tackle another problem, there is a self-help book.

Our preoccupation with self-improvement is nothing new; it's been around since the Bible. Although not exactly known as a self-help book author, Benjamin Franklin dispensed self-improvement advice in *Poor Richard's Almanac*: "Early to bed, early to rise, makes a man healthy, wealthy, and wise." In the 19th century, homemakers read *Married Lady's Companion* for help in managing their houses and families. In the 1930s, Dale Carnegie's *How to Win Friends and Influence People* made him the aspiring business-man's guru. And the 1950s brought us Maxwell Malty's *Psychocybernetics* and dozens of marriage manuals.

Interest in understanding the human psyche and how to improve it heated up in the 1960s and 1970s and was accompanied by a glut of self-help books. *I'm OK, You're*

OK and *Your Erroneous Zones* were read by millions of Americans and made fortunes for their authors. They turned out to be only the tip of the iceberg.

The advent of popular films, the information revolution, and the ascendancy of the Internet have given rise to a dizzying diversity of self-help resources. Millions routinely go to the movies, surf the net, and attend self-help groups for edification and assistance. This book is designed to guide you through this morass of self-help information—and misinformation—by providing quality ratings and brief descriptions of five types of self-help materials: self-help books, autobiographies, movies, Internet sites, and self-help/support groups.

1. Self-Help Books

The self-help book market has yielded an overwhelming, bewildering array of choices. Self-help books appear at the rate of about 2,000 a year (Rosen, 1993), and they routinely occupy prominent places on best-seller lists. Books are written on every conceivable topic, as the following list of titles vividly demonstrates:

> *Dance Naked in Your Living Room*
> *How to Juggle Women Without Getting Killed or Going Broke*
> *I Lost 600 Pounds: I Can Sure Help You Lose 30*
> *Change Your Underwear, Change Your Life*
> *Dated Jekyll, Married Hyde*
> *Boldly Live as You Have Never Lived Before: Life Lessons from Star Trek*
> *The Fairy Godmother's Guide to Dating and Mating*
> *Celestial 911—Call with Your Right Brain for Answers*
> *Don't Bite the Apple 'til You Check for Worms*

The soaring volume of self-help books makes the question of quality—which one will work?—increasingly urgent. More than 95% of self-help books are published without any research documenting their effectiveness (Rosen, 1987, 1993). We hope that they will work, but we do not have any systematic evidence to indicate that they do.

So how do people select self-help books? Until this book—the *Authoritative Guide to Self-Help Resources in Mental Health*—people have largely relied on the opinions of friends, their minister, their doctor, their therapist, guest authors on talk shows, a salesperson at a bookstore, or the promotional information on the book's cover. But even personal contact with professionals, such as physicians and psychologists, provides limited information about which book to purchase. Self-help books have been published at such an astonishing pace that even the well-intentioned professional has difficulty keeping up with them. The professional may be well-informed about books in one or two areas, such as depression or anxiety, but may know little about books in other areas, such as eating disorders, women's issues, relaxation, and parenting.

Some self-help books have been written by professionals who have masterful insights about who we are, what we are about, and how we can improve our lives. Others, to put it mildly, leave a lot to be desired. As a concerned psychologist lamented, "Many self-help books are not worth the paper they are printed on." With literally thousands of books on the market, we wanted to know what the leading psychologists in the United States think are the best and the worst self-help books.

After all, restaurant critics inform us which restaurants are superb and which ones to avoid; automobile guides educate us about the gems and the lemons; and consumer magazines dispense advice on which refrigerators, computers, televisions, and VCRs to buy. Considering the immense number of self-help books, a guide to them based on professional judgments by mental health experts is badly needed. This book is that guide.

The good news from research is that self-help programs can be quite effective. Several reviews of the literature have determined that the effectiveness of self-help program substantially exceeds that of no treatment (Kurtzweil, Scogin, & Rosen, 1996; Scogin, Bynum, Stephens, & Calhoon, 1990). For example, in one analysis of the effectiveness of 40 self-help studies, effect sizes for self-help were nearly as large as for therapist-assisted treatments (Gould & Clum, 1993). Fears, depression, headaches, and sleep disturbances were especially amenable to self-help approaches.

Similarly, *bibliotherapy*—a fancy way of saying using self-help books—has been shown to be valuable for many, but not all, adults. In one thorough review (Marrs, 1995), bibliotherapy was as effective as therapist-administered treatments. Comparable findings have been reported for the effectiveness of self-help books with specific disorders, such as sexual dysfunctions (van Lankveld, 1998), depression (Cuijpers, 1997), anxiety disorders (Weekes, 1996), alcohol problems (Watson & Sher, 1998), and geriatric depression (Scogin, Hamblin, & Beutler, 1987; Scogin, 1998).

Self-help books come in many guises. In this book, we do not evaluate books that are primarily religious in nature or medical in content. Books that focus on physical health and disease, be it AIDS, cancer, or heart disease, were not included. Our target is self-help books on mental health topics.

In Study 1, we asked mental health professionals to rate more than 350 self-help books. We chose these books by examining the shelves of major national bookstore chains, by perusing the wares of large Internet book dealers (Amazon.com, bn.com), by discussing self-help books with psychologists, by consulting the best-seller lists, and by reading numerous books and articles about self-help books. In Study 2 and Study 3, mental health professionals rated an additional 250 self-help books—a few that were missed in Study 1, but mostly books that were published after Study 1 was completed.

2. Autobiographies

Autobiographies provide an inside view of people facing life's problems, drawing on the human capacity for self-description and self-analysis. In this way, memoirs complement research and case studies performed from the outside looking in. Written in the person's own words, an autobiography emphasizes issues that the writer, as distinct from a therapist or researcher, considers important. It describes a disorder in its family and environmental context. Such books are interesting to read as narratives with a strong story line.

Autobiographical authors and their credentials vary tremendously. Some authors are celebrities, already the subject of public interest; others are writers, poets, and artists capable of portraying their inner worlds in words, songs, and drawings. Many accounts are written by ordinary people whose first contact with publishing is writing about their disorder. Some earlier accounts have become classics in mental health education; other books by Kay Jamison (*An Unquiet Mind*), William Styron (*Darkness Visible*), and Mark Vonnegut (*The Eden Express*) are likely to become future classics. Several autobiographies have been made into major films, bringing them to a wide public audience. The books have been used in training mental health professionals and as part of therapy for mental health consumers.

Autobiographies cover virtually all diagnostic categories. There have also been at least 100 published bibliographies and book-length anthologies of first-person accounts of mental disorder (Sommer, Clifford, & Norcross, 1998).

The autobiographies listed and evaluated in this book were selected specifically for their availability. Our earlier research articles on autobiographies contained many historical accounts, often very difficult to obtain. In this resource, we looked for first-person accounts still in print that covered mental health problems and life challenges. We visited bookstores and checked electronic booksellers to make sure that the book was still available. The date listed is that of the most recent edition, often in paperback. Even so, it is likely that some books will no longer be available by the time this book is published. However, it is likely that an out-of-print title can be obtained on the used book market.

An autobiographical account presents a personal view of the disorder and its treatment. When an author says that a mood disorder was relieved by Prozac or blames a family member or therapist for some transgression, this represents the person's view of the situation. Most of the books listed were written by the person with the disorder, but occasionally there is a book by a family member, which provides another perspective on the disorder and the treatment.

The self-help industry is virtually unregulated. The people with the most influence on which autobiographies are published and marketed are the publishers, the owners of large bookstore chains, and a hodgepodge of authors with a vast range of credentials, knowledge, and competencies. We hope our studies and this book help put a corrective influence in the hands of informed, experienced mental health professionals whose competencies are superior to those of the merchandisers.

3. Movies

Watching popular movies toward therapeutic ends—call it *videotherapy*—extends reading self-help books and autobiographies. They have similar aims, but movies typically differ from books in using fiction, rather than nonfiction, and in using the film medium, rather than print.

Films are a powerful and pervasive part of our culture. The widespread availability of movie theaters, VCRs, and videotapes allows most Americans ready access to movies. Gallup polls indicate that watching movies at home and in theaters are amongst adults' favorite pastimes (along with reading, watching television, and participating in family activities). Domestic box office revenues top, according to *Variety*, a staggering $12 billion for the 100 top-performing movies. And movies frequently touch us emotionally more than book. Psychologist Ken Gergen (1991) opines that the movies have become one of the most influential rhetorical devices in the world; "Films can catapult us rapidly and effectively into states of fear, anger, sadness, romance, lust, and aesthetic ecstasy—often within the same two-hour period. It is undoubtedly true that for many people film relationships provide the most emotionally wrenching experiences of the average week" (pp. 56–57).

Movies possess a number of advantages over books and computers. Films are fun to watch, require only a small investment of time, appeal to more people than reading, and are already part of many clients' usual routines (Hesley & Hesley, 1998). Instead of spending days or weeks reading books, people get the thrust in a few hours. As a result, clients may be more compliant with recommendations for movies, which are more accessible, fun, and familiar.

We are not the first to recommend specific movies to enhance self-help, but we may well be the most systematic. Several mental health professionals have penned fine compilations of popular movies to use in understanding psychopathology (Wedding & Boyd, 1999), to use in psychotherapy (Hesley & Hesley, 1998), to help with life's problems (Solomon, 1995), and to illustrate how psychiatry is depicted in the American cinema (Gabbard & Gabbard, 1999). But all of their books essentially present one or two individual opinions. By contrast, in this book we present the consensus of hundreds of mental health experts.

In preparation for Study 5, we compiled a large list of healing films by reviewing movie books (including those listed above), tracking the top-grossing films from the past decade, and throwing in some of our personal favorites. We also used the excellent Internet Movie Database (http://www.imdb.com) and Amazon.com to search for reviews. We then conducted a small pilot study of 25 colleagues to identify movies that a sizable proportion had actually seen. The result was a list of popular, commercially available films that have played in theaters or, in a few cases, only on television. These were then evaluated by hundreds of psychologists.

The movies portray healing stories. The best of them typically increase awareness about a disorder or treatment; *As Good as It Gets* comes immediately to mind for its accurate and humorous depiction of obsessive–compulsive disorder (OCD). The best also show flawed, yet effective role models struggling realistically with problems and ultimately resolving them; two cases in point are *The Color Purple* about overcoming childhood abuse and *On Golden Pond* about accepting the ravages of aging and healing family rifts. The favorably rated movies typically generate hope and inspiration and perhaps give a new perspective on ourselves and our relationships.

As with all of the self-help resources in this book, using movies requires certain warnings and preparation. Viewers are asked to suspend belief and to enter a fantasy world, but not to overidentify or overgeneralize from a single cinematic episode. The young and the squeamish should be directed away from stark, frightening portrayals. People suffering from debilitating psychiatric disorders should be forewarned of possible negative consequences of dramatic films, and those who recently suffered from trauma depicted in films should be careful not to be retraumatized by the experience.

4. Internet Resources

The Internet has opened a whole new world for people seeking information and advice. There are online sites for every aspect of human life and type of psychological suffering. Researchers estimate that half of all Internet users have already sought health care information there.

But which sites and which information should be trusted? Internet sites are unregulated, and their quality varies extensively. Early studies suggest that the quality of mental health sites is not impressive; almost half were judged to be inadequate in terms of accuracy and practicality of information (DiBlassio et al., 1999). Gleaning trustworthy information on the Internet is like taking a 2-year-old on a walk: The toddler picks up a few pretty pebbles, but also lots of garbage and dirt (Skow, 1999) Professionals may know when a beguiling irrelevancy can be dismissed with a click of the mouse, but the average person rarely does. And any single search engine indexes no more than 16% of the public web, according to a recent study published in *Nature* (Lawrence & Giles, 1999).

For this book, Dr. Edward Zuckerman visited approximately 3,000 Internet sites that seemed to be related to the topics covered in this book and might provide assistance to people struggling with mental health problems and life challenges. He chose the 500 or so listed sites on the belief that they would assist people—with or without psychotherapy—by fulfilling two major functions. First, these Internet sites would support the person or client with evidence that they are not alone, that others have overcome similar difficulties, and that much is known about their conditions. Second, the online resources would provide education for patients or parents concerning symptoms and diagnoses, the logic and methods of treatment, and other aspects of treatment.

In using these Internet resources, psychotherapists will have to explore ways to incorporate the materials. Some could be assigned as homework to save time, increase accuracy and completeness of education, enhance adherence and motivation, decrease dropouts and resistance, and provide instruction in the self-administration of some techniques. Online materials could empower people and raise their self-confidence, encourage socializing, enhance lifestyle changes, maintain changes after treatment, reduce the number of sessions, reinforce points or strategies of a session, and the like. A mental health professional should *always* read the materials because their contents may frighten rather than educate some clients, may conflict with a particular treatment plan, or may have changed.

You should assume that all materials on the net are copyrighted. If you find them of value, someone worked hard to make them valuable, and that person deserves your respect. Generally, for multiple copies, educational uses, or commercial distribution, you must get permission from the copyright holder. Therefore, obtain permission to use any of these materials with your patients unless they are specifically indicated as available for reprinting. You must include the copyright holder's information when you reproduce any materials.

There are literally thousands of chat rooms, bulletin boards, and other forms of support for clients to participate in. Many sites offer materials that are simply readings, much like a handout or pamphlet. Many of the better ones are in the form of FAQs (frequently asked questions and their answers). A few sites offer questionnaires that are scored and interpreted online. There are almost no interactive therapeutic activities available.

In selecting sites, we included those that provide people with information, explanations, and introductions to treatments beyond what the clinician could easily supply and that would not compete with or distract the client from the processes of therapy. The material had to be current; we estimate that more than 90% of the sites listed here were written in the last 3 years. All sites were visited as the book was being published and were working at that time. However, the Internet is a famously fluid place, so you might want to visit a site before recommending it.

We excluded sites from this book for a number of reasons. About 2,500 sites have been excluded sites because they

- Are purely commercial, pushing a book, seminar, drug, treatment center, or private practice.
- Are not concerned with the psychology or treatment of a disorder.
- Are essentially popular magazines of loosely related but superficial contents presented for their entertainment value.
- Possess strong religious tones or messages (that may not fit many clients).
- Offer only reading lists or bibliographies, course outlines, reviews, or catalogs for purchasing books, videos, or other self-help materials.
- Are simply a nonprofessional author's opinions or experiences.
- Consist of listserves, mailing lists, and bulletin boards on which anyone can post anything—recommendations, gossip, rumors, diatribes, and suggestions as well as accurate and useful information.
- Are a chat, or real-time equivalent of the mailing lists, chat rooms, and discussion groups. Chat is live, typed statements that appear in sequential order on the viewer's screen. Anyone can join in, and the statements are off-the-cuff and usually unmonitored and contain inappropriate and irrelevant messages from people without providing real names or identities. Professionals are usually not present, often not welcome, and sometimes excluded.
- Offer only materials for professionals and are not suitable for clients' self-help.

In each chapter, Internet sites are listed under these headings:

Metasites. These are rich collections of links (underlined and/or in blue print on the computer screen) to collections of other sites. Generally, clients would be overwhelmed by being referred to metasites because they usually offer hundreds of links. However, for those needing specifics not available through a search engine (because a good question cannot be generated), metasites are a boon.

Psychoeducational Materials for Clients and Families. This is where most of the sites appear. When there are large numbers of good sites, subheadings have been added to simplify searching. The titles of papers are in italics. Where an author's name does *not* appear, we could find no author. This does not mean that the material is not copyrighted; it is.

Biographical and Autobiographical Vignettes. For a few topics, sufferers of a disorder have posted biographical essays that are informative and not too idiosyncratic.

Other Resources. Here are sites and materials that bear on the topic indirectly and have some quality that makes them well worth exploring.

Online Support Groups. Only when these are particularly applicable have they been offered. For those seeking local or real-world meetings of support groups, see the American Self-Help Clearinghouse Sourcebook which is online at http://www.mentalhelp.net/selfhelp (and is also available in print.)

Our compilation of online listings is not exhaustive. If you desire additional or different sites, we heartily recommend that you refer to several other practical sources. An excellent printed resource is John Grohol's latest *Insider's Guide to Mental Health Resources Online*. The CMHC corporation (http://www.cmhc.com) supports two immense and wonderfully rich sites of relevance: Mental Health Net's Disorders and Treatments at http://mentalhelp. net/dxtx.htm is the most comprehensive metasite for all of the problems and disorders addressed in this book. Dr. Ladd's book, *Psychological Self-Help*, at http://www.mentalhelp.net/psyhelp explains most problems in ordinary language, gives practical directions for about 100 self-change methods, and cites 2,000 references. In 15 chapters and about 1,000 pages, Clayton E. Tucker-Ladd, PhD, a clinical psychologist, offers information on all kinds of psychological problems and their treatments. The book can be downloaded, or sections can be read online.

One site, in addition, provides many handouts for clients. Internet Mental Health's site at http://www.mentalhealth.com/book/p40.html lists hundreds of booklets.

If we have missed a site that you have found useful for yourself or patients, please send e-mail to edzuckerman@information4u.com so that we can share it with others in the next edition of this book.

5. Self-Help/Support Groups

Millions of Americans have come to rely on self-help or support groups for assistance with virtually every human challenge or disorder. The most recognizable of these are the 12-step groups patterned after Alcoholics Anonymous (AA) that address a wide spectrum of addictive disorders, such as those to drugs, food, and sex. But self-help groups encompass much more than addictions. There are groups for dealing with death, Alzheimer's, attention-deficit disorder, difficult children, and abusive partners, as even a casual glance of the blue pages of a telephone directory will confirm. In fact, 5% of American adults attended a self-help group in the past year (Eisenberg et al., 1998).

The popularity of self-help groups is easy to understand: They are typically free, widely available, and surprisingly effective. Most of the groups charge nothing or, at most, request a small donation to help cover expenses. Although research studies on these groups are infrequent and plagued with methodological problems, they do generally show positive results. A meta-analysis (Tonigan, Toscoova, & Miller, 1995) found that participation in Alcoholics Anonymous and reduction in drinking were positively related, especially in outpatient populations. Several large and well-controlled evaluations of 12-step programs for addictive disorders have shown that they generally perform as effectively as professional treatment, including at follow-up (Morgenstern, Labouvie, McCrady, Kahler, & Frey, 1997; Ouimette, Finney, & Moos, 1997; Project MATCH Research Group, 1997). Likewise, research has generally found that clients rate 12-step groups as helpful as psychotherapy (Seligman, 1995).

At the end of most chapters of this book, we alphabetically list prominent self-help/support groups for that particular challenge or disorder. These are listed without ratings—and for good reason. The effectiveness of self-help groups largely depend on the local members and leaders, so it is impossible to make general claims about the quality of any particular group. We provide contact numbers for the national office and online sites so that you can identify the mission of the organization and determine whether there is a local group in your locale.

The American Self-Help Clearinghouse's *Self-Help Sourcebook* at http://mentalhelp.net/selfhelp was developed "to act as your starting point for exploring real-life support groups and networks that are available throughout the world and in your community." We strongly recommend that you visit it, particularly if you are searching for a support group on a topic or disorder not covered in this guide

FIVE NATIONAL STUDIES

We have conducted a series of national studies over the past 7 years to determine the most useful self-help resources. In each study, the methodology and the samples were very similar: a lengthy survey mailed to clinical and counseling psychologists residing throughout the United States. Across the five studies, more than 2,500 psychologists contributed their expertise and judgment to evaluate self-help books, autobiographies, and movies. Appendix A presents the methodological details of these studies.

These mental health professionals are all members of the clinical or counseling divisions of the American Psychological Association. To be a member of these divisions, mental health professionals are required to have obtained a doctorate from an accredited university and have been recommended for membership by their colleagues. Their ratings and comments on the books, autobiographies, and movies are based on many years of experience in helping people with particular problems and are an invaluable resource for sorting through the bewildering maze of self-help materials available today.

Our studies are probably the earliest and the most thorough to be conducted on a large-scale, national basis. A number of the mental health professionals who participated in the studies spontaneously commented about the virtual absence of information available to the public about how to select good self-help materials. Their positive comments about the need for our studies and the extensiveness of the materials rated bolstered our motivation for writing this book.

The responding psychologists rated self-help resources with which they were sufficiently familiar on the same 5-point scale:

+2	Extremely good	Outstanding; highly recommended book, best or among best in category
+1	Moderately good	Provides good advice, can be helpful; worth purchasing
0	Average	An average self-help book
−1	Moderately bad	Not a good self-help book; may provide misleading or inaccurate information
−2	Extremely bad	This book exemplifies the worst of the self-help books; worst, or among worst in its category

The wording was slightly modified for rating autobiographies and movies—for example, "an average autobiographical account" and "outstanding; highly recommended movie."

Self-help materials in the following 28 categories were rated by the mental health professionals:

Abuse
Addictive Disorders and Codependency
Adult Development and Aging
Anger
Anxiety Disorders
Assertiveness
Attention-Deficit/Hyperactivity Disorder
Career Development
Child Development and Parenting
Communication and People Skills
Death and Grieving
Dementia/Alzheimer's
Divorce
Eating Disorders
Families and Stepfamilies
Love and Intimacy
Marriage
Men's Issues
Mood Disorders
Pregnancy
Schizophrenia
Self-Management and Self-Enhancement
Spiritual and Existential Concerns
Stress Management and Relaxation
Sexuality
Teenagers and Parenting
Weight Management
Women's Issues

ONE TO FIVE STARS AND A DAGGER

We analyzed the responses to our national studies by computing how often the self-help resources were rated and how high or low the ratings were. All resources not listed at least 10 times were eliminated from the final ratings. Then, based on how often and high or low they were rated, books and movies with positive ratings were given one to five stars; the rare books and movies with a negative rating were given a dagger:

★★★★★   Average rating of 1.25 or higher; rated by 30 or more mental health professionals

★★★★   Average rating of 1.00 or higher; rated by 20 or more mental health professionals

★★★   Average rating of .50 through .99; rated 10 or more times

★★   Average rating of .25 through .49; rated 10 or more times

★   Average rating of .00 through .24; rated 10 or more times

†   Average negative rating; rated by 10 or more mental health professionals

The sole exception to this rating system was the autobiographies. There, we used a cutoff of 8 or more ratings, as opposed to 10, simply because fewer psychologists were sufficiently familiar with autobiographies than with self-help books or movies and because in Study 2 we had previously used 8 as the minimum number of raters. Thus, the rating system for autobiographies was:

★★★★★   Average rating of 1.25 or higher; rated by 24 or more mental health professionals

★★★★   Average rating of 1.00 or higher; rated by 16 or more mental health professionals

★★★   Average rating of .50 through .99; rated 8 or more times

★★   Average rating of .25 through .49; rated 8 or more times

★   Average rating .00 through .24; rated 8 or more times

†   Average negative rating; rated by 8 or more mental health professionals

Internet resources, as previously noted, were individually evaluated and rated by a single clinical psychologist, Edward Zuckerman, PhD. They were not part of the national studies. But we use a similar system to rate their quality and utility:

★★★★★   Quality interactive materials and/or lots of readings with value for patient education and accessibility; accurate, current, clearly presented, and pitched at a common reading and knowledge level

★★★★   Some readings or other material of high quality

★★★   One or two readings that can help extend a client's understanding

★★   One small reading that was, however, all that is available on the Internet on that topic

★   Of limited value for self-help or patient education; sites with this rating have been excluded

In this book, the four-star and five-star self-help resources are Strongly Recommended; the three-star resources are Recommended; the one-star and two-star books are Not Recommended; and the daggered books are Strongly Not Recommended. In addition to these ratings, some self-help books and autobiographies received high ratings but were rated infrequently. These resources were assigned to the Diamonds in the Rough category (♦). They have the potential to become four-star or five-star books if they become more widely known.

HOW THIS BOOK IS ORGANIZED

The following chapters present the self-help categories alphabetically, beginning with "Abuse" and ending with "Women's Issues." Each chapter opens with a brief description of the problem area or disorder and of the audiences to which the self-help resources are addressed. We then provide our Recommendation Highlights for that chapter, which includes all five-star resources, most four-star resources, and many Diamonds in the Rough. Next, we present the expert ratings and our profiles of, in order, self-help books, autobiographies, movies, and Internet sites. Descriptions and contact information are provided for self-help/support groups; however, we do not offer evaluative information or expert ratings on these groups. Not every chapter provides listings of all resources, either because there were too many resources available for that disorder or, conversely, there were too few. Our profile of each resource entails a terse review of its contents, objectives, and organization. In the final chapter, we feature nine strategies for selecting a self-help resource.

The four appendixes contain statistical and methodological data. Appendix A details the methodology of the five national studies. Appendix B presents the experts' average ratings for all the self-help books evaluated by five or more psychologists. Appendix C presents the average ratings for all the autobiographies evaluated by five or more respondents, and in turn, Appendix D does likewise for all the movies.

USING THIS BOOK EFFECTIVELY

The *Authoritative Guide to Self-Help Resources in Mental Health* is intended for both mental health professionals and the general public.

Psychotherapists increasingly recommend self-help resources to their clients In our recent study involving 1,229 psychologists, 82% were recommending self-help groups to their psychotherapy patients, and 85% were recommending self-help books. Almost one-half are prescribing particular movies to patients, and about one-quarter recommend autobiographies.

Moreover, psychotherapists are increasingly convinced of the effectiveness of self-help resources in conjunction with psychotherapy. Table 1.1 presents the results of one of our recent studies; it clearly demonstrates that psychologists find self-help materials to be somewhat helpful or very helpful in 70 to 90% of psychotherapy cases. Psychologists report that these self-help resources exerted a harmful effect on only 2 to 3% of their patients, a deterioration rate similar to or less than that for professional treatment. Indeed, careful review of the evidence on self-administered treatments shows that negative outcomes are rare (Scogin et al., 1996).

Mental health professionals can use the *Authoritative Guide to Self-Help Resources in Mental Health* as a professional resource for information about the quality of self-help resources on a wide-ranging set of behavioral disorders and life transitions. The evaluative ratings and concise reviews will increase therapists' knowledge of the content of hundreds of resources that can be used with or without professional treatment. Since all this information is packed into a single volume, books, autobiographies, movies, and Internet resources can be quickly compared to determine their appropriateness.

TABLE 1.1. Psychologists' Estimated Effects of Self-Help Resources on Patients as Part of Psychotherapy

Effect	Self-help books ($N = 571$)	Autobiographies ($N = 192$)	Movies ($N = 295$)
Very harmful	1%	0%	1%
Somewhat harmful	2%	2%	1%
No effect	4%	29%	30%
Somewhat helpful	74%	60%	61%
Very helpful	19%	9%	7%

The layperson who is or is not engaged in psychotherapy can also use the *Authoritative Guide to Self-Help Resources in Mental Health* to become knowledgeable about a large number of self-help resources and to learn which ones are helpful and which aren't. This is a self-help book on self-help resources. Chapter 30, Strategies for Selecting Self-Help Resources, can help you evaluate self-help more effectively.

Now that we have introduced self-help materials, our national studies, and the organization of this book, let's turn to the ratings in specific areas of mental health, beginning with Abuse.

CHAPTER 2

Abuse

Experiencing abuse can transform a person's life forever. Once victimized, many individuals never again feel quite as invulnerable or trusting. Determining the scope of abuse is difficult because many abused individuals never reveal their experiences. Especially disturbing in the available figures are the abuses perpetuated by close friends and family members. Acquaintances of the victim are implicated in almost 50% of child sexual assaults, romantic partners in 50 to 75% of sexual assaults reported by college-age and adult women. The burden of abuse falls on women unequally: More than 75% of the reported cases of child sexual abuse involve girls, and more than 90% of adult rape victims are women.

Over the past decade, a professional and legal controversy has erupted over the reality of childhood abuse uncovered during psychotherapy. On the one side are those mental health professionals who regularly encounter clients who report being physically or sexually abused as children but who have repressed these traumatic memories because they were too painful. On the other side are some mental health professionals, memory researchers, and accused parents who contend that the "recovered" memories of abuse are frequently fictitious accounts subtly prompted by suggestive and hypnotic therapy techniques and by social hysteria. The storm has spilled over into the professional literature and into the nation's courtrooms. There have been charges and countercharges. But all sides of the debate agree on two fundamental propositions: First, abuse of children is all too common and devastating, and second, the matter of recovered or false memories deserves serious scientific attention.

Following is a capsule summary of the self-help books, autobiographies, movies, and Internet sites that we and our experts recommend on the national epidemic of abuse.

RECOMMENDATION HIGHLIGHTS

Self-Help Books

- On adult women's recovery from child sexual abuse:

    ★★★★★ *The Courage to Heal* by Ellen Bass and Laura Davis

- On adult men's recovery from child sexual abuse:

    ★★★★ *Victims No Longer* by Michael Lew

- For the partners of adult survivors of child sexual abuse:

    ★★★★ *Allies in Healing* by Laura Davis

- On battered women who have been abused by their marital or romantic partners:

    ★★★★ *The Battered Woman* by Lenore Walker

    ★★★★ *Getting Free* by Ginny NiCarthy

- On date or acquaintance rape:

    ★★★ *I Never Called It Rape* by Robin Warshaw

- For women who have endured verbal abuse:

    ★★★ *The Verbally Abusive Relationship* by Patricia Evans

    ◆ *You Can't Say That to Me!* by Suzette Haden Elgin

Autobiographies

- On sexual abuse and incest:

    ★★★   *Daddy's Girl* by Charlotte Vale Allen

- On physical and sexual abuse:

    ★★★ *Sleepers* by Lorenzo Carcaterra

    ★★★ *A Child Called "It"* by Dave Pelzer

- On sexual obsessions following sexual molestation:

    ★★★ *Secret Life* by Michael Ryan

Movies

- On domestic abuse and triumphant survival:

    ★★★★ *Radio Flyer*

    ★★★★ *The Color Purple*

    ★★★★ *This Boy's Life*

- On spousal abuse:

    ★★★ *What's Love Got to Do with It?*

Internet Resources

- On sexual assault:
    - ★★★★★ *Sexual Assault Information Page*
      http://www.cs.utk.edu/~bartley/saInfoPage.html
    - ★★★★★ *AWARE: Arming Women against Rape and Endangerment*
      http://www.aware.org/index.html

- On domestic violence:
    - ★★★★★ *Domestic Violence* http://www.zip.com.au/~korman/dv
    - ★★★★★ *Domestic Abuse* http://www.telalink.net/~police/abuse/index.html
    - ★★★★★ *Shattered Love, Broken Lives*
      http://www.s-t.com/projects/DomVio/content.HTML
    - ★★★★★ *Trust Betrayed* http://meb.marshall.edu/trust/trust-toc.htm
    - ★★★★★ *When Love Hurts* http://home.vicnet.net.au/~girlsown
    - ★★★★★ *Domestic Violence Resources*
      http://homepages.go.com/homepages/d/a/n/danielsonkin
    - ★★★★★ *Why Women Stay* http://www.prevent-abuse-now.com/domviol.htm

- Specific information on date rape:
    - ★★★★ *Coercion, Rape, and Surviving*
      http://www.student-affairs.buffalo.edu/shs/ccenter/violence.shtml
    - ★★★★ *"Friends" Raping Friends—Could It Happen to You?*
      http://www.cs.utk.edu/~bartley/acquaint/acquaintRape.html

- For people who batter and abuse others:
    - ★★★★★ *Excuses* http://comnet.org/adacss/poster.html

- On community responses and interventions to sexual assault:
    - ★★★★★ *A Community Checklist: Important Steps to End Violence Against
      Women* http://www.usdoj.gov/vawo/cheklist.htm
    - ★★★★ *Community Outreach Health Information System*
      http://www.bu.edu/cohis/violence/domesvio.htm

- On child abuse:
    - ★★★★ *Child Abuse FAQs*
      http://www.extension.ualberta.ca/legalfaqs/nat/v-chi-en.htm

- On preventing self-abuse and self-injury:
    - ★★★★★ *Self-Injury: You Are NOT the Only One*
      http://www.palace.net/~llama/psych/injury.html

- On elder abuse:
    - ★★★★ *NY Elder Abuse Coalition* http://www.ianet.org/nyeac

SELF-HELP BOOKS

Strongly Recommended

★★★★★ *The Courage to Heal* (rev. ed., 1992) by Ellen Bass and Laura Davis. New York: Harper Perennial.

This outstanding self-help book has become a bible for many women who were sexually abused as children. Originally published in 1988, a revised edition appeared in 1992. Ellen Bass realized how little help was available to adult survivors of child sexual abuse when she was teaching creative writing workshops in the 1970s. Although not trained as a psychologist, she decided to offer groups for survivors and developed the I Never Told Anyone workshops, creating a safe context where women could face their own pain and anger and begin to heal. Laura Davis was sexually abused as a child and turned to Ellen Bass for help. *The Courage to Heal* begins with a brief introduction about how healing is possible. Readers answer a series of 14 questions that help them determine if they were victims of child sexual abuse. The bulk of the book is divided into five parts: Taking Stock, The Healing Process, Changing Patterns, For Supporters of Survivors, and Courageous Women. Two sections toward the end of the book focus on counseling and healing resources. The 1992 edition includes a list of more than 600 resources for women survivors of child sexual abuse. Any woman who knows she was sexually abused as a child will probably benefit from this book. The writing is clear, the survivors' comments and stories are artfully woven through the book, the writing exercises are valuable therapy tools, and the authors' compassion, understanding, and insight are apparent. Unlike some recovery books that dwell too extensively on the past, this resource moves on in positive ways to help women heal and recover.

As a visible and best-selling book on sexual abuse of children, *The Courage to Heal* has been drawn into the repressed versus false memory storm. The authors contend that women who strongly sense that they were sexually abused but do not have specific memories of it were in fact probably abused. While this position fosters an acceptance and trust toward women whose abuse may have been denied by others, it simultaneously may generate or perpetuate false "memories" of abuse that never occurred. Critics contend that specific memories of early childhood abuse are notoriously unreliable and that encouraging rhetoric might create false memories and thus false accusations against innocent family members. In this specific respect, some psychologists are unhappy that this self-help resource was the top-rated book on abuse in our national studies.

The Courage to Heal Workbook (1990) was authored by Laura Davis to provide in-depth exercises for both women and men who were sexually abused as children. The workbook includes a combination of checklists, open-ended questions, writing exercises, art projects, and activities that take the adult survivor through the healing process. This book is a helpful companion to *The Courage to Heal* and is organized into four main sections: Survival Skills, Taking Stock, Aspects of Healing, and Guidelines for Healing Sexually.

★★★★ *The Battered Woman* (1979) by Lenore Walker. New York: Harper & Row.

This excellent self-help book is written for women who have been or continue to be abused by their husbands or romantic partners. Lenore Walker is widely recognized as one of the leading therapists who study and counsel battered women. The book is divided into three main parts: Psychology of the Battered Woman includes valuable information about the myths and realities of abuse as well as psychological theories that help explain the victimization of the battered woman; Coercive Techniques in Battering Relationships provides vivid, heart-wrenching stories told by battered women themselves; and The Way Out examines not only the dark side of legal, medical, psychological, and other services that tend to keep battered women as victims, but also the services battered women themselves say would be more helpful. Walker asserts that battered women undergo a process of victimization, acquiring a sense of learned helplessness that leaves them prey to abuse, unable to fault their abusers, and unwilling to leave them. The case studies unabashedly present battering from a woman's perspective; indeed, Walker acknowledges that the book is written from a woman's point of view. *The Battered Woman* was written in 1979 and has not been revised. One of its few shortcomings is its age, but a woman in an abusive relationship with a man will likely benefit from this excellent self-help book.

★★★★ *Allies in Healing* (1991) by Laura Davis. New York: Harper Perennial.

The partners of survivors are an overlooked group. This book by one of the coauthors of *The Courage to Heal* is written for partners who may or may not have been abused themselves, but who are living with the effects of abuse. The question and answer format makes the book highly readable, with each question at the top of a page. Questions are organized under basic topics, including My Needs and Feelings, Dealing with Crisis, Intimacy, Family Issues, and Realistic Expectations. Sensitive and difficult questions are asked, and the answers are candid, informative, and useful. A significant part of the book describes the stories of eight partners and their struggles and triumphs.

★★★★ *Getting Free: You Can End Abuse and Take Back Your Life* (3rd ed., 1997) by Ginny NiCarthy. Seattle, WA: Seal Press.

This book is intended for women and is about battering. It is divided into six sections: Making the Decision to Leave or Stay, Getting Professional Help, Helping Yourself to Survival, After You Leave, The Ones Who Got Away, and New Directions. The final section examines topics that do not appear in the other books on battered women listed here and provides valuable analysis and recovery advice for abused teens and abused lesbians. *Getting Free* has an extensive number of exercises for readers and is thus virtually a combination of narrative and workbook.

★★★★ *Victims No Longer: Men Recovering from Incest and Other Sexual Child Abuse* (1990) by Michael Lew. New York: Harper & Row.

While the previous books in this category were designed for women, this splendid self-help book was written for men who experienced childhood incest and other sexual abuse and for the people involved with them. The focus section lends special emphasis or specific experience to the chapter subject (e.g., defining victim and survivor, debt to the women's movement, if the abuser is a woman, and myths that interfere with recovery). Statements and personal accounts from survivors are sprinkled between chapters, bringing a sense of individual realities experienced by survivors. These statements include something about the self, what happened to the survivor, the effects, what is useful in recovery, and messages to other survivors. Topics are clustered into myths and realities of abuse, messages about masculinity, surviving abuse, and recovery. This book provides an emotional journey for the reader and tells the story of courageous journeys.

Recommended

★★★   *Battered Wives* (rev. ed., 1989) by Del Martin. Volcano, CA: Volcano.

This book is intended for women who have been in an abusive relationship with a man or who continue to be abused in the relationship. While the book is titled *Battered Wives*, Martin says that her book applies equally to unmarried women who live with violent men; many of the examples she uses involve unmarried cohabitants. In Martin's view, the underlying problem that has led to the battering of so many women is found not in the husband–wife interaction or immediate triggering events but rather in the institution of marriage itself, historically negative attitudes toward women in society, the economy, and inadequacies in legal and social services systems. The book is at its best in its scathing feminist critiques of a society that discriminates against women and, in this respect, is more a sociological analysis of battered women than an in-depth psychological analysis. The textbook style of writing makes for difficult reading in many places. The riveting case studies and more personal tone in Walker's book will be more attractive to most readers. And even the 1989 revision of *Battered Wives* is dated.

★★★   *I Never Called It Rape* (1994) by Robin Warshaw. New York: Harper Perennial.

A major study conducted by *Ms* magazine and the National Institute of Mental Health as well as interviews of 150 women conducted by the author are cited throughout this book in defining and describing acquaintance rape. The road to recovery of those sexually assaulted by an acquaintance and information on how to prevent assault are featured. The denial of acquaintance rape in our culture and the uphill battle of survivors are thoughtfully chronicled. The book features the acquaintance rape on the college campus, in the workplace, and in other settings. The intended audience is not only the survivors of acquaintance rape, but also family, parents, educators, counselors, and those in the legal system. The book is not widely known among experts in our studies, but those who do know it accord it high ratings. It is probably the best self-help book available on date rape. Any female who has experienced date rape can benefit from Warshaw's portrayal of the healing process; any dating female can benefit from the book's detailed observations about how and why date rape happens; and males can benefit from the book's description of the devastating aftereffects of date rape.

★★★   *Healing the Shame That Binds You* (1988) by John Bradshaw. Deerfield Beach, FL: Health Communications.

This book has appeared on the *New York Times* best-seller list and has sold more than half a million copies. Bradshaw believes that people with a wide array of problems, including addictions, compulsions, and codependencies, developed their problems because of toxic shame. What is toxic shame? Bradshaw never gives a clear definition, but he does provide some hints about its nature. He says toxic shame is present when people believe that things are hopeless and feel that they themselves are worthless. They feel defective and flawed as people, bad, and inadequate. Individuals with toxic shame perceive that they lack power. How can people get rid of shame-based feelings? Bradshaw believes that the healing process involves getting the shame out of hiding and externalizing it. This involves liberating the lost inner child, integrating disowned parts, loving the self, healing memories, improving self-image, confronting and changing inner voices, coping with toxic shame relationships, and spiritual awakening. Bradshaw describes a number of therapy strategies that can be used to help individuals externalize their toxic shame. Although popular with the public, this book received tepid and mixed evaluations by the mental health experts in our national studies.

★★★ *Wounded Boys, Heroic Men: A Man's Guide to Recovering from Child Abuse* (1992) by Daniel Jay Sonkin. Stamford, CT: Longmeadow Press.

The material in this text is presented in a step-by-step manner. It is meant for men who were abused physically, sexually, or psychologically when they were boys as well as for their partners, friends, and family members. Special focus is given to the gender-based roadblocks that men face, including not seeking help and being expected to pull themselves up by their bootstraps, thinking and not feeling, and taking punishment like a real man. Topics are how to begin the journey, types of abuse, breaking the pattern of denial, and healing through attitude and behavior change. Boxed bullet points highlight the message of each chapter (e.g., knowing you're on the right track, how abuse affects you today). This book provides a hopeful and demythologizing message about recovery.

★★★ *Beginning to Heal: A First Book for Survivors of Child Sexual Abuse* (1993) by Ellen Bass and Laura Davis. New York: Harper Perennial.

Beginning to Heal is a condensed version of *The Courage to Heal*, reviewed above, and is meant for those who are just starting to face the abuse they experienced earlier in life. The approach offers an empathic and validating perspective that involves healing, believing it happened, grieving, anger, change, and moving on. Inserts, including quotes, comments, and observations in boxed or bullet form, contribute to clarity on such subjects as surviving the panic stage, how most people begin to remember, breaking the silence, and how to change. A significant section of the book recalls the stories of five women who were abused as children and how they moved through the healing process. This book serves as an invitation and introduction to recovery from child sexual abuse.

★★★ *The Verbally Abusive Relationship* (1996) by Patricia Evans. Holbrook, MA: Adams Media.

The stories in this book were told to the author by women who were verbally abused. Their experiences serve as validation for abused women who have questioned the legitimacy and reality of their thoughts and feelings. Forty verbally abused women between the ages of 21 and 66 were interviewed. Verbal abuse is discussed from the perspective of power and dominance over another person. The first part of the book takes the reader through a self-evaluation questionnaire, and the second part characterizes categories of verbal abuse (e.g., withholding, discounting, accusing, trivializing, denial), using illustrations of typical scenarios. A valuable aspect of the book is that it addresses how to respond effectively to verbal abuse. Examples provide clear and understandable ways to interpret and deal with abusive communication. This edition includes a chapter for therapists that considers verbal abuse from the therapeutic standpoint, and chapters on children in abusive environments and frequently asked questions have been added. The book received a stellar rating of 1.61 in one of our national studies but was rated by only 13 experts, thus leading to its 3-star rating and to an underestimation of its probable usefulness.

Diamond in the Rough

♦ *You Can't Say That to Me!* (1995) by Suzette Haden Elgin. New York: Wiley.

The significance of the language environment in which we relate to others is identified as an important part of the abuse pattern. We are taught to adapt to this pattern rather than to change the language environment. The goals are to learn how to establish a nonabusive language environment and how to deal with verbal abuse when it does happen. The book is written in a stepwise manner with an added feature called "Back Up Material" that offers exercises and activities on the content of each chapter. The book is well organized and addresses the phases of abuse identification and treatment effectively. Victims of verbal abuse and their support systems are the intended readers of this Diamond in the Rough that received good ratings despite low readership.

Not Recommended

★★ *Toxic Parents: Overcoming Their Hurtful Legacy and Reclaiming Your Life* (1989) by Susan Forward. New York: Bantam.

★★ *Abused No More: Recovery for Women from Abusive or Co-Dependent Relationships* (1989) by Robert Ackerman and Susan E. Pickering. Blue Ridge Summit, PA: T. A. B. Books.

★ *Reclaiming the Inner Child* (1990) edited by Jeremiah Abrams. Los Angeles: Jeremy P. Tarcher.

AUTOBIOGRAPHIES

Recommended

★★★ *A Child Called "It": One Child's Courage to Survive* (1995) by Dave Pelzer. Deerfield Beach, FL: Health Communications.

The author's horrifying account of his abuse as a child by a sadistic and alcoholic mother who nearly killed him, and his rescue by an alert schoolteacher. This best-selling book demonstrates how hope and love can overcome extreme adversity in childhood. Pelzer has also written *The Lost Boy: A Foster Child's Search for the Love of a Family.*

★★★ *Daddy's Girl* (1995) by Charlotte Vale Allen. New York: Berkeley.

A professional writer and novelist struggles to free herself from memories of her father's incestuous demands, which started when she was 7 years old and continued until she was 17, and from her image of herself as ugly and unlovable. The author is now active in behalf of victims of child abuse and domestic violence. A compelling autobiography.

★★★ *Sleepers* (1996) by Lorenzo Carcaterra. New York: Ballantine.

As a young man growing up in a poor neighborhood, the author and his friends engaged in petty crimes. When they were caught, the four young men were sent to a juvenile home where they were assaulted and raped by brutal guards. Years later, the men took revenge against their tormenters. The book was made into a popular movie of the same name.

★★★ *Secret Life* (1996) by Michael Ryan. New York: Vintage.

Poet Michael Ryan attributes the sexual obsessions of his adult years to having been molested at age 5 by a neighbor and being physically abused by an alcoholic father. He bares his soul to the reader in this searing autobiography.

MOVIES

Strongly Recommended

★★★★ *Radio Flyer* (1992) produced by Lauren Shuler-Donner and directed by Richard Donner. PG-13 Rating. 120 minutes.

This beautiful but painful film illustrates the denial patterns of a codependent wife and her physically and verbally abusive alcoholic husband. The two boys who are the focus of the story try to protect her and each other from his beatings. While the movie offers no usable guidance for coping with or overcoming the abuse or its denial, the nature of the pathology is clearly displayed and could be the focus of therapy.

★★★★ *The Color Purple* (1986) produced by Steven Spielberg, Kathleen Kennedy, Frank Marshall, and Quincy Jones for Guber–Peters Company and directed by Steven Spielberg. PG-13 Rating. 152 minutes.

This unforgettable movie depicts a magnificent triumph of the human spirit over endless and vile cruelties—physical and sexual—brought about by family separation, abuse, and ignorance. Despite her sufferings, Celie, a poor, unloved, unlovely, African American woman in the turn of the century South, discovers her beauty, her courage, and her potential. If she can do it, we all can. The movie is notable for its superb performances and the Oscars it won.

★★★★ *This Boy's Life* (1994) produced by Art Linson and directed by Michael Caton-Jones. R Rating. 115 minutes.

A mother takes her son and heads west after divorce to the little town of Concrete. Desperate for marriage, she weds a pathetic bully. The heart of the story is the war between a nice kid and his sadistic, lying, con-artist stepfather, who is perfectly portrayed as a sick adult child, always feeling cheated and misunderstood and blaming the boy. The film illustrates the boy's growth in confidence and hope to escape, the mother's passivity, and the loathsome man's character weaknesses. As such, it demonstrates hope and growth despite a terrible childhood.

Recommended

★★★ *Sleeping with the Enemy* (1991) produced by Leonard Goldberg and directed by Joseph Ruben. R Rating. 98 minutes.

A battered trophy wife fakes her own death in order to break away from the total dominance and control of her husband. She runs away to start her life again; he finds her and threatens her again. That is all the film has to offer. It is best used to illustrate the characters and dynamics of the couple.

★★★ *What's Love Got to Do with It?* (1994) produced by Doug Chapin and Barry Krost and directed by Brian Gibson. R Rating. 119 minutes.

A true and completely believable story of a seductive, charming, violent, abusive husband and his talented wife, who stays with him long beyond what reason or love would require. He beats her, flaunts his girlfriends, and abuses cocaine. She excuses him, believes his apologies, and gives him many more chances. The movie is an unflinching and honest look at how such patterns can exist in any family.

Not Recommended

★★ *Mommie Dearest* (1981) produced by Frank Yablans and directed by Frank Perry. PG Rating. 129 minutes.

★★ *Thelma and Louise* (1992) produced by Ridley Scott and Mimi Polk and directed by Ridley Scott. R Rating. 129 minutes.

Strongly Not Recommended

† *The Prince of Tides* (1992) produced by Barbra Streisand and Andrew Karsch for Barwood/Longfellow and directed by Barbra Streisand. R Rating. 132 minutes.

INTERNET RESOURCES

There are an enormous number of resources available online about all kinds of abuse. The sites described here focus on sexual assault and abuse, domestic violence, child abuse, abused males, self-injury, abuse by professionals, trauma, and other kinds of abuse. Excluded are materials primarily about workplace violence; juvenile crime and violence; the legal side (prosecution, suits, advocacy); sexual harassment; sex offenders and their treatment; ritual abuse, torture, and mind control; and sites that combine abuse with materials on dissociation, dissociative identity disorder/multiple personlaity disorder.

Reading some of these sites may trigger memories in those who have experienced abuse.

Metasites

★★★★★ *Sexual Assault Information Page*
            http://www.cs.utk.edu/~bartley/saInfoPage.html

This rich site is a gift from Chris Bartley and offers hundreds of links under about 40 headings. You can find readings and resources on almost any aspect of sexual assault, victims, recovery, trauma, offenders, and posttraumatic stress disorder (PTSD).

★★★★★ *Domestic Violence* http://www.zip.com.au/~korman/dv

An excellent general site with lists of Internet sites with help for victims, fact sheets, what you can do, and so on.

Psychoeducational Materials for Orienting and Educating Clients and Families

Sexual Assault and Abuse

★★★★ *Coercion, Rape, and Surviving*
            http://www.student-affairs.buffalo.edu/shs/ccenter/violence.html

Although it opens with a questionaire, it offers about 10 pages of solid information on date rape and coercion. It is excellent for raising consciousness.

★★★★ *Sexual Abuse* http://www.soulselfhelp.on.ca

There are a half dozen pages on definitions, effects, memory recovery, anger, obesity, and getting support. The section on Tools in Recovery is a good set of tips and advice on relapse prevention, helpful slogans, definitions, and so forth. Ignore the ads.

★★★★ *Becoming Whole Again: Healing from Sexual Assault*
            http://www.utexas.edu/student/cmhc/rape.html

The site provides definitions and information on immediate responses, coping, recovering, and self-care, plus suggestions for family—all in 5 pages. Designed for a college audience, it is an excellent starting point.

★★★★ *Rape Victim Advocacy Program* http://www.uiowa.edu/~rvap

This is a counseling center in Iowa, but its online readings for victims include Facts about Sexual Assault, If You Have Been Assaulted, and What to Say to a Rape Survivor.

★★★★ *Information for Victims of Sexual Assault and Their Families*
            http://www.connsacs.org/infocsa.htm

A comprehensive and informative brochure of 10 pages.

★★★★ *"Friends" Raping Friends—Could It Happen to You?* by Jean O'Gorman
       Hughes and Bernice R. Sandler
       http://www.cs.utk.edu/~bartley/acquaint/acquaintRape.html

Although somewhat dated, this is a superb overview in 16 packed pages.

★★★★ *STDs and Sexual Assault: Information on HIV/AIDS, Hepatitis B, and Other
       Sexually Transmitted Diseases* http://www.connsacs.org/library/hivbook.html

Seven pages of facts.

★★★★ *Abuse-Free List Rules: Principles of Abuse Recovery*
       http://blainn.cc/abuse-free/rules/afh-rules.html

Eight good rules from an online support group.

★★★   *What Is Sexual Assault?* http://www.utexas.edu/student/cmhc/rape.html

About five pages of an overview from a college counseling service. See also the very
similar *For Loved Ones of Sexual Assault/Abuse Survivors* at http://www.couns.uiuc.edu/
friends.htm.

★★★   *Facts about Sexual Assault*
       http://www.ama-assn.org/public/releases/assault/facts.htm

A one-page list with specifics about societal attitudes from the American Medical Association.

★★★   *If Someone You Love Is Sexually Assaulted*
       http://www.cs.utk.edu/~bartley/sacc/ifSomeoneYouLove.html

A quick four-page overview.

Domestic Violence

★★★★★ *Domestic Abuse* http://www.telalink.net/~police/abuse/index.html

This remarkable series of brief but realistic checklists (from the Nashville Police Department) should make the reader much less vulnerable. They are headed Potential Indicators of Domestic Abuse, Stress Related Problems in Children of Abuse, Progression of
Violence, How Abusers Stage a Return, Signs of Rehabilitation, Common Characteristics of the Battered and the Batterer, Similar Stories of Battered Spouses, Dangers After
Separation, Long Term Effects of Abuse, and Make a Separation Safety Plan.

★★★★★ *Shattered Love, Broken Lives* http://www.s-t.com/projects/DomVio

Here are 60 integrated newspaper articles examining all aspects of domestic violence.
They could provide both specific and background information for all readers.

★★★★★ *Trust Betrayed* http://meb.marshall.edu/trust/trust-toc.htm

A superb booklet of about 20 pages teaches what are healthy and controlling relationships and ways of dealing with abusive relationships.

★★★★★ *When Love Hurts: A Guide for Girls on Love, Respect and Abuse*
        in Relationships
        http://home.vicnet.net.au/~girlsown

A superb booklet of about 20 pages that provides information on abusive relationships, help in thinking about respect, effects, and feelings and ideas about changing.

★★★★★ *Domestic Violence Resources* by Daniel Jay Sonken, PhD
        http://homepages.go.com/homepages/d/a/n/danielsonkin

Under General Public Information are 6 sections totaling about 15 pages with solid information, techniques, and advice for abusers.

★★★★★ *AWARE: Arming Women Against Rape and Endangerment*
        http://www.aware.org/index.html

A fine introduction to "effective self-protection for intelligent women who want help, not hype."

★★★★★ *Why Women Stay* by Nancy Faulkner, PhD
        http://www.prevent-abuse-now.com/domviol.htm

In 13 pages, the author describes the 13 types of persons who stay or reasons for staying. Well done and clear, the site could help clarify the issues for a victim.

★★★★★ *Excuses* http://comnet.org/adacss/poster.html

The site lists perhaps 500 short statements used by abusers as excuses. The seemingly endless list is powerful and thus valuable for confrontation of denial, but it can be overwhelming. It is also available as a poster.

★★★★★ *A Community Checklist: Important Steps to End Violence Against Women*
        http://www.ojp.usdoj.gov/vawo/speeches/checklist.htm

From the Department of Justice, this document offers nine pages of concrete suggestions for the religious, academic, law enforcement, health care, sports, media, and workplace communities. It could be a good response to "What can I do?"

★★★★ *Community Outreach Health Information System*
        http://www.bu.edu/cohis/violence/domesvio.htm

The Partner Violence menu has papers that may clarify a client's thinking, such as Characteristics of a Healthy and an Abusive Relationships (a short checklist), and Types of Abuse and Warning Signs (a two-page list).

★★★★ *Family Life Library*
        http://www.oznet.ksu.edu/library/famlf2/#Family%20Living

Page down to Family Violence Series for 13 articles suitable as handouts and brochures from a Kansas State University program. The articles have to be downloaded and opened using Adobe Acrobat.

★★★★   *Domestic Violence Brochure*
      http://www.noda.new-orleans.la.us/source/dv_bro1.html

From the District Attorney of New Orleans, this site offers definitions, myths, information on the legal processes, a checklist of what to take when leaving, and victim's rights, all in about eight pages. A good starting place for advice.

★★★★   *Blain Nelson's Abuse Pages*
      http://www.blainn.cc/abuse

Nelson offers two long questionnaires, which are consciousness raising. Not all abuse is simple or physical.

★★★★   *Is Your Relationship Heading into Dangerous Territory?*
      http://www.utexas.edu/student/cmhc/relaviol.html

Six pages of checklists raise awareness, comparing violent and nonviolent relationships, the cycle of domestic violence, and what to do.

★★★★   *Determining a Safety Plan*
      http://womensissues.miningco.com/library/weekly/
      aa030799.htm?pid=2771&cob=home

Excellent tips, shelters, national hotline numbers, and links to sites from the American Bar Association and the federal government.

★★★   *Domestic Violence Information Manual*
      http://www.infoxchange.net.au/wise/DVIM/index.htm

This Internet book from Australia covers myths blaming the victim, theories, programs, and links.

★★★   *Frequently Asked Questions*   http://www.mincava.umn.edu/faqs.asp

This set of questions and answers is useful as a beginning point primarily because of its links to data sources.

★★★   *Spokane County Domestic Violence Web Site*
      http://www.domesticviolence.net/index.htm

A very rich site funded by the Centers for Disease Control that offers solid information for abusers, victims, and law enforcement.

Child Abuse

★★★★   *Child Abuse FAQs*
      http://www.extension.ualberta.ca/legalfaqs/nat/v-chi-en.htm

About 25 brief, well-written, and clear answers to questions.

Abused Males

★★★ *Myths of Male Sexual Victimization* by the National Organization
on Male Sexual Victimization http://www.malesurvivor.org

A good starting point for resources for male victims. See also the list of sites at http://incestabuse.miningco.com/msubsmen.htm? pid=2791&cob=home and Surviving and Living—Male Survivors of Child Sex Abuse at http://www.vix.com/menmag/sexabupg.htm whose online articles are very informative.

Self-Injury

★★★★★ *Self-Injury: You Are NOT the Only One*
http://www.palace.net/~llama/psych/injury.html

This is a high-quality, rich site. The Quick Primer is very educational, as is Self-Help: Organized and Otherwise. There are a questionnaire, quotes, references, chat, and more. Much of it can be used with Linehan's Dialectical Behavior Therapy program.

Abuse by Professionals

★★★★★ *H.O.P.E. (Help Overcoming Professional Exploitation)*
http://www.advocateweb.com/hope/default.asp

This excellent resource contains links to all the major groups and resources. It includes two clear and informative readings—"Sex between Therapist and Patient is NEVER Acceptable" and "Broken Boundaries: Sexual Exploitation in the Provider–Client Relationship"—and more specific materials. Reading these materials can raise awareness of past exploitation, so be alert in recommending these.

★★★ *Victorious Advocates for Survivors of Therapists (VAST): A Support Group
for Victims of Therapist Sexual Abuse*
http://www.cs.utk.edu/~bartley/other/vast.html

A page of information.

★★★ *SNAP (Survivors Network of those Abused by Priests)*
http://www.teleport.com/~snapmail/index.html

This is a self-help online support group with many resources listed. See also the support group SOSA: Survivors of Spiritual Abuse at http://www.sosa.org.

Other Kinds and Aspects of Abuse

★★★★★ *The Jewish Domestic Abuse and Agunah Problem*
http://users.aol.com/agunah/index.htm

This site provides support and comprehensive information for religious Jews.

★★★★ *Information for Mothers and Other People Concerned about Children Who
Witness Domestic Violence* http://home.vicnet.net.au/~dvirc/Childwit.htm

A brief factual overview and many good links.

★★★★   *WHOA (Working to Halt Online Abuse)*
          http://www.haltabuse.org

This site provides readings, technical suggestions, and support for those harassed or stalked in the online world.

★★★★   *National Center on Elder Abuse* http://www.elderabusecenter.org

The best site for FAQs, definitions, and readings.

★★★   *Domestic Violence in Lesbian Relationships*
          http://www.en.com/users/allison/l_dv.html

A brief statement and some support links.

Trauma

★★★★★   *Post Traumatic Stress Resources Web Page*
          http://www.sni.net/trips/links.html

The best set of links to major pages and metasites.

★★★★   *Trauma Resource Area* http://www.sidran.org/trauma.html

This site provides online resources for survivors, families, and helping professionals. Look under Resources and Articles for information about the Dissociative Experiences Scale (DES); and three brochures—Dissociative Identity Disorder (Multiple Personality Disorder), PsychTrauma Glossary, and Traumatic Memories. These are good but can be retraumatizing.

★★★★   *Post-Traumatic Stress Disorder: An Overview*
          by Matthew J. Friedman, MD, PhD
          http://www.ncptsd.org/treatment/literature/overview/cl_overview.html

Too technical for all but the most sophisticated readers, but it is a good orientation to symptoms and diagnosis for them.

★★★★   *Treatment of PTSD*
          http://www.ncptsd.org/facts/treatment/fs_treatment.html

This good overview by symptoms is three pages in length.

Biographical and Autobiographical Vignettes

There are literally hundreds of sites maintained by victims and former perpetrators of abuse. Please bear in mind that these stories may trigger memories in those who have experienced abuse. At http://www.blainn.cc/abuse/stories/index.html, you will find stories from about a dozen adult victims and abusers; and at http://www.blainn.cc/abuse/mystory/index.html, a wife abuser tells of his path.

Online Support Groups

★★★★ *The Abuse-Free Family of Mail Lists* http://blainn.cc/abuse-free

This is a well-structured support groups for victims, aggressors, and concerned others.

★★★ *Sexual Abuse Support*
http://incestabuse.miningco.com/msubssex.htm?pid=2791&cob=home

Links to about 20 support groups on the Internet for sexual abuse victims and concerned others.

See also Men's Issues (Chapter 19); Women's Issues (Chapter 29).

NATIONAL SUPPORT GROUPS

Batterers Anonymous
8485 Tamarind, #D
Fontana, CA 92335
Phone: 909-355-1100

For men who wish to control their anger and eliminate their abusive behavior.

Believe the Children
PO Box 797
Cary, IL 60013
Phone: 708-515-5432

For parents of children who have been victimized by people outside of the family.

Child Help USA Hotline
http://www.childhelpusa.org
Phone: 800-422-4453 (24 hours)

General information on child abuse and related issues and some crisis counseling. Referrals to local agencies for child abuse reporting.

Domestic Violence Anonymous
DVA, c/o BayLaw
PO Box 29011
San Francisco, CA 94129
Phone: 415-681-4850
E-mail: BayLaw1@ix.netcom.com

Twelve-step spiritual support for men and women who are recovering from domestic violence.

False Memory Syndrome Foundation
3401 Market Street, Suite 130
Philadelphia, PA 19104
Phone: 800-568-8882 or 215-387-1865
Fax: 215-387-1917
E-mail: psp@saul.cis.upenn.edu or
pam@linc.cis.upenn/edu

Research-oriented organization for persons falsely accused of childhood sex abuse based on recovered or repressed memories.

National Child Abuse Hotline
Phone: 800-422-4453

National Domestic Violence Hotline
http://www.ojp.usdoj.gov/vawo/
    newhotline.htm
Phone: 800-799-7233;
    800-787-3224 (TDD)

Information and referrals for victims
of domestic violence.

**National Legal Resource Center
on Children and the Law**
American Bar Association
1800 M Street, NW, Suite 200
Washington, DC 20036
Phone: 202-331-2250

**Network for Battered Lesbians
and Bisexual Women**
Phone: 617-423-7233

Parents Anonymous
675 West Foothill Boulevard, Suite 220
Claremont, CA 91711-3416
Phone: 909-621-6184
Fax 909-625-6304
E-mail:parentsanon@msn.com
http://www.parentsanonymous-natl.org

Professionally facilitated peer-led
group for parents who are having difficulty and would like to learn more effective ways of raising their children.

Parents United International
615 15th Street
Modesto, CA 95354-2510
Phone: 209-572-3446
Fax: 209-524-7780

Provides treatment for child sexual
abuse.

**RAINN (Rape Abuse and Incest
National Network)**
Phone: 800-656-4673
http://www.rainn.org

Offers a national hotline network for
victims and survivors of sexual abuse
who cannot get to a local rape crisis center. (Centers can be searched for online.)

**SAFE (Self-Abuse Finally Ends)
Alternative Information Line**
Phone: 800-DONT-CUT

Provides information on dealing with
self-abuse and self-mutilation and the
treatment options.

**SESAME (Survivors of Educator Sexual
Abuse/Misconduct Emerge)**
681 Route 7A
Copake, NY 12516
Phone: 518-329-1265 or 516-489-6406
Fax: 516-489-6101
E-mail:sesame-w@taconic.net or
    donses@earthlink.net
http://www.sesamenet.org

Support and information network for
families of children (K–12) who have
been sexually abused by a school staff
member.

**Sexual Abuse Survivors Anonymous
(SASA)**
PO Box 241046
Detroit, MI 48224

Twelve-step program for survivors of
rape, incest, or sexual abuse.

**S.I.A. (Survivors of Incest Anonymous)
World Service Office**
PO Box 21817
Baltimore, MD 21222-6817
Phone: 410-282-3400
Fax: 410-282-3400
http://www.siawso.org

Self-help 12-step program for men and
women 18 years and older who have
been victims of child sexual abuse and
want to be survivors.

**SNAP (Survivors Network of Those
Abused by Priests)**
PO Box 438679
Chicago, IL 60643-8679
Phone: 312-409-2720

Support for men and women who
were sexually abused by any clergy person.

Violence Against Women Office
http://www.ojp.usdoj.gov/vawo

From the U.S. Department of Justice, this site offers, under "VAW Online Resources," lots of information on interventions, advocates, and resources concerning all aspects of domestic violence from rape to stalking to child abuse and custody. There is also an up-to-date list of hotlines and local groups.

VOCAL (Victims Of Child Abuse Laws)
7485 East Kenyon Avenue
Denver, CO 80237
Phone: 303-233-5321
http://www.nasvo.org

To protect the rights of persons falsely and wrongly accused of child abuse. Referrals to psychologists.

CHAPTER 3

Addictive Disorders and Codependency

Most self-help authorities, as well as psychotherapists, realize how difficult the process of recovery from an addiction is. Virtually all authors of self-help books, autobiographies, and Internet sites on addiction recognize that some form of treatment or ongoing self-help group is needed for recovery. Therefore, reading a self-help book or watching a movie on addictions is unlikely, by itself, to help an individual conquer or control an addiction. However, good self-help materials can help someone determine the presence of an addictive disorder, can direct a person to the optimal form of self-help group or therapy, can be successfully employed as an adjunct to professional treatment, and can be of immense value to family and friends of a person with an addictive disorder.

In defining the range of addictive disorders for this chapter, we choose to focus on substance abuse (alcohol and drugs). Some mental health professionals would also consider sex or eating disorders as addictions, but these are located in the chapters on Sexuality (Chapter 24) and Eating Disorders (Chapter 15).

In addition to materials on alcohol and drugs, we consider a handful of self-help books devoted to the controversial concept of codependency. Although codependency originally referred to the problems of people married to alcoholics, it spread rapidly, perhaps indiscriminately, to include a host of other circumstances. Agreement on a precise definition of codependency has not been forthcoming, but those who write about the topic agree that the number of women who are codependent is staggering. And they agree that women who are codependent have low self-esteem, grew up in a dysfunctional family, and should focus more on their own inner feelings instead of catering to someone else's needs. In the language of codependency, many women stay with an unreliable partner, usually a male, because they are addicted to the relationship dynamics of being subservient to a male.

RECOMMENDATION HIGHLIGHTS

Self-Help Books

- On Alcoholics Anonymous and related strategies of recovery:

    ★★★★ *Alcoholics Anonymous* by Alcoholics Anonymous
    World Services

    ★★★★ *Twelve Steps and Twelve Traditions* by Alcoholics Anonymous
    World Services

- On maintaining sobriety as alternatives to AA:

    ★★★ *The Truth about Addiction and Recovery* by Stanton Peele,
    Archie Brodsky, and Mary Arnold

    ★★★ *Sober and Free* by Guy Kettelhack

    ★★★ *When AA Doesn't Work for You* by Albert Ellis
    and Emmett Velton

- For adult children of alcoholics:

    ★★★★ *A Time to Heal* by Timmen Cermak

Autobiographies

- On the descent into alcohol abuse and recovery:

    ★★★★ *A Drinking Life* by Pete Hamill

    ★★★★ *Getting Better: Inside Alcoholics Anonymous*
    by Nan Robertson

- On struggling with codependency and substance abuse:

    ★★★★ *Codependent No More* by Melodie Beattie

- On social aspects of drinking in American society:

    ◆ *Note Found in a Bottle* by Susan Cheever

Movies

- On the depressing descent into alcoholism:

    ★★★★★ *Days of Wine and Roses*

- Inspiring story of recovery and the founding of AA:

    ★★★★ *My Name Is Bill W*

- The process of surrender and recovery from cocaine addiction:

    ★★★★ *Clean and Sober*

- Realistic portrayal of alcoholism and families:

    ★★★★ *When a Man Loves a Woman*

    ★★★ *Cat on a Hot Tin Roof*

Internet Resources

- An excellent overview of addictions:

  ★★★★★ *Web of Addictions* http://www.well.com/user/woa

- A cognitive-behavioral therapy and harm-reduction model with interactive exercises:

  ★★★★★ *HabitSmart* http://www.cts.com/crash/habsmrt

- A nonreligious approach for patients using the SOS model:

  ★★★★★ *LifeRing*
            http://www.unhooked.com/toolbox/index.html

- A comprehensive document from the National Institute on Drug Abuse:

  ★★★★ *Cocaine Abuse and Addiction*
          http://www.nida.nih.gov/researchreports/cocaine/cocaine.html

---

In this chapter, we present the experts' consensual ratings on self-help books, autobiographies, movies, and Internet resources on addictive disorders and codependency. The titles and contact information for prominent self-help organizations are included as well.

SELF-HELP BOOKS

Strongly Recommended

★★★★ *Alcoholics Anonymous* (3rd ed., 1976). New York: Alcoholics Anonymous
        World Services.

In our national studies, this and the Cermak book (listed below) emerged as the highest rated self-help books for alcoholism. Revised twice since the first edition was published in 1939, the book is the basic text for Alcoholics Anonymous self-help groups. The principles of Alcoholics Anonymous have been revised and adapted by a number of self-help groups, such as Narcotics Anonymous, Gamblers Anonymous, and Al-Anon (for people with a variety of addictions and their families). Called the Big Book by AA, *Alcoholics Anonymous* is divided into two parts. The first part describes the Alcoholics Anonymous recovery program, which relies heavily on confession, group support, and spiritual commitment to help individuals cope with alcoholism. Extensive personal testimonies by AA members from different walks of life make up the latter two-thirds of the book. Successive editions of the book have expanded the case histories to include examples of alcoholics from a variety of backgrounds in the hope that alcoholics who read the book can identify with at least one of them. Brief appendixes include the Twelve AA Steps and Traditions and several testimonials to AA by ministers and physicians. The book also explains how to join AA and attend meetings.

★★★★ *Twelve Steps and Twelve Traditions* (pocket ed., 1995). New York: Alcoholics Anonymous World Services.

This book is devoted to detailed discussions of the Twelve Steps and Twelve Traditions used in Alcoholics Anonymous. The Steps and Traditions represent the heart of AA's principles, providing a precise guide for members to use in recovery. The strong religious nature of the Twelve Steps and Traditions is apparent in the first five steps:

1. We admitted we were powerless over alcohol . . . that our lives had become unmanageable.
2. We came to believe that a Power greater than ourselves could restore us to sanity.
3. We made a decision to turn our will and our lives over to the care of God as we understood Him.
4. We made a searching and fearless moral inventory of ourselves.
5. We admitted to God, to ourselves, and to another human being the exact nature of our wrongs.

Almost 200 pages are devoted to elaborating the basic principles of the Twelve Steps. The religious orientation of AA takes center stage. Like its sister book, *Alcoholics Anonymous, Twelve Steps and Twelve Traditions* earned a 4-star Recommended rating in the national studies. Because the 12 steps have become so widely used, mental health experts have carefully analyzed them. Criticisms focus mainly on their spiritual basis. Unhappy with the strong religious flavor, some mental health experts have recast the steps in nonreligious terms to appeal to a wider range of people. Before his death, the famous behaviorist B. F. Skinner put together a psychological alternative to AA's Twelve Steps. Here are the first five:

1. We accept the fact that all our efforts to stop drinking have failed.
2. We believe that we must turn elsewhere for help.
3. We turn to our fellow men and women, particularly those who have struggled with the same problem.
4. We have made a list of the situations in which we are most likely to drink.
5. We ask our friends to help us avoid those situations.

★★★★ *A Time to Heal: The Road to Recovery for Adult Children of Alcoholics* (1988) by Timmen L. Cermak. Los Angeles: Jeremy P. Tarcher.

This book attempts to carry the promise of hope. With a time to heal will come a time to belong. Each chapter addresses a specific time along the path of healing which includes a time to heal, to see, to remember, to feel, to separate, to be honest, to trust, to belong, and a time for courage. Included are case histories of the trauma and emotional pain adult children of alcoholics (ACOAs) had to live with as kids and currently as adults. Two important points made are that healing begins with honesty and that the flaws of an ACOA's lifestyle can only be dissolved by making the discipline of recovery a part of daily life. This is a helpful book for adult children of alcoholics, especially with their current relationships, and for the professionals who work with ACOAs.

Recommended

★★★ *It Will Never Happen to Me* (1981) by Claudia Black. New York: Ballantine.

Unlike the Alcoholics Anonymous books that are directed at alcoholics themselves, Claudia Black's book was written to help children—as youngsters, adolescents, and adults—cope with the problem of having an alcoholic parent. Black has counseled many alcoholic clients who were raised in alcoholic families, as well as wives of alcoholics. She comments that virtually every one of them said, "It will never happen to me"; hence the title of her book. Black believes that when people grow up in alcoholic homes, they learn to not talk, not trust, and not feel, whether they drink or not. This book received an impressive rating, but by only a small number of people who were familiar with it, which is why it has a 3-star rating. Black's book is a superb self-help book for children and spouses of alcoholics. Black does a good job of describing the alcoholic cycle, paints a vivid picture of the pitfalls faced by those related to alcoholics, and is upbeat in giving them hope for recovery and positive living. In the final chapter, Black tells readers about a number of resources for relatives of alcoholics.

★★★ *One Day at a Time in Al-Anon* (1988). New York: Al-Anon Family Group Headquarters.

Originated by a group of women with alcoholic husbands, Al-Anon is a support group for relatives and friends of alcoholics. Like a number of self-help support groups for alcoholics and their relatives, Al-Anon members follow AA's Twelve Steps of recovery. This book reflects an important principle of Al-Anon: Focus on one day at a time when living with an alcoholic. Each day is viewed as a fresh opportunity for self-realization and growth rather than for dwelling on past problems and disappointments. Like the other Alcoholics Anonymous books, *One Day at a Time in Al-Anon* has a strong spiritual emphasis. Each page is devoted to one day—from January 1 to December 31—and consists of two parts: a message and a daily reminder. Religious quotations are used frequently throughout the book.

★★★ *Sober and Free: Making Your Recovery Work for You* (1996) by Guy Kettelhack. New York: Simon & Schuster.

This book primarily focuses on maintaining sobriety with discussions of how to manage slips and relapses and relearning how to create significant relationships. The author stresses the importance of finding one's own way of maintaining sobriety, with help from support groups, therapy settings, medication, family, and friends. For those in conventional programs who are looking for more, or for people who do not feel that conventional programs will work for their recovery, this book could be a helpful resource.

★★★ *The Recovery Book* (1992) by Al J. Mooney, Arlene Eisenberg, and Howard Eisenberg. New York: Workman.

This book is written from a professional and personal perspective. The information is designed like a road map from active addiction to recovery and relapse prevention.

Topics covered are understanding recovery, deciding to quit, picking the right treatment and support group programs, knowing the facts and feeling about treatment and support groups, maintaining sobriety and dealing with temptations, relationships (families and social life), dentistry, physical fitness, financial and medical concerns, mind, emotions and spiritual issues, and relapse prevention. A section is devoted to dependency as a family disease. This book is a blend of medical knowledge and practical wisdom. It is also a comprehensive source for patients, families, and professionals dealing with the recovery process.

★★★ *A Day at a Time* (1976). Minneapolis: CompCare.

This is a book of daily reflections, prayers, and catchy phrases that are intended to offer inspiration and hope to recovering alcoholics. The book is based on the spiritual aspects of Alcoholics Anonymous, especially the Twelve Steps and Twelve Traditions. Like Al-Anon's *One Day at a Time in Al-Anon*, each page is devoted to a day—from January 1 through December 31. Each page is divided into three parts: Reflection for the Day, Today I Pray, and Today I Will Remember. The brief daily messages come from poets, philosophers, scholars, psychologists, and members of AA.

★★★ *When AA Doesn't Work for You: Rational Steps to Quitting Alcohol* (1992) by
      Albert Ellis and Emmett Velton. Fort Lee, NJ: Barricade Books.

The authors acknowledge that AA works for many people, but not for everyone. The beginning chapters help readers determine whether they have a drinking problem and introduces Rational Emotive Therapy as the best strategy for recovery. A number of helpful step-by-step methods, including the use of a daily journal and homework assignments, are provided in later chapters. Maladaptive thought patterns and conversations, followed by specific ways to replace them with more adaptive ones, are woven throughout the book. Unlike many of the books in the addiction and recovery category, Ellis and Velton's book does not include spiritual commitment in the recovery process. In fact, Ellis and Velton believe that AA's notion of the alcoholic's powerlessness is an irrational idea. Rational Recovery (RR), one of the increasing number of nonreligious self-help groups for recovering alcoholics and their relatives formed in recent years, traces its roots directly to the ideas of Albert Ellis and his Rational Emotive Therapy. RR teaches that what leads to persistent drinking is a person's belief that he or she is powerless and incompetent. Using Ellis's approach, a moderator (usually a recovered RR member) helps guide group discussion and gets members to think more rationally and act more responsibly. While AA stresses that alcoholics can never fully recover, but instead are always in some phase of recovery, RR tells members that recovery is not only possible but that it can happen in a year or so.

★★★ *Codependent No More: How to Stop Controlling Others and Start Caring for
      Yourself* (2nd ed., 1996) by Melodie Beattie. Center City, MN: Hazelden.

This is Melodie Beattie's personal narrative about being addicted to a certain type of relationship and how she recovered from it. In addition to describing her own personal struggles, she discusses the nature of codependency and how to recover from it. Beattie estimates that upwards of 80 million Americans are emotionally involved with an addict or are addicted themselves, not necessarily to alcohol or drugs but also to sex, work, food, or shopping. What kind of characteristics do codependents have? Beattie says that they are sufferers who feel anxiety, pity, and guilt when other people have a problem and that they overcommit themselves. How do codependents get out of this mess? Beattie endorses insight about the nature of codependent relationships and a version of the spiritually based Twelve Step recovery popularized by AA. Another theme of Beattie's recovery strategy is to begin having a love affair with yourself instead of with someone else to whom you have given too much.

This volume received a 3-star rating and a very mixed reception in our studies. Some respondents called it a great book, others an awful book. Although *Codependent No More* was on the *New York Times* best-seller list for 115 weeks and has sold upwards of 4 million copies, mental health professionals are not uniformly enthusiastic about it—thus the rather tepid three-star rating.

★★★　*Beyond Codependency* (1989) by Melodie Beattie. New York: Harper & Row.

This sequel to Beattie's *Codependent No More* elaborates the self-sabotaging behavior patterns of codependency in which a codependent person overcares for an unreliable, addictive person. Beattie addresses healthy recovery, the role of recycling (falling into old bad habits) in recovery, and how positive affirmations can counter negative messages. Testimonials from people who have used this method to break away from addictive relationships are liberally interspersed throughout the book. This book, too, received a 3-star rating in the national studies, and virtually the same plaudits and criticisms that characterize reviews of Beattie's earlier work apply to *Beyond Codependency* as well.

★★★　*The Truth about Addiction and Recovery* (1992) by Stanton Peele,
　　Archie Brodsky, and Mary Arnold. New York: Fireside.

Drawing on recent research and detailed case studies, the authors conclude that addictions are not diseases and they are not necessarily lifelong problems. Instead of medical treatment or a 12-step program, Peele, Brodsky, and Arnold recommend a life process program that emphasizes coping with stress and achieving one's goals. The book is a calm and reasoned alternative to the disease model of addiction that can prove very helpful. While it does include a number of case studies, it is more like a textbook than the other books in this category. A number of research studies and academic sources are cited to support the author's interpretations and recommendations. The book is well-documented but somewhat difficult to digest. It is particularly applicable to people seeking or valuing an alternative to the 12-step approach.

★★★　*Out of the Shadows: Understanding Sexual Addiction* (1983) by Patrick Carnes.
　　Minneapolis: CompCare.

This book is a guide to understanding sexual addictions using a 12-step program as a means to recovery. Important milestones are discovered, for example, the moment that comes for every addict, the cycle and levels of the addictive process, and the family's relationship to the world of a person and his or her addiction. Charts and diagrams are used to elucidate the system's levels, beliefs, and the Twelve Steps of AA and their adaptation to sexual addiction. The author states that like other addictions, sexual addiction is also rooted in a complex web of family and marital relationships and that part of therapy is to discover the role of the previous generation in the addiction. The author examines the tangled web of love, addictive sex, hate, fear, and relationships. Ultimately, this book is about hope. If you are a sex addict or suspect you are and have the courage to face yourself, this book is intended for you.

★★★ *Addiction and Grace* (1988) by Gerald C. May. New York: HarperCollins.

This volume combines spiritual and psychological principles to help combat any type of addiction, whether to alcohol, other drugs, sex, love, food, work, gambling, and so on. Reflecting his belief in the roles that relationships with others and spirituality play in addiction, May has subtitled his book *Love and Spirituality in the Healing of Addictions*. He states that the deepest human need is to be in a loving relationship with God and others. However, says May, our freedom to satisfy this need is restricted by many different addictions (including fame as well as drugs) that use up our desire. This book may particularly appeal to individuals with a strong spiritual orientation, and many people will find its writing style too abstract and technical to benefit them.

★★★ *Adult Children of Alcoholics* (expanded ed., 1990) by Janet Woititz. Deerfield Beach, FL: Health Communications.

Janet Woititz, the "mother" of the ACOA (adult children of alcoholics) movement, describes basic problems and vulnerabilities of adult children of alcoholics. Woititz says that reading her book can be the first step to recovery, along with Al-Anon and its Twelve Step program. The key to recovery is learning the principle of detachment. In her view, because adult children of alcoholics received inconsistent nurturing as children, as adults they hunger for nurture and are too emotionally dependent on their parents. They have to separate themselves from their parents in the least stressful way possible. Although this book was on the *New York Times* best-seller list for more than 45 weeks and has sold more than 2 million copies, the ratings by the mental health experts in our studies were mixed.

Not Recommended

★★ *The Alcoholic Man* (1990) by Sylvia Carey. Los Angeles: Lowell House.

★★ *How to Break Your Addiction to a Person* (1982) by Howard Halpern. New York: McGraw-Hill.

★ *Love Is a Choice* (1989) by Robert Helmfelt, Frank Minirth, and Paul Meier. Nashville, TN: Thomas Nelson.

★ *Co-Dependence: Healing the Human Condition* (1991) by Charles Whitfield. Deerfield Beach, FL: Health Communications.

Strongly Not Recommended

†   *Healing the Addictive Mind* (1991) by Lee Jampolsky. Berkeley, CA: Celestial Arts

†   *The Miracle Method: A Radically New Approach to Problem Drinking* (1995) by Scott D. Miller and Insoo Kim Berg. New York: Norton.

AUTOBIOGRAPHIES

Strongly Recommended

★★★★   *A Drinking Life: A Memoir* (1995) by Pete Hamill. Boston: Little, Brown.

Noted journalist and novelist Hamill, now sober for two decades, discusses without sentimentality the critical role alcohol played in his life. He argues that alcohol is not necessary to stimulate literary creativity. This is the book that inspired Caroline Knapp, author of *Drinking: A Love Story* (listed below), to sober up.

★★★★   *Codependent No More: How to Stop Controlling Others and Start Caring for Yourself* (2nd ed., 1996) by Melodie Beattie. Center City, MN: Hazelden.

The second edition of the author's best-selling *Codependent No More*, this edition updates Beattie's views on how to break away from destructive codependent relationships. She tried various self-help groups, including AA, Al-Anon, and Sex Addicts Anonymous, and she advocates their use for those in codependent relationships. Also reviewed in this chapter as a self-help book.

★★★★   *Getting Better: Inside Alcoholics Anonymous* (1988) by Nan Robertson. New York: William Morrow.

The author chronicles the growth of Alcoholics Anonymous, provides descriptions of meetings, and recounts her own struggle with alcoholism. A moving and factual tale.

Recommended

★★★   *Drinking: A Love Story* (1997) by Carolyn Knapp. New York: Delta.

Daughter of a psychoanalyst, the author grew up in a well-to-do family. She graduated magna cum laude from Brown University before becoming a reporter and later an editor. She was an anorexic and a high-functioning alcoholic who kept her addiction hidden from her associates. She bottomed out, checked into a rehab center, joined AA, and started on the slow path to recovery.

★★★   *Now You Know* (1990) by Kitty Dukakis (with J. Srovell). New York: Simon & Schuster.

The wife of a former governor of Massachusetts and presidential candidate discusses her bouts with bipolar disorder and her addiction to alcohol and pills.

Diamond in the Rough

♦ *Note Found in a Bottle: My Life as a Drinker* (1998) by Susan Cheever. New York: Simon & Schuster.

Daughter of a famous writer with serious drinking problems, Susan Cheever discusses the role that alcohol played in her own life and in her three failed marriages. She started early in life identifying cocktails with sophistication and sociability, but soon alcohol controlled her life. Now in recovery, Cheever reflects on social aspects of alcohol use in our society.

MOVIES

Strongly Recommended

★★★★★ *Days of Wine and Roses* (1962) produced by Martin Manulis and directed by Blake Edwards. 108 minutes.

This film is a portrait of a successful middle-class couple's agonizing struggles with progressive alcoholism in the 1950s. The husband recovers with AA, but the wife cannot, and he must leave her. The movie is depressing, with its depiction of job loss, repeated lapses, descent into ugliness, and the eventual dissolution of the marriage. Useful as a warning and illustration of the patterns of alcoholic couples.

★★★★ *My Name Is Bill W.* (1989) produced by Peter K. Duchow, James Garner, and Paul Rubell and directed by Daniel Petrie. 100 minutes.

This superbly acted film is the true story of the founder of AA, Bill W, a successful financial manager who gradually lost his job, friends, self-respect, and all he valued to alcoholism. Finally, he met Dr. Bob, and they kept each other sober and invented AA. Nothing is held back, and their success is highly inspirational.

★★★★ *Clean and Sober* (1988) produced by Tony Ganz and Deborah Blum and directed by Glenn Gordon Caron. R Rating. 124 minutes.

To escape the police for a murder he did not commit and a large theft from his employer, a young cocaine-addicted real estate salesman enters a drug rehabilitation program. He is in massive denial, but despite valiant attempts, he cannot escape the insights, confrontations, and caring of the counselors. The process of surrender and recovery by an ordinary and less-than-perfect client is well illustrated and believable.

★★★★ *When a Man Loves a Woman* (1994) produced by Jordan Kerner and Jon Avnet and directed by Luis Mandoki. R Rating. 124 minutes.

A film about alcoholism and families that is not overly simple, stereotyped, or designed with a happy ending. After extensive drinking and denial the wife enters treatment and recovery, and that is when her loving and accepting husband, a born enabler, must also change. He must give up handling all the responsibilities and making the decisions. His world is thus shaken up, too. No quick or final fixes are offered, but the movie portrays treatment adequately and recovery from denial with rare realism.

Recommended

★★★   *Cat on a Hot Tin Roof* (1958) produced by Lawrence Weingarten and directed by Richard Brooks. 108 minutes.

A superb writer's portrayal of the greedy family of a dying Southern patriarch. The family members all try to please him for their selfish benefits, except for the guilt-ridden ex-jock son and his sexually frustrated wife. The film is the classic story of family conflict and confrontation.

★★★   *Mask* (1986) produced by Martin Starger and directed by Peter Bogdanovich. PG-13 Rating. 120 Minutes.

A teenager, horribly disfigured by a rare disease, remains unbowed in the face of cruelties with the love and help of his gutsy mother. He succeeds at school, begins a relationship with a blind girl, relates normally to his mother's boyfriend, and lectures his mother on drug abuse. She protects and loves him so intensely that you believe he will somehow survive his fatal condition. The film makes the love between a mother and son palpable and inspirational.

★★★   *Leaving Las Vegas* (1995) produced by Jean Cazes and Phillipe Geoffroy and directed by Mike Figgis. R Rating. 112 minutes.

A poignant film about doomed losers. He is irretrievably dedicated to drinking himself to death, and she is a prostitute, abused and misused daily. He has no choices left, but she chooses to stay with him and care for him because he is her redemption. The film illustrates her unselfish love, charity, and gentleness despite the hardness of their lives and the weaknesses of their characters.

★★★   *Drugstore Cowboy* (1989) produced by Nick Wechsler and Karen Murphy and directed by Gus Van Sant, Jr. R Rating. 100 minutes.

A junkie and his four-person "family" rob drugstores to support their habits, which consume their empty lives. The excitement of drugs and the staged robberies alternate with the ennui of their highs and the routines of moving around the country. They are all sick and try ineffectively to help each other. After the death of a member of the group and a meeting with a haunted and haunting old addict, the junkie plans to get into treatment. His wife cannot understand a world without drugs and tries to pull him back. Utterly realistic, even to its junkie logic, and wonderfully acted, this movie might help clients see what the road ahead looks like and the possibility of difficult change.

★★★   *Postcards from the Edge* (1991) produced by Mike Nichols and John Calley and directed by Mike Nichols. R Rating. 101 minutes.

A drug-addicted young actress is falling apart, barely surviving at work, sleeping around with strangers, misplacing her days, and awaiting her next fix. Her mother is a famous actress and is addicted more acceptably to alcohol. The daughter enters rehab. Her mother visits her but responds only to the attentions of her fans. Mother–daughter rivalry is dramatized, and the ladies have many parallels. Well written and acted, the film drifts and does not reveal much about recovery. It might illustrate a not uncommon mother–daughter relationship for some clients.

★★★ *Jungle Fever* (1991) produced and directed by Spike Lee. R Rating. 132
        minutes.

On its surface, this is a film about an interracial romance between a successful, middle-class, married African American architect and a white working-class temp in his office. Lee, the director, calls this interracial attraction Jungle Fever and portrays it as based on media-enhanced stereotypes and America's focus on skin color. However, the film is much more. It portrays many of the effects of this relationship on the members of the families and communities from which the lovers come. It might be a suitable film for exploring interracial relationships and their contexts.

★★★ *The Gambler* (1974) produced by Irwin Winkler and Robert Chartoff and
        directed by Karel Reisz. R Rating. 111 minutes.

Despite his education and position as a college professor, the central character is a compulsive gambler sacrificing all to his addiction. He is pursued by the mob. Desperate, he gets money from his mother, which he then gambles away. He tries to end it all in one last attempt. This film might be useful to show gamblers or their families how compulsive and destructive this addiction is.

INTERNET RESOURCES

There are literally thousands of sites on these topics. Many are devoted to prevention; they are not cited here because only those about treatment are relevant to self-help.

Metasites

★★★★★ *Web of Addictions* http://www.well.com/user/woa

A superb source of accurate information. The Facts offers links to hundreds of fact sheets from many trustworthy sources.

★★★★ *Another Empty Bottle* http://www.alcoholismhelp.com

An enormous collection of links to health, drunk driving, organizations, support, treatment, and so on. Available in six languages.

Psychoeducational Materials for Clients and Families

Alcohol

★★★★★ *HabitSmart* http://www.cts.com/crash/habtsmrt

Using the best cognitive-behavioral therapy and harm reduction models, this site offers a dozen long essays and several interactive exercises for overcoming ambivalence, introducing cognitive-behavioral therapy ideas, and other solid materials by Robert Westermeyer.

★★★★★   *LifeRing* http://www.unhooked.com/toolbox/index.html

If you accept the evidence of the ineffectiveness of the Minnesota Model and want a nonreligious approach, this page offers several fine long pieces for patients using the Secular Organization for Sobriety/Save Our Selves model, the empirical evidence, and links to groups.

★★★★★   *Alcohol Dependence* http://www.mentalhealth.com/dx/fdx-sb01.html

There are reprints and booklets from the best sources. They are solidly informative, and most can be very educational to clients.

★★★★   *Concerned about Your Drinking?* http://www.carebetter.com

The most obvious feature of this site is an interactive, anonymous test of drinking and confidential feedback of results. However, the information under FAQs is good. Both the FAQs and the Related Sites encourage self-control treatment models.

★★★★   *Alcohol—An Interactive Assessment*
            http://www.mayohealth.org/mayo/9707/htm/alcohol.htm

Starting with a nine-item test and feedback, the next four pages guide one through taking off the blinders to treatments (only 12-step programs). It might be a simple place to have clients begin.

★★★★   *Common Sense* http://www.pta.org/commonsense

A section of the Parent Teachers Association site with material aimed at parents. Solid information, support, and good advice.

★★★★   *JACS—Jewish Alcoholics, Chemically Dependent Persons and Significant Others*
            http://www.jacsweb.org

The Library contains 10 articles that can be of help in breaking down denial and ignorance.

★★★   *Adult Children of Alcoholics* http://www.couns.uiuc.edu/brochures/adult.htm

A three-page handout on adult children for college students. See also *Children of Alcoholics* http://www.aacap.org/publications/factsfam/Alcoholc.htm

★★★   *SMART: Self-Management And Recovery Training*
            http://www.smartrecovery.org

Based on Ellis's rational-emotive behavior therapy, this approach eschews war stories, sponsors, and meetings for life for structured meetings run by trained advisors. Their Four-Point Program is: (1) building and maintaining motivation to abstain; (2) coping with urges; (3) managing thoughts, feelings, and behavior; and (4) balancing momentary and enduring satisfactions.

★★★ *Al-Anon and Alateen* http://www.Al-Anon-Alateen.org

The usual AA literature in a dozen languages may serve as a good introduction to the naive or those in denial.

★★★ *Drug/Alcohol Brochures* http://www.uiuc.edu/departments/mckinley/
health-info/drug-alc/drug-alc.html

Ten single-page handouts from a university counseling center with guidelines and facts. Basic information.

Drug Abuse

★★★★ *Cocaine Abuse and Addiction*
http://www.nida.nih.gov/researchreports/cocaine/cocaine.html

A comprehensive, recent (May 1999) document from the National Institute on Drug Abuse.

★★★★ *Public and Research Views of Dual-Diagnosis Explored* by Leslie Knowlton
http://www.mhsource.com/pt/p950536.html

A four-page introduction written for an educated public that explains some of the interactions of substance use and mental illness.

★★★★ *Preveline–Prevention Online* http://www.health.org

This is SAMHA's clearing house of information on all aspects. Designed to be accessed by drug name, audience, or publication series.

★★★ *Commonly Abused Drugs: Street Names for Drugs of Abuse*
http://www.nida.nih.gov/DrugsofAbuse.html

A chart with current names, medical uses, periods of detection, and so forth.

★★★ *National Institute on Drug Abuse* http://www.nida.nih.gov

Many publications that can be useful for patients. The Research Reports are large and sophisticated, but for a thorough overview they are of high quality. The NIDA Infofax— Science Based Facts on Drug Abuse and Addiction contains three- to five-page summaries available online and by fax. There are a dozen summaries about different chemicals and four on treatments.

★★★ *The Do It Now Foundation* http://www.doitnow.org/pages/pubhub.html

Here you will find readable and printable copies of approximately a hundred brochures about smoking, drugs, alcohol, street drugs, and drugs and kids. The style is often hip and striking.

Codependency

★★★★ *The Issues of Codependency* http://www.soulselfhelp.on.ca/coda.html

This site includes a full explanation of each step, materials on the codependent personality, and similar essays.

Compulsive Gambling

★★★ Compulsive Gambling
       http://www.drkoop.com/wellness/mental_health/compulsive_gambling

Many excellent links and materials in the Library.

Other Resources

★★★★ *National Inhalant Prevention Coalition* http://www.inhalants.org

About a dozen one- to two-page informational resources. Well-done information about a growing area of abuse.

★★★ *Software for Recovering People* http://christians-in-recovery.org/software

Mainly Bible study and 12 steps, but also journaling, references, and goal setting.

★★★ *Addiction Resource Guide* http://www.addictionresourceguide.com

To assist with choosing a rehabilitation program, this guide has descriptions of about 100 inpatient and three outpatient programs, guidelines, and definitions.

See also Eating Disorders (Chapter 15).

NATIONAL SUPPORT GROUPS

Adult Children of Alcoholics World Services Organization
PO Box 3216
Torrance, CA 90510
Phone: 310-534-1815
http://www.adultchildren.org or E-mail:info@adultchildren.org

A Twelve Step and Twelve Tradition program of recovery for adults raised in a dysfunctional environment that included alcohol or other family dysfunctions.

Alateen and Al-Anon Family Groups
1600 Corporate Landing Parkway
Virginia Beach, VA 23454-56127
Phone: 757-563-1600 or 888-425-2666
Fax: 757-536-1655
E-mail:wso@al-anon.org
http://www.al-anon.org
   or http://www.alateen.org

A fellowship of young persons whose lives have been affected by someone else's drinking.

Alcoholics Anonymous
Box 459, Grand Central Station
New York, NY 10163
Phone: 212-870-3400
http://www.alcoholics-anonymous.org

American Council on Alcoholism
Hotline: 800-527-5344
Referrals to treatment centers and DWI
classes.

Chemically Dependent Anonymous
PO Box 423
Severna Park, MD 21146
Phone: 410-647-7060

Twelve-step program for friends and
relatives of people who are chemically
dependent.

Cocaine Anonymous
3740 Overland Avenue, Suite C
Los Angeles, CA 90034-6337
For local chapters, call 800-347-8998 or
310-559-5833
Fax: 310-559-2554
E-mail:cawso@ca.org
http://www.ca.org

Debtors Anonymous
PO Box 400, Grand Central Station
New York, NY 10163-0400
Phone: 212-642-8220

Fellowship that follows the AA Twelve
Step program for mutual help in recovering from compulsive indebtedness.

Gamblers Anonymous
PO Box 17173
Los Angeles, CA 90017
Phone: 213-386-8789
Fax: 213-386-0030
E-mail: isomain@gamblersanonymous.org
http://www.gamblersanonymous.org

Gam-Anon Family Groups
PO Box 157
Whitestone, NY 11357
Phone: 718-352-1671

Twelve-step program of recovery for
relatives and friends of compulsive gamblers.

Marijuana Anonymous (MA)
PO Box 2912
Van Nuys, CA 91404
Phone: 800-766-6779

Twelve-step program of recovery from
marijuana addiction.

Mothers Against Drunk Driving
http://www.madd.org

This large organization provides support though local chapters, education,
political activism, and victim assistance.

Moderation Management (MM)
PO Box 1752
Woodinville, WA 98072
Phone: 888-561-9834
http://moderation.org

Self-management, moderation, and a
balanced lifestyle are emphasized. Not
intended for alcoholics or those severely
dependent on alcohol.

Narcotics Anonymous
PO Box 9999
Van Nuys, CA 91409
Phone: 818-773-9999
Fax: 818-700-0700
E-mail:info@na.org
http://www.na.org

Nar-Anon World Wide Service
PO Box 2562
Palos Verdes, CA 90274-0119
Phone: 310-547-5800

Twelve-step program of recovery for
families and friends of addicts.

National Clearinghouse for Alcohol and Drug Information
Hotline: 800-788-2800 (Touch-Tone);
800-729-6686 (rotary)

Information on alcohol and drug
abuse, prevention, and treatment centers.

National Institute on Alcohol Abuse and Alcoholism
6000 Executive Boulevard
Bethesda, MD 20892
Phone: 301-443-3860
http://www.niaaa.nih.gov

Rational Recovery (RR)
PO Box 800
Lotus, CA 95651
http://www.rational.org/recovery
Phone: 530-621-2667

Founded 1986. Abstinence-based. Addictive Voice Recognition Training is emphasized.

Recovery Online
http://www.onlinerecovery.org/
index.html

A set of 100 links to 12-step, religious, and secular support groups for all kinds of addictions.

Self Management and Recovery Training (SMART)
24000 Mercantile Road, Suite 11
Beachwood, OH 44122
http://www.smartrecovery.org
Phone: 216-292-0220

An abstinence-based, cognitive-behavioral approach.

CHAPTER 4

Adult Development and Aging

For too long, psychologists believed that development was something that happens only to children. To be sure, growth and development are dramatic in the first two decades of life, but development goes on in the adult years, too. In this chapter, we consider self-help resources for people in the middle adult and older years.

The adult years are important not only to the adults who are passing through them but also to their children, who often want to better understand their parents and improve their relationships with them. Changes in body, personality, and ability can be considerable during the adult years. Adults want to know how to adjust to these changes and how to make transitions more smooth.

More than a century ago, Oliver Wendell Holmes said, "To be seventy years young is sometimes far more cheerful and hopeful than to be forty years old." In Holmes's day, being 70 years young was unusual, as the average life expectancy was less than 45 years. In the ensuing century, we have gained an average of more than 30 years of life, mainly because of improvements in sanitation, nutrition, and medical knowledge.

For too long, the aging process was thought of as an inevitable, irreversible decline. Aging involves both decline and growth, loss and gain. The previous view of aging was that we should passively live out our final years. The new view stresses that, although we are in the evening of our lives, we are not meant to live out our remaining years passively. Everything we know about older adults suggests that the more active they are, the happier and healthier they are.

Here, then, are the evaluative ratings and reviews of self-help books, autobiographies, movies, and websites devoted to adult development and aging. We begin with a snapshot of our primary recommendations.

RECOMMENDATION HIGHLIGHTS

Self-Help Books

- For adult daughters seeking to understand and improve relationship with their mothers:

    ★★★★ *Necessary Losses* by Judith Viorst

- For young adults looking to understand and improve relationships with their parents:

    ★★★ *How to Deal with Your Parents When They Still Treat You Like a Child* by Lynn Osterkamp

- For men wanting to learn about stages of adult development and the midlife crisis:

    ★★★★ *Seasons of a Man's Life* by Daniel J. Levinson

- For women wanting to learn about stages of adult development:

    ★★★ *Passages* by Gail Sheehy

- On menopause:

    ★★★ *The Silent Passage* by Gail Sheehy

- On aging in general, with emphasis on the medical and physical dimensions:

    ★★★ *Complete Guide to Health and Well-Being after 50* by Robert Weiss and Genell Subak-Sharpe

    ★★★ *Aging Well* by James Fries

- On aging in general with emphasis on the lifestyle dimensions:

    ★★★ *It's Better to Be over the Hill Than under It* by Eda LeShan

- On making environmental changes to improve life quality:

    ◆ *Enjoy Old Age* by B. F. Skinner and M. E. Vaughan

Autobiographies

- Moving conversations about dying (and living):

    ★★★★★ *Tuesdays with Morrie* by Mitch Albom

- For older people wanting to remain active and contribute to society:

    ★★★★ *The Virtues of Aging* by Jimmy Carter

- On turning 50 and passing through menopause:

    ◆ *Getting Over Getting Older* by Letty Cottin Pogrebin

Movies

- On accepting the limitations of age and repairing relationships before death:
  ★★★★★ *On Golden Pond*

- On living with adult children while maintaining one's independence and goals:
  ★★★★★ *The Trip to Bountiful*

- The pompous aging doctor becomes a caring patient:
  ★★★★★ *The Doctor*

- Inspiring fable on life paths and second chances:
  ★★★★ *It's a Wonderful Life*

Internet Resources

- A great site with links to health and retirement concerns:
  ★★★★ *Geropsychology Central*
  http://www.premier.net/~gero/geropsyc.html

- A training program online to teach the basics of geriatric care:
  ★★★★★ *Multidisciplinary Education in Geriatrics and Aging*
  http://cpmcnet.columbia.edu/dept/dental/
  Dental_Educational_Software/
  Gerontology_and_Geriatric_Dentistry/introduction.html

- On understanding aging in a fuller context:
  ★★★★★ *Social Gerontology* http://www.trinity.edu/~mkearl/geron.html

- Useful publications for health concerns:
  ★★★★★ *Booklets for Health Professionals and Public*
  http://www.nih.gov/nia/health/general/general.htm

- A great site for those who are retired:
  ★★★★★ *The American Association of Retired Persons (AARP)*
  http://www.aarp.org

SELF-HELP BOOKS

Strongly Recommended

★★★★ *Necessary Losses* (reprint ed., 1998) by Judith Viorst. New York: Fireside.

This book, on best-seller lists for more than a year, describes how we can grow and change through the losses that are an inevitable part of our lives. When we think of loss, we often think of the death of people we love. But Viorst talks about loss as a far more encompassing theme of life. She says we lose not only through death but also by leaving and being left, by changing and letting go and moving on. Viorst also describes the losses we experience as a result of impossible expectations, illusions of freedom and power, illusions of safety, and the loss of our own younger self, the self we always thought would be unwrinkled, invulnerable, and immortal. Although most of us try to avoid loss, Viorst gives a positive tone to the emotional struggles we go through. She believes that through the loss of our mother's protection, the loss of impossible expectations we bring to relationships, and the loss of loved ones through separation and death, we gain a deeper perspective, true maturity, and fuller wisdom about life. This fine self-help book was the highest-rated book in the adult development category. Viorst writes extraordinarily well, and her sensitive voice comes through clearly. Most adults can benefit from reading this book and will relate to the examples of loss.

★★★★ *Seasons of a Man's Life* (reissue ed., 1986) by Daniel J. Levinson. New York: Ballantine.

This national bestseller is an adult development book that outlines a number of stages adults pass through, with a special emphasis on the midlife crisis. The book's title accurately reveals that *Seasons of a Man's Life* is more appropriate for men than for women. In this book, Levinson and his colleagues summarize the results of their extensive interviews with 40 middle-aged men. Conclusions are bolstered with biographies of famous men and memorable characters from literature. Although Levinson's main interest is midlife change, he describes a number of stages and transitions in the life cycle between ages 17 and 65. Levinson believes that successful adjustment requires mastering developmental tasks at each stage. He sees the 20s as a novice phase of adult development. At the end of the teenage years, people need to make a transition from dependence to independence, a transition marked by the formation of a dream—an image of the kind of life desired, especially in terms of career and marriage. From about 28 to 33, people go through a transition period in which they must face the more serious question of determining their development. In the 30s, individuals enter the phase of "becoming one's own man" (or BOOM). By age 40, they have reached a stable location in their careers, have outgrown their tenuous attempts at learning to become adults, and now must look forward to the kind of lives they will lead as middle-aged adults. Levinson reports that 70 to 80% of the men he interviewed found the midlife transition (ages 40 to 45) tumultuous and psychologically painful. This book is one of several that helped form the American public's image of a midlife crisis. The book is two decades old now and tends to overdramatizes the midlife crisis. However, it remains a classic self-help resource.

Recommended

★★★ *It's Better to Be over the Hill Than under It: Thoughts on Life over Sixty* (1990) by Eda LeShan. New York: Newmarket.

This book consists of what LeShan believes are her best columns from *Newsday* on a wide range of aging topics, related mainly to the social, psychological, and lifestyle aspects of aging. The articles are divided into three sections: Loving and Living, Memories, and Growing and Changing. The 75 essays range from "An Open Letter to the Tooth Fairy" to "Nothing Is Simple Anymore" and "Divorce after Sixty." Many life issues that have to be dealt with in old age are covered: money, love, sex, anger, facing mortality, work, marriage, friendship, retirement, holidays, grandparenting, children, and so on. Woven through the essays is hope for older adults, hope that will allow them to love and grow and to keep their minds and bodies active and alive. The real test for older adults, LeShan says, is not looking back but rather dealing with the present, no matter what the inevitable aspects of aging are, and anticipating each coming day. This 3-star book was favorably reviewed, deserving of 4 stars were it not for the small number of experts evaluating it, and is enjoyable reading. LeShan is a masterful writer who mixes wit with sage advice. The book is especially good for older adults who feel caught in a rut and need their spirits lifted.

★★★ *Making Peace with Your Parents* (1983) by Harold Bloomfield. New York: Random House.

This book is about adults' relationships with their parents. According to Bloomfield, to become a fulfilled and competent person, you need to resolve the conflicts surrounding your relationship with your parents. Drawing on insights from his clinical practice, research in the area of adult children–parent relationships, and personal experiences in his own family, Bloomfield describes the problems many adults encounter in expressing love and anger toward their parents. *Making Peace with Your Parents* contains exercises and case studies that help adults improve their communication with their parents; cope effectively with difficult parents; unravel parental messages about love, sex, and marriage; and deal with parents' aging, dying, and death. The author especially believes that adults have to become their own best parent by nurturing themselves and engaging in self-responsibility instead of relying on their parents to satisfy important needs. This book just missed making the 4-star category. It is an excellent book for adults who have a great deal of anger toward their parents. The message of self-responsibility and the clear examples can help adults become aware of how their relationships with their parents have continued to shape their lives as adults.

★★★ *The Silent Passage* (rev. ed., 1998) by Gail Sheehy. New York: Random House.

This best-seller concerns menopause, the time in middle age—usually in the late 40s or early 50s—when a woman's menstrual periods and childbearing capability cease and production of estrogen drops considerably. Journalist Gail Sheehy is also the author of the widely read adult development book, *Passages*, reviewed below. To better understand menopause, Sheehy interviewed many middle-aged women and talked with experts in a number of fields. Sheehy argues that the passage through menopause is seldom easy for women because of distracting symptoms, confusing medical advice, unsympathetic reactions from loved ones, and the scornful attitudes of society. For these reasons, menopause has been a lonely and emotionally draining experience for many women. Sheehy's goal is to erase the stigma of menopause and help women understand that it is a normal physical process. She describes her own difficult experiences and reports the frustrations of many women she interviewed. Sheehy's optimism comes through in her hope that menopause will come to be known as "the gateway to a second adulthood" for women. Sheehy is a masterful writer and the book is quick and easy reading (it's a small-format book, only about 150 pages long). Few self-help writers' books ring with the clear-toned prose that Sheehy's do. At the same time, many medical and psychological experts simply don't believe that menopause is the widespread problem Sheehy thinks it is. Critics contend that just as Sheehy overdramatizes midlife as a crisis, she has done the same with menopause.

★★★ *Passages: Predictable Crises of Adult Life* (1976) by Gail Sheehy. New York: Dutton.

Like *Seasons of a Man's Life*, *Passages* is about stages of adult development that all adults supposedly pass through. In the mid-1970s Sheehy's book was so popular that it topped the *New York Times* best-seller list for 27 weeks. Sheehy argues that we all go through developmental stages roughly bound by chronological age. Each stage brings problems people must solve before they can progress to the next stage. The periods between the stages are called passages. Sheehy uses catchy phrases to describe each stage: "the trying 20s," "catch 30," "the deadline decade" (35 to 45 years of age), and "the age 40 crucible." Sheehy's advice never waivers: Adults in transition may feel miserable, but those who face up to agonizing self-evaluation, who appraise their weaknesses as well as their strengths, who set goals for the future, and who try to be as independent as possible will find happiness more often than those who do not fully experience these trials. Sheehy believes that these passages earn people an authentic identity, one that is not based on the authority of one's parents or on cultural prescriptions. Not surprisingly, given its popularity with the public, this was one of the most frequently rated books in our national studies. But the experts' evaluations, while largely positive, were mixed. On the positive side, some mental health experts believe the book has given people in their 30s, 40s, and 50s new insights about developmental stages and transitions in adult development. On the negative side, some experts on adult development believe that Sheehy's book describes midlife as too much of a crisis and does not adequately consider the many individual ways people go through midlife. Dilemmas in adult development do not spring forth at 10-year intervals as Sheehy implies.

★★★ *When You and Your Mother Can't Be Friends* (1990) by Victoria Secunda. New York: Delacorte.

As the title of this book suggests, Secunda writes about the problems that can unfold in mother–daughter relationships when daughters become adults—daughters who have not resolved unhappy childhood attachments to their mothers and who continue to have unhappy relationships with them. Secunda believes that many adult women won't admit or explore their emotional confusion about their mothers. Yet honesty is exactly what is needed to go beyond mother–daughter bitterness, she says. One problem is that many adult daughters may not recognize how their relationships with their mothers have skewed their adulthood. Such women may play out their unresolved disaffection with husbands and lovers, coworkers and friends, and especially with their own children. Adult daughters can resolve unhappy relationships with their mothers and develop affectionate truces. Friendship can even develop. Excerpts from 100 interviews with adult daughters are interspersed throughout the book to help adult daughters come to know, understand, and accept their mothers. This is an excellent book for adult daughters who have problematic relationships with their mothers. It is also easy to read with an optimistic tone and many real-life examples. On the other hand, other mental health professionals marked down the book, citing it as stereotyping adult daughter–mother relationships and giving too little attention to individual variations.

★★★   *The Fountain of Age* (1993) by Betty Friedan. New York: Simon & Schuster.

The book looks at new possibilities and new directions for aging of both men and women. Some topics covered are women's living longer than men; physical, emotional, and environmental changes; and age as adventure. The author encourages older people not to buy into the myth that aging is a problem, a plight, a time of rapidly declining physical and mental faculties. Friedan provides research and anecdotal evidence that the older adult years may be a period of true creativity. She discusses the tragic practice of early retirement, myths about menopause, early preparation for death, and over-protectiveness of family, friends, professionals, and the government. Creative ideas about health care, housing, work, and relationships are discussed. A book for all adults, but a critique of our society and aging that will definitely move the over-60 crowd.

★★★   *Ageless Body, Timeless Mind: The Quantum Alternative to Growing Old* (1993) by
       Deepak Chopra. New York: Harmony Books.

Chopra, a best-selling author, offers an Eastern philosophical approach to the problems of aging. He combines mind–body medicine with current antiaging research. He states that a prolonged fruitful life is not a question of mind over matter, but rather of mind and matter, mind and body, together as one with the universe. By intervening at the level where belief becomes biology, we can achieve our potential: Mental, social, and intellectual activity can keep people vital and alert as they age. Chopra offers step-by-step exercises to help create a healthy life. A separate chapter examines India's traditional medical system of Arurveda. The book reveals how we can learn to direct the way our bodies metabolize time and reverse the aging process. A book for the layperson and professional interested in a blend of Eastern philosophy and Western scientific research.

★★★   *How to Deal with Your Parents When They Still Treat You Like a Child* (1992) by
       Lynn Osterkamp. New York: Berkley Books.

This book was written for adult children who want to understand and improve their relationships with their parents. Author Lynn Osterkamp helps the reader answer several important questions:

- Why are so many adults still worrying about what their parents think?
- Why can't I talk to my parents the way I talk to other people?
- Why do we keep having the same arguments?
- How can I stop feeling guilty?
- How can I change family gatherings and holidays?
- What role would I like for my parents to play in my life today?

Osterkamp's analysis of adult children–parent relationships can especially benefit adults in their 20s and 30s who want to get along better with their parents. The book is filled with personal accounts and identifies problems readers may be having. Osterkamp suggests ways to communicate more effectively with parents. And she motivates the reader to develop a step-by-step action plan to accomplish relationship goals. Well written and well researched, this book is full of helpful examples and wise advice.

★★★   *Complete Guide to Health and Well-Being after 50* (1988) by Robert Weiss and Genell Subak-Sharpe. New York: Times Books.

The full title of this book is actually *The Columbia University School of Public Health Complete Guide to Health and Well-Being after 50*. The book was produced under the auspices of the Columbia University School of Public Health. The word *complete* in the title is appropriate: The book provides information about an encyclopedic number of physical and mental health issues that older adults face. The topics range from medical and physical concerns such as heart disease, arthritis, and cosmetic surgery to psychological and lifestyle concerns such as coping with stress and retirement. Most self-help books don't have elaborate charts and tables, but this one is filled with them, along with many illustrations, exercises, diets, and self-tests. This excellent guide provides solid descriptions of the health problems of the elderly and the best ways to deal with them. As would be expected in a book written by public health experts, *Complete Guide to Health and Well-Being after 50* is strongly tilted toward a presentation and exploration of physical health issues. Coverage of the psychological and social dimensions of aging is not as thorough and not as insightful.

★★★   *Aging Well* (1989) by James Fries. Reading, MA: Addison-Wesley.

Fries believes that we have the capability to age well, with grace, wisdom, energy, and vitality. Aging well is not an easy task, he says. It requires a basic understanding of the aging process, a good plan, work, and persistence. Part I, Vitality and Aging, communicates the value of pride and enthusiasm in preventing disease and maintaining vitality and provides a wealth of understanding about specific diseases such as arthritis and osteoporosis. Part II, General Concerns, describes the five keys to a healthy senior lifestyle: selecting and dealing with doctors, sexual issues, retirement, chronic illness, and completing a plan that will ensure that your wishes are carried out after you die. Part III, Solutions, is a step-by-step guide to managing a full range of medical problems, including pain, urinary tract problems, and heart ailments. The book is optimistic, well-written, and thorough. Fries's expertise on aging clearly comes through. The book is especially helpful as a guide to consult when physical and medical problems arise.

★★★   *How to Live Longer and Feel Better* (1986) by Linus Pauling. New York: W. H. Freeman.

This book provides a regimen that the author believes will add years to your life and make you feel better. Linus Pauling, a two-time Nobel Prize winner, shows how vitamins work and how to make them work for you. Pauling especially believes that vitamin C is responsible for producing and maintaining the body's supply of collagen, which he calls the glue that holds the body together. He argues that megadoses of vitamin C and other critical vitamins can slow down the aging process, make us look younger, and help us feel better. This book received 3 stars in the national studies, barely making it into the Recommended category. In the past, Pauling's ideas clashed with those of the medical establishment, but recently researchers are finding that vitamin supplements of C, E, and betacarotene may help slow the aging process and improve the health of older adults. Pauling portrays himself as a misunderstood, maligned maverick whose ideas will eventually be accepted by the medical community.

Diamonds in the Rough

♦ *Your Renaissance Years* (1991) by Robert Veninga. Boston: Little, Brown.

This volume, subtitled *Making Retirement the Best Years of Your Life,* begins by describing the secrets of successful retirement and urging the reader to consider early retirement. Subsequent parts of the book focus on the following retirement concerns: money, housing, health, leisure, relationships, and spirituality. Case histories of 135 retirees are interspersed throughout. *Your Renaissance Years* was positively rated in the national study, but by only five psychologists; few of the mental health professionals were familiar with it. Nonetheless, it is a valuable, well-written, and in-depth resource for coping effectively with retirement.

♦ *Enjoy Old Age: A Program of Self-Management* (1993) by B. F. Skinner
  and M. E. Vaughan. New York: Norton.

Vaughan, a former Harvard research associate and well-known expert on aging, and Skinner, a pioneer in behaviorism, combine their talents to assist older adults in making environmental changes to improve the quality of their lives. Specific areas covered include forgetfulness, thinking clearly and creatively, doing something about old age, getting along better with people, and dealing with the new emotions of aging. Advanced planning and a positive approach can provide solutions to the problem of age. Skinner describes his own solutions, and Vaughan contributes selections from the literature on aging. The book is written in a nonscientific way using everyday English. It is useful for people approaching or already in their 60s or 70s, or for those living or working with older people. Its eight raters evaluated it very positively, resulting in its placement in the Diamond in the Rough category.

Not Recommended

★ *The 50+ Wellness Program* (1990) by Harris McIlwain, Debra Fulghum,
  Robert Fulghum, and Robert Bruce. New York: Wiley.

AUTOBIOGRAPHIES

Strongly Recommended

★★★★★ *Tuesdays with Morrie: An Old Man, a Young Man, and Life's Greatest Secrets*
  (1997) by Mitch Albom. New York: Doubleday.

Sportswriter Albom had been a student of sociology professor Morrie Schwartz 20 years earlier. Reunited after he saw Schwartz on *Nightline*, Albom finds that his former professor is dying from Lou Gehrig's disease. The book describes fourteen Tuesday visits Albom made to his dying mentor and the content of their conversations. It is a moving best-seller.

★★★★ *The Virtues of Aging* (1998) by Jimmy Carter. New York: Ballantine Books.

The former president discusses aging in America, with special attention to the state of the Social Security system, health, exercise, and financial planning. Carter discusses the importance of family ties and describes ways in which older people can remain active and contribute to social betterment.

Recommended

★★★ *The Fountain of Age* (1994) by Betty Friedan. New York: Touchstone.

One of the major figures in the modern feminist movement and author of *The Feminine Mystique,* Friedan deconstructs current beliefs about aging while maintaining that it can be a time of adventure, exploration, fulfillment, and creativeness. Also rated earlier in this chapter as a self-help book.

Diamonds in the Rough

◆ *Getting Over Getting Older* (1997) by Letty Cottin Pogrebin. New York: Berkley.

Well-known feminist writer Letty Cottin Pogrebin describes her reactions to turning 50 and her concerns about her appearance, health, relationships, sex, and going through menopause.

◆ *I'm Not as Old as I Used to Be* (1998) by Frances Weaver. New York: Hyperion.

A sprightly account of life after 70, in which NPR commentator and senior editor of the *Today Show* Frances Weaver describes her battle with alcoholism after her husband's death. She went to a detox center and eventually achieved sobriety. Weaver returned to school, traveled, and began writing. She employs her keen wit to demonstrate how to be active and productive during life's later years. A recent book, probably not widely known by mental health experts—and thus classified as a Diamond in the Rough—but a good account of developing new interests after the age of 70.

MOVIES

Strongly Recommended

★★★★★ *On Golden Pond* (1981) produced by Bruce Gilbert and directed
          by Mark Rydell. PG Rating. 109 minutes.

An 80-year-old retired teacher becomes preoccupied with death and losing his faculties as his birthday is celebrated. He becomes anxious, irritable, and difficult to live with, but his wife knows how to handle him and helps his alienated daughter make the connections needed by both for resolution before his death. All three actors received Oscars. This film might be most useful to those alienated from parents and trying to communicate and to those parents. It might reinforce that there may not be time for healing unless one acts now.

★★★★★ *The Trip to Bountiful* (1985) produced by Sterling Vanwagenen and Horton Forte and directed by Peter Masterson. PG Rating. 106 minutes.

A country woman forced by circumstances to live with her son and daughter-in-law in a small city apartment is surprised to discover how old she has become and decides to revisit her girlhood home in Bountiful, Texas. She stubbornly persists, evading her family's fears about this trip, and makes the journey to reminisce and imagine her parents in the old house. In a subplot, she relates with a young girl during the brief bus trip to Bountiful, and we see her learn to accept her life and choose to make the best of it. This film can illustrate but not resolve the conflicts between the goals of people in different generations and helps demonstrate what they hold of value and what aging is like.

★★★★★ *The Doctor* (1991) produced by Laura Ziskin and directed by Randa Haines. PG-13 Rating. 125 minutes.

A pompous surgeon develops throat cancer and experiences what it is like to be a patient in an uncaring and mechanical system. He discovers his disconcerting mortality, and gets a reprieve to lead a life of caring and compassion. This may be useful for all those lacking empathy, struggling with what the health care system has become, or needing an example of how to communicate with a spouse made distant.

★★★★ *It's a Wonderful Life* (1946) produced and directed by Frank Capra. 129 minutes.

A man who has done the right thing all his life, living by his values and those of his neighbors, is brought low by a relative's accidental misplacement of bank funds and contemplates suicide. An angel appears and shows him how badly his town, its families, and its ordinary citizens would have suffered had he not been there to lend them funds and advice. The movie works as an inspiring fable encouraging people to examine their lives, gain perspective, and take a second chance.

Recommended

★★★ *Field of Dreams* (1989) produced by Lawrence Gordon and Charles Gordon and directed by Phil Alden Robinson. PG Rating. 106 minutes.

A couple choose a simple farming lifestyle instead of the hectic modern world. The husband then hears a voice telling him to "build it and he will come." Despite his doubts, the threat of foreclosure, and family opposition, with his wife's support he builds a baseball diamond in a cornfield, and the legends of a simpler time in professional baseball emerge and toss a few around. This movie may inspire self-doubters to cling to their dreams and others to take the risk of supporting their loved one's dreams. At the same time, it is important to recognize the fantasy and insubstantiality of the plot.

★★★   *Cocoon* (1986) produced by Richard D. Zanuck, David Brown, and
       Lili Fini Zanuck and directed by Ron Howard. PG-13 Rating. 117 minutes.

Disregard the subplot of visiting intergalactic aliens and focus on how the senior citizens of a Florida retirement community find an actual fountain of youth. They experience new vigor and possibilities. The movie is, of course, a fantasy and a denial of the negatives and losses of aging; nonetheless, it is an inspiring and perhaps helpful picture about what may still be felt and lived.

★★★   *A Christmas Carol* (1938) produced by Joseph L. Mankiewicz and directed by
       Edwin L. Marin. 69 minutes.

Ideal for reminding those too focussed on making money that family can provide enormous satisfaction. But this theme can be expanded to include examining any of one's values: relationships, seeking fame, accepting invitations to become different, and generally looking at the future outcomes of current choices (the three ghosts' visits).

INTERNET RESOURCES

While there are vast numbers of sites of data on aging, medical problems, and geriatric information, there is much less self-help on the Internet. These are the most clinically useful sites.

Metasites

★★★★★   *Booklets for Health Professionals and Public*
          http://eb-174105.od.nih.gov/cgi-bin/nia/search_publication.pl

The National Institute on Aging has made these useful publications available online, including "Exercise: A Guide from the National Institute on Aging," "The Resource Directory for Older People," "Alzheimer's Disease: Unraveling the Mystery," "In Search of the Secrets of Aging," "Talking with the Doctor: A Guide for Older People," and "Hearts and Arteries: What Scientists Are Learning about Age and the Cardiovascular System." Unfortunately, they are behind a search engine and so you must know what you are looking for.

★★★★   *Friendly4Seniors*
         http://www.friendly4seniors.com

Very likely the largest site for finding any information or resources on the Internet on the issues of aging. After the 10 major sections, thousands of sites are listed alphabetically, so finding a particular resource may be difficult.

★★★★   *Geropsychology Central*
         http://www.premier.net/~gero/geropsyc.html

Slow loading because of graphics, the Senior's Corner offers the best short lists of links on health, retirement, news, and bulletin boards. The next section offers many valuable links to professional resources.

★★★ *Ask NOAH About: Aging and Alzheimer's Disease*
http://www.noah-health.org/english/aging/aging.html

The section on aging contains links to about 100 brochures on the physiology of aging and medical problems and care and treatment of the elderly.

★★★ *ElderWeb* http://www.elderweb.com

This research site for professionals and family members contains more than 4,500 links to eldercare and long-term care information, including legal, financial, medical, and housing issues and policy, research, and statistics.

★★★ *Administration on Aging* http://www.aoa.dhhs.gov

This is a federal site with lots of information. National Institute on Aging Age Pages offer many brochures with accurate information about health, alcohol, exercise, sexuality, and so on. About 20 AoA Fact Sheets provide facts and references designed for the educated reader.

Psychoeducational Materials for Clients and Families

★★★★★ *Multidisciplinary Education in Geriatrics and Aging*
http://cpmcnet.columbia.edu/dept/dental/Dental_Educational_Software/
Gerontology_and_Geriatric_Dentistry/introduction.html

Although intended for professionals, this 12-module training program is an online textbook with wider uses. The modules on Normal Aging and Mental Health (mainly assessment) are perhaps the most relevant, but the others may be right for some caregivers and clients. "The purpose of this series of learning modules is to teach graduate and undergraduate students in the health sciences those basic concepts in geriatric care. For each discipline, information is provided on relevant changes brought about by the normal aging process, geriatric assessment, common problems encountered among the elderly, and how to deal with these problems. After using these modules, the student should be better able to identify problems relevant to disciplines other than their own and therefore to make appropriate referrals."

★★★★★ *Social Gerontology* http://www.trinity.edu/~mkearl/geron.html

Written for the college-educated, this page offers an introductory context and links for understanding aging from a social psychological perspective. The sections and the links allow one to come to understand aging in a fuller context than is presented elsewhere.

★★★★ *Alcohol and the Elderly* http://alcoholism.about.com/library/weekly/
aa981118.htm?pid=2750&cob=home

This page has links to many others of relevance to alcohol and drug overuse in the elderly population. They may help overcome denial in clients or families. Similarly, the upstream site, http://alcoholism.tqn.com/msubelder.htm offers a dozen articles on different aspects of this issue. If this URL changes, try http://about.com and choose Health/Fitness, then Diseases/Conditions, and then Alcohol.

★★★ *Alcohol, Medications and Aging: Use, Misuse and Abuse*
      http://www.asaging.org/nlc/onlineframe.html

A web-based training program designed for professionals but usable by anyone. It could be useful for those in denial or the uninformed.

★★★ *If You're over 65 and Feeling Depressed . . . Treatment Brings New Hope*
      http://www.nimh.nih.gov/publist/964033.htm

"Many older people believe that their age alone is responsible for feelings of exhaustion, helplessness, and worthlessness. This brochure discusses the causes of depression in the older years, symptoms, type of treatment, and where to go for help." About six pages of general information on depression.

Other Resources

★★★★★ *Attitudes: Key to Health, Happiness and Longevity*
        http://www.attitudefactor.com

The 20-item, five-minute questionnaire asks about feelings of well-being, happiness, and hopefulness, and scores and returns information on the longevity consequences of your answers. This could be useful feedback for unhappy persons who cannot commit to therapy or change. The site offers empirical support citations for this relationship and many readings.

★★★★★ *The American Association of Retired Persons (AARP)* http://www.aarp.org

AARP offers many self-help materials (which must be searched for under their "Topic Guides") such as a Reminiscence Training Kit; Where Did I Put My Keys? A Self-Help Guide for Improving Memory; If Only I Knew What to Say: Ideas for Helping a Friend in Crisis; So Many Friends Have Moved Away or Died: Suggestions for Making New Friends; I Wonder Who Else Can Help? Questions and Answers about Counseling Needs; On Being Alone: A Guide for Widowed Persons; Is Drinking Becoming a Problem? Older Women and Alcohol; If Only I Could Get a Good Night's Sleep: Self-Help Guide to Understanding Insomnia; So Many Pills and I Still Don't Feel Good: Suggestions for Preventing Problems with Medication; If You're over 65 and Feeling Depressed; Distinctions between Depressive Grief and Clinical Depression; The Suicide of Older Men and Women: How You Can Prevent a Tragedy.

★★★ *Spirituality and Aging—Bibliography* http://www.usc.edu/isd/locations/
      science/gerontology/MLA/mlabib-god.html

Lists about 40 books, without annotations.

★★★ *Caregiving—Special Topics* http://www.usc.edu/isd/locations/science/
      gerontology/MLA/mlabib_care.html

An unannotated list of about 40 books.

Online Support Groups

Seniors-Site http://seniors-site.com

About 30 message boards on all topics of relevance to seniors, their children, and caregivers.

Internet and E-mail Resources on Aging: Index of Listserv and Mailing Lists http://www.aoa.dhhs.gov/jpost/ListServs.html

This site offers direct connection to about 50 mailing lists for information and support.

See also Dementia/Alzheimer's (Chapter 13).

NATIONAL SUPPORT GROUPS

American Association of Retired Persons (AARP)
601 E Street NW
Washington, DC 20049
Phone: 202-434-2260

American Parkinson's Disease Association
60 Bay Street
Staten Island, NY 10301
Phone: 800-223-APDA
Fax: 718-981-4399

American Society on Aging
833 Market Street, Suite 511
San Francisco, CA 94103-1824
Phone: 415-974-9600

Arthritis Foundation
1314 Spring Street, NW
Atlanta, GA 30309
Phone: 800-283-7800

Department of Veterans Affairs
Phone: Ms. Susan Cooley
   at 202-535-7531

   Publishes a resource guide for working with older adults.

Grey Panthers
2025 Pennsylvania Avenue NW, #821
Washington, DC 20006
Phone: 202-466-3132

   For young and old adults working together.

National Council on Aging
600 Maryland Avenue SW,
   West Wing 100
Washington, DC 20024
Phone: 202-479-1200 or 800-424-9046

National Eldercare Institute on Health Promotion
601 E Street NW, Fifth Floor
Washington, DC 20049
Phone: 202-434-2200
Fax: 202-434-6474

National Family Caregivers Association
9223 Longbranch Parkway
Silver Spring, MD 20901-3642
Phone: 301-949-3638
Fax 301-949-2302

National Hispanic Council on Aging
2713 Ontario Road NW
Washington, DC 20009
Phone: 202-745-2521
Fax 202-745-2522

National Parkinson Foundation
1501 NW 9th Avenue
Bob Hope Road
Miami, FL 33136
Phone: 305-547-6666 or 800-327-4545
Fax: 305-548-4403

National Stroke Association
8480 East Orchard Road, #1000
Englewood, CO 80111-5015
Phone: 303-771-1700 or 800-STROKES
Fax: 303-771-1886

Older Women's League
666 11th Street NW
Washington, DC 20001
Phone: 202-783-6686

Membership organization that advocates on behalf of various economic and social issues for midlife and older women.

CHAPTER 5

Anger

Anger is a powerful emotion. People who have fiery tempers—who become furious when they are criticized, get angry when they are slowed down by others' mistakes, say nasty things when they get mad, feel like hitting someone when they are frustrated, and whose blood boils when they are under pressure—hurt not only others but themselves as well. Everybody gets angry sometimes, but for most of us, it's mild anger a couple of times a week. Mild anger often emerges if a loved one or a friend performs what we perceive to be a misdeed, whether it is being late, promising one thing and doing another, or neglecting a duty, for example. Anger disorders, on the other hand, are characterized as enraged, agitated, uncontrollable, and frequent.

In this chapter, we present the ratings and descriptions of anger self-help books and Internet resources, respectively.

SELF-HELP BOOKS

Strongly Recommended

★★★★ *The Dance of Anger: A Woman's Guide to Changing the Patterns of Intimate Relationships* (reissue ed., 1997) by Harriet Lerner. New York: Harper Perennial.

This popular and prized book was written mainly for women about the anger in their lives, both their anger and that of the people they live with, especially men. It has sold more than a million copies and deservedly has been on the *New York Times* best-seller list. Lerner maintains that expressions of anger are not only encouraged more in boys and men than in girls and women but may be glorified to maladaptive extremes. By contrast, girls and women have been denied even a healthy and realistic expression of anger. Lerner argues that to express anger—especially openly, directly, or loudly—traditionally is considered to make a woman appear unladylike, unfeminine, unmaternal,

RECOMMENDATION HIGHLIGHTS

Self-Help Books

- For women who want to understand and moderate their anger:

    ★★★★★ *The Dance of Anger* by Harriet Lerner

- On coping with anger in many different facets of life:

    ★★★★ *Anger: The Misunderstood Emotion* by Carol Tavris

- For practical advice and methods based on the cognitive-behavioral orientation:

    ★★★★ *The Anger Workbook* by Lorrainne Bilodeau

    ★★★★ *How to Control Your Anger before It Controls You* by Albert Ellis and Raymond Chip Tafrate

    ★★★★ *Letting Go of Anger* by Ron Potter-Efron and Pat Potter-Efron

- For helping children control their anger:

    ◆ *A Volcano in My Tummy* by Eliane Whitehouse and Warwick Pudney

- On the relationship of hostility to health problems and how to decrease vulnerability:

    ◆ *Anger Kills* by Redford Williams and Virginia Williams

- For understanding and reducing anger in the workplace:

    ◆ *Anger at Work* (1995) by Hendrie Weisinger

Internet Resources

- For overviews on conceptualizing and treating anger:

    ★★★★★ *Controlling Anger* http://www.apa.org/pubinfo/anger.html

    ★★★★★ *Anger* http://incestabuse.about.com/library/weekly/aa010598.htm?pid=2791&cob=home

- For multiple articles offering guidelines on anger management:

    ★★★★ *Get Your Angries Out* http://members.aol.com/AngriesOut

and sexually unattractive. Lerner explains the difficulties women have in showing anger and describes how they can use their anger to gain a stronger, more independent sense of self. Rooted in both family systems and psychoanalytic theory, *The Dance of Anger* has nine chapters and an epilogue. Lerner describes the circular dances of couples, such as the all-too-familiar situation of the nagging wife and the withdrawing husband. The more she nags, the more he withdraws, and the more he withdraws, the more she nags. Lerner goes on to provide valuable advice about how to deal with anger when interacting with "impossible" mothers, with children, and in family triangles.. In the Epilogue, she gives wise guidelines for going beyond self-help, believing that trying to deal with anger should not be an isolated task. This excellent guide is a careful, compassionate exploration of women's anger and an insightful guide for turning anger into a constructive force that can reshape women's lives.

★★★★ *Anger: The Misunderstood Emotion* (revised and updated, 1989) by
Carol Tavris. New York: Touchstone Books.

This excellent self-help book covers the wider terrain of anger and its manifestations. Indeed, it is hard to come up with any facet of anger—from wrecked friendships to wars—that Tavris does not address. The revised and updated edition includes new and expanded coverage of highway anger, violence in sports, young women's anger, and family anger, and it suggests strategies for getting through specific anger problems. The book consists of 10 well-written, entertaining chapters. In the first several chapters, Tavris debunks a number of myths about anger and highlights anger's cultural rules. She persuasively argues that "letting it all out" is not the best solution for defusing anger and effectively coping with stress. She dislikes pop-psychology approaches that tell people that anger is buried within them, and she argues that such notions are dangerous to the mental health of participants and to the social health of the community. She also sharply criticizes psychotherapy approaches that are based on the belief that inside every tranquil soul is a furious person screaming to get out. Later chapters present helpful ideas about anger in marital relationships and situations involving justice. In the final two chapters, Tavris tells readers how to rethink anger and make more adaptive choices. The book is well-researched, and Tavris's delivery is witty and eloquent. Anyone wanting to cope more effectively with the anger in their lives will find this book a welcome tonic.

★★★★ *The Anger Workbook* (1992) by Lorrainne Bilodeau. Minneapolis: CompCare.

This information manual and workbook is written for adults and explains how to think about anger, understand anger, see its usefulness, and have healthier anger. A cognitive-behavioral approach to anger is taken. The book presents a self-assessment questionnaire, followed by information, discussion, questionnaire and answers, and recommended changes in thought pattern and/or behavior. The chapters are structured effectively for instruction; the several questionnaires are followed by chapters that address the potential clusters of answers the reader could have given and responds to them in a decision-making format. Concepts include taking a new perspective on anger, acknowledging the complexities of anger, understanding how anger goes awry, changing the experience of anger, and responding to another person's anger. This valuable and practical book clearly explains how to understand anger problems and how to move toward their resolution.

★★★★ *How to Control Your Anger before It Controls You* (1997) by Albert Ellis and
Raymond Chip Tafrate. Secaucus, NJ: Birch Lane Press.

The treatment model of rational-emotive behavior therapy (REBT) developed by Albert Ellis has evolved over the years into many applications, all with the same underlying goal of controlling thoughts in order to control feelings. Ellis and his coauthor have adapted the REBT model to create a self-help approach to reducing or eliminating anger. They consider myths about dealing with anger, rational and irrational aspects of anger, and identifying self-angering beliefs. Multiple techniques are taught for thinking ways out of anger, as are well-described relaxation exercises and self-help forms that allow the reader to record experiences and self-guide through the cognitive-behavioral aspects of anger reduction. This practical volume is easy to read, understand, and apply. The REBT principles are presented with clarity in an inviting manner.

★★★★ *Letting Go of Anger: The Ten Most Common Anger Styles and What to Do about Them* (1995) by Ron Potter-Efron and Pat Potter-Efron. Oakland, CA: New Harbinger.

The authors take a systematic approach to identifying and treating types of anger, often using cognitive-behavioral strategies. A questionnaire allows readers to categorize themselves into anger styles: masked anger, explosive anger, or chronic anger. Each chapter further describes several ways of manifestating anger within each of the three primary styles. Clarity and conciseness are strengths of this self-help resource. Each chapter outlines the characteristics of the anger style, typical examples of how the anger plays out, and remedies for counteracting anger. The suggested treatments are under-standable and easily conducted by nonprofessionals.

Recommended

★★★ *When Anger Hurts* (1997) by Matthew McKay, Peter Rogers, and Judith McKay. Oakland, CA: Fine Communications.

This book presents a cognitive-behavioral approach to coping with anger. Subtitled *Quieting the Storm Within*, it is divided into three main sections that focus on under-standing anger, building skills to cope with anger, and dealing with anger at home. The section on building skills to cope with anger contains a number of helpful strategies, including how to control stress step-by-step, how to keep anger from escalating, how to use healthy self-talk to deal with angry feelings, and how to engage in problem-solving communication when anger is harming relationships. The authors instruct readers in the specifics of keeping an anger journal.

★★★ *Angry All the Time: An Emergency Guide to Anger Control* (1994) by Ron Potter-Efron. Oakland, CA: New Harbinger.

This book was written for and about people who regularly function at a high level of anger. Candid descriptions of the angry lifestyle, myths, and excuses for anger are revealed, along with a road map for breaking the cycle. Validating checklists enable the reader to clearly understand how to change. These include The Six Main Reasons People Stay Angry, The Violence Ladder, and a chapter for Partners of Angry People. This book hits anger behavior head on with a no-nonsense, but understanding approach. The mental health experts in our study preferred Potter-Efron's later work, *Letting Go of Anger*, slightly more than this book. Refer to its review above in the Strongly Recommended listing.

★★★ *Anger: How to Live with and without It* (1986) by Albert Ellis. New York:
       Lyle Stuart.

This is one of pioneering cognitive therapist's Albert Ellis's many books on how to cope more effectively. Here, Ellis applies his rational-emotive therapy to help people deal with anger. He provides step-by-step instructions for how to cognitively and behavioral-ly rearrange anger. Readers are given a number of homework assignments to help them rethink how they deal with anger. This book is a bit dated, and our mental health experts preferred Ellis's (and Tafrate's) newer book on the same topic, *How to Control Your Anger before it Controls You*, reviewed above in the Strongly Recommended category.

★★★ *The Angry Book* (1969) by Theodore Rubin. New York: Macmillan.

This early, psychoanalytically oriented book advocates the "let it all out" catharsis approach to anger. Rubin warns readers about the dangers that await them if they bottle up their anger and "twist" or "pervert" it. He says that a "slush fund" of accumulated, unexpressed anger builds up in the body, waiting for the opportunity to produce high blood pressure, depression, alcoholism, sexual problems, and other diseases. At the end of *The Angry Book*, Rubin asks readers 103 questions that are intended to give them therapeutic guidance. One of these questions is whether readers have ever experienced the good, clean feeling that comes after expressing anger, as well as the increased self-esteem and feeling of peace that such expression brings. The "let it all out" approach was widely accepted by many clinicians in the past, but it is less accepted today. Rubin's recommendations directly contradict the approaches advocated by Carol Tavris in *Anger* and the cognitive-behaviorists in multiple books reviewed above. This book barely makes it into the 3-star category, and many experts probably see it as seriously dated.

Diamonds in the Rough

◆ *A Volcano in My Tummy—Helping Children to Handle Anger* (1996) by Eliane
   Whitehouse and Warwick Pudney. Gabriola Island, BC: New Society Publishers.

This valuable workbook is written in a lesson-plan format that structures key concepts related to anger into activities for children age six through teens. The book is written for parents and teachers, with emphasis on use by teachers. Activities lend themselves to small groups. The activities are well-designed for the targeted age groups and they demonstrate creativity and variety that could hold the attention of children, whether in school or at home. The purpose of the book is to help children become aware of their anger and learn safe, alternate responses to anger, how to handle other people's anger, and how to deal with authority. Listed as a Diamond in the Rough because the few rat-ings it received were consistently high.

◆ *Anger Kills: Seventeen Strategies for Controlling the Hostility That Can Harm Your
   Health* (1994) by Redford Williams and Virginia Williams. New York:
   Harper Perennial.

The health costs to a person who experiences ongoing anger is the focus of *Anger Kills*, cited as a Diamond in the Rough for its modest number of raters but very high ratings. Hostility and its effect on individuals and those around them are outlined in factual terms and through scientific study. This area of study was pioneered by coauthor Redford Williams. A self-administered hostility questionnaire is followed by a road map of strategies to overcome hostility. Chapters are grouped by recommendations to alter thinking patterns, cope with volatile situations, react to others' hostility, improve relationships, and adopt positive attitudes. Cognitive-behavioral strategies are suggested and demonstrated through decision-making diagrams, making this book a good companion to cognitive-behavioral work on anger.

◆ *Anger at Work* (1995) by Hendrie Weisinger. New York: Morrow.

This book is distinctive in that it focuses on anger in the workplace. Anger and cognition, feelings, communication, emotions, and behavior are each addressed in a chapter. Each chapter systematically considers definitions, manifestations, management recommendations, and key concepts of anger. The art of anger management is described, and scenarios that include typical anger situations are played out, including harassment, favoritism, insensitivity, unfair performance appraisals, and lack of trust. This approach makes use of self-management and cognitive-behavioral techniques and teaches the reader how to make decisions in stressful circumstances in the workplace. The book does a good job of differentiating anger situations and how to interpret them. It is placed in the Diamond in the Rough category for high ratings in the face of low numbers of raters.

Not Recommended

★★ *Anger: Deal with It, Heal with It, Stop It from Killing You* (1981) by Bill Defoore. Deerfield Beach, FL: Health Communications.

INTERNET RESOURCES

Psychoeducational Materials for Clients and Families

★★★★★ *Controlling Anger—Before It Controls You*
　　　　http://www.apa.org/pubinfo/anger.html

A five-page overview from the American Psychological Association that offers several approaches.

★★★★★ *Anger—Part I: Identifying Anger* http://incestabuse.about.com/library/ weekly/aa010598.htm?pid=2791&cob=home

　　　　Anger—Part II: Using Anger's Power Safely http://incestabuse.about.com/ library/weekly/aa011298.htm?pid=2791&cob=home

These sites present an excellent overview with many quotations and guidelines from books. No great psychological sophistication is required; material is accessible to the average reader.

★★★★ *Get Your Angries Out* http://members.aol.com/AngriesOut

The 40 or 50 articles by Lynn Namaka offer guidelines and directions for adults, kids, parents, and teachers. They are comprehensive and speak directly and productively.

★★★   *When Anger Hurts* by Mathew McKay, Peter D. Rogers,
        and Judith McKay http://www.alzwell.com/Clues.html

A three-page list of the verbal, gestural, facial, and other behaviors that trigger anger.
Could be useful for clients who do not recognize their triggers.

★★★   *Anger and Aggression* http://mentalhelp.net/psyhelp/chap7

This chapter of an online book offers a wide-ranging presentation (for example, marriage, prejudice, distrust, and gender) and cites a dozen therapeutic approaches and
techniques.

★★★   *Temper Tantrums: What Causes Them and How Can You Respond?* by
        Dawn Ramsburg http://npin.org/pnews/pnew997/pnew997g.html

Two useful pages from *Parent News*.

★★★   *Plain Talk About . . . Dealing with the Angry Child*
        http://npin.org/library/pre1998/n00216/n00216.html

About three pages from the U.S. Department of Health and Human Services.

★★★   *Why Am I So Angry?* http://arthritis.about.com/library/weekly/
        aa022498.htm?COB=home&terms=anger&PM=113_300_T

Anger is a major component in flare-ups of rheumatoid arthritis. These four pages are a
good introduction to the topic of anger for patients.

CHAPTER 6

Anxiety Disorders

Anxiety is a highly unpleasant feeling that comes in different forms. Sometimes it is a diffuse, vague feeling; at other times, it is a fear of something specific. People who have an anxiety disorder often feel motor tension (they are jumpy, trembling, or can't relax), are hyperactive (they feel dizzy, their heart races, or they perspire), and are apprehensive.

All these anxiety symptoms exist, to a lesser or greater degree, in the spectrum of anxiety disorders: phobias, obsessive–compulsive disorder (OCD), panic disorders, hypochondriasis, and posttraumatic stress disorder (PTSD). Also falling into this category is the controversial and rare diagnosis of dissociative identity disorder (DID), previously known as multiple personality.

Controversy swirls around the reasons people suffer from clinical levels of anxiety. Some mental health experts, especially in the medical field, believe that anxiety is biologically determined and should be treated with medications. Other mental health experts, including many psychologists, argue that anxiety is primarily caused by what we experience and how we think. They maintain that helping people reduce anxiety involves rearranging their environment and how they cognitively interpret their world. The following self-help resources include both schools of thought.

As with the other chapters, we begin with a synopsis of our primary recommendations, and proceed through the ratings and descriptions of the respective self-help books, autobiographies, movies, Internet resources, and national support groups.

SELF-HELP BOOKS

Strongly Recommended

★★★★★ *The Anxiety and Phobia Workbook* (1995) by Edmund J. Bourne. Oakland, CA: New Harbinger.

In this workbook, the author's intentions are to (1) describe specific skills needed to overcome problems with panic, anxiety, and phobias and (2) provide step-by-step proce-

RECOMMENDATION HIGHLIGHTS

Self-Help Books

- For step-by-step cognitive, behavioral, and social tools to reduce anxiety:

  ★★★★★ *The Anxiety and Phobia Workbook* by Edmund J. Bourne

  ★★★★★ *Mastery of Your Anxiety and Panic II* by David H. Barlow and Michelle J. Craske

- For clinicians and others with a fairly sophisticated knowledge of psychological problems:

  ★★★★ *Anxiety Disorders and Phobias* by Aaron Beck and Gary Emery

- On reducing or eliminating panic attacks:

  ★★★★ *Don't Panic* by Reid Wilson

- On coping more effectively with an obsessive–compulsive disorder:

  ★★★★★ *S.T.O.P. Obsessing* by Edna B. Foa and Reid Wilson

  ★★★★ *Obsessive–Compulsive Disorders* by Steven Levenkron

- On the biological basis of anxiety and its treatment through drug therapy:

  ★★★ *The Good News about Panic, Anxiety, and Phobias* by Mark Gold

- On treating phobias, panic, and obsessive–compulsive behaviors:

  ◆ *The Sky Is Falling* by Raeann Dumont

Autobiographies

- For recovering from dissociative identity disorder:

  ★★★★ *A Mind of My Own* by Chris Costner Sizemore

- A treatment program for agoraphobia:

  ★★★ *The Panic Attack Recovery Book* by Shirley Swede and Seymour S. Jaffe

- For a humorous and acerbic recounting of OCD and phobias:

  ★★★ *Memoirs of an Amnesiac* by Oscar Levant

Movies

- On OCD and its interpersonal impact:

  ★★★★ *As Good as It Gets*

- On war-related anxiety and PTSD:

  ★★★ *Born on the Fourth of July*

  ★★★ *Full Metal Jacket*

  ★★★ *The Deer Hunter*

- On recovery from PTSD:
    - ★★★ *Fearless*

- On the development and treatment of dissociative identity disorder:
    - ★★★ *Sybil*

Internet Resources

- Comprehensive site with strong emphasis on cognitive-behavioral therapy:
    - ★★★★★ *Panic and Anxiety Hub*
      *http://*www.paems.com.au/index.html

- Sites with humor and knowledge about specific anxiety disorders:
    - ★★★★★ *the Anxiety Panic internet resource (tAPir)*
      www.algy.com/anxiety/index.shtml
    - ★★★★★ *Self-Help Corner: Anxiety*
      http://www.queendom.com/selfhelp/index.html

- All kinds of traumatic experiences and their reactions:
    - ★★★★★ *David Baldwin's Trauma Information Pages*
      http://www.trauma-pages.com/index.phtml

- On OCD and its resources:
    - ★★★★★ *Expert Consensus Treatment Guidelines*
      for Obsessive–Compulsive Disorder: A Guide for Patients and Families
      http://www.psychguides.com/oche.html
    - ★★★★ *Obsessive–Compulsive Disorder Web Sites*
      http://www.interlog.com/~calex/ocd
    - ★★★★ *About OCD* http://www.ocfoundation.org

- Great overview written by experts for their clients:
    - ★★★★★ *The Causes of Anxiety and Panic Attacks* by Ron Rapee,
      Michelle Craske, and David Barlow
      http://www.algy.com/anxiety/files/barlow/html

- Explicit detail on the development of panic:
    - ★★★★★ *Panic Disorder*
      http://lexington-on-line.com/naf.panic2.html#anchor333635
    - ★★★★ *Understanding Panic Disorder*
      http://www.nimh.nih.gov/anxiety/upd.cfm

dures and exercises for mastering these skills. The book contains a fair amount of descriptive material but emphasizes coping strategies, skills, and exercises to foster recovery. Its approach is strongly holistic, focusing on multiple dimensions (e.g., body, behavior, feelings, mind, interpersonal relations, self-esteem, and spirituality). For the layperson, this is a concise, practical, and comprehensive directory on how to reduce anxiety. A highly regarded and widely known resource.

★★★★★ *Mastery of Your Anxiety and Panic II* (1994) by David H. Barlow and Michelle G. Craske. Albany, NY: Graywind.

Barlow and Craske, nationally known researchers in the treatment of anxiety disorders, have updated their original self-help offering. This edition is easier to read, includes new methods for providing exposure to feared sensations, and has a separate manual titled the *Agoraphobia Supplement*. The book is based on empirically supported and clinically proven treatments that cover the cognitive, behavioral, physical, and social aspects of anxiety. Record forms, case vignettes, and self-assessments are both numerous and useful. Questions and answers about medications are reviewed. An excellent and scientifically based self-help approach for anxiety-ridden patients, either as an independent self-help book or as an adjunct to psychotherapy.

★★★★★ *S.T.O.P. Obsessing: How to Overcome Your Obsessions and Compulsions* (1991) by Edna B. Foa and Reid Wilson. New York: Bantam.

Two authorities on the treatment of anxiety disorders present a cognitive-behavioral approach in this book. The book begins with a questionnaire to help understand and analyze the severity of obsessions and compulsions. Included is a self-help program to overcome the milder symptoms and a more intensive 3-week program for severe symptoms. Guidelines to help determine whether a person needs professional help are presented with clarity and practicability. Our mental health experts consistently agree that this book is very useful for people suffering from obsessions and compulsions.

★★★★ *Anxiety Disorders and Phobias: A Cognitive Perspective* (1985) by Aaron Beck and Gary Emery. New York: Basic Books.

This sophisticated book provides information about different types of anxiety and how sufferers can rearrange their thoughts to overcome crippling anxiety. Author Aaron Beck is an internationally acclaimed expert on anxiety disorders and depression and one of the founders of cognitive therapy. Beck and Emery describe the nature of anxiety and how it is distinguished from fear, phobia, and panic. They believe that the core problem for anxiety sufferers is their sense of vulnerability and their ineffective cognitive strategies for coping with anxiety. The latter portion of the book contains a treatment program based on cognitive therapy that can help individuals cope effectively with anxiety and phobias. Separate chapters tell readers how to change the way they develop images of themselves and their world, how to change feelings, and how to modify behavior. This highly rated volume received rave reviews in the academic community, but it is not primarily a self-help book. It is written at a very high level that is appropriate for psychotherapists or for graduate students in psychology. Only lay readers who are already fairly sophisticated about the nature of psychological problems and how they can be treated or who seek an intellectual challenge will want to tackle this volume.

★★★★　*Feel the Fear and Do It Anyway* (reissue ed., 1992) by Susan Jeffers. New York: Fawcett.

This book offers positive and concrete techniques for turning fear, indecision, and anger into power, action, and love. The author helps people reach, understand, and convert negative paths of thinking that feed fear and inactivity. Jeffers uses a 10-step program to help convert negative thinking. Visualization techniques are one of the cognitive exercises that help people rid themselves of destructive anger and fear. Other methods entail power vocabulary, turning decisions into no-lose situations, and adoption of an optimistic perspective about life. The author's belief is that fear can be dealt with through reeducation. For those who struggle with their feelings of fear and indecision, this is a useful book.

★★★★　*Don't Panic: Taking Control of Anxiety Attacks* (rev. ed., 1996) by Reid Wilson. New York: Harper & Row.

This books covers the diagnosis and treatment of panic, an anxiety disorder in which the main feature is recurrent panic attacks marked by the sudden onset of intense apprehension or terror. People who suffer from panic disorder may have feelings of impending doom but aren't necessarily anxious all the time. Wilson describes a self-help program for coping with panic attacks. In Part I, readers learn what panic attacks are like, how it feels to undergo one, and what type of people are prone to panic attacks. Advice is given on how to sort through the physical and psychological aspects of panic attacks. In Part II, readers learn how to conquer panic attacks, especially by using self-monitoring, breathing exercises, focused thinking, mental imagery, and deep muscle relaxation.

★★★★　*Obsessive–Compulsive Disorders* (1992) by Steven Levenkron. New York: Warner.

As the title implies, this book is about one category of anxiety—obsessive–compulsive disorders (OCD)—in which an individual has anxiety-provoking thoughts that will not go away (obsession) and/or feels the urge to perform repetitive, ritualistic behaviors usually designed to prevent or produce a future situation (compulsion). Obsessions and compulsions are different problems, but often both are displayed by the same person. Levenkron believes OCD is the personality's attempt to reduce anxiety, which may stem from a painful childhood or a genetic tendency toward anxiousness. Levenkron developed therapy techniques to help people who suffer from OCD that include the help and support of parents, teachers, physicians, and friends. Levenkron argues that people can reduce their obsessions and compulsions if they follow four basic steps: (1) rely on a family member or a therapist for support and comfort, (2) unmask their rituals, (3) talk in depth to trusted family members or a therapist, and (4) control their anxiety.

Recommended

★★★ *Panic Disorder: The Facts* (1996) by Stanley Rachman and Padmal de Silva.
New York: Oxford University Press.

This self-help resource book covers the experience, assessment, and treatment of panic attacks. The authors provide sound, practical advice to family members about choosing a therapist, and self-help. Some of the common questions asked by people with panic disorder are reviewed. This book is a valuable and scientific resource for sufferers of this disorder as well as their families. It can be integrated into a patient's treatment and is easy to read.

★★★ *An End to Panic* (1995) Elke Luerchen-White. Oakland, CA: New Harbinger.

The author's goal is to teach the cognitive-behavioral methods that have proven effective for panic disorders. In other words, changing one's style of thinking, believing, and behavior (e.g., breathing style) can help reduce anxiety. Medication is also discussed, as is a combination of medication and cognitive-behavioral therapy. Part I explains panic disorder and agoraphobia and sets the stage for the work ahead. Parts II and III review theory and practical methods to overcome panic. Part IV works on mastery of the techniques taught. This book is for people with panic disorders with or without agoraphobia and for people who want to prevent further panic attacks. Highly regarded by the psychologists in our national studies but not well known, leading to the 3-star rating.

★★★ *Life without Fear: Anxiety and Its Cure* (1988) by Joseph Wolpe with
David Wolpe.

Joseph Wolpe, an internationally known expert in the field of behavior therapy, provides a clear and authoritative account of the essential features of behavior therapy and its application to anxiety. With the help of his son David, a playwright, the two translated into nontechnical language information and concepts about behavior therapy and anxiety. Topics include useful and useless fears, how useless fears are developed, how thoughts and feelings are controlled by habit, how habits are formed and extinguished, coping in real-life situations, special behavior techniques for anxiety, getting help for behavior analysis, and the advantages and limits of behavior therapy. This book can be a useful self-help manual for adults engaged in behavior therapy for anxiety.

★★★ *How to Control Your Anxiety before It Controls You* (1998) by Albert Ellis.
Secaucus, NJ: Carol.

Ellis, one of the world's most influential psychologists, bases this book on his particular brand of cognitive-behavior therapy known as rational–emotive behavior therapy. He talks about how anxious feelings and behaviors go with specific kinds of anxiety-provoking thinking. You think, act, and feel together. That's the way, as a human, you behave. In the final three chapters, the author emphasizes rational maxims and beliefs that can help change anxiety-provoking thinking, emotions, and actions. This book can be valuable for the average reader or can be used as a self-help resource during psychotherapy.

★★★   *Peace from Nervous Suffering* (1972) by Claire Weekes. New York: Hawthorn
Books.

This book concerns itself with one type of phobia—agoraphobia, the fear of entering
unfamiliar situations, especially open or public spaces. It is the most common type of
phobic disorder. Weekes maintains that the cure for agoraphobia involves four simple
rules: (1) face the phobia, don't run away from it; (2) accept it, don't fight it; (3) float
past it, do not stop and listen in; and (4) let time pass, and don't be impatient. Weekes
includes an extensive number of case studies from around the world in which
agoraphobics have successfully overcome their fear of leaving the safety of their homes.
Peace from Nervous Suffering was given 3 stars: On the positive side, Weekes's book was
one of the first to deal with agoraphobia, and it helped many people recognize their
problem; on the negative side, it is dated and misses many of the advances in cognitive
and medical treatments.

★★★   *Anxiety and Panic Attacks: Their Cause and Cure* (1985) by Robert Handly.
New York: Fawcett Crest.

This text, about both panic attacks and agoraphobia, begins with the author's describing his own struggle with agoraphobia and the successful strategies he used to overcome it. Handly believes that five basic methods are involved in coping with anxiety and
panic attacks: (1) Use the creative powers of your unconscious mind to help yourself; (2)
use visualizations and affirmations to improve your self-image; (3) engage in rational
and positive thinking; (4) act as if you are already who you want to be; and (5) set goals
to be the person you want to be. Handly also stresses the importance of physical health,
fitness, and good nutrition in overcoming anxiety. This book has an easy-to-read writing
style and provides in-depth analysis of one person's experience. However, it suffers
from inattention to current developments in treating panic disorder and agoraphobia
and from the rather loose inclusion of many different ideas that have not been well
tested.

★★★   *The Anxiety Disease* (1983) by David Sheehan. New York: Scribner.

This book astutely reviews the biological factors involved in anxiety and how anxiety
can be conquered through the use of appropriate drugs and behavior therapy. Sheehan
describes a number of case studies from his psychiatry practice to illustrate how to recognize anxiety problems and successfully treat them. He believes that anxiety disorders
progress through seven stages—spells, panic, hypochondriacal symptoms, limited phobias, social phobias, agoraphobia/extensive public avoidance, and finally depression—
and that recovery from an anxiety disorder occurs in four phases—doubt, mastery,
independence, and readjustment. Individuals go through the phases as their medications eliminate chemically induced panic attacks and therapy overcomes their avoidance tendencies.

★★★   *The Good News about Panic, Anxiety, and Phobias* (1990) by Mark Gold.
New York: Bantam.

This text, like that above, stresses the biological basis of anxiety disorders and their
treatment with medications. Gold asserts that if a person has an anxiety disorder, it is

not the person's fault. Instead, the disorder is the fault of inherited dysfunctions in the biochemistry of the person's body. Gold recommends variations in drug therapy for different types of anxiety disorders. At the end of the book, he provides a state-by-state listing of resources and medical experts on anxiety disorders.

Diamond in the Rough

♦ *The Sky Is Falling* (1996) by Raeann Dumont. New York: Norton.

This author provides information that will help the reader understand and cope with phobias, panic, and obsessive-compulsive behavior. Using case vignettes, Dumont alerts the reader to the danger of forming conclusions that increase anxiety without the benefit of rational thought. She explains how magic thinking evolves out of faulty cause-and-effect understanding. The book provides directions on how to plan one's own treatment program with charts and diaries. Clients, family members, and professionals will find this book to be informative and practical. Highly but infrequently rated in our national studies, leading to its placement in the Diamonds in the Rough category.

AUTOBIOGRAPHIES

Strongly Recommended

★★★★ *A Mind of My Own* (1989) by Chris Costner Sizemore. New York: William Morrow.

The protagonist of *Three Faces of Eve* describes her successful battle with multiple personality disorder. Now married with two children, the author has become a lecturer on mental health topics. A tale of hope and the success of psychotherapy, it has become a perennial favorite of those fascinated by—or suffering from—dissociative identity disorder.

Recommended

★★★ *The Panic Attack Recovery Book* (1989) by Shirley Swede and Seymour S. Jaffe. New York: New American Library/Dutton.

Jointly written by a former agoraphobic and her psychiatrist, the book outlines a seven-step treatment program along with dietary suggestions and stress reduction exercises. The PASS program is based on seven steps to recovery from panic attacks: (1) a healthy balanced diet; (2) relaxation; (3) exercise; (4) a positive attitude; (5) imagination (pretending to feel confident); (6) social support; and (7) spiritual values (faith, hope, and forgiveness). The book is an informative blend of personal experience (Swede) and medical knowledge (Jaffe) that panic attack sufferers may find enlightening and helpful.

★★★ *Memoirs of an Amnesiac* (1990) by Oscar Levant. Hollywood, CA: Samuel French Trade Books.

A famed pianist recounts a life with many mental and physical disorders. In a humorous and acerbic style, Levant describes his obsessive–compulsive disorder, phobias, and addiction to barbiturates. Chapter titles include "Total Recoil," "My Bed of Nails," and

"Stand Up and Faint." Levant was treated with an enormous number of different drugs and had psychotherapy, several hospitalizations, and electric shock therapy. Through it all, he appeared to lack the motivation to get well.

★★★　*Phantom Illness: Recognizing, Understanding, and Overcoming Hypochondria* (1997) by Carla Cantor with Brian Fallon. New York: Houghton Mifflin.

Cantor's serious problems began when she crashed her car, killing a passenger. She became depressed and was briefly hospitalized. In the hospital, her diagnosis was changed to hypochondria. The book describes her intense struggle with bodily preoccupations and the lessons she learned on the road to recovery.

★★★　*Afraid of Everything: A Personal History of Agoraphobia* (1984) by Daryl M. Woods. Saratoga, CA: R & E Publishers.

A first-person account by a young woman with agoraphobia, the book includes information on what is known about causes and treatment of the disorder. A helpful memoir in the self-help tradition, though dated with respect to treatments.

Not Recommended

★★　*Sybil* (1995) by Flora Rheta Schreiber. New York: Warner.

A reissue of a book that has become a classic in the multiple personality literature, now more accurately known as dissociative identity disorder (DID). Sybil Dorsett had 16 separate personalities before her recovery. The dissociation is attributed to childhood abuse by her schizophrenic mother, which also produced unusual blackouts. Mental health experts give the television movie higher marks than the book.

★★　*When Rabbit Howls: The Troops for Truddi Chase* (1987) by Truddi Chase. New York: Dutton.

The troops are the approximately 90 personalities of the author. She did not know they existed until adulthood. Troop members speak of their empathy for Chase, who was abused from age 2 until age 16 by her stepfather. A controversial but enthralling tale.

MOVIES

Strongly Recommended

★★★★　*As Good as It Gets* (1997) produced by James L. Brooks, Bridget Johnson, and Kristi Zea and directed by James L. Brooks. PG-13 Rating. 138 minutes.

Jack Nicholson's portrayal of a nasty, selfish bigot with a mix of anxiety symptoms (compulsions and phobias) won him an Oscar because of the humanizing experiences with his neighbor and the only waitress he can trust. Probably useful to show that even a person crippled by symptoms can find the courage to reach out and improve (if not cure) his relationships, especially with the help of caring others (Helen Hunt, who won a Oscar as the waitress; an ugly dog; and Jack's suffering neighbor).

Recommended

★★★ *Born on the Fourth of July* (1990) produced by A. Kitman Ho and Oliver Stone and directed by Oliver Stone. R Rating. 145 minutes.

The true story of a patriotic and excitement-seeking small-town boy who volunteers to fight in Vietnam only to return wheelchair bound. Abandoned and condemned by his fellow citizens, he falls into drug use and anxiety disorder but eventually finds himself by understanding the larger political picture and participating in antiwar activism. The movie might be used to show the possibility of redemption and making the best of a terrible situation by facing reality and seeing the truth beyond the culturally supported images.

★★★ *Fearless* (1994) produced by Paula Weinstein and Mark Rosenberg and directed by Peter Weir. R Rating. 122 minutes.

An ordinary man survives a plane crash that kills many. He realizes that assumptions about how life works and should be lived can be questioned. He comes to feel invulnerable but is laid low by a tiny accident. His wife offers loving support for his withdrawal and confusions, but only a fellow survivor can offer understanding. Their relationship avoids the sexual, and the movie shows how each grows. His PTSD and anxiety symptoms are shown and treated in group therapy. The film richly illustrates the psychic consequences of traumatic experiences and the ways we can overcome them with the help of our friends.

★★★ *Sybil* (1976, Made for TV) produced by Jacqueline Brown and directed by Daniel Petrie.

The horrific physical and psychological abuse Sybil experienced as a child led to multiple personalities that served as protection, comfort, and survival through her tormented years. She commits herself to the journey of therapy and healing with a caring and courageous therapist who essentially reparents Sybil and gives her the healthier relationship that Sybil never had. This is a moving and complex movie about the human spirit, the extraordinary ways in which people survive, and the miraculous healing power of human connection.

★★★ *Full Metal Jacket* (1988) produced and directed by Stanley Kubrick. R Rating. 118 minutes.

The film moves from the induction into the military of naive recruits, though hellish training to toughen them, and into the war in Vietnam—the battles, killing, prostitution, drugs, and alcohol. A haunting film that may demonstrate the genesis of posttraumatic stress disorder, but not much else of clinical utility. Vivid scenes of the horrors of war and warriors mark a realistic, apolitical, and complex film.

★★★ *The Deer Hunter* (1978) produced by Barry Spikings, Michael Deeley, Michael Cimino, and John Peverall and directed by Michael Cimino. R Rating. 182 minutes.

Three working-class guys from a small town go to war and are greatly and differently affected by the experience. We witness the most graphic of atrocities as they change.

One is scarred but matures and can no longer kill even the deer he used to hunt. The other two are damaged, one physically and the other mentally. The film illustrates the way a person can endure and develop, even in the most hostile of environments, into a better human being. Winner of five Academy Awards.

Not Recommended

★ *What about Bob?* (1992) produced by Laura Ziskin and directed by Frank Oz. PG Rating. 99 minutes.

Strongly Not Recommended

† *High Anxiety* (1977) produced and directed by Mel Brooks. PG Rating. 94 minutes.

INTERNET RESOURCES

Metasites

★★★★★ *Panic and Anxiety Hub*
        http://www.paems.com.au/index.html

Enormously comprehensive, with sections on treatment, chat, resources, support, and so on. Especially strong on cognitive-behavior therapy—including cost comparisons, outcomes, methods, and questions and answers. See also *The Politics of Anxiety Disorder Treatments* at http://www.healthyplace.com/Communities/Anxiety/paems/articles/treatment_politics.htm.

★★★★★ *the Anxiety Panic internet resource (tAPir)*
        http://www.algy.com/anxiety/index.shtml

A dry sense of humor underlies a rich site with chat, listserv, and loads of good quality links. Each of the anxiety disorders has section with a brief but meaningful description and authoritative materials and handouts. The URL http://www.algy.com/anxiety/LINKS/websearch2.pl?category=an will bring you to a annotated list of links addressing many questions about the anxiety disorders.

★★★★★ *Self-Help Corner: Anxiety* http://www.queendom.com/selfhelp/index.html

If necessary, click on Anxiety in the left column. Here is a little of everything: online tests, recommended books, case studies and advice, newsgroups and chat, organizations online, and about 20 very good articles from major organizations. Not all of the site can be recommended to patients because of the extensiveness and variety, but for the sophisticated patient who can be selective, it is a major online resource.

★★★★★ *David Baldwin's Trauma Information Pages*
        http://www.trauma-pages.com/index.phtml

This is the premier trauma resource on the Internet, with articles, resources, support, and books. It is not specific for PTSD and covers all kinds of traumatic experiences and reactions, so you may have to do some digging.

★★★★ *Obsessive–Compulsive Disorder Web Sites*
http://www.interlog.com/~calex/ocd

Has a large list of links to bulletin boards, treaters, humor, music, religion and scrupulosity, and so on.

★★★ *False Memory Sundrome Facts* http://fmsf.com

For those concerned with any side of this debate, this site offers access to almost all of the gigantic literature of relevance. Therapists can find materials to educate clients, peers, lawyers, and others.

★★★ *Duke University's Program in Child and Adolescent Anxiety Disorder (PCAAD)* http://www2.mc.duke.edu/pcaad

A very large site with a number of materials on every aspect of anxiety disorders in children.

★★★ *The Sidran Foundation* http://www.sidran.org

The site focuses on traumatic memories and dissociation. Sidran is a publisher and supplier of books, and their annotated catalog is at http://www.sidran.org/bookshelf.html.

Psychoeducational Materials for Clients and Families

★★★★★ *The Causes of Anxiety and Panic Attacks* by Ron Rapee,
Michelle J. Craske, David H. Barlow
http://www.algy.com/anxiety/files/barlow.html

Probably the best overview written by noted experts for their clients. The aim is to teach about the physical and mental components of anxiety so that "(1) you realize that many of the feelings which you now experience are the result of anxiety and (2) you learn that these feelings are not harmful or dangerous."

★★★★★ *Panic Disorder*
http://lexington-on-line.com/naf.panic2.html#anchor333635

These eight pages clearly explain the development of panic and its treatment. Recommended.

★★★★ *National Institute of Mental Health's Library*
http://www.nimh.nih.gov/anxiety/library/brochure/pubs.htm

NIMH offers six booklets (most about 20 pages long) on anxiety disorders and their treatment. They can be read online or ordered (call 1-888-8-ANXIETY). Authoritative and very well done.

★★★★ *How to Treat Your Own Panic Disorder* by Bert Anderson, PhD
http://www.eadd.com/~berta/

About 60 printable pages on hyperventilation syndrome and its treatment with a simple common device.

★★★★ *Obsessive–Compulsive Disorder (OCD)*
  http://lexington-on-line.com/naf.ocd.2.html

A good but brief (five page) explanation.

★★★★ *Managing Traumatic Stress: Tips for Recovering From Disasters and Other Traumatic Events* http://www.apa.org/practice/traumaticstress.html

From the American Psychological Association, a good set of guidelines in five pages.

★★★★ *Obsessive–Compulsive Disorder*
  http://www.mayohealth.org/mayo/9809/htm/ocd.htm

About five pages from the Mayo Clinic with solid information.

★★★★ *Understanding Panic Disorder*
  http://www.nimh.nih.gov/anxiety/upd.cfm

A 20-page comprehensive brochure from NIMH.

★★★★ *Obsessive Compulsive Disorder* http://www.nursece.com/OCD.htm

This site includes the readings for a continuing education course for nurses. In about 20 pages, it is very comprehensive as to the features and treatments.

★★★★ *Caregiver Series* http://www.bcm.tmc.edu/civitas/caregivers.htm

About a dozen rather sophisticated articles on childhood trauma's effect on relationships and brain development.

★★★★ *FAQ: Panic Disorder* http://www.algy.com/anxiety/panicfaq.html

An excellent overview with many resources in just 12 pages.

★★★ *Panic Disorder, Separation, Anxiety Disorder, and Agoraphobia in Children and Adolescents* by Jim Chandler, MD
  http://www.klis.com/chandler/pamphlet/panic/panicpamphlet.htm

About 15 pages from a medical perpective, filled with vignettes. The site can also provide a basis for educational materials.

★★★ *The Trauma Response* http://www.trauma-pages.com/t-facts.htm

A two-page listing of symptoms and ways to cope by Dr. Patti Levin.

★★★ *Getting Treatment for Panic Disorder*
  http://www.nimh.nih.gov/anxiety/getpd.cfm

Eight pages with an emphasis on cognitive-behavioral therapy and medications.

★★★ *Anxiety Disorders–The Caregiver* http://www.pacificcoast.net/~kstrong

A site offering advice, support, and information.

★★★ *Answers to Your Questions about Panic Disorder*
       http://www.apa.org/pubinfo/panic.html

A good four-page overview from the American Psychological Association.

★★★ *Agoraphobia: For Friends/Family*
       http://panicdisorder.about.com/msubagora05.htm?pid=2791&cob=home

Seven articles with guidance for those assisting people with agoraphobia.

★★★ *For the Support Person: Helping Your Partner Do In-Vivo Exposure* by
       Edmund J. Bourne, PhD http://www.npadnews.com/support.htm

Brief and clear guidelines.

★★★ *Obsessive-Compulsive Disorder*
       http://www.nimh.nih.gov/publicat/ocdmenu.cfm

Four booklets of well-written information suitable for an introductory handout. Treatment recommendations are medications and behavior therapy.

★★★ *Guidelines for Families Coping with OCD* Adapted from *Over and Over Again* by
       Nesiroglu and Yaryura-Tobias http://www.ocdhope.com/gdlines.htm

A very good list for families.

★★★ *Menu for Understanding Panic Attacks*
       http://www.anxietypanic.com/menuunderstanding.html

This offers six to eight very useful and simple sets of advice for coping with panic attacks, dealing with relatives with panic, and the dynamics and symptoms of panic.

★★★ *Anxiety and Phobias*
       http://www.rcpsych.ac.uk/public/help/anxiety/anx_frame.htm

A five-page introductory brochure with lots of good information in a friendly presentation.

★★ *Anxiety Disorders* http://www.psych.org/public_info/anxiety.cfm

About eight pages from the American Psychiatric Association, with an emphasis on diagnostic criteria. The treatment suggested at this site is combined behavior therapy and medication.

Treatment

★★★★★ *Expert Consensus Treatment Guidelines for Obsessive–Compulsive Disorder:*
          A Guide for Patients and Families http://www.psychguides.com/oche.html

Based on *The Expert Consensus Guideline Series: Treatment of Obsessive–Compulsive Disorder* by John S. March, MD, Allen Frances, MD, Daniel Carpenter, PhD, and David A. Kahn,

MD (available at http://www.psychguides.com/ocgl.html), it tells almost everything about treatment in 16 pages. It leans heavily on behavior therapy and medications.

★★★★ *The Systematic Desensitization Procedure* by R. Richmond, PhD
       http://members.aol.com/avpsyrich/sysden.htm

An excellent presentation of the logic and methods of systematic desensitization in about eight pages.

★★★★ *Relaxation* http://www.algy.com/anxiety/relax.html

A dozen good lists of tips and suggestions for coping with anxiety, including tools, tips, advice, and wisdom.

★★★★ *About OCD* http://www.ocfoundation.org (top of left side of page)

Here are brochures offering a very good quality and appropriately full presentation of the nature of OCD and its treatment (cognitive-behavior therapy and medications for adults and children) and a screening test. Overall somewhat heavier on pills, but each article has solid information in about 10 to 12 pages.

★★★★ *A Fuller Explanation of Cognitive-Behavioral Therapy* by John Winston Bush, PhD http://www.cognitivetherapy.com/fuller.html

These five pages can be used as an introduction.

★★★ *Basics of Cognitive Therapy* http://mindstreet.com/cbt.html

An overview with references in two or three pages. This is part of a cognitive-based treatment program.

★★★ *Instructions for Breathing Exercises* http://www.transformbreathing.com/STET

See also http://www.algy.com/anxiety/A2Z/diaph.html

★★★ *Anxiety and the Workplace* http://www.pacificcoast.net/~kstrong/work.html

This is a discussion and list of suggestions for modifying the workplace for the anxious worker.

Other Resources

★★★★ *Post-Traumatic Stress Disorder: A Bibliographic Essay* by Lisa S. Beall
       http://www.lib.auburn.edu/socsci/docs/ptsd.html

This is a fuller, contextualized, expanded, and annotated bibliography.

★★★★ *Traumatic Stress and Secondary Traumatic Stress*
       http://www.isu.edu/~bhstamm/ts.htm

The site of Dr. Beth Hudnall Stamm, a major worker in this area. Her materials on traumatic stress and secondary or vicarious traumatization of helpers (family and professionals) are thorough, and the links are invaluable.

★★★★ *Social Anxiety Test: Are You a Social Animal?*
http://www.queendom.com/tests/soc_anx.html

A 25-item interactive test for social anxiety. This resource might prove useful in helping a client to organize his or her symptoms.

★★★★ *Self-Help Brochures* http://www.couns.uiuc.edu/Brochures/brochure.htm

These may be relevant to people with an anxiety disorder: Dissertation Success Strategies, Overcoming Procrastination, Perfectionism, Stress Management, Test Anxiety, and Time Management.

★★★ *Panic Disorder Treatment and Referral: Information for Health Care Professionals*
http://www.algy.com/anxiety/files/treatref.html

If you need to educate referral sources, this eight-pager will do it. It includes How to Recognize Panic Disorder, Biological and Psychological Causes, Treatment and Referral, and Sources of Further Information.

★★★ *Out Damn Spot: The Nature and Treatment of Contamination Fears* by Dean McKay, PhD http://www.ocdonline.com/articlesmckay.htm

A 10-page presentation on the contamination anxiety of OCD.

★★★ *The National Center for PTSD: Research and Education on Post-Traumatic Stress Disorder* http://www.dartmouth.edu/dms/ptsd/Index.html

Although oriented to military veterans, there are many readings of value for families and survivors. There are also assessment instruments, fact sheets, and the world's largest index to trauma literature.

★★ *Anxiety: Theoretical Views and Therapeutic Techniques* by David W. Ayer
http://www.algy.com/anxiety/files/outline.html

If you need notes for a lecture or presentation.

★★ *Obsessive Compulsive Personality Disorder: A Defect of Philosophy, not Anxiety* by Steven Phillipson, PhD http://www.ocdonline.com/articlephillipson6.htm

A 14-page discussion of OC personality disorder in a folksy style by a cognitive-behavioral therapist with his own point of view.

Online Support Groups

Club OCD http://www.ocdresource.com

A place for kids to learn about OCD with some games and puzzles, an art gallery, links for kids, and information for parents.

OCD and Parenting Mailing List
http://www.onelist.com/subscribe.cgi/ocdandparenting

An e-mail list that serves as online support group for parents of children with OCD.

Friends and Family
http://forums.cmhc.com/forums/jnjbbs.cgi?uid=GUEST&config=friends

A support bulletin board for those caring for people with mental disorders.

Meet Other Support People http://www.pacificcoast.net/~kstrong/meetsp.html

An e-mail support group for caregivers for people with anxiety.

Support People Need Understanding Friends Too
http://www.pacificcoast.net/~kstrong/meetsp.html

An e-mail support group for caregivers to those with anxiety disorders.

Silver Umbra's Haven http://www.geocities.com/HotSprings/1497/index.html

A site for chat and discussions.

Victim Services: Links That Can Help
http://www.victimservices.org/reflink.html

This is an enormous list of national and New York-area organizations that focus on the victims of various crimes, such as assault, stalking, elder abuse, and domestic violence.

See also Stress Management and Relaxation (Chapter 26).

NATIONAL SUPPORT GROUPS

Agoraphobics Building Independent Lives (ABIL)
3805 Cutshaw Avenue, Suite 415
Richmond, VA 23230
Phone: 804-353-3964
E-mail: abil1996@aol.com

Agoraphobics in Action
PO Box 1662
Antioch, TN 37011-1662
Phone: 615-831-2383

Agoraphobics in Motion (AIM)
1729 Crooks
Royal Oak, MI 48067
Phone: 810-547-0400

Anxiety Disorders Association of America (ADAA)
11900 Parklawn Drive, Suite 100
Rockville, MD 20852-2624
Phone: 301-231-9350
http://www.adaa.org

Their bookstore is excellent for its prices and the wide range of books.

Emotions Anonymous
PO Box 4245
St. Paul, MN 55104-0245
Phone: 612-647-9712

Twelve-step program of recovery from emotional difficulties.

National Anxiety Foundation
3135 Custer Drive
Lexington, KY 40517-4001
Phone: 606-272-7166
http://lexington-on-line.com/naf.html

Neurotics Anonymous
PO Box 12
Casa, AR 72025-0012

Twelve-step program of recovery from mental and emotional disturbances.

Obsessive–Compulsive Foundation
PO Box 70
Milford, CT 06460-0070
Phone: 203-878-5669
Fax: 203-874-2826
E-mail: info@ocfoundation.org
http://www.ocfoundation.org

Their Internet site is very broad, with research, book reviews, chat, newsletters, and conferences.

Obsessive–Compulsive Anonymous
PO Box 215
New Hyde Park, NY 11040
Phone: 516-741-4901

Twelve-step self-help group for people with obsessive–compulsive disorders.

Phobics Anonymous
PO Box 1180
Palm Springs, CA 92263
Phone: 619-322-COPE

An international fellowship for people with anxiety and panic disorders. Follows the 12-step program of recovery. Group development manual and worksheets available. Publications *From Anxiety Addict to Serenity Seeker* and *Twelve Steps of Phobics Anonymous* are available.

Recovery
802 North Dearborn Street
Chicago, IL 60610
Phone: 312-337-5661
Fax: 312-337-5756
E-mail: spot@recovery-inc.com
http://www.recovery-inc.com

"Self-help method of will training; a system of techniques for controlling temperamental behavior and changing attitudes toward nervous symptoms, anxiety, depression, anger and fears."

tAPir Registry
http://www.algy.com/anxiety/registry/index.html

This is a search engine for support groups. Although new, it is a wonderful idea and helps locate many people and organizations.

CHAPTER 7

Assertiveness

The famous behavior therapist Joseph Wolpe said that there are essentially three ways to relate to others. The first is to be aggressive, considering only ourselves and riding roughshod over others. You count, but others don't. The second is to be nonassertive, always putting others before ourselves and letting others run roughshod over us. Others count, but you don't. The third approach is the golden mean—to be assertive, placing ourselves first, but taking others into account. That is, you count *and* other people count.

In most cultures, women have traditionally been socialized to be nonassertive and men to be aggressive. In today's world, an increasing number of women have stepped up their efforts to reduce their passivity and be more assertive, and more men are choosing to be less aggressive. Many mental health professionals believe that our society would benefit from increased assertiveness by women and decreased aggression by men. Breaking out of traditional patterns, though, can be difficult and stressful. In the case of working hard to become more assertive, it's clearly worth the effort.

In this chapter, we present evaluative ratings and brief descriptions of self-help books and Internet resources on assertiveness.

SELF-HELP BOOKS

Strongly Recommended

★★★★★ *Your Perfect Right: A Guide to Assertive Living* (7th ed., 1995) by
Robert Alberti and Michael Emmons. San Luis Obispo, CA: Impact.

This national best-seller, periodically updated, emphasizes the importance of developing better communication skills in becoming more assertive. Initially published in 1970, *Your Perfect Right* is divided into two main parts: Part I speaks to the self-help reader who wants to learn how to become more assertive; Part II is a guide for assertiveness

---

RECOMMENDATION HIGHLIGHTS

Self-Help Books

- For practical and comprehensive training in assertion and communication skills:

  ★★★★★ *Your Perfect Right* by Robert Alberti and Michael Emmons

  ★★★★ *Asserting Yourself* by Sharon Anthony Bower and Gordon H. Bower

  ★★★★ *Stand Up, Speak Out, Talk Back* by Robert Alberti and Michael Emmons

  ★★★★ *When I Say No, I Feel Guilty* by Manuel Smith

- For women who want to become more assertive:

  ★★★ *The Assertive Woman* by Stanlee Phelps and Nancy Austin

- For training in assertion and communication skills for 8- to 12-year-old children:

  ◆ *Stick Up for Yourself* by Gershen Kaufman and Lev Raphael

Internet Resources

- For quality information on assertion from a rights perspective:

  ★★★★ *Assertiveness* http://www.couns.uiuc.edu/Brochures/assertiv.htm

- For an assertion scale scored online:

  ★★★★ *Are You Assertive?* http://www.queendom.com/assert2.html

---

training leaders that teaches techniques to help others become more assertive. In Part I, the reader learns how to distinguish assertive, nonassertive, and aggressive behavior and why assertive behavior is the best choice. Among the key components of assertive behavior are self-expression, honesty, directness, self-enhancement, not harming others, being socially responsible, and learned skills. Readers complete a questionnaire to evaluate their own level of assertiveness, and they learn about the obstacles they will face in trying to be more assertive. Step-by-step procedures are presented for getting started and for gaining the confidence to stand up for their own rights. An excellent chapter on soft assertions gives information about how to be more assertive with friends and family members. Being assertive with friends and family members makes relationships more open and honest and less harmful. Interactions in school, work, and community are also covered, with tips on how to be assertive in those contexts. Readers learn how anger needs to be expressed in assertive, nonaggressive ways. An extensive annotated list of readings about assertiveness is provided toward the end of the book. *Your Perfect Right* received the highest rating in the Assertiveness category and is widely respected; almost 300 respondents rated it. Indeed, some mental health professionals call it the assertiveness bible, they think so highly of it.

★★★★★   *The Assertive Woman* (3rd ed., 1997) by Stanlee Phelps and Nancy Austin.
          San Luis Obispo, CA: Impact.

This book is about how women can become more assertive. The third edition addresses
the challenge for women to be assertive in the workplace, socially, at home, and with
various sets of people with whom they come into contact. The topics of body image,
attitude, power, compliments, saying no, and anger, among others, are approached with
illustrative scenarios, checklists, and exercises that readers may use to learn the concepts presented. A strength of the book is that the authors adapt the assertion principles to relevant contemporary contexts rather than to conventional scenarios. An effective question and answer section at the end of the book presents the questions that the
authors have found women to most frequently ask.

★★★★   *Asserting Yourself: A Practical Guide for Positive Change* (1991) by Sharon
         Anthony Bower and Gordon H. Bower. Reading, MA: Addison-Wesley.

The authors maintain that individuals lack communication and coping strategies for
everyday living and that these deficits are often the root of interpersonal conflict and
general unhappiness. The purpose of their program is to help individuals learn to
change behavior in positive ways and to relate to others more effectively. Several self-
tests help the reader identify desired areas of change and goals. Then, the text focuses
on success exercises that the reader can do initially, followed by sample scripts for common situations that can be practiced and, finally, ways to handle situations when people
react negatively to new assertive behaviors. In addition to the major focus of assertiveness training, the authors address the often-accompanying problem of self-esteem and
deficit coping skills and conclude with a chapter on how to develop friendships.

★★★★   *Stand Up, Speak Out, Talk Back* (1975) by Robert Alberti and
         Michael Emmons. New York: Pocket Books.

This book tackles the same problem as its sister publication, *Your Perfect Right*: how to
become more assertive by improving communication skills. The authors discuss developing self-confidence and specific strategies that will help you become more assertive.
Alberti and Emmons give artful advice on how to become assertive without stepping on
others. Their 13-step assertiveness training program is based on the idea that it is easier to
change people's behavior than to change their attitudes. The steps are clearly described
and easy to understand. Readers learn some fascinating strategies for using nonverbal
behavior—eye contact, body posture, gestures, facial expressions, voice, and timing—to
present themselves more assertively. Readers are also taught how to handle potential
adverse reactions to their assertiveness, and situations are presented in which they might
not want to assert themselves (such as when interacting with overly sensitive people). Not
as well-known or as highly regarded by our mental health experts as the authors' *Your Perfect Right*, this book nonetheless is a solid, practical text on assertiveness training.

★★★★   *When I Say No, I Feel Guilty* (1975) by Manuel Smith. New York: Bantam
         Books.

This volume was especially written for people who feel that they are always being talked
into doing something they don't want to do. It falls into the category of assertiveness
books that emphasize the importance of learning better communication skills to

become more assertive. Its 11 chapters cover such important assertiveness topics as how other people violate our rights, an assertiveness bill of rights, the importance of persistence in becoming assertive, how to assertively cope with supervisors and experts, how to work out compromises and say no, and how to be assertive in sexual encounters. Interspersed through the book are 34 annotated dialogues that illustrate basic assertive skills, such as using calm persistence to get what we want, disclosing our worries to others, agreeing with critical truths and still doing what we want, asserting our negative points, prompting criticism, and keeping our self-respect. Many mental health professionals praise the book, commenting about the down-to-earth advice and the many examples of timid people who gained assertive skills; however, some find that the book oversimplifies some issues related to becoming more assertive.

Recommended

★★★ *Don't Say Yes When You Want to Say No* (1975) by Herbert Fensterheim and Jean Baer. New York: Dell Books.

This behaviorally oriented book contains 13 chapters, 7 of which are devoted to the behavioral approach to assertiveness training. In the early chapters, the reader learns how to target assertiveness difficulties, use behavioral rehearsal and other strategies to learn to say no, call on assertiveness training techniques to develop a social network of friends and acquaintances, develop self-control, and learn assertiveness skills that help at work. Other chapters explore a wide range of topics, some of which are not found in other assertiveness self-help books, including using assertiveness to combat depression, reduce eating disorders, and improve sexual relationships. The book was published more than two decades ago and has become dated in some ways; for example, in discussing mental disorders the outmoded category of neurosis is used.

★★★ *Good-Bye to Guilt* (1985) by Gerald Jampolsky. New York: Bantam Books.

This self-help book presents an emotionally and spiritually based approach to becoming more assertive. Jampolsky uses the term *good-bye* for the process of letting go of guilt, fear, and condemning judgments. In Part I, the reader learns about the spiritual transformations involved in moving from fearfulness (of love, death, having fun, and much more) to forgiveness (letting go) to unconditional love (for and from God, for self, and for others). In Part II, the majority of the book, 14 lessons apply the knowledge of Part I to real-life situations. Among the chapters are "Only My Condemnation Injures Me" and "In My Defenselessness My Safety Lies." Exercises such as becoming one with a flower introduce vivid images of the spiritual healing process.

★★★ *The Gentle Art of Verbal Self-Defense* (1980) by Suzette Elgin. Englewood Cliffs, NJ: Prentice-Hall.

This self-help book presents a communication skills approach to becoming more assertive. The 18 chapters train readers in verbal judo, which involves using an opponent's strength and momentum as tools for self-defense. Elgin describes four basic principles of verbal self-defense that are important to master: (1) know that you are under attack; (2) know what kind of attack you are facing; (3) know how to make your defense fit the attack; and (4) know how to follow through. A number of examples and exercises help readers learn to use these principles. Tips for verbal self-defense are provided for men and women. On the positive side, the book includes effective verbal strategies for seizing control of a situation, and the extensive exercises are good learning devices. However, the consensus of the mental health experts in the national studies was that the 4-star and 5-star books listed earlier do a better job of teaching the communication skills necessary to becoming more assertive.

Diamond in the Rough

♦ *Stick Up for Yourself: Every Kid's Guide to Personal Power and Positive Self-Esteem* (1990) by Gershen Kaufman and Lev Raphael. Minneapolis: Free Spirit.

Written for children ages 8 to 12, this book begins with the elusive concept of sticking up for yourself. The authors very effectively use cognitive techniques in walking the child through definitions, explanations, and numerous scenarios with which the child can identify, thereby breaking down these concepts to clear thinking and behaving choices for the child. Getting to know yourself is a central idea of the book, and the breadth and intensity of human feelings are discussed using short narratives, illustrations, short writing exercises, and questions to generate thinking (e.g., write about a time when you felt angry; tell what happened and what you did). A strength of this text is the inclusion of a section on learning to like yourself, which includes a self-esteem self-quiz, do's and don'ts, and good things to do for yourself. This book is cited as a Diamond in the Rough because few of our mental health experts were familiar with it, but it is particularly well presented and appropriate for the young.

Not Recommended

★★ *Creative Aggression: The Art of Assertive Living* (1974) by George Bach and Herb Goldberg. Garden City, NY: Doubleday.

★ *Pulling Your Own Strings* (1977) by Wayne Dyer. New York: Crowell.

★ *Control Freaks: Who Are They and How to Stop Them from Running Your Life* (1991) by Gerald Piaget. New York: Doubleday.

Strongly Not Recommended

† *Looking Out for Number One* (1977) by Robert Ringer. Beverly Hills, CA: Los Angeles Book Company.

† *Winning through Intimidation* (1973) by Robert Ringer. Beverly Hills, CA: Los Angeles Book Company.

INTERNET RESOURCES

Psychoeducational Materials for Clients and Families

★★★★ *Assertiveness* http://www.couns.uiuc.edu/Brochures/assertiv.htm

A three-page brochure with many specific self-statements from a rights perspective.

★★★★ *Are You Assertive?* http://www.queendom.com/assert2.html

A 32-item questionnaire on assertiveness scored online. A simpler questionnaire can be found at http://www.srg.co.uk/areyouassert.html.

★★★ *Learn to Be Assertive—In a Positive Way*
http://www.utexas.edu/student/cmhc/assertips.html

Three brief pages, including 4 Types of Assertion and What Is Being Assertive?

★★ *Basic Strategies for Behaving More Assertively*
http://www.unc.edu/depts/unc_caps/Assert.html

A one-page listing.

★★ *Assertiveness: What It Is* http://members.aol.com/sitaofIl/Assertiveness.html

One page of definitions in terms of mental abilities.

See also Communication and People Skills (Chapter 11).

CHAPTER 8

Attention-Deficit/ Hyperactivity Disorder

The diagnosis of attention-deficit/hyperactivity disorder (ADHD) has proliferated over the past decade, with some experts asserting that this neurobehavioral disorder is finally being effectively diagnosed and other experts claiming that we are unduly labeling fidgety or misbehaving children The attention deficit part of the disorder is characterized by inability to pay attention to details or to sustain attention over time, failure to complete tasks, easy distractibility, and forgetfulness in daily activities. Hyperactivity is characterized by fidgeting, squirming, talking excessively, moving around during sedentary activity, and impulsiveness, such as interrupting and displaying impatience. Adolescents and adults report restlessness and inability to engage in quiet activities. ADHD is estimated to affect 3 to 5% of school-age children and occurs between 4 and 9 times more frequently in males than in females.

Children's lives can be dramatically affected in both school and home and, correspondingly, parents find their lives and families in turmoil. The symptoms become evident during early school years, when adjustment to group activities and norms become important. Academic achievement often declines, and behavioral problems in school develop. This results in frequent interaction with school authorities, affecting the parents and the relationship between parents and child. The child's inability to apply himself or herself to concentrated work often has the appearance of disinterest, lack of discipline, and contrary behavior. The symptoms of ADHD can shift in intensity and frequency, resulting in the parents' and teachers' perception of willfulness and deliberateness in oppositional behavior. The fallout from this condition includes family discord, training and discipline problems, and frustrations of not knowing what to do, while the child feels isolated, misunderstood, sometimes rejected, and different.

The self-help books, autobiographies, websites, and support groups described in

---

RECOMMENDATION HIGHLIGHTS

Self-Help Books

- For parents of ADHD children:

  ★★★★★ *Taking Charge of ADHD* by Russell Barkley

- For adults with ADHD:

  ★★★★★ *Driven to Distraction* by Edward M. Hallowell and John J. Ratey

- For teens with ADHD:

  ★★★ *ADHD and Teens* by Colleen Alexander-Roberts

- For children with ADHD:

  ★★★ *Learning to Slow Down and Pay Attention* by Kathleen G. Nadeau and Ellen B. Dixon

Autobiographies

- Coping strategies from two parents of ADHD children:

  ★★★★ *Parenting a Child with Attention Deficit/Hyperactivity Disorder* by Nancy S. Boyles and Darlene Contadino

- A parent's compilation of ADHD information:

  ◆ *Maybe You Know My Kid* by Mary Fowler

Internet Resources

- Excellent general information about ADHD:

  ★★★★★ *National Attention Deficit Disorder Association* http://www.add.org

  ★★★★★ *Attention Deficit Hyperactivity Disorder* http://www.nimh.nih.gov/publicat/adhd.cfm

- A site that offers materials for diagnosis, outcomes, and medications:

  ★★★★★ *ADHD Assessment Services* http://www.svr.com/addhelp/index.htm

---

this chapter target parents of children with ADHD, the children themselves, and adolescents and adults grappling with special aspects of the problem.

SELF-HELP BOOKS

Strongly Recommended

★★★★★ *Taking Charge of ADHD* (1995) by Russell A. Barkley. New York: Guilford Press.

The author adopts an empathic stance toward parents of ADHD children, offering illustrations of how parents and children are misunderstood and misinformed. The purpose is to describe how ADHD impairs the lives of parents and children and to empower parents to be proactive and take an executive role in decisions about their children. The theme of the book is upbeat in that the author offers parents many practical and effective ideas about how to manage their children, take care of themselves as parents, become effective as advocates for their children, and implement techniques to help ADHD children succeed at school and feel better about themselves. This stellar book, which received a ringing endorsement from our mental health experts, is written for beleaguered parents who have not given up hope.

★★★★★ *Driven to Distraction: Recognizing and Coping with Attention Deficit Disorder from Childhood through Adulthood* (1994) by Edward M. Hallowell and John J. Ratey. New York: Simon & Schuster.

This superb book is written for all people with ADHD, family members, and others in their lives, with special focus on adults suffering from ADHD. The experience of ADHD is realistically portrayed through numerous case studies that illustrate specific problems, such as secondary symptoms of depression, low self-esteem, fear of learning new things, and the fear of diagnosis as an educational death sentence. The reader is taught how to further a diagnosis (e.g., an expanded symptom/criteria list is identified for adults and children), what one can do when the diagnosis is suspected, how to explain the diagnosis to children, and how to structure the child's daily life. There is a thorough description of treatment possibilities. The experience of ADHD and its effects on the relationships of adults, couples, the family, and schoolchildren are addressed. The book also presents an informative description of ADHD effects when coupled with anxiety, depression, learning disabilities, substance abuse, conduct disorders, and other conditions.

Recommended

★★★ *ADHD and Teens* (1995) by Colleen Alexander-Roberts. Dallas TX: Taylor.

This volume is written for parents and, secondarily, for those working with ADHD teens. The roller-coaster ride of going through adolescent development with ADHD is described by identifying problem areas, offering warning signs, suggesting coping techniques, and explaining improved parenting skills. The approach assumes a partnering of behavioral and educational models with medication (for moderate to severe cases). The larger context of the effect on family dynamics, school and peer interactions, and stages of development are addressed. This book also includes helpful chapters on coexisting special problems, such as substance abuse, sexuality, suicide risk, and oppositional defiance/conduct disorder.

★★★ *Learning to Slow Down and Pay Attention: A Book for Kids about ADD* (2nd ed., 1997) by Kathleen G. Nadeau and Ellen B. Dixon. Washington, DC: Magination Press.

This second edition of *Learning to Slow Down and Pay Attention* retains the fundamental elements of the first but adds several strong content areas, including many more "things I can do to help myself," increased focus on attentional problems without hyperactivity, and a greater emphasis on problems experienced by girls. The writing style, page layout, drawings, and cartoons lend themselves effectively to the interests of children. A checklist about the child at home, at school, with friends, and about the child himself or herself allows children to identify specific concerns and frustrations on which they can work with parents and teachers. "Things I can do for myself" is an excellent activity list that includes getting ready for school, how to pay attention, homework, controlling anger, solving problems, and making friends. A section on special projects that children can do with parents adds positive experiences for the parents and child together.

★★★ *Living with ADHD Children: A Handbook for Parents* (1998) by
      Peter H. Buntman. Los Alamitos, CA: Center for Family Life.

This handbook is written in a workbook format that presents the major topics very concisely, but thoroughly. The focus areas start with how it feels to be a parent and how the child feels to be coping with ADHD, moves into symptoms, other causes of hyperactivity that need to be ruled out, and then targets behavioral change. The instructional chapters teach the parent how to change the child's behavior, how to get the child to listen, how to work with self-esteem and school problems, and about medication. The last chapter is a compendium of questions from parents that is quite comprehensive. Scenarios and hypothetical situations are presented that convey realistic and typical problems encountered by the child and parent.

Diamond in the Rough

◆ *Distant Drums, Different Drummers: A Guide for Young People with ADHD* (1995) by
   Barbara D. Ingersoll. Bethesda, MD: Cape.

The author has written this book for the ADHD child between 6 and 10 with about a second-grade reading level. The narrative talks directly to the child and describes what its like to have ADHD, explains what it is, and speculates about how children might feel about taking medicine. A central focus is individual differences among children, the evolutionary role of action-oriented adventurers, and how it is hard to be an action-oriented person in today's controlled and detailed environment. The explanation is likely to give children a sense that there is not something wrong with them after all and may make clearer, in fantasy terms, the frustrations they feel. The book receives a Diamond in the Rough rating in that it was rated favorably but infrequently. ADHD books tend to be written about but not for children, and this book gives professionals and parents a reference for the child.

AUTOBIOGRAPHIES

Strongly Recommended

★★★★ *Parenting a Child with Attention Deficit/Hyperactivity Disorder* (1996) by
       Nancy S. Boyles and Darlene Contadino. Los Angeles: Lowell House.

The two authors, both parents of children with ADHD working as professionals in the field, have also collaborated on *The Learning Differences Sourcebook*. Here they present management, coping, and advocacy strategies for parents based on their own experiences and those of other parents. A highly valued and practical volume with a strong insider's voice.

Recommended

★★★ *ADHD Handbook for Families: A Guide to Communicating with Professionals* (1999) by Paul L. Weingartner. Washington, DC: Child Welfare League of America.

An experienced therapist who works with children who have ADHD, Weingartner brings a personal perspective in that he has ADHD himself. He describes his coping mechanisms and the methods he uses to work with children and educate parents about the disorder. A central theme of the book, encapsulated in its subtitle, is enhancing the family's ability to communicate and lobby effectively with health care professionals.

Diamond in the Rough

◆ *Maybe You Know My Kid: A Parents' Guide to Helping Your Child with Attention Deficit Hyperactivity Disorder* (3rd ed., 1999) by Mary Fowler. Secaucus, NJ: Birch Lane Press.

Faced with the challenge of raising a son with ADHD, Mary Fowler researched the topic. The book describes theories in the field, available treatments, educational programs, and advocacy techniques related to the Americans with Disabilities Act. The new edition features recent material on treatments and sources of assistance for families. Named a Diamond in the Rough because of its high rating but low number of ratings; our experts may have not been familiar with the revised edition.

INTERNET RESOURCES

Metasites

★★★★ *The National Attention Deficit Disorder Association*
  http://www.add.org/content/menu1.html

While this site offers dozens of articles under Treatment, ABCs, and Research, some are scientifically weak, so read them before recommending them. The following seem solid: Basic Information About Attention Deficit Disorders by Rebecca Chapman Booth; An Update on Medications Used in the Treatment of Attention Deficit Disorder by John Ratey, MD; Some Basic Facts about ADD Medications; and What Causes ADD?

★★★ *CHADD: Children and Adults with Attention Deficit/Hyperactivity Disorder*
  http://www.CHADD.org

CHADD is both an educational and an advocacy organization. Their Fact Sheets (online are two-page versions of their booklets) are a starting place.

Psychoeducational Materials for Clients and Families

★★★★★ *National Attention Deficit Disorder Association* http://www.add.org

The six essays under The ABCs of ADHD: General Information are excellent introductory materials. The other dozen headings under ADD Information are also very informative, but many are speculative. Altogether an excellent site for anyone exploring ADD. A similar site is *One ADD Place* at http://www.oneaddplace.com. The *Attention*

Deficit Disorder and Parenting site at http://LD-ADD.com is more focused on learning disabilities and interventions and is designed for parents of children with ADD.

★★★★★ *Attention Deficit-Hyperactivity Disorder (ADHD)* by Jim Chandler, MD
http://www.klis.com/chandler/pamphlet/adhd/adhdpamphlet.htm

About 25 pages of solid information with lots of cases. An excellent educational product because it offers more than medications for treatment.

★★★★★ *Attention Deficit Hyperactivity Disorder*
http://www.nimh.nih.gov/publicat/adhd.cfm

This 30-page booklet from the federal government is packed with factual information. A good start for many who want to know all the science as of 1996. Also available in Spanish at http://www.nimh.nih.gov/publicat/spadhd.htm.

★★★★★ *ADHD Assessment Service* http://www.svr.com/addhelp/index.htm

This is the site of a psychologist who markets evaluation materials, but it also offers many useful, accurate, informative brochure-sized pages about diagnosis, educational rights, outcomes, medication, and behavioral treatments.

★★★★ *110 Diagnosis and Treatment of Attention Deficit Hyperactivity Disorder*
http://odp.od.nih.gov/consensus/cons/110/110_intro.htm

This is a Consensus Conference Statement from November 1998 on the scientific data on diagnosis, effects, effective treatments, risks of treatments, and so forth. For those who need this level of professional evidence, this is the best and latest available.

★★★★ *What Is ADHD? A General Overview* http://www.svr.com/addhelp/over.htm

Nine pages of well-written and accurate questions and answers.

★★★★ *Attention Deficit Disorder without Hyperactivity: ADHD, Predominantly Inattentive Type* by Jennifer Wheeler, MA, and Caryn L. Carlson, PhD
http://www.kidsource.com/LDA-CA/ADD_WO.html

A solidly research-based seven-page article on this subtype.

★★★★ *Attention-Deficit Hyperactivity Disorder* by Russell A. Barkley, PhD
http://www.sciam.com/1998/0998issue/0998barkley.html

The best-known writer in the field presents a new theory suggesting that "the disorder results from a failure in self-control. ADHD may arise when key brain circuits do not develop properly, perhaps because of an altered gene or genes." Worthy of consideration, it is written for the college-educated reader.

★★★★ *ADD FAQ* http://www3.sympatico.ca/frankk

Although last revised in August 1996, this contains lots of good information with some humor and perspective. About 200 pages.

★★★★ *Attention Deficit Disorder* http://add.miningco.com

Dozens of headings offer hundreds of sites. The breadth is amazing, and almost any need can be met here—from medications to allopathy, from doing homework to college work, from Ritalin to saying no to Ritalin.

★★★★ *Bob's Little Corner of the Web*
        http://www.bobseay.com/littlecorner/newurl/homepage.html

A fine combination of completeness and humor—easy to use, informative, and fair-minded. The sections How Are We Different, Traits of ADDers, and The Secret Lives of ADDers give a good sense of differences.

★★★ *Attention-Deficit/Hyperactivity Disorder in Children and Adolescents*
        http://www.mentalhealth.org/publications/allpubs/Ca-0008/ADHD.HTM

A three-page fact sheet perhaps useful as a handout because it lists the symptoms very fully.

★★★ *Attention Deficit Disorder: Beyond the Myths*
        http://www.catalog.com/chadd/doe/doe_myth.htm

Three pages of facts and myths are introductory and yet quite informative.

★★★ *A Journey into Attention Deficit Disorder*
        http://hometown.aol.com/BevKPrice/HTML/index.html

Under Strategies and Intervention are six pages on how to modify the school setting and four pages on coping at home.

★★★ *ADDvance Magazine* http://www.addvance.com

The "Resource Site for Women and Girls with Attention Deficit Disorder. . . . " Some of the articles and resources are specific to females—girls, students, mothers, workers—and the site also has chat, links, and support groups.

★★★ *Special Education Rights and Responsibilities* http://adhdnews.com/sped.htm

Here a child advocate will find all the federal rules and policies and advice for writing IEPs and TIEPs for pursuing special educational services. See also the guidance in *Advocating for Your Child* at http://adhdnews.com/advocate.htm.

★★★ *Born to Explore! The Other Side of ADD* http://borntoexplore.org

"ADD is a difference not a defect" is the theme here. Start with the site map. Creativity, Positive Quotes, and The Other Side are highlights. Lots of loose hypotheses about causation and treatments, so be cautious.

★★ *Social Security* http://adhdnews.com/ssi.htm

For advice on applying for Social Security disability benefits for a child with ADHD.

Especially for Kids

★★★★ *Questions from Younger Children about ADD*
http://users.aol.com:80/jimams/answers1.html

★★★★ *Questions from Adolescents about ADD*
http://users.aol.com:80/jimams/answers2.html

Here are responses to actual children's questions. Ideal for kids who have experienced the name-calling and distorted ideas of their peers.

Other Resources

★★★★ *Forms* http://www.add-plus.com/forms.html

Devised by John F. Taylor, PhD, these five data collection forms can enhance communication with teachers and physicians. They are not available online but can be ordered at no cost. Their titles are: Academic Problem Identification Checklist; Classroom Daily Report Form; Hyperactivity Screening Checklist; Medication Effectiveness Report Form (Parents' and Teachers' versions); and Social/Emotional/Academic Adjustment Checklist. Also consider ordering Preventing Misbehavior from Boredom: The Fun Idea List, which is also free.

★★★ *Amen Clinic ADD Subtype Test*
http://www.amenclinic.com/ac/addtests/default.asp

An interactive test to diagnose five subtypes of ADD and a checklist for adult ADD.

★★★ *Job Information for People with ADD*
http://add.about.com/msubjobs.htm?pid=2791&cob=home

Nine articles to assist in managing work issues, and a list of careers and information about each.

★★★ *ADDitude: The Happy Healthy Lifestyle Magazine for People with ADD*
http://www.additudemag.com

Articles, information, and encouragement.

NATIONAL SUPPORT GROUPS

Attention Deficit Disorder Association (ADDA)
PO Box 1303
Northbrook, IL 60065-1303
E-mail: mail@add.org
http://www.add.org

Also an online support group at
http://www.add.org/content/group1.htm

Attention Deficit Information Network (Ad-IN)
475 Hillside Avenue
Needham, MA 02194
Phone: 781-455-9895

CHADD: Children and Adults with Attention Deficit/ Hyperactivity Disorder
8181 Professional Place, Suite 201
Landover, MD 20785
Phone: 800-233-4050
Fax: 301-306-7090

Council for Exceptional Children
11920 Association Drive
Reston, VA 22091
Phone: 703-620-3660

Federation of Families for Children's Mental Health
1021 Prince Street
Alexandria, VA 22314
Phone: 703-684-7710

HEATH Resource Center
American Council on Education
1 Dupont Circle, Suite 800
Washington, DC 20036
Phone: 800-544-3284

National Information Center for Children and Youth with Disabilities
PO Box 1492
Washington, DC 20013
Phone: 800-695-0285

Learning Disabilities Association of America
4156 Library Road
Pittsburgh, PA 15234
Phone: 412-341-1515 and 412-341-8077

For people with learning disabilities and their families.

CHAPTER 9

Career Development

Too often we perceive developing a career plan as a one-time event, the steps toward making a single, major commitment. But each of us probably experiences life changes that require modifications in employment, adjustments in career goals, and sometimes a change of careers. In fact, the average worker now makes five to six job transitions in a lifetime.

Careers are occupying an increasingly crucial role in our life satisfaction and our family relationships. Cost reduction and downsizing by businesses have translated into displacement and job loss. The work force is rapidly becoming increasingly diverse, service-oriented, and internationally linked. Many jobs are more complex and technically demanding. Workers are increasingly perceiving the workplace as a means of enhancing their health and well-being, not simply as a place for earning a living. Dual-career couples predominate. And now, more than ever, people are concerned about the role of work in their lives, wanting to strike the best balance between work and other life tasks.

Self-help resources on career development transverse a number of topics, including career choice, job hunting, interviewing, career changes, dual-career families, and effective communication in the workplace. A large number of self-help books on specific components of work have been written—how to become a better salesperson, how to be an effective manager, how to improve the corporate workplace—but such books are not included here.

What follows are national ratings and evaluative descriptions of self-help books and Internet resources devoted to career development.

SELF-HELP BOOKS

Strongly Recommended

★★★★★ *What Color Is Your Parachute?* (30th edition, 1999) by Richard Bolles. Berkeley, CA: Ten Speed.

This extremely popular book about job hunting was first published in 1970. Since 1975, an updated edition has appeared annually. This is an enormously successful self-help

RECOMMENDATION HIGHLIGHTS

Self-Help Books

- On career choice, job hunting, and interviewing:
    - ★★★★★   *What Color Is Your Parachute?* by Richard Bolles
    - ★★★   *Knock 'Em Dead* by Martin Yate

- On work and its meaning for traditional males and traditional females:
    - ★★★★   *Staying the Course* by Robert Weiss

- On turning conflict into career and interpersonal advancement:
    - ★★★★   *Win–Win Negotiating* by Fred Jandt

- On the meaning of work:
    - ◆ *Lives without Balance* by Steven Carter and Julia Sokol

- On clarifying career and life values:
    - ◆ *Career Anchors* by Edgar H. Schein

- On diversity and women's career:
    - ◆ *Diversity and Women's Career Development* by Helen Farmer and Associates

Internet Resources

- Everything you want to know about college and graduate school:
    - ★★★★★   *Petersons.com* http://www.petersons.com

- Great suggestions for a career:
    - ★★★★   *Career Interests Game!*
      http://web.missouri.edu/~cppcwww/holland.shtml

- Everything you need to know about career planning:
    - ★★★★★   *Career Development Manual*
      http://www.adm.uwaterloo.ca/infocecs/CRC/manualhome.html

book that has become the career seeker's bible. Bolles tries to answer concerns about the job-hunting process and gives many sources that can provide further valuable information. Unlike many books on job hunting, *What Color Is Your Parachute?* does not assume that readers are recent college graduates seeking their first jobs. He spends considerable time discussing job hunting for people seeking to change careers. Bolles describes a number of myths about job hunting and successfully debunks them. He also provides invaluable advice about where jobs are, what to do to get hired, and how to cut through the red tape and confusing hierarchies of the business world to meet the key people who are most likely to make hiring decisions. The book has remained appreciably the same over the years with updates as appropriate. Recent editions have added material on job hunting for handicapped workers, how to effectively use career counselors, and how to find a mission in life. In recent editions, Bolles's discussion of finding a mission in life has been moved from the appendixes to an epilogue. This 5-star book was one of the most frequently rated books in our national studies—more than 300 mental health professionals evaluated it. It is indeed an excellent self-help book about job hunting and career change. Bolles writes in a warm, engaging, personal tone. His chatty comments are often witty and entertaining, and the book is attractively packaged with cartoons, drawings, and many self-administered exercises.

★★★★ *Staying the Course: The Emotional and Social Lives of Men Who Do Well at Work* (1990) by Robert Weiss. New York: Free Press.

This book is based on Weiss's interviews with 80 men, aged 35 to 55, in upper-middle-class occupations. Weiss explores the nature of the men's work and nonwork lives—their activities, relationships, goals, and stresses. He also delves into their psychological lives to discover what has motivated them to meet their obligations year after year after year. Weiss found that men who stayed the course had established social status and self-worth at work, had experienced emotional and social support from their marriages and families, and had benefited from loyal friendships. Weiss says that all too often in our society, successful men are portrayed as exploiters. He found this not to be the case. Successful men had made compromises with their youthful dreams and had developed respectful and caring relationships both in and out of the workplace. Their lives revolved around steady career advancement instead of ruthless ambition, and they cared more about family stability than sexual conquest. *Staying the Course* contains high-quality research, careful interpretation, and useful insights. However, there is something of an old-fashioned cast to Weiss's men and his interpretation of their lives. Feminists especially do not appreciate some of the conclusions that can be drawn from Weiss's work, such as: If wives work, their jobs are secondary in terms of economics and status.

★★★★ *Win–Win Negotiating: Turning Conflict into Agreement* (1987) by Fred Jandt. New York: Wiley.

The main themes of this book are that conflict is inevitable but is not always bad and that, if everyone involved makes an honest effort, the conflict can be resolved. In the first four chapters, Jandt describes the basic nature of conflict and includes a self-assessment so that readers can determine how they deal with conflict and identify sources of conflict. He shows the reader how to keep minor disagreements from turning into major battles. Jandt makes the important point that when one party is the "winner" in a conflict, in the long run both parties often lose when the losing party avoids future contact or tries to get even. Ultimately, the relationship dies. Thus, the goal is to develop a solution that will satisfy both parties and let the relationship continue in much the same way as in the past. *Win–Win Negotiating* is a good introduction to learning how opponents or adversaries think and how they negotiate their positions. Anyone who wants to learn about negotiating techniques and resolving conflict in the workplace can benefit from reading it.

Recommended

★★★　*Shifting Gears* (1990) by Carole Hyatt. New York: Simon & Schuster.

Hyatt calls attention to data that suggest that most people go through several career changes. She uses the results of interviews with 300 individuals who succeeded in career transitions to develop a framework for self-guidance in making career transitions. She advises how to:

- Adapt to today's marketplace.
- Determine your work style.
- Identify trigger points that require change.
- Explore the psychological barriers to change, and overcome them.
- Learn strategies to define an appropriate career path and repackage yourself.

This recent addition to the self-help literature was not well-known among the mental health professionals—only 20 rated it—but they accorded it moderately positive points.

★★★　*Knock 'Em Dead* (9th ed., 1996) by Martin Yate. Holbrook, MA: Bob Adams.

This regularly updated guide to job interviewing is subtitled *With Great Answers to Tough Interview Questions*. Yate gives the best answers to a number of key questions likely to be asked in a job interview, such as:

- Why do you want to work here?
- How much money do you want?
- What can you do that someone else can't?
- What decisions are the most difficult for you?
- What is your greatest weakness?
- Why were you fired (if you lost your last job)?

According to Yate, the best jobs go to the best-prepared rather than to the best-qualified candidates. Yate prepares the potential interviewee with the inside scoop on stress interviews, salary negotiations, executive search firms, and drug testing. He also provides advice about how to respond to illegal questions and other hardball tactics. In the most recent editions, Yate has added sections on dress and body language. This 3-star book was not well known among the mental health professionals, but the experts who did rate it thought it gives sound advice for job interviewing, especially on handling tough interviews.

★★★　*Do What You Love, the Money Will Follow* (1987) by Marsha Sinetar. New York: Dell.

This book is subtitled *Discovering Your Right Livelihood,* and that is what Sinetar tries to encourage readers to do. Sinetar strongly believes that people should try to find jobs that fulfill their needs, talents, and passions. She provides a step-by-step guide to doing this and includes dozens of real-life examples of how people have overcome their fears, taken risks, and found work that allows them to express themselves and grow. Readers learn how to get in touch with their inner selves and true talents, evaluate and build their self-esteem, get rid of their "shoulds," overcome resistance, and get out of unfulfilling jobs and into fulfilling ones. *Do What You Love, the Money Will Follow* barely received a 3-star rating; that is, it was given mixed reviews. Some of the mental health professionals felt that Sinetar does a good job of helping people stuck in jobs they don't like to break free and find jobs they truly enjoy doing. Others said that Sinetar's approach borders on naïveté and might encourage people to leave jobs they probably shouldn't in search of the ultimate, perfect job.

Diamonds in the Rough

♦ *Lives without Balance* (1992) by Steven Carter and Julia Sokol. New York: Villard.

The authors describe the problem of having an unbalanced life because of outdated values and false premises. Among the modern destructive myths highlighted are the limitless credit card; you are the master of your own fate; think and grow rich; you can have it all; and you can do it all. Using catchy phrases themselves, the authors evaluate four types of unbalanced lives: the downward slide, the never-ending treadmill, the uncontrollable escalator, and the roller coaster. Carter and Sokol also analyze image fixes, power fixes, glamour fixes, buying and selling fixes, job perks fixes, and status fixes— along with the problems entangled in the fixes. *Lives without Balance* was published between our national studies and, unfortunately, we neglected to secure experts' ratings on it. But the book raises important issues and stimulates thought about various dimensions of work, careers, and meaning in life.

♦ *Career Mastery* (1992) by Harry Levinson. San Francisco: Berrett-Koehler
    Publishers.

This introspective exploration of career choices is not a how-to book, nor does it give advice on specific, practical aspects of a job search. Rather it is a psychological self-assessment and a values clarification that enables readers to decide how to direct themselves through a lifetime of careers. Topics involve a larger context of decision-making, not a specific job but the direction the individual wants to go in shaping a professional future. Some of these topics include how to cope with change in an organization, how to avoid self-blame, how to make sense of a defeat or failure, how to cultivate good work relationships with coworkers, and how to relate to a good and to a problem boss. This book falls into the Diamonds in the Rough category because it received positive but infrequent ratings and because it reflects on the psychological aspects of work.

♦ *Diversity and Women's Career Development* (1997) by Helen S. Farmer and
    Associates. Thousand Oaks, CA: Sage.

The results of a longitudinal study of career paths of culturally diverse women from adolescence to adulthood are recounted through their stories. Each chapter focuses on a subset of the interviews conducted with 57 women and 48 men related to the theme of that chapter (e.g., socioeconomics, rural women, gender differences, ethnic discrimination). An overview of the themes, illustrations, and representative quotes are presented and then related to the social learning theory framework woven throughout the book. This book is an excellent resource for those interested in career development of women, diversity, ethnicity and family effect on career; it offers insight into the courage and perseverance demonstrated by these career women. Rated favorably but infrequently in our national studies, this book is unique in that it incorporates a data-based perspective on the changing role of women in the workplace. The target population is professionals: psychologists, social workers, teachers, professors, and career counselors. A tough read for a layperson.

♦ *Career Anchors: Discovering Your Real Values* (1990) by Edgar H. Schein. San Francisco, CA: Jossey-Bass/Pfeiffer.

This self-assessment inventory workbook is structured around the concept of career anchors representing areas of competence, personal motivations for work, and values. The purpose of the assessment is to determine the relative importance of the eight identified career anchors in the person's life and thereby to make better career decisions. The sources of self-awareness are the career-orientation inventory and the career interview, which a person takes in cooperation with a partner (friend). The eight anchors—technical competence, managerial competence, autonomy, security, entrepreneurial creativity, service, challenge, and lifestyle—are thoroughly explained and are the continuing themes throughout the verbal interview with the partner. This workbook does not focus on career preferences or on special interests, but rather the underlying personal qualities that affect career satisfaction. Accorded Diamond in the Rough status because of its favorable but infrequent ratings in one of the national studies.

Not Recommended

★★ *The Portable MBA* (1990) by Eliza Collins and Mary Devanna. New York: Wiley.

★★ *The 100 Best Companies to Work for in America* (1984) by Robert Levering, Milton Moskowitz, and Michael Katz. New York: Signet.

INTERNET RESOURCES

There are numerous sites to post resumes and search for openings, sites of recruiters, virtual job fairs, and specialized job area sites. None of these have been included here because they are not direct self-help resources and because they do not assist in psychotherapy.

Metasites

★★★★★ *Petersons.com* http://www.petersons.com

If a client needs college, this is the place to start. Just about anything and everything you could want to learn about college and graduate school is here: selecting a college, studying abroad, financing school, job searching, admission tests, adult students, executive education programs, and so on.

★★★★ *Yahoo—Careers* http://www.yahoo.com

Searching Yahoo under Careers produces about 60 sections, including information about each of 100 careers (at http://dir.yahoo.com/Business_and_Economy/ Companies/Corporate_Services/Human_Resources/Recruiting_and_Placement/ Career_Fields) and career planning (at http://dir.yahoo.com/Business_and_ Economy/Employment_and_ Work/Career_Planning).

★★★★ *Career Interests Game*! http://web.missouri.edu/~cppcwww/holland.shtml

Using Holland's six types of personality, this site will suggest careers. Neat.

★★★ *Graduate and Professional School Guides*
        http://www.jobweb.org/catapult/gguides.htm

Links to sites about applying to and financing graduate school and about making the transition to graduate school.

★★★ *Monster.com* http://www.monster.com

If you are seeking a job, this is the largest list of job openings. The readings can be very helpful.

Psychoeducational Materials for Clients and Families

★★★★★ *Career Development Manual*
        http://www.adm.uwaterloo.ca/infocecs/CRC/manualhome.html

This small, book-sized site covers all the steps in detail: self-assessment, researching occupations, making decisions, contacting employers, working, and life planning. From the University of Waterloo.

★★★★★ *JobTrak: Job Search Tips*
        http://www2.jobtrak.com/help_manuals/jobmanual

This is actually a small book on how to find a job aimed at college students but of value to anyone. It covers all the area, such as networking, business letters, resumes, and interviewing.

★★★★★ *Developing A Career Transition Strategy*
        http://www.doi.gov/octc/strategy.html

An interactive guidebook with 10 sections on career transitions, it offers assessment tools, areas of occupational growth, interviewing tips, resumes, and retirement information.

★★★★★ *The Student Guide* http://www.ed.gov/prog_info/SFA/StudentGuide

This online book is the most comprehensive resource on student financial aid. From the U.S. Department of Education.

★★★★★   *The Riley Guide: Research for Career and Work Options*
         http://www.dbm.com/jobguide/research.html

This site is eight collections of links to the very best sites for job and career research. If you need the facts, here is how to find them on employers, education, pay, the future of different careers, career counselors, and so on. From DBM, a major placement service.

★★★★   *Career Adviser: Your Channel Guide to Career Resources*
        http://www.careeradviser.com

If you know what you want to explore but don't know where to start, this site will take you to just about all the online information about the job.

★★★★   *Your Self-Assessment* http://cscwww.cats.ohiou.edu/careers/self.htm

A worksheet to assess interests, skills and values. This may help clarify issues in an open-ended way.

★★★★   *Feminist Career Center* http://www.feminist.org/911/911jobs.html

Listings of available positions with about 200 feminist and progressive organizations.

★★★★   *Job Hunters Bible* http://www.jobhuntersbible.com

This site is designed to supplement the valuable book *What Color Is Your Parachute?* Best if the client is familiar with the book, but the 25 articles in the Parachute Library are of value by themselves.

★★★★   *Out on Your Own: From Corporate to Self-Employment* by Robert W. Bly
        and Gary Blake http://www.smartbiz.com/sbs/arts/bly66.htm

About four pages on the fears that being suddenly self-employed bring and how to cope with them.

★★★★   *Career Shift Coach*
        http://www.ivillage.com/content/categories/0,1825,1946~41,00.html

Many useful articles on improving and changing jobs in the Library and hundreds more in the left-hand column.

★★★   *Career Goals* http://www.careernet.state.md.us./goalsetting.htm

For those who cannot decide on goals, this essay and worksheet will help them focus.

★★★   *Birkman Quiz* http://www.review.com/birkman

An interactive test to determine a person's most likely interests and work style to help choose fields, jobs, and organizations best suited to strengths and occupational preferences.

★★★ *iVillage Work from Home* http://www.ivillage.com/work

Support and information for those who work at home, especially women.

★★★ *Conference Calls in Your Pajamas: The Pros and Cons of Working from Home*
by Bradley Richardson
http://campus.monster.com/articles/onthejob/workfromhome

A two-page summary to help a person decide.

★★★ *ACCESS: Networking in the Public Interest* http://www.accessjobs.org

Some articles and a large listing of jobs in the nonprofit area. "An excellent resource for anyone seeking jobs, internships, volunteer positions, and career development in nonprofit organizations." See also *Opportunity NOCs: Nonprofit Organization Classifieds* http://www.opportunitynocs.org where jobs can be searched by region, state, or keyword.

★★★ *The Red Guide to Temp Agencies: Tips for Temps; Strategies for Successful Temping* http://www.panix.com/~grvsmth/redguide/tips.html

Lots of guidance for seeking and using temporary employment agencies.

Other Resources

★★ *Job Searching* http://dir.yahoo.com/Business_and_Economy/Companies/ Employment/Software/Titles/Career_Information_System

Here are online searching programs for the following states: Idaho, Illinois, Minnesota, Montana, Nebraska, and Oregon.

CHAPTER 10

Child Development and Parenting

Playwright George Bernard Shaw once commented that although parenting is a very important occupation, no test of fitness for it is ever imposed. If a test were imposed, some parents would turn out to be more fit than others. Most parents hope that their children will grow into socially mature individuals, but they often are not sure how to help their children reach this goal.

Child development and parenting are probably the largest categories of self-help resources. If parents are not confused about what to do before they visit a bookstore or surf the Internet to obtain information on parenting, they may become confused when they see the bewildering array of advice, all promising to help them turn out a happier, more competent child. The ratings of the mental health experts in the national studies provide valuable advice about how to navigate the maze of parenting self-help books.

In this chapter we evaluate self-help resources focusing on parenting infants and children. Other chapters consider closely related topics, notably Pregnancy (Chapter 21), Families and Stepfamilies (Chapter 16), and Teenagers and Parenting (Chapter 27). An entire chapter (8) is also devoted to attention-deficit/hyperactivity disorder.

Infancy is a special period of growth and development, requiring extensive time and support by caregivers. Unlike the newborn of some species (the newborn wildebeest runs with the herd moments after birth!), the human newborn requires considerable care. Good parenting requires long hours, interpersonal skills, and emotional commitment. Many parents learn parenting practices and baby care from their parents—some of which they accept, some of which they discard. Unfortunately, when parenting practices and baby care are passed on from one generation to the next, both desirable and undesirable practices are perpetuated.

Many parents eagerly, perhaps anxiously, want to know the answer to such ques-

---

RECOMMENDATION HIGHLIGHTS

Self-Help Books

- On parenting infants:

  ★★★★★ *Infants and Mothers* by T. Berry Brazelton

  ★★★★★ *What Every Baby Knows* by T. Berry Brazelton

  ★★★★★ *Dr. Spock's Baby and Child Care* by Benjamin Spock and Michael Rothenberg

- Developmental milestones with month-to-month descriptions of infant development and care:

  ★★★★★ *What to Expect the First Year* by Arlene Eisenberg and Associates

- A broad-based nonmedical approach to parenting infants and young children:

  ★★★★★ *The First Three Years of Life* by Burton White

  ★★★★★ *The First Twelve Months of Life* by Frank Caplan

- Information on the normal course of child development and coping with problems:

  ★★★★★ *To Listen to a Child* by T. Berry Brazelton

  ★★★★★ *Your Baby and Child* by Penelope Leach

- For parents of toddlers:

  ★★★★★ *Toddlers and Parents* by T. Berry Brazelton

- On general parenting skills and better communication with children:

  ★★★★★ *Between Parent and Child* by Haim Ginott

  ★★★★★ *How to Talk So Kids Will Listen and How to Listen So Kids Will Talk* by Adele Faber and Elaine Mazlish

  ★★★★ *Parent Effectiveness Training* by Thomas Gordon

- On effective discipline for children:

  ★★★★★ *Children: The Challenge* by Rudolph Dreikurs

  ★★★★★ *1-2-3 Magic* by Thomas W. Phelan

  ★★★★ *Parenting the Strong-Willed Child* by Rex Forehand and Nicholas Long

  ★★★ *Living with Children* by Gerald Patterson

- On the problem of children growing up too soon:

  ★★★★ *The Hurried Child* by David Elkind

- On the effect of emotionally unavailable, narcissistic parents on children's development:

  ♦ *The Drama of the Gifted Child* by Alice Miller

- For African-American parents:

  ♦ *Raising Black Children* by James P. Comer and Alvin E. Poussaint

Movies

- A morality tale on pushing children and on children trying to please their parents:

   ★★★★ *Searching for Bobby Fischer*

- On discovering what is in the gifted child's best interest:

   ★★★★ *Little Man Tate*

Internet Resources

- Comprehensive sources of parenting:

   ★★★★★ *ABCs of Parenting* http://www.abcparenting.com

   ★★★★★ *NPIN: National Parent Information Network*
   http://ericps.crc.uiuc.edu/npin/index.html

- An informative site for families with substance abuse concerns:

   ★★★★★ *Common Sense: Strategies for Raising Alcohol- and Drug-Free Children*
   http://www.pta.org/commonsense

---

tions as: How should I respond to the baby's crying? Is there a point at which I can spoil the baby? What are normal developmental milestones for my child? How should I stimulate my young child intellectually? How do I deal with the terrible twos? What discipline methods are most effective and yet most humane? Many parents turn to self-help resources on parenting for answers and advice on the best way to handle their children. And those who do find no shortage of written and Internet resources.

Because there are so many resources, we had to make some decisions about which to include and exclude. We primarily included resources that deal with parenting in general rather than parenting strategies for specific problems. For example, we evaluate parenting books on discipline, but for the most part we do not rate books that exclusively cover such topics as learning disabilities or mental retardation. Of course, some of the general parenting books include such specific topics in their overview of parenting and child development.

Even with these exclusions, be forewarned: this is the lengthiest chapter in the book. It is also, rewardingly, the chapter with the largest number of strongly recommended self-help resources.

SELF-HELP BOOKS

Strongly Recommended

★★★★★ *Infants and Mothers* (rev. ed., 1983) by T. Berry Brazelton. New York: Delta/Seymour Lawrence.

This book concerns the infant's temperament, developmental milestones in the first year of life, and the parents' (especially the mother's) role in the infant's development.

Author T. Berry Brazelton, MD, a pediatrician, has recently been crowned America's baby doctor, a title once reserved for Benjamin Spock. Brazelton describes three different temperamental or behavioral styles: active baby, average baby, and quiet baby. He takes readers through the developmental milestones of these three different types of babies from birth to 12 months. Most of the chapters are titled with the babies' ages: The Second Month, The Third Month, and so on. In every chapter, Brazelton tells mothers the best way to parent the three different types of babies. He advises the mother to be a sensitive observer of her baby's temperament and behavior, believing that this strategy will help the mother chart the best course for meeting the infant's needs. This 5-star book is now considered a classic. Brazelton's approach is well-informed, warm, and personal.

★★★★★ *What Every Baby Knows* (1987) by T. Berry Brazelton. Reading, MA: Addison-Wesley.

This self-help book is based on the Lifetime cable television series that Brazelton hosts, and like the series, it is a broad approach to parenting infants that is organized according to the experiences of five different families. Brazelton presents in-depth analyses of five families and their child-rearing concerns, such as how to handle crying, how to discipline, how to deal with the infant's fears, sibling rivalry, separation and divorce, hyperactivity, birth order, and the child's developing sense of self. The descriptions of each family include the circumstances of the family's visits to Dr. Brazelton and lengthy excerpts of pediatrician–parent dialogues, interspersed with brief explanatory notes. Each family also is portrayed two years later to see how they resolved their child-rearing difficulties and where they are at that point. In this 5-star book, Brazelton dispenses wise advice to parents. He does an excellent job of helping parents become more sensitive to their infants' needs and of providing parents with sage recommendations on how to handle a host of problems that may arise

★★★★★ *Dr. Spock's Baby and Child Care* (1997) by Benjamin Spock and Michael Rothenberg. New York: Pocket Books.

Initially published in 1945, this is one of the classics of self-help literature. Author Benjamin Spock, MD, was considered America's baby doctor for decades, and this book was perceived by many to be the bible of self-help books for parents of infants and young children. *Dr. Spock's Baby and Child Care* is a broad approach to infant and child development. It has more medical advice than most of the other books in the infant and parenting category, but it also includes a number of chapters of child-rearing advice. Most of the material in earlier editions has been carried forward into the 1997 edition. This material includes advice on feeding, daily care, illnesses, first aid, nutrition, and a myriad of other topics. The revision gives more attention to divorce, single-parent families, stepparenting, and the role of fathers in the infant's development. An expanded section on breast feeding for mothers who work outside the home appears in the new edition. And there are new chapters on child abuse, neglect, permissiveness, and children's fears of nuclear war. The book has retained its political flavor. The authors fervently state that children should not play with toy guns or watch cowboy movies, advocate a nuclear freeze, and argue for abolishing competitiveness in our society. Across almost 5 decades, more than 30 million copies of this book have been sold, placing it second on the nation's overall best-seller list (after the Bible). The book's enthusiasts say that it is extremely well-organized and serves as a handy guide for parents to consult when they run into a problem with their infant or child. The medical advice is outstanding. However, some critics maintain that Spock's approach to discipline is still too permissive and is not the best strategy for developing young children's self-control.

★★★★★ *The First Three Years of Life* (20th rev. ed., 1995) by Burton White.
New York: Fireside.

This book presents a broad-based, age-related approach to parenting infants and young children. White strongly believes that most parents in the United States fail to provide an adequate intellectual and social foundation for their children's development, especially between the ages of 8 months and 3 years. White provides in-depth discussion of motor, sensory, emotional, sociability, and language milestones. He divides the first 3 years into seven stages. For each of the seven stages, White describes the general behavior and educational development of the young child and parental practices that he does and does not recommended. His goal is to provide parents with the tools to help every child reach his or her maximum level of competence by structuring early experiences and opportunities in appropriate ways. White presents advice about such child-rearing topics as sibling rivalry, spacing children, types of discipline, and detection of disabilities. Appropriate toys and materials are listed and how to obtain professional testing of a child is outlined. White also provides a list of recommended readings for parents. His recommendations about which toys parents should and should not buy, how to handle sibling rivalry, and how to discipline children are also excellent. This 5-star book has been a very popular self-help book; however, White has especially been criticized because he essentially does not think mothers should work outside the home during the child's early years. Critics say White's view places an unnecessary burden of guilt on the high percentage of working mothers with infants.

★★★★★ *What to Expect the First Year* (1996) by Arlene Eisenberg, Heidi Murkoff, and Sandee Hathaway. New York: Workman.

This is an encyclopedic (almost 700 pages) volume of facts and practical tips on how babies develop, how to become a better parent, and how to deal with problems as they arise. The authors give chatty answers to hypothetical questions arranged in a month-by-month format. The book is full of questions commonly asked by parents. What to buy for a newborn, first aid, recipes, adoption, low birth-weight babies, and the father's role also are discussed. Some of the book's enthusiasts called it the best one on the market for parents of infants in their first year of life. The book covers an enormous array of topics that concern parents and generally provides sound advice.

★★★★★ *To Listen to a Child* (1984) by T. Berry Brazelton. Reading, MA: Addison-Wesley.

Brazelton's focus here is primarily on problematic events that arise in the lives of children. Fears, feeding and sleep problems, stomachaches, and asthma are among the problems that Brazelton evaluates. He assures parents that it is only when they let their own anxieties interfere that problems such as bedwetting become chronic and guilt-laden. Each chapter closes with practical guidelines for parents. This 5-star book is easy to read, includes extremely well-chosen and clearly explained examples, and is warm, personal, and entertaining. The book's descriptions are not as detailed as those in some other books that focus on specific periods of development—for example, Brazelton's own *Toddlers and Parents*—but it is a very good resource for parents to refer to throughout the childhood years when normal problems emerge.

★★★★★ *Toddlers and Parents* (2nd ed., 1989) by T. Berry Brazelton. New York: Delacorte.

This Brazelton contribution traces normal child development and advises parents on how to handle typical problems and issues that arise during the toddler years. Each of the 11 chapters interweaves the narrative of an individual child's experiences (e.g., the birth of a sibling or a typical day at a day-care center) with Brazelton's moment-by-moment descriptions of what the child may be feeling, explanations of the child's behavior, and supportive suggestions for parents that help them cope with their own feelings as well as their child's behavior. Among the topics addressed by Brazelton:

- The toddler's declaration of independence from parents at about 1 year of age, a time when the toddler becomes alternately demanding and dismissing.
- The nature of working parents' family life and their toddler's development at 18 and 30 months.
- Life with a toddler of different ages in nontraditional families (divorced, step-family).
- Special considerations for withdrawn, demanding, and unusually active toddlers.
- Coping with the 18-month-old's frequent no's.
- Day-care centers.
- The 30-month-old's developing self-control and self-awareness.

All told, this is an excellent self-help book for the parents of toddlers. The writing is clear; the examples are extraordinarily well-chosen; and the tone is warm and personal. Brazelton not only provides parents with a guide to survival but helps them develop a sense of delight in the struggles and triumphs their toddler is experiencing.

★★★★★ *Between Parent and Child* (1965) by Haim Ginott. New York: Avon.

This aging classic provides parents with a guide to improving communication with their children and understanding their children's feelings. Ginott's aim is to help parents understand the importance of listening to the feelings behind their child's communication. Ginott says that children who feel understood by their parents do not feel lonely and develop a deep love for their parents. Toward this end, he describes a communication technique he calls "childrenese," which is based on parents' respect for the child and statements of understanding preceding statements of advice or instruction. Since its publication in 1965, millions of copies of the book have been sold. It was never revised. *Between Parent and Child* has been praised for being simple and clear. Many mental health professionals believe that it provides important advice for parents in helping them understand children's feelings and how to communicate more effectively with their children. Although more than three decades old, *Between Parent and Child* continues to be one of the books that many mental health professionals recommend for parents. The age of the book is a problem: For example, the material on sex education and sex roles is severely outdated, as are the appendixes on further reading and where to get help; mothers are always at home, and fathers are off at work.

★★★★★   *Children: The Challenge* (1964) by Rudolph Dreikurs. New York: Hawthorn.

This aging classic is centrally concerned with effective and loving discipline. Dreikurs believes that parents have to learn how to become a match for their children by becoming wise to their children's ways and capable of guiding them without letting them run wild or stifling them. Unfortunately, says Dreikurs, most parents don't know what to do with their children. Dreikurs teaches parents how to understand their children and meet their needs. He stresses that the main reason for children's misbehavior is discouragement. Discouraged children often demand undue attention. Parents usually respond to this negative attention-getting behavior by trying to impose their will on the children, who in turn keep misbehaving. Dreikurs says that parents who get caught up in this cycle are actually rewarding their children's misbehavior. He tells parents to instead remain calm and pleasant when disciplining the child. Each of the 39 brief chapters involves a different type of discipline problem in which children misbehave and parents respond inappropriately. Dreikurs clearly spells out effective ways to handle each of these situations. He teaches parents to be firm without dominating, to induce respect for order and the rights of others, to stay out of power struggles and conflict, to refrain from being overprotective, and to have the courage to say no. He also recommends a "family council" for solving family problems. This book remains an excellent guide for parents to use in learning how to discipline their children more effectively. It is easy to read; the examples are clear and plentiful; the strategies for discipline are good ones. Although written over three decades ago, *Children: The Challenge* still is a widely recommended book on parental discipline.

★★★★★   *Your Baby and Child: From Birth to Age Five* (rev. ed., 1997) by
          Penelope Leach. New York: Knopf.

This book describes normal child development from birth to 5 years of age and provides suggestions for parents about how to cope with typical problems at different ages in infancy and the early childhood years. Leach describes the basics of what parents need to know about feeding, sleeping, eliminating, teething, bathing, and dressing at each period of early development—during the first 6 months, 6 to 12 months, 1 to 2½ years, and 2½ to 5 years. Nontechnical graphs of growth rates are easy to interpret. Leach also explores the young child's emotional world, telling parents what children are feeling and experiencing in different periods of development. Despite describing normal development in different periods, Leach carefully points out individual variations in growth and development. She concludes that when parents have a decision to make about their child, their best choice is usually to go "by the baby"—their sensitive reading of what the child's needs are—rather than "by the book" or what is generally prescribed for the average child. The index in *Your Baby and Child* cleverly doubles as a glossary of terms. The final pages of the book are a handy illustrated guide to first aid, accidents, safety, infectious diseases, and nursing. Leach also suggests developmentally appropriate games and toys. Leach's extensive experience with children comes through in her sensitive, 5-star suggestions for how to handle children at different developmental levels in the early years of life. The material is extensive, well-organized, and packed with more than 650 well-executed charts, drawings, and photographs.

★★★★★ *How to Talk So Kids Will Listen and Listen So Kids Will Talk* (20th ed., 1999) by Adele Faber and Elaine Mazlish. New York: Avon.

This is a how-to book written with the goal of teaching methods that affirm the dignity and humanity of parents and children. After years of conducting workshops on communication skills for parents, the authors assembled the many ideas, activities, and lessons learned into this book. Each chapter presents ways to put principles and concepts into action and addresses topics such as dealing with children's feelings, cooperation, alternatives to punishment, autonomy and praise, and putting it all together. These approaches include situations with open-ended answers for reader response, cartoons that teach key principles, feeling and context exercise, parent-child role play, and questions and answers. This is a good book for parent–child interaction in that it is clear and understandable.

★★★★★ *1-2-3 Magic: Effective Discipline for Children 2–12* (2nd rev. ed., 1996) by Thomas W. Phelan.

This humorous book takes the reader through the explanation of the 1-2-3 disciplinary approach with colorful and applicable illustrations. How to successfully start behaviors (e.g., cleaning room) and stop them (e.g., tantrums) are clearly described. The false assumption that the child is a little adult and the big mistakes parents make of showing too much emotion and explaining too much are played out in lighthearted but all too familiar scenarios. Established behavioral and Adlerian principles are employed in a novel and interesting context. The book is written to instruct parents in accomplishing the program, but also to demonstrate empathic support of the challenges of discipline in contemporary families.

★★★★★ *The First Twelve Months of Life* (rev. ed., 1995) by Frank Caplan. New York: Bantam.

This is a broad-based, developmental milestone approach to the infant's development in the first year of life. A month-by-month assessment of normal infant development is provided. The timetables in the book are presented in a rather rigid way. The author does warn the reader not to use them that way but rather as indicators of appropriate sequences of growth. Feeding, sleeping, language, physical skills, guidance, parental emotions, and learning stimulation are among the topics covered in depth. Each chapter contains a detailed developmental chart outlining the appropriate sensory, motor, language, mental, and social developmental milestones for that month. The book also includes 150 photographs. This 5-star book is well-organized, well-written, and easy to follow. Although Caplan warns readers not to take the timetables for developmental milestones as gospel, it's almost impossible not to do so because that is the way the book is organized.

★★★★ *Parent Effectiveness Training: The Tested New Way to Raise Responsible Children*
(1975) by Thomas Gordon. New York: Peter Wyden.

First published in 1970, this book was revised 1975. It is designed to educate parents
about the nature of children's development and to help them communicate more effectively with their children. The book opens with a discussion of how parents are blamed
but not trained (which underscores the rationale for Gordon's Parent Effectiveness
Training program). Gordon tells parents what they should and can be. He advocates an
authoritative parenting strategy that involves being neither permissive nor punitive but
that rather emphasizes nurturing and setting clear limitations. Gordon provides especially good advice about how to communicate more effectively with children. Included
in his recommendations are how to engage in active listening, how to make frank statements of feeling without placing blame, and how to deal with children's problems.
Gordon's approach enables parents to show children how to solve their own problems
rather than inappropriately accusing or blaming children or making them feel guilty.
Strategies for modifying a child's behavior and setting limits are discussed under the
topics of how to change unacceptable behavior by changing the environment and the
nature of parental power. The widespread popularity of this 4-star book was reflected in
the large number of respondents who rated the book—more than 250. The book and
the Parent Effectiveness Training course, taught through numerous parenting groups
and classes across the country, have helped millions of parents gain a better understanding of their children and learn to communicate more effectively with them.
Despite its age, it remains one of the best books available for improving parent–child
communication.

★★★★ *Parenting the Strong-Willed Child* (1996) by Rex Forehand and Nicholas Long.
Chicago, IL: Contemporary Books.

Parents of strong-willed children will learn a system of techniques and interactive skills
that have been shown by research to be effective in significantly improving child behavior. Well-accepted behavioral interventions and strategies are taught in very clear and
understandable terms. A 5-week program is outlined with step-by-step instructions,
examples, and scenarios that teach attending to the child, rewards, when to ignore the
behavior, how to give directions, and how to implement an effective time-out. The program is then integrated with a focus on improved relationship, communication, and
how to deal with specific problem behaviors (e.g., tantrums, aggression, lying). This
book will capture the interest of frustrated parents and will effectively lead parents
through steps to improve their children's behavior.

★★★★ *The Hurried Child: Growing Up Too Fast Too Soon* (rev. ed., 1988) by
David Elkind. Reading, MA: Addison-Wesley.

This book describes a pervasive and harmful condition that all too many children experience—growing up too fast and too soon. Elkind believes that many parents place too
much pressure on children to grow up too soon. He says that parents too often push
children to be superkids, competent to deal with all of life's ups and downs. He believes
that parents have invented the superkid to alleviate their own anxiety and guilt. But he
doesn't just blame parents; he also faults schools and the media. Elkind argues that too

many parents expect their children to excel intellectually and demand too much achievement early in their lives. Excessive expectations are both academic and athletic: Parental pressures let children know that to be fully loved they have win. In response, Elkin recommends respecting children's own developmental timetables and needs, encouraging children to play and fantasize, making sure that expectations and support are in reasonable balance, and being polite. This 4-star book highlights an important theme and provides insightful analysis: Too often, parents want children to be stars but don't give them the necessary time and support. One criticism of the book is that it fails to give parents day-to-day prescriptions for remedying hurried children's lives.

★★★★ *Dr. Spock on Parenting* (1988) by Benjamin Spock. New York: Simon & Schuster.

This book is primarily a collection of articles that Dr. Spock wrote for *Redbook* magazine in the 1970s and 1980s. Topics are anxieties in our lives, being a father today, divorce and its consequences, the new baby, sleep problems, discipline, stages of childhood, difficult relationships, behavior problems, influencing personality and attitudes, and health and nutrition. In a chapter on discipline, Spock rebuts the criticism leveled at *Dr. Spock's Baby and Child Care* that he encourages parents to be too permissive. Spock says that he never had such a philosophy and believes that parents should deal with their children in firm, clear ways. This 4-star book is easy to read and generally dispenses sound parenting advice. The consensus of our experts in the national studies was that several of the preceding books would be better choices on general approaches to parenting.

Recommended

★★★ *Positive Discipline A–Z* (1993) by Jane Nelsen, Lynn Lott, and H. Stephen Glenn. Rocklin, CA: Prima.

This book addresses 1,001 solutions to everyday parenting problems. The text covers parenting any age child but focuses on children younger than teenage. Part I consists of helpful parenting tools that set the stage for use of the positive discipline solutions to everyday problems (Part II). The tools are well-explained and include how to affect your child's behavior using concepts such as natural consequences, honesty, saying no, and using your sense of humor. The book also covers beliefs behind behavior. The text is guided by Adlerian principles and implements the approach effectively.

★★★ *Living with Children* (3rd ed., 1987) by Gerald Patterson. Champaign, IL: Research Press.

This behavior modification approach to disciplining children has an unusual style for a self-help book. It is written in a programmed instruction format that makes the material easy to learn, according to Patterson. In this approach, main ideas are broken down into small units or items. Parents are asked to respond to the items actively, rather than just read them. Four sections tell parents how learning takes place, how to change undesirable behavior, how normal children have normal problems, and what the problems of more seriously disturbed children are like. Patterson explains how reinforcement works and the importance of rewarding children immediately. Parents learn to develop a plan for changing their child's undesirable behavior. They begin by observing and recording the child's behaviors, detecting what led up to the behaviors and what followed them as well as how the parents responded when the child behaved in undesirable ways. Parents then learn to respond to the child's behaviors differently than they have in the past. Time out from positive reinforcement figures prominently in replacing the child's negative behaviors with positive ones. This simple but powerful book helps parents replace a child's undesirable behaviors with desirable ones by rearranging the way they respond to the child. Its 3-star rating is somewhat misleading: The book secured very positive ratings but was not rated frequently enough to reach the 4-star or 5-star categories.

★★★   *The Father's Almanac* (2nd ed., 1992) by S. Adams Sullivan. Garden City, NY: Doubleday.

The Father's Almanac is a guide for the day-to-day care of children written primarily for fathers. It begins before the child is born and includes a discussion of childbirth classes. The father's role at birth and infancy is chronicled, as his relationship with the child during the preschool years. The traditional role of the father is emphasized by Sullivan. For example, one chapter devoted to "Daddy's Work" describes how business travel or commuting cuts into the time available to the father to spend with his children. Another chapter stresses the importance of the father's being supportive of the mother. Other chapters focus on the father's play with children, building things with them, learning with them, and hints about photographing the family. This 3-star resource includes a great deal of practical advice for helping fathers interact with their young children effectively.

★★★   *How to Discipline Your Six- to Twelve-Year-Old without Losing Your Mind* (1991) by Jerry Wyckoff and Barbara Unell. New York: Doubleday.

As its title suggests, this book falls into the category of discipline techniques for parents. The authors define discipline as a teaching system that leads to orderliness and control. Chapters focus on such topics as social problems, school problems, noise, children wanting their own way, irresponsibility and disorganization, sleeping and eating, hygiene problems, self-image problems, and activities. Each chapter begins with the statement of a problem followed by a brief description of how the problem can be prevented. Then the authors tell parents how to solve the problem. A "what not to do" section is also included. Although the book's title indicates that it is about discipline, in reality the book is a general parenting guide that provides suggestions for how to prevent or solve typical childhood problems. The experts' 3-star ratings convey the impression that the book does a good job of providing parents with concrete advice in an easy-to-read format.

Diamonds in the Rough

◆   *The Drama of the Gifted Child* (1981) by Alice Miller. New York: Basic Books.

Originally published in German as *Prisoners of Childhood*, this book is about how disturbed parent–child relationships negatively affect children's development. Miller tries to get parents to recognize the dangers of misusing their power. The title of the book is somewhat misleading in that *gifted* does not mean talented in ability or intellect; rather, it means sensitive and alert to the needs of others, especially to the feelings and needs of parents. As a result of parents' unintentional or unconscious manipulation of them, gifted children's feelings are stifled. While gifted children become well-behaved, reliable, empathic, and understanding in order to keep their parents happy, they end up never having experienced childhood at all. Miller believes that gifted children's sensitivity, empathy, and unusually powerful emotional antennae predispose them to be used by people with intense narcissistic needs. Miller argues that narcissistic individuals do not experience genuine feelings, and ultimately they destroy the authentic experiencing of genuine feelings in their children. *The Drama of the Gifted Child* was positively rated, but by only five respondents. It is beautifully written and can help gifted readers gain insight into their own feelings.

♦ *Helping the Child Who Doesn't Fit In* (1992) by Stephen Nowicki and
  Marshall Duke. Atlanta, GA: Peachtree.

The traumatic effects on children of nonverbal communication deficits are described as the most common reason for social rejection and alienation suffered by children beyond their or their parents understanding. The authors present sets of skills and accompanying exercises for the parents and children to practice together. Receptive or expressive deficits in the areas of facial gestures, body gestures, tone of voice and intonation (paralanguage), use of timing, and style of dress are identified through assessment exercises conducted by the parents. Once the problem is targeted, remedial exercises are recommended and explained. This book registers as a Diamond in the Rough for its favorable but few ratings and for its understandable and effective materials that can be useful in helping children build the interpersonal skills they need.

♦ *Common Sense Parenting* (1996) by Ray Burke and Ron Herron. Boys Town, NB:
  Boys Town.

Many parents doubt their effectiveness as parents. This book is written for those parents who wish to improve their parenting skills with what the authors call a blueprint for parenting: practical, down-to-earth teaching and unconditional love coupled with spending time together. The skills material is systematically presented in a clear, understandable way using the following format: presentation of skill, examples and illustrations of how to use it, and how not to, and a variety of typical situations. The book is applicable to children of any age and developmental stage and includes skill development topics such as positive and negative consequences, praise, clear expectations, making decisions, and teaching self-control. This book is included as a Diamond in the Rough because it received very high ratings albeit from a small number of psychologists.

♦ *Raising Black Children* (1992) by James P. Comer and Alvin E. Poussaint.
  New York: Plume.

Written by two highly respected experts on black children, this book argues that African American parents face additional difficulties in raising emotionally healthy children because of problems related to minority status and income. Comer and Poussaint's guide contains almost 1,000 child-rearing questions they have repeatedly heard from black parents across the income spectrum. Among the issues on which they offer advice are how to improve the child's self-esteem and identity; how to confront racism; how to teach children to handle anger, conflict, and frustration; and how to deal with the mainstream culture and still retain a black identity. This is an excellent self-help book that includes pertinent suggestions that are not found in most child-rearing books. Virtually all other child-rearing books are written for white, middle-class parents and do not deal with many of the problems faced by black parents, especially black parents from low-income backgrounds.

♦ *Systematic Training for Effective Parenting* (3rd ed., 1976) by Don Dinkmeyer and Gary McKay. Circle Pines, MN: American Guidance Service.

This is the accompanying text for the STEP (Systematic Training for Effective Parenting) program that has trained thousands of parents across the country to become more effective communicators with their children. Dinkmeyer and McKay believe that democratic child-rearing is the best strategy for parents. In democratic child-rearing, both parent and child are socially equal in the family and mutually respect each other. The authors explain why children misbehave (to get attention, achieve power, mete out revenge, or display inadequacy). They suggest family activities and encourage parents to develop parenting goals. Parents are told how to get in touch with their own emotions and understand their children better. Encouragement, communication skills, and discipline methods that develop responsibility are advocated. One chapter is exclusively devoted to the family meeting, in which all members of the family have an equal opportunity to discuss issues of concern. Every chapter includes a guide for parents to use in constructing goals for improving family relationships. *Systematic Training for Effective Parenting* received a very high positive rating but was evaluated by only eight respondents. The book is brief (less than 100 pages) and somewhat sketchy without the accompanying parenting course that it is designed to supplement. Several mental health professionals mentioned that its exercises and goal-setting strategies are especially effective, but that the depth of coverage and extensive examples in other books make them more attractive on their own. The best use of this book is in conjunction with the parent training workshops developed by the authors.

Not Recommended

★★ *Parent Power! A Common Sense Approach to Parenting in the 90's and Beyond* (1990) by John K. Rosemond. Kansas City, MO: Andrews and McMeel.

MOVIES

Strongly Recommended

★★★★ *Searching for Bobby Fischer* (1994) produced by Scott Rudin and William Horberg and directed by Steven Zaillian. PG Rating. 110 minutes.

When a 7-year-old boy and his father discover that he has a gift for the game, the boy begins a conflicted journey to become the next Bobby Fischer. His father and coach relentlessly drive him to become ruthless, single-minded, and competitive beyond a level of decency that the boy and his mother value. The boy accommodates the wishes of his father and coach for a while, but when he and his mother realize that his very life is at stake, he returns to playing chess in the local park and makes difficult but confirming choices. This is a compelling morality tale about and for parents who drive their children, children who feel the pressure and desire to please their parents, and families learning to cherish the true value of nurturance.

★★★★ *Little Man Tate* (1991) produced by Scott Rudin and Penny Rajski and directed by Jodie Foster. PG Rating. 99 minutes.

Young Fred Tate and his single-parent mother are a working-class family. They love each other and find great enjoyment in their lives. Tension and uncertainty arise when the mother realizes that Fred is a genius and, though she can give him the safety and caring, she cannot provide the intellectual stimulation he requires. She sends him to a school for the gifted where his teacher focuses only on his intellectual abilities. Only when the two women work together for Fred's welfare will he truly grow and learn. The film is about the decision of what is best for one's child and how to balance the many dimensions of a child's growth.

Recommended

★★★ *Big* (1989) produced by James L. Brooks and Robert Greenhut and directed by Penny Marshall. PG Rating. 104 minutes.

Twelve-year-old Josh yearns to be older so that he can be taken more seriously, especially by Cynthia, who has stolen his heart. After being rejected by Cynthia at the carnival, he wanders over to the wish machine, where his wish to grow up fast is granted. The next morning, he wakes up as an adult. He remains an imaginative, fun-loving, spontaneous youngster in an adult existence. We are reminded that adults could use a good dose of Josh's qualities in order to enjoy life more and to truly connect with others and with life. Josh's compelling honesty and virtuosity play out in a corporate advertising environment to remind us of the power of basic morality and good deeds.

★★★ *Splendor in the Grass* (1961) produced and directed by Elia Kazan. 124 minutes.

This is the story of a blue-collar girl and rich boy who fall in love in the 1920s. They are young, passionate, and very conflicted about where their relationship is leading. The girl, played by Natalie Wood, attempts suicide and is placed in a mental institution. In the meantime, the devil-may-care boy, played by Warren Beatty, continues with his free-spirited, fast-paced lifestyle. The film presents the very personal moral conflicts and gender differences characteristic of the 1920s. The moral of the story, however, is in the awakening and maturing of Natalie Wood's character to see the shallowness and limitations of her boyfriend as she develops herself.

★★★ *Parenthood* (1990) produced by Brian Grazer and directed by Ron Howard. PG-13 Rating. 124 minutes.

The common yet terribly difficult challenge of raising children is effectively illuminated through the eyes of the main character, Gil (played by Steve Martin). Gil is the son of Frank, whose other three adult children continue to bring their problems home to father, and Gil has three children of his own for whom he wants to be a better dad than his was. Frank discovers that not rescuing his adult children is in fact the only way to help save them. Gil learns that bringing home the bacon and being home for the family are in a continuing balance. This is a film that lets parents know they are not alone in their uncertainties, anxieties, and dreams.

INTERNET RESOURCES

There are hundreds of websites about parenting, almost all of them commercial. They are essentially magazines with advertisements and are generally not reported on here.

Metasites

★★★★★ *ABCs of Parenting* http://www.abcparenting.com

A comprehensive source of pregnancy, parenting, and child care articles and websites. Categories include child care, education, health, fatherhood, finance, nutrition, organizations, safety issues, product recalls, infertility, and online shopping. Includes special sections on attention-deficit disorder (ADD) and how to deal with the death of a child.

★★★★★ *BabyCenter* http://www.babycenter.com/rcindex.html

A truly enormous site! Although very commercial, it has thousands of pages of information from before pregnancy to the end of toddlerhood. A good site to start with when you are unsure just what you want to learn.

Psychoeducational Materials for Clients and Families

★★★★★ *The Natural Child Project* http://www.naturalchild.com/home

The aim of this site seems to be to encourage simple and close bonding parenting. It offers perhaps a hundred of the very best articles by experts under these topic headings: Attachment, Parenting, Babies, Breast-Feeding, Child Advocacy, Learning, Living with Children, and Sleeping. If an intelligent and interested parent wants to enlarge his or her perspective on children, this is the place to go.

★★★★★ *NPIN: National Parent Information Network*
          http://ericps.crc.uiuc.edu/npin/index.html

A product of ERIC, this site has endless high-quality information on the education of children for parents, professionals, and researchers. Click for the bimonthly magazine *Parent News* with first-class articles on a variety of topics from sexuality and sportsmanship to school safety. One of the best features is that parents can AskERIC and get answers.

★★★★★ *NPIN Resources for Parents: Full Texts of Parenting-Related Materials*
          http://ericps.crc.uiuc.edu/npin/library/texts.html

Full-text electronic versions of pamphlets, brochures, digests, guides, and other materials. Dozens of articles are available under the following headings: Assessment and

Testing, Child Care (all ages), Children and the Media, Children with Special Needs, Children's Health and Nutrition, Early Childhood—Family/Peer Relationships, Early Childhood—Learning, Gifted Children, Helping Children Learn at Home, Older Children, Pre-Teens and Young Adolescents (ages 9–14), Parents and Families in Society, Parents and Schools as Partners, and Teens (14–20).

★★★★★ *Today's Parent Online* http://www.todaysparent.com

For lots of high-quality information on each developmental stage, go to Step and Stages, select an age (from 0 to 12) and use the popup menus to choose an article, then click on Go.

★★★★ *ParenthoodWeb* http://www.parenthoodweb.com

A magazine with all kinds of information and advice focusing on the early years.

★★★★ *Parenting: Child Care*
http://www.kidsource.com/kidsource/pages/parenting.childcare.html

About 20 annotated links to articles on selecting child care providers, safety, nutrition, training, and more.

★★★★ *Family Relations*
http://www.personal.psu.edu/faculty/n/x/nxd10/family3.htm

This site must have a thousand papers written by students at Penn State, all clearly organized and in accessible English. There are hundreds under these headings: (1) Relationships, including dating, marriage, and breaking up; (2) Parenting, from pregnancy and dealing with infertility to parenting teenagers; (3) Grandparents and brother–sister relationships; (4) Family problems, including grieving, alcohol and drug use, and divorce; and (5) Intimate violence. When you go to any of these, all the papers in that section will be on one page and indexed at the top, so finding relevant ones is easier. The papers generally summarize an area, and many offer links. Their best use may be for people needing general information to get them thinking rather than for those searching for the answer to a specific question.

★★★★ *KidSource Online* http://www.kidsource.com

This is basically a magazine with a gigantic collection of good-quality readings. It is perhaps best used by people who need an orientation to the world of children. It is organized by age of children, followed by some general articles.

★★★★ *Parenting: General Parenting Articles*
http://www.kidsource.com/kidsource/pages/parenting.general.html

About 100 articles described and rated and available online. They cover almost everything and will guide parents well.

★★★★ *Family Life Library*
      http://www.oznet.ksu.edu/library/famlf2/#Family%20Living

Page down to Managing Time, Work, and Family for a series of nine articles suitable as handouts and brochures from a Kansas State University program. They have to be downloaded and opened in Adobe's Acrobat Reader.

★★★ *Parent City Library* http://www.parentcity.com/read/library

About 50 several-page articles on many aspects of marriage, parenting, children, and so on. Arranged alphabetically by title, so look around.

Specific Aspects of Parenting

★★★★★ *Project NoSpank* http://www.nospank.org/toc.htm

A superb site for those who wish to campaign against paddling in the schools and the like. Lots of research, cases, links, and logic. Numbers 3 and 6 are of direct use in protecting one's children. For those partial to James Dobson's views, see section 47.

★★★★★ *Common Sense: Strategies for Raising Alcohol- and Drug-Free Children*
      http://www.pta.org/commonsense

A project of the National PTA, the site is simple and pretty. The contents are well-designed for effectiveness. The Parent's Center offers hard-hitting interactive quizzes, drug facts and risk, warning signs, guidance on discipline, being a role model, and getting closer. A nice package of materials that should have an effect on families with drug and alcohol concerns.

★★★★ *People, Places, and Things That Help You Feel Better*
      http://www.kidshealth.org/kid/feel_better/index.html

If you need readings for children about going to the hospital, dentist, or other medical service, the 7 here are good.

★★★★ *Contact a Family* http://www.cafamily.org.uk

Information and support for people caring for children with rare disorders. If parents need this kind of material, this is the only place to get it.

★★★★ *Dealing with Feelings* http://www.kidshealth.org/kid/feeling/index.html

There are 10 readings here of about four pages each. They really deal with contexts, not just labeled emotions. Examples are A Kid's Guide to Divorce, Am I Too Fat or Too Thin?, Are You Shy? Find Out Why, and Why Am I So Sad?

★★★★ *Daddys Home* http://www.daddyshome.com/departments/index.cfm

A collection of about 50 articles from the online magazine for stay-at-home dads. A supportive introduction to the benefits, costs, joys, and risks of this lifestyle.

★★★★ *So What are Dads Good For?* http://www.io.com/~duanev/family/dads.html
A fine essay with insight and guidance for the confused.

★★★★ *National Center for Fathering* http://www.fathers.com
Under about 30 practical tips are hundreds of brief and sometimes sappy essays on stages, roles, responsibilities, and functions. It is best as a source of beginning ideas or expanding some men's ideas of what it could mean to be a father.

★★★ *Full Texts of Parenting-Related Materials: Gifted Children*
http://ericps.crc.uiuc.edu/cgi-bin/texis/webinator/npinvlft1search
Search for the word "gifted" to find the relevant readings. These readings vary from 3 to about 10 pages and address ADHD and Children Who Are Gifted; College Planning for Gifted and Talented Youth; How Can I Help My Gifted Child Plan for College?; How Parents Can Support Gifted Children; and Should Gifted Students Be Grade Advanced?

★★★ *The Fatherhood Project* http://www.fatherhoodproject.org
"The Fatherhood Project is a national research and education project that is examining the future of fatherhood and developing ways to support men's involvement in child-rearing. Its books, films, consultation, seminars, and training all present practical strategies to support fathers and mothers in their parenting roles."

Other Resources

★★★★★ *HealthyKids.com* http://www.healthykids.com
This is the online version of *Healthy Kids Magazine*, the official consumer publication of the American Academy of Pediatrics. It is a health resource for children up to age 10. Use the menu selection under Site Areas for more.

★★★ *CareGuide: Child and Elder Care Directory* http://166.90.133.173
For those in need of information and direction in taking care of an elderly person or a child, this somewhat commercial site has good links and information under Resources. A good starting place.

CHAPTER 11

Communication and People Skills

We get things done by talking with family, friends, colleagues, and neighbors. When someone doesn't quite grasp what we are saying, we often let it go, the talk continues, and nobody pays much attention. But some conversations have critical outcomes that hinge on the effectiveness of the conversation—a job interview, a business meeting, a marriage proposal. In these circumstances, ineffective communication can have serious negative consequences: We don't get the job, don't convince our business colleagues that our ideas are worth adopting, and are turned down for marriage.

Sometimes strained conversations reflect real differences between people: They are angry with each other; one person is a liberal, the other a conservative; and so on. On many occasions, though, strained conversations develop when people simply are miscommunicating. Their conversations could readily be improved by understanding the nature of interpersonal communication.

Communication and people skills are hot items on self-help lists. Whether it is people skills in general, or female–male communication, or negotiating agreements, humans seem to crave "knowing" one other. In this chapter, we review self-help books, movies, and Internet sites devoted to these quintessentially human skills.

SELF-HELP BOOKS

Strongly Recommended

★★★★ *You Just Don't Understand: Women and Men in Conversation* (1990) by Deborah Tannen. New York: Ballantine.

As its title implies, this book is about how women and men communicate—or all too often miscommunicate—with each other. *You Just Don't Understand* reached number one

RECOMMENDATION HIGHLIGHTS

Self-Help Books

- On a wide range of communication and people skills:
    - ★★★★ *How to Communicate* by Matthew McKay and Associates
    - ★★★★ *People Skills* by Robert Bolton
    - ◆ *The Talk Book* by Gerald Goodman and Glenn Esterly

- For improving female–male communication:
    - ★★★★ *You Just Don't Understand* by Deborah Tannen
    - ★★★★ *Intimate Strangers* by Lillian Rubin

- On defining boundaries and clarifying responsibilities:
    - ★★★★ *Boundaries* by Henry Cloud and John Townsend

- On negotiating agreements:
    - ★★★★ *Getting to Yes* by Roger Fisher and William Ury

- On the healing power of confiding in others:
    - ★★★ *Opening Up* by James Pennebaker

- On overcoming shyness and being less lonely:
    - ★★★★ *Shyness* by Philip Zimbardo
    - ★★★★ *Intimate Connections* by David Burns

- On friendship and its important roles in our lives:
    - ★★★★ *Just Friends* by Lillian Rubin

Movies

- A story of love, triumph over adversity, and struggle for control:
    - ★★★★★ *Children of a Lesser God*

- Brilliant teacher inspires creativity and individuality at a cost:
    - ★★★★ *Dead Poets Society*

Internet Resources

- Comprehensive workbook in communication skills:
    - ★★★★★ *Cooperative Communication Skills*
      http://www.coopcomm.org/fswcover.htm

on several best-seller lists. Tannen shows that friction between women and men in conversation often develops because as girls and boys they were brought up in two virtually distinct cultures and continue to live in those two very different cultures. The two gender cultures are rapport talk (female culture) and report talk (male culture). Rapport talk is the language of conversation and a way of establishing connections and negotiating relationships, which women feel more comfortable doing. Report talk is public speaking, which men feel more comfortable doing. Women enjoy private speaking, talk that involves discussing similarities and matching experiences. Tannen illustrates miscommunication in male–female relationships with several cartoons about a husband and wife at the breakfast table. Harmful and unjustified misinterpretations might be avoided by understanding the conversational styles of the other gender. The problem, then, may not be an individual man or even men's styles but the difference between women's and men's styles. If so, both women and men need to make adjustments. In the public context, a woman can push herself to speak up without being invited or begin to speak at even the slightest pause in talk. Men can learn that women are not accustomed to speaking up in groups. They can make women feel more comfortable by warmly encouraging and allowing them to speak rather than hogging public talk for themselves. This excellent 4-star self-help book has been especially taken up by women who, after reading the book, want their husband or male partner to read it too. Tannen presents a balanced approach to female–male communication problems by focusing on the different ways females and males communicate and a positive approach by emphasizing that women and men can get along better by understanding each other's different styles. Tannen's book is solidly written, well-researched, and entertaining.

★★★★ *Boundaries: When to Say Yes, When to Say No to Take Control of Your Life* (1992) by Henry Cloud and John Townsend. Grand Rapids, MI: Zondervan.

A boundary is a personal line that defines identity and responsibility. In this fine book, Cloud and Townsend define several types of boundaries (e.g., physical, mental, emotional, and spiritual) and help people clarify their boundaries. This is accomplished in various ways, such as setting limits and changing how one feels about setting boundaries. The authors take a biblical and psychological approach to defining and constructing healthy boundaries. Under the Law of Exposure, the authors remind us that the entire concept revolves around the fact that we exist in relationships. An excellent resource for individuals looking to clarify boundaries, especially for those interested in blending psychology and scripture.

★★★★ *Intimate Strangers* (rev. ed., 1990) by Lillian Rubin. New York: Harper & Row.

This book focuses on intimacy and communication difficulties between women and men. Rubin tackles a relationship problem that confronts many women and men—their inability to develop a satisfying intimate relationship with each other. Rubin says that male–female differences in intimacy are related to the fact that it is primarily mothers who raise children and are the emotional managers of the family. Because girls identify with mothers and boys with fathers, females develop a capacity for intimacy and an interest in managing emotional problems, and males do not. Rubin supports her ideas with a number of case studies derived from interviews with approximately 150 couples.

Many different dimensions of close relationships are analyzed in *Intimate Strangers*. Rubin especially provides detailed insights about the nature of intimacy and communication problems in sexual matters and in raising children. She concludes that the only solution to the intimacy gulf between females and males is for every child to be raised and nurtured by two loving parents, not just the mother, from birth on. That is, Rubin's culprit is the nonnurturant father, who, she says, has to change his ways and serve as a nurturing, intimate role model committed to managing emotional difficulties. Only then will boys have an opportunity to develop these important qualities. While this 4-star resource is reviewed in this chapter, its contents also apply to several other categories, including marriage, love, and intimacy.

★★★★ *How to Communicate: The Ultimate Guide to Improving Your Personal and Professional Relationships* (1997) by Matthew McKay, Martha Davis, and Patrick Fanning. New York: Fine.

The premise of this book is that communication makes life work. The book tells what to do about communicating rather than what to think about. The emphasis is on skills (e.g., basic skills, advanced skills, conflict skills, social skills, family skills, public skills). The authors recommend that you read the basic and advanced skills chapters first, then go on to the specific chapters appropriate to your relationships and position in life. Contained in the basic skills section are listening, self-disclosure, and expressing skills. In the advanced skills section is information on body language, paralanguage (vocal component), hidden agendas, and clarifying language skills. For adults and older adolescents looking to improve their communication style, this 4-star book is worthwhile.

★★★★ *Getting to Yes: Negotiating Agreement without Giving In* (1981) by Roger Fisher and William Ury. New York: Penguin.

This concise book (only about 150 pages) offers a step-by-step method for arriving at mutually acceptable agreements in many different types of conflict, whether between parents and children, neighbors, bosses and employees, customers and business managers, tenants and landlords, or diplomats. Fisher and Ury describe how to:

- Separate people from the problem.
- Emphasize interests, not positions.
- Develop precise goals at the outset of negotiations.
- Work together to establish options that will satisfy both parties.
- Negotiate successfully with opponents who are more powerful, refuse to play by the rules, or resort to dirty tricks.

The book is based on the method of principled negotiation developed as part of the Harvard Negotiation Project. This method helps people evaluate issues based on their merits instead of regressing to a haggling process in which each side says what it will and won't do. It teaches negotiators to look for mutual gains whenever possible. The method of principled negotiation is hard on the merits of the issues, soft on the people. It uses no tricks and no posturing. Although written more than a decade ago, this 4-star book remains one of the best easy-to-read resources for learning how to negotiate effectively in a wide range of situations.

★★★★ *Shyness* (1987) by Philip Zimbardo. Reading, MA: Addison-Wesley.

This book is dedicated to overcoming social isolation and becoming more gregarious. Shyness is a widespread problem that affects as many as four out of every five people at one time or another in their lives. What does Zimbardo say shy people can do about their situation? First, they have to analyze their shyness and figure out how they got this way. Possible reasons include negative evaluations, fear of being rejected, fear of intimacy, and lack of adequate social skills, among others. Second, they need to build up their self-esteem. To help with this, Zimbardo spells out 15 steps to becoming more confident. Third, shy people need to improve their social skills. To accomplish this, Zimbardo describes several behavior modification strategies, tells how to set realistic goals, and advocates working hard toward achieving these goals. *Shyness* received a robust 4-star rating as a well-known (164 respondents), excellent self-help book for shy people. It gives sound advice, is free of psychobabble, and is easy to read.

★★★★ *Intimate Connections: The New Clinically Tested Program for Overcoming Loneliness* (1985) by David Burns. New York: Morrow.

This book, a program for overcoming loneliness, is authored by David Burns, famous for *Feeling Good*, on depression. Burns believes that loneliness is essentially a state of mind that is primarily caused by the faulty assumption that a loving partner is needed before one can feel happy and secure. Burns says that the first step in breaking free from the loneliness pattern is learning to like and love oneself. He also distinguishes between two types of loneliness: situational loneliness, which lasts for only a brief time and can be healthy and motivating, and chronic loneliness, which persists and results from problems that have plagued people for most of their lives. Burns says that to overcome chronic loneliness, a person has to change the patterns of perception that created the loneliness and continue to perpetuate it. Among the topics Bums touches on are how to make social connections, how to get close to others, and how to improve one's sexual life. Checklists, worksheets, daily mood logs, and a number of self-assessments are found throughout the book, which received a 4-star rating. This is a good self-help book—full of straightforward advice and helpful examples—for helping people overcome their loneliness.

★★★★ *People Skills* (reissue ed., 1986) by Robert Bolton. New York: Touchstone.

This book, dedicated to improving human communication, is divided into four main parts. Part I, the Introduction, describes a number of skills for bridging gaps in interpersonal communication and barriers to communicating effectively. Part II, Listening Skills, explains how listening is different from merely hearing, how to develop the important skill of reflective listening, and how to read body language. Part III, Assertion Skills, outlines a number of valuable techniques to help a person become more assertive in relationships. Part IV, Conflict Management Skills, discusses how to effectively manage conflict in many different circumstances. *People Skills* received a 4-star rating in our studies despite the fact that the book was originally published in 1981. However, a number of the mental health professionals concluded that it remains one of the best general introductions to communication skills.

★★★★ *Just Friends: The Role of Friendship in Our Lives* (1985) by Lillian Rubin. New York: Harper & Row.

Author Lillian Rubin, who penned *Intimate Strangers* evaluated earlier in this chapter, examines the nature of intimacy and friendship in this book. Rubin analyzes the nature of the valued yet fragile bond of friendship between women, between men, between women and men, between best friends, and in couples. She says that unlike many other relationships, friendship is a private affair with no rituals, social contracts, shared tasks, role requirements, or institutional supports of any kind. Rubin believes friends are central players in our lives, not just in childhood but in adulthood as well. Friends give us a reference outside of our families against which we can judge and evaluate ourselves; they help us develop an independent sense of self and support our efforts to adapt to new circumstances and stressful situations. This is an insightful analysis of the important and often overlooked role that friends play in our lives. However, some critics said that Rubin exaggerates sex differences in the intimacy of friendships.

Recommended

★★★ *That's Not What I Meant! How Conversational Style Makes or Breaks Relationships* (1986) by Deborah Tannen. New York: Ballantine.

This book provides a broader understanding of the inner workings of conversation than Tannen's earlier-reviewed book, *You Just Don't Understand*. Tannen believes that different conversational styles are at the heart of miscommunication. But conversational confusion between the sexes is only part of the picture. Tannen shows that growing up in different parts of the country, having different ethnic and class backgrounds, being of different ages, and having different personality traits all contribute to different conversational styles that can cause disappointment, hurt, and misplaced blame. *That's Not What I Meant!* received a 3-star rating in the national study, just missing a 4-star rating. This is a good self-help book that provides a rich understanding of how conversational styles make or break relationships. Compared to *You Just Don't Understand*, this book, includes more basic information about communication skills in general, which are covered in other books, although Tannen does a better job of describing these skills than most other authors.

★★★ *Opening Up: The Healing Power of Confiding in Others* (1997) by James Pennebaker. New York: Guilford Press.

As its subtitle indicates, this book concerns the healing power of confiding in other people. It deals with the following issues:

- Why suppressing inner turmoil has a devastating effect on health.
- How denial of mental pain can cause physical pain.
- Why talking or writing about troubling thoughts protects us from the internal stresses that cause physical illness.

Pennebaker's advice is not based only on his own opinions. For more than a decade, he has studied thousands of people in many different contexts to learn how confessing troubling thoughts, feelings, and experiences benefited their physical and mental health. What is surprising about Pennebaker's findings is that the benefits of confession occur whether you tell your secrets to someone else or simply write about them privately. Pennebaker is especially adept at pinpointing how the hard work of inhibiting troublesome thoughts and feelings gradually undermines the body's defenses. *Opening Up* received a 3-star rating in our national study, probably because it was not well-known at the time it was rated. One of the rare self-help books that is based on hard science, this contribution deserves to be better known and more frequently read.

★★★   *Coping with Difficult People* (1981) by Robert Bramson. New York: Dell.

In this resource, Bramson describes and presents strategies for coping with the following types of difficult people:

- The Hostile Aggressive, who bullies by bombarding, making cutting remarks, or throwing tantrums.
- The Complainer, who gripes incessantly but never gets any closer to solving the problem.
- The Silent Unresponsive, who is always reasonable, sincere, and supportive to your face but never comes through.
- The Negativist, who responds to any proposal with statements like "It will never work."
- The Know-It-All, who is confident that he or she knows everything there is to know about anything worth knowing.
- The Indecisive, who delays any important decision until the outcome is certain to be what he or she wants and refuses to let go of anything until it's perfect—which is never.

Bramson outlines a six-step plan to cope with any of these people and make life less stressful. This 3-star book is entertaining reading, and the author uses a lot of catchy labels to get his points across and grab the reader's attention, such as describing Know-It-Alls as bulldozers and balloons and Hostile Aggressives as Sherman tanks, snipers, and exploders. Written almost two decades ago, *Coping with Difficult People* has been successful, with sales of more than 500,000 copies. The mental health experts in the national survey recommended the book for improved understanding of people in work settings rather than family settings; since the author's background is in managerial consulting, many of the examples come from work settings.

★★★   *Games People Play* (1964) by Eric Berne. New York: Grove.

Eric Berne, MD, was the founder of transactional analysis, an approach to understanding interpersonal relationships that emphasizes communication patterns. He maintained that people live their lives by playing out games in their interpersonal relationships. People play games to manipulate others, avoid reality, and conceal ulterior motives. Berne analyzes 36 different games, which he divides into seven main categories:

- Life games, which pervade every person's behavior.
- Marital games, which partners may use to maintain a frustrating and unrewarding life.

- Sexual games, in which one person provokes sexual reactions in another and then acts like an innocent victim.
- Party games, which are highly social and include perpetual gossip.
- Consulting room games, played by a patient with a doctor to avoid cure (as in psychiatry).
- Underworld games, most often played for material gain, but can also be played for psychological gain.
- Good games, which involve social contributions that outweigh the complexity of underlying motivation and manipulation.

Games People Play received a 3-star rating in one of our national studies. On the positive side, many characterize the book as a self-help classic that has been a huge best-seller. It was one of the most frequently rated books in our studies. Berne's book singles out an important dimension of communication that had not before been detected as critical to intimate relationships. People who read it will find numerous examples that apply to their own lives. And Berne connects with readers through catchy, witty writing. You can read about the sweetheart, the threadbare, the schlemiel, the stocking game, the wooden leg, and the swymd (see what you made me do). Although the book is more than three decades old, some psychotherapists continue to strongly recommend it to clients who are having communication problems and use Berne's transactional analysis in their practice. On the other side, this book has steadily faded in professional popularity, and many will find it dated in content and tone. Some critics opine that Berne overdramatizes the role of game playing in intimate relationships, that the parent–adult–child aspect of Berne's approach is overly simplistic, and that the games reiterate traditional male and female orientations.

★★★ *Difficult People: How to Deal with Impossible Clients, Bosses and Employees* (1990) by Roberta Cava. Toronto: Key Porter.

This book addresses the stress of dealing with rude, impatient, emotional, persistent, and aggressive people. You learn to control your moods by not allowing other people to give you negative feelings, which you do by improving your people skills. The author first helps identify and understand emotional behavior by having you answer specific questions, examine techniques for specific stressful situations, look at consequences of behavior, and examine approaches to conflict resolution. Reviewed are basic communication skills, communication skills for specific situations, gender influences, and ratings of your listening and speaking skills. Three chapters address difficult clients, supervisors, coworkers, and subordinates. For adults finding themselves faced with difficult people, this book could provide some informative advice and skills to practice.

★★★ *Stop! You're Driving Me Crazy* (1979) by George Bach and Ronald Deutsch. New York: Berkley.

This book covers a broad array of communication strategies to help, in the authors' words, "keep the people in your life from driving you up the wall." It spells out Bach's catchy concept of "crazymaking." Crazymaking describes a wide variety of harmful communication patterns that are passive–aggressive in nature. Passive–aggressive individuals consciously like, love, or at least respect each other but unconsciously undermine rather than build up the morale and mental well-being of friends, lovers, or spouses. Some examples of passive–aggressive crazymaking:

- A husband stirs up a screaming fight, then wants to make passionate love.
- A boss gives an employee a promotion, then says, "You're worthless."
- A young woman tells her mother that she is on a crash diet, and a day later her mother brings her a chocolate cake.

The authors help you identify, cope with, and eliminate such crazymaking techniques. On the borderline between 2 and 3 stars, this book just managed the 3-star rating. An early success that achieved best-seller status in the early 1980s, its popularity has waned. Several mental health experts criticized the book for being too sensational, gender-biased, and difficult to read in places.

Diamonds in the Rough

◆ *The Talk Book: The Intimate Science of Communicating in Close Relationships* (1988) by Gerald Goodman and Glenn Esterly. New York: Ballantine.

Talk is an essential tool for ensuring the success of all close relationships, and *The Talk Book* is about ways to improve face-to-face communication. If people don't know how to use talk to benefit themselves, the cost can be high. The authors describe six communication tools that contribute to using talk more effectively: disclosures, reflections, interpretations, advisements, questions, and silences. These talk tools fashion most of the meaning in everyday conversation. Understood well, they can help improve close relationships. Part I, The Intimate Science Explained, explores the inner workings of person-to-person talk. Natural conversations are used to illustrate events, habits, and hidden rules that go unnoticed in the flow of conversation. Part II, The Intimate Science Mastered, tells how to initiate self-change and improve talk. Each chapter in Part II ends with a section that includes several tested methods for improving mastery of talk and making sense of another person's talk. This resource made the Diamonds in the Rough category: it was rated positively but by too few experts. This is a solid book on conversation skills written by a leading expert. *The Talk Book*'s main drawbacks are its length (almost 400 pages of small type) and encyclopedic tendencies.

◆ *Peoplemaking* (1972) by Virginia Satir. Palo Alto, CA: Science and Behavior Books.

This book is aimed at improving communication with a select group of people in your life—family members. Virginia Satir, a pioneer in family therapy, believes that all important aspects of a family can be changed and improved: individual self-worth, communication, the family system, and rules. By reading *Peoplemaking*, couples can learn better communication skills; parents can learn to improve communication with their children; single parents and stepparents can learn ways to cope with the special issues; and individuals can learn how to communicate more effectively with extended family members. Satir's book was positively rated in one of our studies, but by only seven respondents. The book is now almost three decades old but was popular in the 1970s. It still contains some valuable advice, especially for couples who want to communicate effectively and for parents who want to communicate with their children.

Not Recommended

★★ *How to Start a Conversation and Make Friends* (1983) by Don Gabor. New York: Simon & Schuster.

★★ *Men Are from Mars, Women Are from Venus* (1992) by John Gray. New York: HarperCollins.

★★ *How to Argue and Win Everytime* (1995) by Gerry Spence. New York: St. Martin's Press.

★ *Body Language* (1970) by Julius Fast. New York: Pocket Books.

★ *How to Win Friends and Influence People* (rev. ed., 1981) by Dale Carnegie. New York: Simon & Schuster.

★ *Are You the One for Me?* (1998) by Barbara DeAngelis. London: Thorsons.

Strongly Not Recommended

† *Mars & Venus on a Date: A Guide for Navigating the Five Stages of Dating to Create a Loving and Lasting Relationship* (1997) by John Gray. New York: HarperCollins.

MOVIES

Strongly Recommended

★★★★★ *Children of a Lesser God* (1987) produced by Burt Sugarman and Patrick Palmer and directed by Randa Haines. R Rating. 119 minutes.

Marlee Matlin, who is hearing impaired, won an Academy Award for her performance as a young hearing-impaired woman who refuses to read lips or try to learn to speak. She encountered a teacher of the deaf who is both attracted to her and single-minded in implementing his ideas that the deaf should read lips and speak. The film is a love story, but more a story of triumph over adversity and the struggle for control between two people. Those who live with physical or emotional obstacles will find spirit and love winning out in this excellent 5-star film.

★★★★ *Dead Poets Society* (1990) produced by Steven Haft, Paul Junger Witt, and Tony Thomas and directed by Peter Weir. PG Rating. 129 minutes.

John Keating is a brilliant and inspiring English teacher who returns to the New England private school that he attended as a youth. He brings poetry, literature, and pursuit of life for to his students and in so doing, brings to life their spirit, self-confidence, and independence. The school doesn't approve of his teaching style. When a student is encouraged to confront his parents about his career direction and the parents remove him from the school, the boy commits suicide. The death is subsequently blamed on

Keating. The film reminds us that the exhilaration of learning through spontaneity, nurtured curiosity, and creativity is to be cherished; the rebelliousness and individuality that often result from unbridled growth must be handled conscientiously. Also reviewed under Teenagers and Parenting (Chapter 27).

Not Recommended

★★ *He Said, She Said* (1990) produced by Frank Mancuso, Jr., and directed by Ken Kwapis and Marisa Silver. PG-13 Rating. 115 minutes.

INTERNET RESOURCES

Surprisingly there is little material on the web regarding communication and other people skills. There are many sites about marital and sexual relationships, and those can be found in Marriage (Chapter 18) and Families and Stepfamilies (Chapter 16). The numerous sites about communication in business and in groups are not included here, nor are the commercial sites with nothing of value to self-changers or psychotherapy clients.

Psychoeducational Materials for Clients and Families

★★★★★ *Cooperative Communication Skills* http://www.coopcomm.org/fswcover.htm

Here you will find a seven-chapter workbook and reader in communication skills by Dennis Rivers, MA. Each topic takes only two to three pages and is stated as a challenge: listening more attentively and responsively; explaining your conversational intent and inviting consent; expressing yourself more clearly and completely; translating complaints and criticisms into requests; asking more open-ended and more creative questions; expressing more appreciation; and making better communication an important part of everyday living. This might be assigned as self-help exercises or downloaded and used in therapy.

★★★★ *Arguing and Relationships: Introduction*
   http://www.queendom.com/articles/arguing_intro.html

Four pages presenting guidelines for constructive arguing and a list of books on improving communication skills.

★★★★ *Virtual Presentation Assistant*
   http://www.ukans.edu/cwis/units/coms2/vpa/vpa.htm

This is an online tutorial of nine one-page papers for improving public speaking skills.

★★★ *Communicating When Anger Is Involved*
   http://www.topchoice.com/~psyche/love/misc/communicate.html

Only one page, but very clear on how anger is to be expected, that disagreements are normal and escalation is not. Useful as a starting point.

★★★ *Do You Get Your Message Across? Interpersonal Communication Skills*
http://www.psychtests.com/communic.html

Thirty-four questions with interactive feedback. Most useful for the breadth of the questions in sensitizing a client.

★★★ *Nonverbal Q & A* http://socpsych.lacollege.edu/givens.html

Three pages of questions and answers about nonverbal behavior. A good scientific introduction.

★★★ *Improving Communication in Relationships* by Michael Smith, PhD
http://www.casafuturatech.com/Book/Practice/relationships.html

Two pages of basic ideas, but it may be useful for just that reason: seeing the basics in print.

Other Resources

★★ *Toastmasters International* http://www.toastmasters.org

This international voluntary group offers free or low-cost training, feedback, and practice making speeches to business, civic, and other groups. There are chapters everywhere. Click on "Speaking Tips" for 10 tips for successful public speaking.

See also Child Development and Parenting (Chapter 10); Love and Intimacy (Chapter 17); Marriage (Chapter 18).

CHAPTER 12

Death and Grieving

The famous therapist Erich Fromm once commented that "man is the only animal that finds his own existence a problem he has to solve and from which he cannot escape." He went on to say that "in the same sense man is the only animal who knows he must die." Our life does ultimately end, reaching the point when, as Italian playwright Salvadore Quasimodo says, "Each of us stands alone at the heart of the earth pierced through by a ray of sunlight, and suddenly it is evening!" In the end, the years do steal us from ourselves and from our loved ones.

Compared to people in many other cultures around the world, Americans are death avoiders and death deniers. Although each of us must face his or her own death and the loss of loved ones, we are rarely prepared to cope with the overwhelming emotions and upheavals that fear, despair, and grief bring into our lives. Because we are such a death-avoiding and death-denying culture, many people might expect this chapter to be depressing. We think you will not find that to be the case. Self-help writers who dispense advice on how to cope with the sadness of one's own death or the death of a loved one balance the sadness with love, support, and spiritual healing.

In this chapter, we review self-help books, autobiographies, movies, and Internet sites on the topics of death, loss, and grief. These resources address coping with loss of any kind, including death, responding to impending death (one's own or someone else's), committing suicide, and grieving in general, including its stages and recovery. A listing of pertinent support and self-help groups concludes the chapter.

SELF-HELP BOOKS

Strongly Recommended

★★★★★ *How to Survive the Loss of a Love* (2nd ed., 1991) by Melba Colgrove, Harold Bloomfield, and Peter McWilliams. Los Angeles: Prelude.

This book provides suggestions for coping with the loss of a loved one, through death or otherwise. Since the first edition appeared in 1976, the authors have experienced,

RECOMMENDATION HIGHLIGHTS

Self-Help Books

- On coping with loss of any kind, including death:

  ★★★★★ *How to Survive the Loss of a Love* by Melba Colgrove and Associates

- A spiritually based approach to death, dying, and grief:

  ★★★★★ *When Bad Things Happen to Good People* by Harold Kushner

- On coping with death (your own or someone else's):

  ★★★★ *Working It Through* by Elisabeth Kübler-Ross

  ★★★ *On Death and Dying* by Elisabeth Kübler-Ross

- On how to grieve, the stages of grief, and recovery from grief:

  ★★★★★ *How to Go on Living When Someone You Love Dies* by Therese Rando

  ★★★★ *The Grief Recovery Handbook* by John W. James and Frank Cherry

- On working with dying children, their families, and their friends:

  ★★★★★ *On Children and Death* by Elisabeth Kübler-Ross

- On sudden infant death syndrome:

  ★★★ *Sudden Infant Death* by John DeFrain and Associates

- On helping a child cope with grief:

  ★★★★ *Learning to Say Good-By* by Eda LeShan

  ★★★★ *Talking about Death* by Earl Grollman

  ★★★★ *Helping Children Grieve* by Theresa Huntley

Autobiographies

- On grieving a spouse's death:

  ★★★★★ *A Grief Observed* by C. S. Lewis

- On grieving the death of a mother:

  ★★★★ *Motherless Daughter* by Hope Edelman

- On grieving the loss of a child:

  ★★★ *After the Death of a Child* by Ann Finkbeiner

Movies

- On denial of grief and eventual recovery for some:

  ★★★★★ *Ordinary People*

  ★★★ *The Accidental Tourist*

- On women sharing life and grief:

  ★★★★ *Steel Magnolias*

- On choosing how to live one's life:
  ★★★★ *A River Runs through It*

- On unfinished business and leaving a legacy:
  ★★★ *My Life*

Internet Resources

- For advice on grief and loss:
  ★★★★★ *Death and Dying Grief Support* http://www.death-dying.com

- For information and links on end-of-life care:
  ★★★★★ *Growth House* http://www.growthhouse.org
  ★★★★ *Partnership for Caring* http://www.partnershipforcaring.org

- For hospice information:
  ★★★★ *What Is Hospice?* http://www.nho.org/general.htm

among them, the death of a parent, a major stroke, two serious car accidents, a bank-ruptcy, a lawsuit, and an impending divorce. Consequently, the authors view loss broadly. They subdivide loss into four categories: (1) obvious losses, such as death of a loved one, divorce, robbery, and rape; (2) not-so obvious losses, such as moving, loss of a long-term goal, and success (loss of striving); (3) loss related to age, such as leaving home, loss of youth, loss of hair, and menopause; and (4) limbo losses, such as awaiting medical tests, going through a lawsuit, and having a loved one missing in action. The presentation is unusual for a self-help book. Poetry, common sense, and psychologically based advice are interwoven throughout more than a hundred very brief topics that are organized according to the categories of understanding loss, surviving, healing, and growing. Topics include it's OK to feel, tomorrow will come, seek the comfort of others, touching and hugging, do the mourning now, when counseling or therapy might be helpful, nutrition, remaining distraught is no proof of love, pray, meditate, contem-plate, keep a journal, take stock of the good, and your happiness is up to you. This has been a highly successful book, selling more than 2 million copies. The content is clear, succinct, and helpful, and it covers a vast range of situations involving loss. It has helped people cope with many different types of loss.

★★★★★ *How to Go on Living When Someone You Love Dies* (1991) by
        Therese Rando. New York: Bantam.

Originally published as *Grieving* in 1988, this book advises people about ways to grieve effectively when someone they love dies. Rando believes that there is no wrong or right way to grieve because people are so different. She describes a variety of ways to grieve and encourages readers to select the coping strategy best for them. Part I, Learning about Grief, identifies what grief is, how it affects people, what factors influence grief, and how women and men experience grief differently. Part II, Grieving Different Forms of Death, explains how grief often varies depending on what caused the death. Part III, Grieving and Your Family, addresses the inevitable family reorganization following a family member's death and how to cope with the death of specific family members: spouse, adult loss of a parent, adult loss of a sibling, and loss of a child. Part IV, Resolving Your Grief, offers specific recommendations for getting through bereavement rituals and funerals, including information about funeral arrangements and talking about loss to others. Part V, Getting Additional Help, explains how to find effective professional and self-help groups. This 5-star resource is an excellent self-help book for learning how to cope with the death of a loved one. There are no pat, overgeneralized suggestions on how to grieve. Rando covers a variety of grief circumstances and dispenses easy-to-understand, practical advice for each.

★★★★★ *When Bad Things Happen to Good People* (1981) by Harold Kushner.
New York: Schocken.

Kushner, a rabbi, provides a spiritual perspective on death, dying, and grief. He addresses the historic question: If God is just and all-powerful, why do good people suffer? Some conventional explanations of why bad things happen are that it's God's punishment for our sins, God is teaching us a lesson, or it's all part of a divine plan that is beyond our comprehension. Kushner writes that God provides us with the strength to endure. Although theologically guided, this is not a book about God and theology but rather about one man's personal tragedy and his view of God, humans, and life, written in an informal and easy reading style. The mystery of tragedy is not answered, but readers are brought a little closer to accepting the mystery and, in turn, feel a little more comforted. A book for any adult, but especially for those experiencing the emotional and spiritual conflicts that accompany life's many tragedies. A highly regarded, best-selling source of solace.

★★★★★ *On Children and Death* (reprint ed., 1997) by Elisabeth Kübler-Ross.
New York: Collier.

This psychiatrist and internationally known thanatologist writes about how children and their parents can cope with death. Death is the culmination of life, the graduation, the good-bye before another hello, the great transition. The material in this book represents a decade of working with dying children of all ages, their families, and friends. Kübler-Ross advises not to shield surviving children from the pains of death, but to let them share to the extent that they can. Among the topics addressed are death's influence on having other children, the spiritual aspects of working with dying children, and attending funerals. A valuable 4-star book for the general public, particularly for people caring for a dying child.

★★★★ *The Grief Recovery Handbook: A Step-by-Step Program for Moving beyond Loss* (1988) by John W. James and Frank Cherry. New York: Harper & Row.

The coauthors stress that grief is a growth process. In this book, acceptance of grief is presented as a positive reaction to loss that helps prepare the griever for recovery. The five stages of grief are gaining awareness, accepting responsibility, identifying recovery communications, taking action, and moving beyond loss. This book is for adults who are dealing with the approaching reality of death or in the process of dealing with loss. Although it received a 4-star rating in the national studies, its rating was high enough for 5-stars, but insufficient numbers of experts were familiar with it. A fine, practical resource.

★★★★ *Learning to Say Good-By* (1976) by Eda LeShan. New York: Macmillan.

This book was written to help children cope with the death of a parent. LeShan believes that children are resilient and can live through anything as long as they are told the truth and are allowed to share their suffering with loved ones. The book is a letter to children from LeShan, and it helps children understand what they are probably feeling, what their surviving parent is probably feeling, and why family members are behaving so strangely. Topics addressed include what happens immediately following a parent's death, feelings of grief, recovering, and how death teaches us about life. Although written for children, *Learning to Say Good-By* can help a surviving parent better understand children's feelings during this time of emotional upheaval. In our death-avoiding culture, LeShan's message is an important one: Children should be allowed to see our grief and should have the privilege of expressing their own grief in their own time. LeShan is an excellent writer, and she sensitively communicates with children.

★★★★ *Talking about Death: A Dialogue between Parent and Child* (3rd ed., 1991) by Earl Grollman. Boston: Beacon.

This brief book (about 100 pages) is appropriate for children of all faiths. It consists of dialogues between parents and children and is divided into two main parts: The Children's Read-Along, which uses simple language so that even 5- to 9-year-olds can understand its messages about death and dying; and The Parent's Guide to Talking about Death, which provides answers for children's anticipated questions about death. Parents are urged to be straightforward with their children and are also helped to come to terms with their own feelings of loss. Highly regarded by our mental health experts, it received a 4-star rating and is a solid self-help resource.

★★★★ *Recovering from the Loss of a Child* (1982) by Katherine Donnelly. New York: Macmillan.

This book tells parents and other family members how to cope with the death of a child. It features excerpts from interviews with parents and siblings of children who died from illness, accident, and suicide. It is divided into two main parts. Part I describes family members' and friends' experiences with grief. Part II is devoted to organizations that help bereaved families. A basic theme of the book is that the loss of a child of any age is tragic and a terrible loss for all members of the family. This 4-star book present a sensitive portrayal of a family's struggle to cope with the loss of a child; there is also an extensive list of support organizations.

★★★★ *Working It Through* (1982) by Elisabeth Kübler-Ross. New York: Macmillan.

Another and an earlier Kübler-Ross book on death and grieving, *Working It Through* is based on workshops for people dealing with death, people who are terminally ill, people who have lost a loved one, and people who are involved with the dying. Sensitive photographs by Mal Warshaw compliment the personal and emotional stories. The varied narratives cover a wide range of grieving experiences, such as emotions as our friends, the significance of music, the loss of a child, suicide, and spiritual awareness. A book especially for those touched by death or wishing to understand the dying process more fully.

★★★★ *Helping Children Grieve* (1991) by Theresa Huntley. Minneapolis: Augsburg
     Fortress.

As the title suggests, this book is about helping children cope with death—their own and the death of a loved one. Huntley presents a developmental approach to helping children cope with death. She begins by discussing how children under 3 years of age understand death. She then describes how death is perceived by children aged 3 to 6 years, 6 to 10 years, 10 to 12 years, and in early and late adolescence. Huntley says that children of different ages have different thoughts about the nature of death. For example, toddlers come to understand death as an extension of "all gone," while 10-year-olds often view a loved one's death as a punishment for some misdeed. Advice is given on how to talk about death with children, and common behaviors and feelings children show when faced with death are discussed. Adults are advised to encourage children to ask them questions about death and to answer these questions as honestly as possible. Fears of the dying child are presented, as are ways for adults to care for the dying child's basic emotional needs. This 4-star resource gives adults sound, clear advice about helping children cope with their own death or the death of a loved one.

Recommended

★★★ *A Time to Say Good-Bye: Moving Beyond Loss* (1996) by Mary McClure Goulding.
     Watsonville, CA: Papier-Mache.

In this book, a psychotherapist recounts her own journey of mourning the death of her husband. This author shares what she has learned in her years of experience, covering such topics as grief, loneliness, and retirement unshared with the mate who she worked beside for so long. The book is her narrative of her 3½ years of mourning at her own speed. She speaks about the love of family, friends, and community and the love of self that nurtured her and still supports her today. She no longer defines herself solely by who she lost. For widows and widowers working out feelings of mourning and at the same time going on with living, this book can be encouraging and a reminder to be patient and loving to themselves. Highly rated but not yet well-known by mental health professionals.

★★★ *How We Die* (1993) by Sherwin B. Nuland. New York: Knopf.

The author attempts to show that death with dignity is a myth and talks about the painful realities of death. His intention is to depict death in its biological and emotional reality, as seen by those who are witness to it and felt by those who experience it. His hope is that frank discussion will help us deal with the aspects of death that frighten us the most. Nuland also talks about responsibility and choices that we have as we exit our own lives. Ultimately, the dignity that we see in dying must grow out of the dignity with which we have lived our lives. For those interested in the physiological process of death, and the accompanying emotions, this is a very informative and insightful book.

★★★   *Living through Personal Crisis* (1984) by Ann Stearns. Chicago: Thomas More
        Press.

This book provides advice about coping with many different kinds of loss, especially the
death of a loved one. Using case studies to document her ideas, Stearns stresses that it is
common for the bereaved to blame themselves and that the grieving person will undoubt-
edly experience such physical symptoms as aches and pains or eating and sleeping problems. Stearns advises readers not to hide their feelings but to get them out in the open, to
be good to themselves, and to surround themselves with caring, sensitive people. Stearns
suggests when to seek professional help, how to find it, and how to evaluate progress. She
closes the book with the image of a bird rising from the ashes as a metaphor for successfully overcoming the sense of loss, but she reminds readers that their scars will never completely disappear. An appendix answers commonly asked questions about grieving. This
book provides a good overview of how grief works in variety of loss circumstances (loss of
limb, rape, loss of personal possessions in a fire, as well as the death of a loved one).

★★★   *Sudden Infant Death: Enduring the Loss* (1991) by John DeFrain, Linda Ernst,
        Deanne Jakub, and Jacque Taylor. Lexington, MA: Heath.

Sudden infant death (SIDS) occurs when an infant stops breathing, usually during the
night, and dies suddenly without apparent cause. SIDS is the major cause of infant
death from birth to 1 year of age, claiming as many as 10,000 infants a year in the
United States alone. The tragic loss of a baby to SIDS affects families in many ways, and
it is the authors' intention to help these families recapture the meaning and direction of
their lives. The book's contents are based on interviews with 392 mothers, fathers, and
siblings who have directly experienced the devastation of SIDS. The book recounts stories of the day the baby died and how parents mistakenly feel an overwhelming sense of
guilt that their baby died of neglect. Grief symptoms, the effects of SIDS on marital
relationships, and the suffering of grandparents are also covered. Suggestions for how
friends and family members can be supportive during this difficult time are given. The
fear of having another child and having it die is dealt with at length. This 3-star book
provides extensive knowledge about SIDS. The many personal stories can help family
members who experience SIDS understand and cope better. The book also will prove
helpful to friends of a family who experience SIDS, providing them with knowledge of
SIDS and support strategies.

★★★   *On Death and Dying* (1969) by Elisabeth Kübler-Ross. New York: Macmillan.

This extremely well-known book is about how to cope when facing one's own death and
about the stages dying people go through. In the 1960s, Kübler-Ross and her students
studied terminally ill patients to learn how they faced and coped with the crisis of their
own impending death. Kübler-Ross and her staff interviewed 200 patients, focusing on
them as human beings rather than bodies to be treated. Kübler-Ross concluded that
people go through five stages as they face death:

1. Denial and isolation: The person denies that death is really going to take place.
2. Anger: The dying person's denial can no longer be maintained and gives way to
   anger, resentment, rage, and envy.
3. Bargaining: The person develops the hope that somehow death can be post-
   poned or delayed.

4. Depression: The person accepts the certainty of death but is unhappy about it.
5. Acceptance: The person develops a sense of peace about accepting the inevitable and often wants to be left alone.

Kübler-Ross presents the five stages in considerable detail and discusses the effects of impending death on the dying person's family. Suggestions for therapy with the terminally ill are included. *On Death and Dying* received a 3-star rating in our national study, just missing the 4-star category. The book was one of the most frequently rated in the entire study: 355 mental health professionals evaluated it. It is a classic in the field of death and dying, and Kübler-Ross's approach has helped millions of people cope effectively with impending death. Critics of the book say that no one has been able to confirm that people go through the stages of dying in the order Kübler-Ross proposes, but Kübler-Ross feels that she has been misinterpreted, saying that she never intended the stages to be taken as an invariant sequence of steps toward death. Her other two books reviewed in this chapter fare better in the national studies.

★★★ *The Widows Handbook* (1988) by Charlotte Foehner and Carol Cozart. Golden, CO: Fulcrum.

Following the deaths of their husbands, Foehner began studying financial investment and tax preparation, and Cozart started her first full-time job. The book provides emotional support for widows, offers suggestions for rearing children, tells widows how to care for themselves, and discusses changes in relationships, but its main emphasis is on the financial and procedural issues widows are likely to encounter. Making funeral arrangements, selecting an attorney and a financial advisory team, performing an executor's duties, filing claims for life insurance and survivor benefits, getting credit and checking accounts in order, and maintaining a house and car are some of the practical topics covered. The authors include sample letters widows need to write and examine questions that crop up. This 3-star book is very good at what it attempts—providing widows with sound advice about financial and procedural matters—but it includes only minimal advice about the psychological and emotional dimensions of coping with the loss of a husband.

Strongly Not Recommended

† *Widowed* (1990) by Joyce Brothers. New York: Simon & Schuster.

† *Final Exit: The Practicalities of Self-Deliverance and Assisted Suicide for the Dying* (1991) by Derek Humphrey. Eugene, OR: The Hemlock Society.

AUTOBIOGRAPHIES

Strongly Recommended

★★★★★ *A Grief Observed* (1961) by C. S. Lewis. New York: Seabury.

This is a spiritual account of one person's experience with grief following the death of a spouse. C. S. Lewis, a professor at Cambridge University in England and a prominent writer, describes briefly (only 60 pages) his grief following the death of his wife from cancer. Originally published under the pseudonym of N. W. Clerk just before Lewis's own death, *A Grief Observed* reveals the inner turmoil of his grief. The author says that he wrote these memoirs as a "defense against total collapse, a safety valve." This 5-star autobiography presents profound human experience from the spiritual perspective of a gifted writer. It offers no advice for recovery but rather presents a moving description of human vulnerability and powerful emotions.

★★★★ *Motherless Daughter* (1995) by Hope Edelman. New York: Delta.

The author was 17 when she lost her mother. After finishing college and working as a journalist, Edelman realized that she was still grieving. She turned this experience first into a magazine article and then into this book, which attracted a large amount of media attention. Often described as the first book specifically on loss of a mother, *Motherless Daughter* discusses the experience of women who lost their mothers either as children or as adults.

Recommended

★★★ *After the Death of a Child: Living with Loss through the Years* (1998) by Ann Finkbeiner. Baltimore: Johns Hopkins University Press.

The author's only child died in 1987. She describes her grief and the methods she used to cope with the loss. She interviewed other parents who had lost children to collect additional material for this book. Highly rated, but infrequently so, in our national studies.

Diamond in the Rough

♦ *Letting Go: Morrie's Reflections on Living While Dying* (1997) by Morrie Schwartz. New York: Dell.

Also published under the title *Morrie: In His Own Words,* this book describes the last years of sociologist Morrie Schwartz after he learned at age 75 that he had Lou Gehrig's disease, which is progressive and incurable. Schwartz became a participant-observer as his physical abilities declined, tape recording his observations, impressions, and memories. He became widely known after appearing three times on Ted Koppel's TV show *Nightline* to discuss his life, dying, and Lou Gehrig's disease.

MOVIES

Strongly Recommended

★★★★★ *Ordinary People* (1980) produced by Ronald L. Schwary and directed by Robert Redford. R Rating. 124 minutes.

This is a movie about grieving and the denial of grief. A well-to-do family loses its prize son, and the parents' withdrawal becomes too extreme for their other son. In his isolation, he cuts his wrists and is hospitalized for months. When he returns, nothing has changed. His father's cheerfulness is all pretense; his mother's self-preoccupation is a stone wall. This stirring but ultimately hopeful film, winner of four Academy Awards, tragically illustrates how some families respond psychologically and interpersonally to loss and how the stress of loss makes them more of what they were before.

★★★★ *Steel Magnolias* (1990) produced by Ray Stark and directed by Herbert Ross. PG Rating. 118 minutes.

This is both a woman's picture and a picture of women. Six friends joke, gossip, and support each other for several years in a small Louisiana town in the early 1980s. They cry and fight and make up and get their hair done at the beauty parlor that is the center of their lives. When a tragic death strikes, their grieving is wonderful to watch: character tells, and strength is required. This may be an excellent movie to show survival in the face of tragedy, although the comedy is the main focus of the movie.

★★★★ *A River Runs through It* (1988) produced by Robert Redford and Patrick Markey and directed by Robert Redford. PG Rating. 123 minutes.

This movie is about how one can chose to live one's life. In the words of movie critic Roger Ebert (*Chicago Sun-Times*, October 9, 1992), "Fly-fishing stands for life in this movie. If you can learn to do it correctly, to read the river and the fish and yourself, and to do what needs to be done without one wasted motion, you will have attained some of the grace and economy needed to live a good life. If you can do it and understand that the river, the fish and the whole world are God's gifts to use wisely, you will have gone the rest of the way."

Recommended

★★★ *My Life* (1993) produced by Bruce Joel Rubin and Hunt Lowry and directed by Bruce Joel Rubin. PG-13 Rating. 112 minutes.

A successful advertising executive whose wife is pregnant learns that he is dying and doesn't know how to deal with the unfinished business in his life (particularly his feelings of anger toward his family) or the fact that he may never see his child. He is able to reach out to his unborn child by making videotapes. His wife is shown as a pillar of strength, his doctors as automatons. There are many truthful and poignant moments in this unabashed tearjerker, but contrivances ultimately take over, especially toward the end. The film could be used to illustrate loss, grief, and unfinished business if the responses to them are not taken too realistically.

★★★ *The Accidental Tourist* (1989) produced by Lawrence Kasdan, Charles Okun, Michael Grillo, Phyllis Carlyle, and John Malkovich and directed by Lawrence Kasdan. PG Rating. 121 minutes.

On the surface, this acclaimed film is about a man who is shattered by the death of his son and withdraws from any emotional contact. His wife leaves him, and he lives a safe but routine life until he meets a kooky, assertive woman who draws him out of his shell. Sounds like a typical Hollywood romance. This film could illustrate a style of coping with death and its negative consequences. It also shows how the man brings himself finally to choose between isolation and routine in his shell or love and risk in a new relationship. The film can be used with couples because it illustrates how the nature of the man's marriage, calm but distant, is too weak to support the couple's needs after their tragedy. The wife needs to talk, but the husband needs to be alone and deny his feelings.

★★★   *The Summer of '42* (1971) produced by Richard Alan Roth and directed by Robert Mulligan. PG Rating. 103 minutes.

A nostalgic look back at an adolescent boy's infatuation with an older woman who shares a sexual experience with him after her husband is killed in World War II and then disappears. The film illustrates how she, desperate for companionship in her despair over her husband's absence and then his sudden and tragic death, reaches out to the boy.

★★★   *The Lion King* (1995) produced by Don Hahn, Thomas Schumacher, Sarah McArthur, and Alice Dewey, and directed by Roger Allers and Robert Minkoff. G Rating. 87 minutes.

Sure, it is a cartoon, and one without people in it, too. But the story is a wonderful one of how courage, assumption of adult responsibilities, and friends can triumph over loss, evil, and treachery. The evil Scar has the king killed and drives the young prince out so that he can become king. The prince lives a carefree life until his father's ghost commands him to return and seek revenge. The film can illustrate how an individual need not be defeated by deaths and losses and can prevail by "growing up" and taking on social responsibilities.

★★★   *My Girl* (1992) produced by Brian Grazer and directed by Howard Zieff. PG Rating. 102 minutes.

An 11-year-old girl has become hypochondrical and as eccentric as her father. He copes with her mother's death in childbirth by isolation and contact only with the dead; she by a preoccupation with death, the meaning of life, and her imaginary diseases. She becomes close to a boy and shares puppy love, philosophical questions, and much of her time. When he dies, she is submerged in guilt—she feels like she killed him and her mother—and she is alone. Through her grieving and sharing with others, she becomes able to have new friends and to accept her father's new girlfriend. She struggles and achieves a normal (early) adolescent's life. While imperfect, this film can be valuable in suggesting the complexities of grief, adolescence, and families.

Not Recommended

★★   *Ghost* (1991) produced by Lisa Weinstein and directed by Jerry Zucker. PG-13 Rating. 122 minutes.

INTERNET RESOURCES

Metasites

★★★★★   *Death and Dying Grief Support* http://www.death-dying.com

A rich site with much advice and information on all kinds of grief and loss. *After Loss* includes many guidelines, and the *Planners* (for grief, funerals, legal issues, emotions, etc.) are especially fine tools. *A Dying Person's Guide to Dying* by Roger C. Bone, MD, on the *Planners* page is superb. *Featured Articles* address many aspects intelligently.

★★★★★ *Growth House* http://www.growthhouse.org

This rich site has thousands of links covering all aspects of end-of-life care. Although there are few publications available here and the resources require clicking through several levels, the organization is functional and clear, and the resources are well described. This site should be the starting point for searches.

★★★★ *GriefNet* http://rivendell.org

In the *Library* under Articles and Manuscripts are many useful papers on gender differences, helping others cope with loss, and so on.

★★★★ *The Compassionate Friends* http://www.compassionatefriends.org

This is the major organization for those who have lost a child. The 15 small brochures are excellent and comprehensive. They publish many books and booklets (see Resources) for all who are bereaved.

Psychoeducational Materials for Clients and Families

These resources are grouped separately under Grieving and Dying.

Grieving

★★★★ *Counseling for Loss and Life Changes* http://www.counselingforloss.com

Under Articles, Jane Bissler's site offers reprints of about 30 short writings and links to perhaps 50 more.

★★★★ *Life after Loss: Dealing with Grief*
          http://www.utexas.edu/student/cmhc/grief.html

A six-page overview written for college students.

★★★★ *Grief and Loss* http://www.couns.uiuc.edu/grief.htm

A three-page set of guidelines suitable as a handout for explaining the nature and process of grief and loss.

★★★★ *Safe Crossings* http://www.providence.org/safecrossings

This site is operated by a hospice and is for children who are facing the loss of a loved one. Not cute and very clear, it interactively explores many feelings, and offers activities and ways to memorialize the loss. See also *Julie's Place* at http://www.juliesplace.com a site for children who have lost a brother or sister that is perhaps too cute, but does offer support and chat.

★★★ *Grief and Bereavement*
          http://www.psycom.net/depression.central.grief.html

Many links of value, including material on teens, pet loss, and widowhood.

★★★   *Bereavement* http://www.rcpsych.ac.uk/public/help/bereav/ber_frame.htm

A good overview in six pages aimed at general readers.

★★★ *Mothers in Sympathy and Support* http://www.misschildren.org

Oriented around the loss of a child, this site includes several useful articles and advice for friends and professionals.

★★★ *WidowNet* http://www.fortnet.org/WidowNet

The first three articles are helpful: Dumb Remarks and Stupid Questions, Getting through the Holidays, and You Know You're Getting Better When. . . .

★★★ *Grief Journey* http://www.grieftalk.com/help1.html

The five articles by Bill Webster would be useful, short basic readings for clients.

Dying

★★★★ *Partnership for Caring* http://www.partnershipforcaring.org

The site offers readings about end-of-life issues, legal aspects, and state-specific advance directives.

★★★★ *What Is Hospice?* http://www.nho.org/general.htm

The four brochures here will answer almost all questions.

★★★★ *FAMSA: Funeral Consumers Alliance* http://www.funerals.org/famsa

A consumer-oriented site with lots of information to help make responsible and efficient choices about funerals, cemeteries, and caskets.

Other Resources

★★★★ *Melanie's Rainbow Bridge*
         http://www.geocities.com/Heartland/Ranch/8291

The pain of the death of a beloved pet is often underappreciated. This site has some resources. This is a valuable collection of articles, books, and links about coping with the death of a beloved pet. A good example is *When a Pet Dies: Coping with Loss* at http://www.olywa.net/peregrine/petloss.html.

★★★★ *Hospice Net* http://www.hospicenet.org

This site provides more than 100 articles on end-of-life issues.

★★★ *A Heartbreaking Choice* http://www.erichad.com/ahc

"For parents who have terminated a pregnancy after learning their baby has severe birth defects."

Online Support Groups

GriefNet http://rivendell.org

There are 32 support groups here addressing all kinds of losses, including KIDSAID for grieving children. There is a charge, but you can try the group for a month before paying.

Bereavement and Hospice Support Netline http://www.ubalt.edu/www/bereavement

There is a list of support groups by state.

NATIONAL SUPPORT GROUPS

Choice in Dying
1035 30th Street NW
Washington, DC 20007
Phone: 202-338-9790
Fax: 202-338-0242

"The inventor of living wills in 1967, it is dedicated to fostering communication about complex end-of-life decisions. The nonprofit organization provides advance directives, counsels patients and families, trains professionals, advocates for improved laws, and offers a range of publications and services."

Compassionate Friends
PO Box 3696
Oak Brook, IL 60522-3696
Phone: 708-990-0010
Fax: 708-990-0246
http://www.compassionatefriends.org

This is the major organization for parents who have lost a child.

Concerns of Police Survivors (COPS)
COPS National Office
PO Box 3199
Camdenton, MO 65020
Phone: 573-346-4911
Fax: 573-346-1414

This group was created to reach out to surviving families of America's law enforcement officers killed in the line of duty.

Mothers against Drunk Driving (MADD)
511 East John Carpenter Freeway, Suite 700
Irving, TX 75062
Phone: 800-GET-MADD; 214-744-6233

For victims of drunk drivers.

National SIDS Foundation
2 Metro Plaza, Suite 205
8240 Professional Place
Landover, MD 20785
Phone: 800-211-SIDS

Parents of Murdered Children (POMC)
100 East Street, B-41
Cincinnati, OH 45202
Phone: 513-721-5683

Pet Loss Hotline
College of Veterinary Medicine
Washington State University
Pullman, WA 99164-7010
Phone: 509-335-5704
E-mail: plhl@vetmed.wsu.edu
http://www.vetmed.wsu.edu/PLHL/index.htm

"It's okay to love and miss your pet." Provides a support mechanism for grieving people who have experienced pet loss.

Sudden Infant Death Syndrome Alliance (SIDS Alliance)
1314 Bedford Avenue, Suite 210
Baltimore, MD 21208
Phone: 800-221-SIDS
Fax: 410-659-8709

THEOS Foundation
322 Boulevard of the Allies, Suite 105
Pittsburgh, PA 15222-1919
Phone: 412-471-7779
Fax: 412-471-7782

"An international support network for recently widowed men and women."

SHARE Office (Pregnancy and Infant Loss Support)
St. Joseph Health Center
300 First Capitol Drive
St. Charles, MO 63301-2893
Phone: 800-821-6819
Fax: 314-947-7486
http://www.NationalSHAREOffice.com

Society of Military Widows (SMW)
5535 Hempstead Way
Springfield, VA 22151
Phone: 703-750-1342, ext. 30071
Fax: 703-354-4380
E-mail: mconaus@aol.com

TAPS (Tragedy Assistance Program for Survivors)
2001 S Street NW, Suite 300
Washington, DC 20009
Phone: 800-959-TAPS
Fax: 907-274-8277
E-mail: tapsak@aol.com

"TAPS serves all those affected by a death in the line of military duty and works with parents, children, spouses, and friends."

CHAPTER 13

Dementia/Alzheimer's

The majority of older adults are living longer, more active, and fulfilling lives, but some older adults are declining mentally and physically to the point of needing continuous help. Many of these older adults are suffering from dementia, which commonly refers to global cognitive decline involving impairment in more than one aspect of cognitive functioning, always including memory dysfunction and personality alterations (Lezak, 1995).

By far, the most prevalent and best known of the dementias is Alzheimer's disease, a progressive and irreversible brain disorder. Characteristics are a gradual deterioration of nerve cells within the brain with deterioration in memory, reasoning, language, and physical functioning. Some data suggest that as people live longer, the incidence of Alzheimer's could triple within the next 50 years.

A family caring for a dementia patient assumes a great deal of responsibility. The condition typically begins so gradually that often the family is unaware that anything is wrong until work problems pile up or a sudden disruption in routine leaves the patient disoriented, confused, and unable to deal with the unfamiliar situation. Families caring for loved ones diagnosed with Alzheimer's or one of the other dementias need to be educated and prepared to cope with a number of predictable and unpredictable behaviors. Family distress tends to be chronic and high. There will come a time when the family has to decide what level of care their family member needs and the most appropriate setting in which to provide that care.

In this chapter, we present the experts' consensual ratings and our brief descriptions of self-help books, autobiographies, and movies on this crippling disease. Listings of Internet resources and national support groups round out the resources.

RECOMMENDATION HIGHLIGHTS

Self-Help Books

- A family guide to caring for a person with Alzheimer's:

  ★★★★★ *The 36-Hour Day* by Nancy Mace and Peter Rabins

- A caregiver's guide to the daily problems of Alzheimer's:

  ★★★ *The Hidden Victims of Alzheimer's Disease* by Steven Zarit and Associates

  ◆ *When Your Loved One Has Alzheimer's* by David L. Carroll

Autobiographies

- Recognizing the signs of a loved one's decline:

  ◆ *Alzheimer's, A Love Story* by Ann Davidson

- Moving accounts of caring for a spouse afflicted with Alzheimer's:

  ★★★ *The Diminished Mind* by Jean Tyler and Harry Anifantakis

  ◆ *Elegy for Iris* by John Bayley

Movies

- A superb portrayal of early Alzheimer's and it impact on the spouse:

  ★★★ *Do You Remember Love?*

- A humorous film about repairing a father–son relationship while father descends into dementia:

  ★★★ *Memories of Me*

Internet Resources

- Extensive materials for patients and caregivers:

  ★★★★★ *The Alzheimer's Association* http://www.alz.org

  ★★★★★ *Alzheimer's Association of NSW* http://www.alznsw.asn.au/library/libtoc.htm

- Practical information about caregiving, nursing homes, and health care:

  ★★★★★ *Alzheimer's Outreach* http://www.zarcrom.com/users/alzheimers

- Great ideas for caregivers of Alzheimer's patients:

  ★★★★ *The Caregiver's Handbook* http://www.acsu.buffalo.edu/~drstall/hndbk0.html

SELF-HELP BOOKS

Strongly Recommended

★★★★★ *The 36-Hour Day: A Family Guide to Caring for Persons with Alzheimer's Disease, Related Dementing Illness and Memory Loss in Later Life* (3rd ed., 1999) by Nancy Mace and Peter Rabins. Baltimore: Johns Hopkins University Press.

This book, now in its third edition, is a family guide to caring for persons with Alzheimer's and related diseases. The authors say that for those who care for a person with Alzheimer's or related diseases, every day seems as if it is 36 hours long. This is a guide for the home care of older adults in the early and middle stages of these diseases. The family is helped to recognize the point beyond which home care is no longer enough, and guidance in choosing a nursing home or other care facility is provided. Various support groups that have been formed to help families with an Alzheimer's member are also described. This 5-star book is an excellent guide for families who have an Alzheimer's relative. It provides practical advice with specific examples that help readers learn how to care for an impaired relative on a day-to-day basis. One of the highest rated self-help books in our national studies.

Recommended

★★★ *The Hidden Victims of Alzheimer's Disease: Families under Stress* (1985) by Steven Zarit, Nancy K. Orr, and Judy M. Zarit. New York: New York University Press.

The authors tell families how to cope with the day-to-day problems in the care of a person with Alzheimer's disease. Specific situations and interventions are addressed, including stealing, incontinence, asking repetitive questions, lowered sexual inhibitions, inappropriate public behavior, and how to cope with the guilt and emotional stress of caregiving. Also covered are positive psychosocial approaches to dementia, causes of memory loss, and how to assess for dementia. This book has been written primarily for practitioners working with patients and their families in community settings. It may also serve the needs of students and of family members working with organizations devoted to Alzheimer's disease. Besides discussing understanding, recognizing, and dealing with Alzheimer's disease, the book also covers individual counseling, family meetings, support groups, and special treatment concerns (e.g., drugs, placement, and patients without families). A valuable 3-star resource that would have received 4-stars if it had been more frequently rated.

★★★ *The Alzheimer's Caregiver: Dealing with the Realities of Dementia* (1998) by Harriet Hodgson. Minneapolis: Chronimed.

The chronic and debilitating nature of Alzheimer's is sensitively captured in Hodgson's book. As an Alzheimer's patient's mental abilities deteriorate, the caregiver's responsibilities and emotional challenges escalate. The caregiver needs to learn how to cope with this consuming process and to care for himself or herself without guilt. Various problems covered in the book are home care, assisted living, anticipatory grief, legal complications, personal struggles, Alzheimer's depression, health care costs, and the family system. Appendixes provide self-assessment. This 3-star book is clearly and effectively aimed at caregivers.

Diamond in the Rough

♦ *When Your Loved One Has Alzheimer's: A Caregiver's Guide* (1989) by David L. Carroll. New York: Harper & Row.

The author covers a variety of Alzheimer topics, notably understanding the disease, reviewing medical care and coverage, preparing the family home, maintaining the caregiver's emotional health, and getting help. The information and techniques in these pages are designed to be used on several levels—practical, psychological, and spiritual. Some of the day-to-day problems discussed in the book are the person's temper tantrums, incontinence pads, embarrassing scenes in public settings, motor difficulties, and impaired memory. This book is written expressly for caregivers as a how-to manual to use in conjunction with quality professional care and directions. Favorably rated but not widely known by the mental health experts in our studies.

AUTOBIOGRAPHIES

Recommended

★★★ *The Diminished Mind: One Family's Extraordinary Battle with Alzheimer's* (1991) by Jean Tyler and Harry Anifantakis. Blue Ridge Summit, PA: TAB Books.

Jean Tyler tells the true story of her husband Manley's devastating battle with Alzheimer's disease. Manley Tyler was a loving husband and a respected elementary school principal before the onset of Alzheimer's. Jean Tyler sensitively describes the pain and grief of her husband's slow 15-year decline and his eventual death. Alzheimer's hits most older adults much later than it did Manley Tyler. He was only 42 years old when he first showed symptoms. His case is also special because he fought the disease longer than most do. Jean Tyler relates the progressive deterioration of memory and judgment that made it impossible for him to complete even the simplest of tasks and made him increasingly prone to hostile behavior and paranoia. This 3-star autobiography not only speaks volumes about the emotionally draining experiences and losses involved in Alzheimer's, but it also carries some important messages for the survivors of an Alzheimer's victim, who can emerge from the experience with fond memories of their loved one and a stronger understanding of what it means to be human.

Diamonds in the Rough

♦ *Alzheimer's, A Love Story: One Year in My Husband's Journey* (1997) by Ann Davidson. Secaucus, NJ: Birch Lane.

In a series of 56 vignettes moving from initial puzzlement and uncertainty about what was happening to eventually acceptance, Ann Davidson documents the year in which her husband, a professor of physiology at Stanford Medical School, experienced the onset of Alzheimer's. A good book, but a recent one, not yet well-known by our mental health experts.

♦ *Elegy for Iris* (1999) by John Bayley. New York: St. Martin's Press.

A moving account of the literary courtship and unconventional union between Oxford don and literary critic John Bayley and renowned philosopher and novelist Dame Iris Murdoch. Using his talents for elegant prose, Bayley recounts his wife's descent into unknowing darkness and the caretaking role he was forced to take and performed nobly. An impressive book not only for the perceptive account of Alzheimer's, but also because the author and the subject are important literary figures. Accorded the designation of a Diamond in the Rough because it was very new at the time of the study.

MOVIES

Recommended

★★★ *Do You Remember Love?* (1985, made for TV) produced by Dave Bell, James Thompson, and Wayne Threm and directed by Jeff Bleckner.

Joanne Woodward won an Emmy for her portrayal of a middle-aged college professor who begins to suffer from Alzheimer's disease. The effect on her husband and family are superbly shown in an Emmy-winning script. Realistic and touching at the same time.

★★★ *Memories of Me* (1989) produced by Billy Crystal and Michael Hertzberg and directed by Henry Winkler. PG-13 Rating. 105 minutes.

After his own heart attack, a heart surgeon seeks to reconcile with his father in order to put his own life back in order. That fathers and sons have superficial and (especially in this movie) joking relationships is not news, but the way they struggle and partly succeed in deepening their relationship is funny and memorable. The son's response to his father's early Alzheimer's is also illuminating at times.

INTERNET RESOURCES

Metasites

★★★★★ *The Alzheimer's Association* http://www.alz.org

The informational materials are extensive and address all the right issues for patients and caregivers. This is the best place to start learning about all aspects of the disease.

★★★★★ *Alzheimer's Outreach* http://www.zarcrom.com/users/alzheimers

Go to the four Alzheimer's directories: Caregiving, Alzheimer's, Nursing/Nursing Home Information, and Health Care Issues to find massive, detailed, and, best of all, practical information.

★★★★★ *Alzheimer's Association of NSW*
http://www.alznsw.asn.au/library/libtoc.htm

The 38 Help Notes on the site seem to be the best-quality information on the Internet. "Our information on dementia is divided into 6 main types: Information about the dementias, Information written for people diagnosed with a dementia, Information written for carers, Management of problem behaviors (also written for carers), Information in languages other than English, and Annotated bibliographies to allow you to read about other resources available on dementia."

★★★★ *Washington University Alzheimer Disease Research Center (ADRC)*
        http://www.biostat.wustl.edu/alzheimer

Links are under headings (under the full list of Aging and Dementia) such as Caregiver Resources, Clinical Care Guides, Research Discussions and Opportunities, Commercial Products and Services, Job Listings in Aging and Dementia, Personal Home Pages, Nursing Homes/Assisted Living, Resources Not in English. The sites are not alphabetical or clustered, and there are hundreds of them, making finding a particular item difficult.

Psychoeducational Materials for Clients and Families

★★★★ *Alzheimer's Center Reference List*
        http://www.mayohealth.org/mayo/common/htm/alzheimpg2.htm

From the Mayo Clinic, this site offers about a dozen one- to three-page guidelines about different aspects of the disease. The sections on risk assessment and genetics seem unique. The papers on caregiving are well done but brief. A good start.

★★★★ *Memory and Dementia*
        http://www.rcpsych.ac.uk/public/help/memory/mem_frame.htm

A seven-page brochure discussing appropriate memory expectations, the role of anxiety and depression in lessening recall, aspects of dementia, self-help tips, and readings.

★★★★ *ALZwell Alzheimer's Caregivers' Page* http://www.alzwell.com

A comprehensive site with many resources especially designed for supporting caregivers.

★★★★ *The Elderly Place* http://www.geocities.com/~elderly-place

A Caregiver's Guide to Alzheimer's and the information on nursing homes is practical and specific.

★★★★ *Ageless Design* http://www.agelessdesign.com

Alzheimer's-proofing your house, special products, a newsletter, and the like. See also http://www.isl.net/~hoffcomp/homesol.html for a good article on this.

★★★★ *The Caregiver's Handbook: Assisting Both the Caregiver*
        and the Elderly Carereceiver by Robert S. Stall, MD
        http://www.acsu.buffalo.edu/~drstall/hndbk0.html

This is a book of about 100 pages with detailed and practical ideas for caregivers about nutrition, emotions, personal care, and legal and financial issues.

★★★ *Alzheimer's Disease Fact Page* by David S. Geldmacher, MD
http://www.ohioalzcenter.org/facts.html

A good four-page overview.

★★★ *The Alzheimer's Disease Education and Referral (ADEAR)*
http://www.alzheimers.org

This is the Alzheimer's section of the National Institute on Aging of the National Institutes of Health. The nine Fact Sheets (under Publications) offer solid information and are a good starting place. A list of the 29 federally funded Alzheimer's disease centers for referral, evaluation, and treatment appears at http://www.alzheimers.org/pubs/adcdir.html.

Biographical and Autobiographical Vignettes

★★★★ *A Year to Remember* http://www.zarcrom.com/users/yeartorem

Created by the daughter of a woman with Alzheimer's disease, this rich site is a memorial, as well as a metasite for all kinds of concerns: research, home pages, the arts, poetry, films, books and book reviews, memorials, genealogy, and so on. A labor of love that can help many.

Other Resources

★★★★★ *The Alzheimer's Disease Bookstore*
http://www.alzheimersbooks.com/102.Alzheimerbookstore.html

This site has every book for caregivers and children, on designing a safe environment, legal issues, activities, and other practical advice. A real find. Other books can be found at http://www.caregiver911.com/html/caregiver_books.html. Videotapes are available at http://www.alzheimersbooks.com/AlzVideos.html.

★★★ *Practice Guidelines for the Treatment of Patients with Alzheimer's Disease and Other Dementias of Late Life*
http://www.psych.org/clin_res/pg_dementia.cfm

This is the Practice Guideline from the American Psychiatric Association. It is a mini-textbook, and the sections on features, natural history, treatments, and treatment planning may be useful.

NATIONAL SUPPORT GROUPS

Alzheimer's Association National Office
919 North Michigan Avenue, Suite 1000
Chicago, IL 60611-1676
Phone: 800-272-3900, 312-335-8700
Fax: 312-335-1110

Alzheimer's Disease and Related Disorders Association
919 North Michigan Avenue, #1000
Chicago, IL 60611-8700
Phone: 312-335-8700

For caregivers of Alzheimer's patients.

Alzheimer's Disease Education and Referral Center
Hotline: 800-438-4380

Information, referrals, publications, and information about clinical trials.

National Family Caregivers Association
10605 Concord Street, Suite 501
Kensington, MD 20895-2504
Phone: 1-800-896-3650
Fax: 301-942-2302
E-mail: info@nfcacares.org

National Niemann–Pick Disease Foundation
22201 Riverpoint Trail
Carrollton, VA 23314
Phone: 804-357-6774

CHAPTER 14

Divorce

Divorce has become epidemic in our society. Until recently, it was increasing annually by 10 percent, although its rate of increase has now leveled off. For those involved, separation and divorce are complex and emotionally charged, and its stresses place men, women, and children at risk for psychological and physical difficulties. Separated and divorced adults have higher rates of behavioral disorders, admission to psychiatric hospitals, substance abuse, suicide, and depression than their married counterparts. Many separations and divorces immerse children in conflict, and as a consequence, the children are more likely to have school-related problems, especially at the beginning of the separation and divorce.

Self-help resources on divorce fall into four main categories: for divorced or divorcing parents; for the children of divorced or divorcing parents; for divorced or divorcing adults in general; and child custody. This chapter presents self-help books, movies, Internet resources, and national support groups directed to all those involved in the epidemic of divorce.

SELF-HELP BOOKS

Strongly Recommended

★★★★★ *The Boys and Girls Book about Divorce* (1985) by Richard Gardner. New York: Bantam.

This treasured book is written for children to help them cope with their parents' separation and divorce. It is appropriate for children of average or better intelligence who are 10 to 12 years of age or older. Most of what Gardner tells children in the book comes from his therapy experiences with divorced children. Gardner talks directly to children about their feelings after the divorce, who is and is not to blame for the divorce, parents' love for their children, and how to handle angry feelings and the fear of being left

RECOMMENDATION HIGHLIGHTS

Self-Help Books

- For young children in divorced families:

    ★★★★★ *Dinosaurs Divorce* by Laurene Brown and Marc Brown

- For older children and adolescents in divorced families:

    ★★★★★ *The Boys and Girls Book about Divorce* by Richard Gardner

    ★★★★ *How It Feels When Parents Divorce* by Jill Krementz

- For divorced parents to use with children:

    ★★★★ *Growing Up with Divorce* by Neil Kalter

    ★★★ *Helping Your Kids Cope with Divorce* by M. Gary Neuman
    with Patricia Romanowski

- For those undergoing divorce:

    ★★★ *Crazy Time* by Abigail Trafford

Movies

- On the pain of custody battles and the need to attend to children's needs:

    ★★★★ *Kramer vs. Kramer*

- On women making the difficult postdivorce transition and redefining themselves:

    ★★★★ *An Unmarried Woman*

- On inevitable changes in marriages and friendships:

    ★★★ *The Four Seasons*

Internet Resources

- An excellent site with hundreds of helpful links:

    ★★★★ *Divorce Magazine* http://www.divorcemag.com

- Complete and supportive sites for people going through divorce:

    ★★★★★ *Divorce Central* http://www.divorcecentral.com

    ★★★★ *Divorce Support* http://www.divorcesupport.com

    ★★★★ *Frequently Asked Questions on Surviving the Emotional Trauma
    of Divorce*
    http://www.divorcecentral.com/lifeline/life_ans.html#Notsaved

- A short course about avoiding the courtroom:

    ★★★★★ *Divorce Helpline: Tools to Keep You Out of Court*
    http://www.divorcehelp.com/index.html

- A guide to the stressors on children who go through divorce:

    ★★★★ *Focus on Kids: The Effects of Divorce on Children* http://
    muextension.missouri.edu/xplor/hesguide/humanrel/gh6600.htm

alone. Then he tells children about how to get along better with their divorced mother and their divorced father. Gardner also covers the important topic of how to get along with parents who live apart, sensitively handling such difficult issues as playing one parent against the other and what to do when parents try to use the child as a tool or weapon. The final chapter explains to children what to expect if they have to see a therapist. Written at an appropriate reading level for its intended audience, the book also features a number of cartoon-like drawings, which adds to its appeal for children. It has survived the test of time and remains a superb resource for divorced or divorcing parents to give to their 10- to 12-year-old or older children to read.

★★★★★ *Dinosaurs Divorce: A Guide for Changing Families* (1986) by Laurene Brown and Marc Brown. Boston: Little, Brown.

This book, designed for children living in divorced families, grew out of the Browns' experiences with divorce as parent and stepparent, and for Laurene, as a child herself. *Dinosaurs Divorce* is a 30-page, full-color picture book that takes children through the experience of divorce in a dinosaur family. The topics covered include why parents divorce, how children feel when their parents divorce, what happens after the divorce, what it's like to live with one parent, what it's like to visit the other parent, having two homes, celebrating holidays and special occasions, telling friends, meeting parents' new friends, and having stepsisters and stepbrothers. The book is simple and easy for children to understand. Much of it can be read and understood by children who are in elementary school. Parents can read and discuss the pictures and words with younger children.

★★★★ *How It Feels When Parents Divorce* (1984) by Jill Krementz. New York: Knopf.

Jill Krementz, a writer and photographer, presents 19 children's experiences with the divorces of their parents. Krementz interviewed and photographed 19 children aged 7 to 16. The title of each of the chapters is a child's name. Each chapter opens with a full-page photograph of the child, followed by the child's experience in a divorced family. The children talk about the changes in their lives, their hurt, the confusion they had to cope with, and the knowledge they gained. The book is mainly geared toward children and adolescents—it is at about the same reading level as Gardner's *The Boys and Girls Book about Divorce*—although divorced parents can also benefit from the children's descriptions of their experiences. The children's stories reflect their vulnerability and resilience. Thirteen-year-old Zach comments, "It's very sad and confusing when your parents are divorced." Eight-year-old Lulu reflects, "I suppose they needed the divorce to be happy, but there were times when I thought it was stupid and unfair and mean to me." Many mental health professionals find it a good self-help book for older children and adolescents.

★★★★ *Growing Up with Divorce* (1990) by Neil Kalter. New York: Free Press.

This book is written for divorced parents and provides information to help their children avoid emotional problems. It is especially designed to counteract the long-term effects of divorce on children, many of whom struggle with emotional difficulties for years after the actual divorce itself. Kalter's book offers parents practical strategies for helping children cope with the anxiety, anger, and confusion that can occur immediately or develop over a number of years. Kalter nicely shows how a child's level of psychological development influences the specific ways that he or she experiences, understands, and reacts to the stress of divorce. The book includes in-depth accounts of the experiences of children from infancy through adolescence. There is practical advice about how to minimize children's stress in many situations, such as feeling caught by divided loyalties and coping with the dislocation of new household arrangements. Kalter gives step-by-step instructions to parents about how to speak to their children in indirect and nonthreatening ways and tells them what to say in specific situations. This was the highest-rated book for parents in the divorce category, and it is an excellent self-help book for divorced parents.

Recommended

★★★ *Crazy Time: Surviving Divorce* (1982) by Abigail Trafford. New York: Harper & Row.

As a result of her own painful experience with divorce, Trafford, who is a journalist, began recording the many stories she heard from others who were going through divorce. Each story was different, yet each fit a pattern. Trafford identifies and describes the developmental stages of divorce, crazy time, and the recovery. *Crazy Time* is the author's term for the two years immediately following a divorce, in which unpredictable and inexplicable emotions take over and the roller-coaster ride begins. Each topic is approached through the true-life experiences of many interviewees. The personalized style of the book gives an intimate feeling to the stories and the people who lived them. *Crazy Time* received a sterling evaluation from those experts familiar with it, but the low number of ratings reduced its overall evaluation.

★★★ *Helping Your Kids Cope with Divorce* (1998) by M. Gary Neuman with Patricia Romanowski. New York: Times Books.

This parents' book on divorce through a child's eyes explains how children think and feel about divorce and, more importantly, how they interpret what has happened and how they make sense of the experience. The central concept is that more often than not the child is thinking about and interpreting experiences differently than the parent thinks. The result is that children blame themselves and make distorted attributions about why it happened, what their role was, and what will happen to them now. Activities teach parents how to stop explaining and reasoning and to start communicating by knowing how to find out what the child thinks and feels through art, play, activities, and simply asking different questions. A chapter each is devoted to age-specific information on the infant and toddler to the 17-year-old. Other topics include fighting, the first day of the divorce, moving, custody and visitation, and divorce-related changes (e.g., finances, home, changing schools, child care).

★★★ *Second Chances: Men, Women, and Children a Decade after Divorce* (rev. ed., 1996) by Judith S. Wallerstein and Sandra Blakeslee. New York: Ticknor & Fields.

This book is based on a long-term study of divorced couples and their children. Wallerstein and associates examined how 60 families fared 5 years after divorce. In *Second Chances*, Wallerstein and Blakeslee describe the reevaluation of 90% of the original

60 families 10 years after divorce, with some analysis of their lives at the 15-year mark. Additional commentary is included about divorced families who are seen at the California clinic Wallerstein directs. The authors argue that divorce is emotionally painful and psychologically devastating for a large proportion of children, even 10 to 15 years after the divorce takes place. In their view, divorced parents who are struggling to meet their own needs often fail to meet their children's needs; through their own instability and continuing conflict with each other, divorced parents add to the psychological burdens of their children. Interview excerpts are interwoven with clinical interpretations and research findings to tell the emotionally difficult story of the long-term negative effects of divorce on children. The book, though recommended, is sobering reading for many divorcing parents.

★★★　*Creative Divorce* (1973) by Mel Krantzler. New York: Signet.

This book, anchored in the 1970s, is about divorced individuals' opportunities for personal growth. When he was 50 years of age, Krantzler and his wife separated after 24 years of marriage. He describes his ordeal—self-pity, guilt, loneliness, and helplessness—and how it helped him grow as a person. The author also draws on the experiences of his male and female clients. Krantzler considers divorce the death of a relationship, requiring a mourning period followed by reflective self-evaluation and planning. The self-destructive patterns that many divorced adults engage in are portrayed, as when men say they want companionship but pursue women as sexual objects. While Krantzler's description of divorce is better when he is dispensing advice for men, he is sympathetic to some of the problems divorced women face—economic difficulties, for example. The book was a best-seller in the 1970s, but its popularity has declined since then, and many readers may regard it as both dated and too optimistic.

Diamonds in the Rough

◆　*The Parents Book about Divorce* (1977) by Richard Gardner. New York: Doubleday.

This resource is the sequel to Gardner's *The Boys and Girls Book about Divorce*, reviewed earlier in this chapter. Gardner provides sage advice to divorced parents about what to tell children, how to help children cope with the separation period, and the best strategies for dealing with children in the aftermath of divorce. Parents are advised about how to get effective counseling and legal assistance, determine custody, cope with unreasonable demands of the former spouse, deal with the new mate of a former spouse, reduce guilt, make visitation less stressful, introduce a new lover into the family routine, and not make the mistake of picking the wrong mate again. Although positively evaluated in the national studies, it was rated by too few respondents to make a rating category. We find it to be a well-written and insightful self-help book for parents; however, the book is more than 20 years old now and is dated in its handling of gender roles and sexual orientation.

◆　*Dumped: A Survival Guide for the Woman Who's Been Left by the Man She Loved* (1999) by Sally Warren and Andrea Thompson. New York: HarperCollins.

Sally Warren, left by her husband after a 19-year marriage, collaborates with freelance writer Andrea Thompson on this survival guide. Research for the book included interviews with 108 women who had been abandoned by their partners. The book includes tips about what is happening (cues and intimations), explaining what is happening to oneself and others, the emotional stages passed through, ways to avoid destructive actions, and the path to healing and new relationships. The stages of being dumped are addressed with humor, candor, and respect. Validation and reality testing for women as well as reassurance and support are pluses for this book, which, along with the very current publication date, is why this well-researched book earned the Diamond in the Rough status.

Not Recommended

★ *Mars and Venus Starting Over* (1998) by John Gray. New York: HarperCollins.

MOVIES

Strongly Recommended

★★★★ *Kramer vs. Kramer* (1979) produced by Richard C. Jaffe and directed by
         Robert Benton. PG Rating. 105 minutes.

Wife leaves marriage; husband assumes care of their 5-year-old son; in doing so, he discovers the responsibilities and joys of parenting. Wife returns and fights for custody of son. The ensuing legal proceedings are bitter and cruel, resulting in a decision favoring the mother and ordering the father to relinquish custody. But then the Kramers negotiate a mature arrangement on their own that attends to the needs of the child and themselves. A powerful film, recipient of five Academy Awards, that vividly demonstrates multiple realities of marriage, divorce, and custody: adult self-involvement with work (the father), search for identity (the mother), avoiding heartrending custody battles, attending to the child's needs during custody, the pain of nasty legal battles, and ultimately the superiority of working cooperatively.

★★★★ *An Unmarried Woman* (1978) produced by Paul Mazursky and Tony Ray and
         directed by Paul Mazursky. R Rating. 124 minutes.

An affluent Manhattan lawyer suddenly informs his steadfast wife that he doesn't love her and is leaving their 20-year marriage. The wife, accustomed to defining herself in terms of her husband, makes the difficult transition to being an unmarried woman, developing a mature identity, and learning to love without losing herself. One of the earliest and still best films that realistically depict women redefining their postdivorce identities. Also beautifully explores the loving relationship between a mother and her teenage daughter.

Recommended

★★★ *The Four Seasons* (1981) produced by Martin Bregman and directed by
       Alan Alda. PG Rating. 107 minutes.

Three middle-aged couples are lifelong friends and vacation together until one of the men decides to divorce his wife. He brings his young girlfriend on their next vacation, a cruise around the Virgin Islands, and the other two couples are both disturbed and envious of the couple's romantic relationship. The divorced wife subsequently accuses her lifelong friends of deserting her, and the three couples continue to support one another, adapt, and struggle through the travails of life and marriage. The film uses Vivaldi's *Four Seasons* as a metaphor for the development and inevitable changes in their lives and marriages. Useful for illustrating the interpersonal ramifications of divorce and accepting changes in friends.

★★★   *The Good Mother* (1989) produced by Arnold Glimcher and directed by Leonard Nimoy. R Rating. 104 minutes.

A divorced mother falls in love with a man who naively allows the woman's young daughter to touch his penis, resulting in the divorced father's filing a suit for custody. Although the psychologists conclude that the child has suffered no harm and that she is securely attached to the mother, the lawyer convinces the mother to make her boyfriend the scapegoat in order to maintain the relationship with her daughter. A provocative and sad film showing the challenges of intimacy for single parents and the charge of sexual molestation being used as a weapon by a former spouse.

★★★   *Mrs. Doubtfire* (1994) produced by Marcia Garces Williams, Robin Williams, and Mark Radcliffe and directed by Chris Columbus. PG-13 Rating. 119 minutes.

An idealistic and fun-loving father clashes with a sensible and sedate mother in marriage and then in divorce when the mother is awarded custody of their three children. The father transforms himself into an elderly English nanny, Mrs. Doubtfire, and is hired to care for the children. That's when the high-jinks begin. Nicely demonstrates the genuine pain and loss of divorce, parental devotion to children despite the end of a marriage, and the realistic struggles to accommodate everyone's needs in postdivorce families.

★★★   *Bye Bye Love* (1995) produced by Gary David Goldberg, Brad Hall, and Sam Weisman and directed by Sam Weisman. PG-13 Rating. 106 minutes.

Three divorced California fathers attempt to juggle their children's and their own needs over a weekend. No enviable role models here, but the film will trigger discussion of the difficult postdivorce adjustment and balancing multiple needs in limited time.

Not Recommended

★   *First Wives' Club* (1996) produced by Noah Ackerman, Thomas Almperato, Heather Neeley, Craig Perry, Scott Rudin, Adam Schroeder, and Ezra Swedlow and directed by Hugh Wilson. PG Rating. 102 minutes.

Strongly Not Recommended

†   *The War of the Roses* (1990) produced by James L. Brooks and Arnon Milchan and directed by Danny DeVito. R Rating. 116 minutes.

INTERNET RESOURCES

Metasites

★★★★ *Divorce Magazine*
http://www.divorcemag.com

This is the printed magazine's online commercial site, with articles and links to all kinds of sites. There is much repetition, puffery, and irrelevancy here, but there are many excellent resources for those willing to examine the links with a goal in mind.

Psychoeducational Materials for Clients and Families

So much information is available online for this topic that we review the most valuable sites under four subtopics: Major Sites (general); Separating; Legal Aspects (e.g., alimony, child support); and Kids, Custody, and Divorce.

Major Sites

★★★★★ *Divorce Central*
http://www.divorcecentral.com

Clever (the Steam Room is for venting anger), complete, and supportive (Chat, New Dawn Cafe), this site provides materials on legal, financial, parental, and personal (Personal Ads) aspects of divorce. Resources (organizations, lawyers) can be found by state. The frequently asked questions in the Resource Guide contain solid and complete information, and the Laws by State contain much information that is not available elsewhere.

★★★★ *Divorceinfo.com*
http://www.divorceinfo.com

This site claims that more than 100,000 documents are available though it. Simple and plain, it addresses all the issues with good, if short, readings, all cross-linked. This might be a good site to recommend to those needing a lot of orienting information that they can comfortably explore. They should read the entire home page.

★★★★ *Divorce Support*
http://www.divorcesupport.com

This site offers lots of readings, chats, information links, and other resources. Somewhat commercialized (mainly selling books) and busy, it covers every aspect of divorce from laws to men's issues and affairs to insurance. This might be a good site to recommend to those who need a lot of information.

★★★★ *Divorce Support Online*
http://www.divorcesupport.com

In the title bar, click on Articles to reach about 25 professionally written articles taken mainly from books for sale. Although we have not read them all, they seem impressive and appear to be a fine survey and introduction to all the aspects of divorce.

Separating

★★★★ *Frequently Asked Questions on Surviving the Emotional Trauma of Divorce*
by Mitchell A. Baris, PhD
http://www.divorcecentral.com/lifeline/life_ans.html#Notsaved

A 10-page FAQ that is well-done and complete. A good starting place for looking at the likely consequences of a divorce.

★★★★ *Guidelines for Separating Parents* http://home.clara.net/spig/guidline.htm
Only three pages, but solid, sensitive, and inclusive directions.

★★★ *The Relationship and Personal Development Center*
http://www.realtionshipjourney.com

Five good quality articles on divorce by Dawn Lipthrott, LCSW, among other articles on relationships.

★★★ *Bill Ferguson's How to Divorce as Friends* http://www.divorceasfriends.com
Ferguson combines legal and relationship advice in brief selections from his book.

★★★ *Divorce Ceremonies* http://www.globalideasbank.org/1993/1993-35.HTML
Based on a book, this site offers one page with a few ideas of a ceremony for marking the end of a marriage. This might be useful for anyone divorcing because our culture does not have a ceremony for marking the end of a marriage and going on.

Legal Aspects

★★★★★ *Divorce Helpline: Tools to Keep You Out of Court*
http://www.divorcehelp.com/index.html

Although this is a commercial site designed to sell books and make referrals, the brief articles in the Reading Room are very educational both legally and emotionally. The Short Divorce Course is an alternative to the courts and should certainly be considered.

★★★★ *Nolo Press* http://www.nolo.com/encyclopedia/mlt_ency.html
The site of Nolo Press sells do-it-yourself legal guides. Their Legal Encyclopedia offers about 30 complete and well-written readings on various legal aspects of divorce.

★★★★ *Annulment* http://marriage.about.com/msubanul.htm?pid=2817&cob=home
At this site are links to a dozen other sites with all the information one might need for seeking an annulment.

★★★★ *Flying Solo* http://www.flyingsolo.com
Click on Divorce Separation in the text or the left column. Here are perhaps 100 articles primarily on the legal and financial side of divorce, taxes, some tips, FAQs, and so

on. Some are too wordy or hard to read, but most are to the point. A fine site to which to refer those who can read a lot and need a lot of information on multiple aspects of divorce. Click on Mediation for several good introductions to mediation and its benefits.

★★★   *DivorceNet* http://www.DivorceNet.com

"The Net's largest divorce resource since May 1995" includes chat and by-state information. The site is legally oriented and searchable.

Kids, Custody, and Divorce

★★★★   *Focus on Kids: The Effects of Divorce on Children* by Karen B. DeBord
          http://muextension.missouri.edu/xplor/hesguide/humanrel/gh6600.htm

In about nine pages, this guide discusses the stresses on kids and their likely reactions.

★★★★   *Coping with Separation and Divorce: A Parenting Seminar* by Judy Branch, MS,
          and Lawrence G. Shelton, PhD
          http://www.nnfr.org/curriculum/topics/sep_div.html

Covers all the issues in about 45 pages of a handbook and curriculum guide.

★★★★   *Still a Dad* http://www.divorcedfather.com

Although designed to sell a book, this site provides focused readings, advice, resources, and so on for divorced fathers.

★★★★   *Child Custody and Access—US Legislation*
          http://home.clara.net/spig/us-law/detail-1.htm#top

If you want to understand the laws of most states, this site of nine pages will explain them in ordinary English.

★★★   *Child Custody and Divorce Resources State by State*
          http://www.custodysource.com/state.htm

The lists of links and resources under each state are a mixed bag of commercial sites, support groups, and public organizations. However, those seeking information or referral can likely find something of value here.

★★★   *Breaking the News* http://www.fsbassociates.com/fsg/whydivorce.html#Excerpt

Part of a book chapter, this site gives clear rules on how to tell and not to tell the kids about a divorce.

★★★   *Your Parents' Divorce* http://www.couns.uiuc.edu

A brief but good pamphlet from a university counseling service.

★★★ *Helping Your Child Cope with Separation and Divorce*
    http://www.cfc-efc.ca/docs/00000095.htm

Less that two pages, this site offers simple but practical rules.

★★★ *Learning to "Get Along" for the Best Interest of the Child* by Hedy Schleifer, MA
    http://www.magicnet.net/~hedyyumi/child.html

A four-page essay suitable as a handout to explain the value of counseling for kids after a divorce. Parts of it push Imago Relationship therapy.

See also Child Development and Parenting (Chapter 10); Families and Stepfamilies (Chapter 16); Marriage (Chapter 18).

NATIONAL SUPPORT GROUPS

ACES (Association for Children for Enforcement of Support)
2260 Upton Avenue
Toledo, OH 43606
Phone: 800-537-7072
Fax: 419-472-6295

Children's Rights Council
220 I Street NE, #200
Washington, DC 20002
Phone: 202-547-6227

Concerned parents provide education and advocacy for reform of the legal system regarding child custody.

Joint Custody Association
10606 Wilkins Avenue
Los Angeles, CA 90024
Phone: 310-475-6962

North American Conference of Separated and Divorced Catholics
80 St. Mary's Drive
Cranston, RI 02920
Phone: 401-943-7903

Rainbows
1111 Tower Road
Schaumburg, IL 60173
Phone: 708-310-1880

Establishes peer support groups in churches, schools, and social agencies for children and adults who are grieving after a death, divorce, or other painful transition in their family.

CHAPTER 15

Eating Disorders

We are a nation obsessed with food, spending an extraordinary amount of time thinking about it, gobbling it, and avoiding it. Eating disorders include compulsive overeating, anorexia nervosa (the relentless pursuit of thinness through starvation), bulimia (a binge-and-purge eating pattern), and a general obsession with weight and body image. Eating disorders are far more common in women than in men, the most extreme case being anorexia nervosa, in which about 95% of cases are female.

In this chapter, we critically review self-help books, autobiographies, movies, and Internet resources on eating disorders. Chapter 28 on Weight Management covers overlapping materials as well. Both chapters conclude with a listing of national support groups on these topics.

SELF-HELP BOOKS

Strongly Recommended

★★★★ *Dying to Be Thin: Understanding and Defeating Anorexia Nervosa and Bulimia— A Practical, Lifesaving Guide* (1987) by Ira M. Sacker and Marc A. Zimmer. New York: Warner.

This book is about the secrets and private worlds of the anorexic and bulimics. The authors have included sections on personal histories; information for the person with an eating disorder and their families, friends, and teachers; and resources. By reading this book, you will see how people can carry dangerous secrets for a long time before they admit that the secret has taken control of their lives. For the person who may think or know they suffer from an eating disorder, or those connected with someone with an eating disorder, this book provides insight, motivation, and knowledge about the complexity of eating disorders. The highest rated self-help book for eating disorders in our national studies.

RECOMMENDATION HIGHLIGHTS

Self-Help Books

- On the dangerous secrets and practical treatment of eating disorders:

  ★★★★ *Dying to Be Thin* by Ira M. Sacker and Marc A. Zimmer

- From compulsive eating to a healthy lifestyle:

  ★★★ *The Hunger Within* by Marilyn Ann Migliore with Philip Ross

  ★★★ *Healing the Hungry Self* by Deirdre Price

- A research-supported treatment for binge eating:

  ★★★ *Overcoming Binge Eating* by Christopher G. Fairburn

Autobiographies

- On the development of anorexia and its treatment:

  ★★★ *Am I Still Visible?* by Sandra Harvey Heater

- Harsh realities of anorexia and bulimia:

  ◆ *Good Enough* by Cynthia N. Bitter

Movies

- On the familial origins and drastic consequences of anorexia:

  ★★★★★ *The Karen Carpenter Story*

  ★★★★ *Best Little Girl in the World*

- A very serious comedy about women and food:

  ★★★★ *Eating*

Internet Resources

- Factual and well-organized sites for therapist and client alike:

  ★★★★★ *Something Fishy* http://www.something-fishy.org

  ★★★★ *Anorexia Nervosa and Related Eating Disorders*
  http://www.anred.com

- An excellent source of educational materials:

  ★★★★ *Eating Disorders Awareness and Prevention*
  http://www.edap.org

Recommended

★★★ *The Hunger Within: A Twelve-Week Guided Journey from Compulsive Eating to Recovery* (1998) by Marilyn Ann Migliore with Philip Ross. New York: Main Street.

This book shows the on-and-off dieter how his or her individual struggle with eating and weight is a response to feelings of emotional deprivation established in childhood. It provides a step-by-step program that explores the core reasons for overeating, identifies triggers that precipitate bingeing, and shows how to break the cycle of yo-yo dieting. The book includes motivational sayings, guided weekly sessions, exercises to help stay on track, a hunger awareness diary, a vicious cycle worksheet, and weekly food for thought programs. A person who eats compulsively is enacting an emotional script, and the script is what has to be changed. This is a twelve-week program with three stages. For people who have ridden the roller coaster of dieting, this book may prove to be helpful. A favorably evaluated book that, probably due to its recent publication, is not yet known by many mental health professionals.

★★★ *Healing the Hungry Self: The Diet-Free Solution to Lifelong Weight Management* (1998) by Deirdre Price. New York: Plume.

This book provides a comprehensive program for healthy eating using a variety of physical, mental, emotional, and spiritual concepts. The author addresses the difference between physical and emotional hunger, the importance of three meals a day, recognizing danger zones, alternatives to food in coping with emotions, and sensible exercise programs. There are case studies, self-help tests, charts to monitor progress, checklists, and a 6-week plan. Adults or adolescents wishing to modify their dietary lifestyles will find practical and useful advice in this 3-star resource, which was only recently published.

★★★ *Overcoming Binge Eating* (1995) by Christopher G. Fairburn. New York: Guilford Press.

Fairburn is a well-known authority on eating disorders. The book has two main parts. The first part reviews the current scientific literature about binge eating, and the second part offers a structured cognitive-behavior self-help manual to treat binge eating problems. This book speaks to the debate of addiction and eating disorders, which seems to be of particular interest in the United States. Given the reluctance of people with eating disorders to reveal their problem to anyone, the book could be a safe and helpful first step in accepting help and beginning treatment. The author advises friends and therapists on how they can use this book most effectively. A 3-star resource with research-supported treatment strategies.

★★★ *The Twelve Steps and Twelve Traditions of Overeaters Anonymous* (1995). Rio Rancho, NM: Overeaters Anonymous.

This book is devoted to detailed discussions of the Twelve Steps and Twelve Traditions used in Overeaters Anonymous (OA). This is a program of physical, emotional, and spiritual recovery based on the original Alcoholics Anonymous principles. The often-moving writing explains how OA's principles help members recover and the fellowships function. The common bonds shared by OA members are the disease of compulsive eating from which all have suffered, and the solutions found are in the principles embodied in the 12 steps. This book, in concert with an OA group and probably therapy, will prove helpful to people who find the spiritual emphasis of 12-step programs congenial.

★★★ *Fat Is a Family Affair* (1996) by Judi Hollis. Cedar City, MN: Hazelden.

This book covers a number of eating disorders, including the bingeing and vomiting of bulimia, the starvation of anorexia nervosa, and compulsive overeating. Hollis recommends a 12-step program as the best treatment for eating disorders. The book is divided into two main parts: Part I, The Weigh In, and Part II, The Weigh Out. The Weigh In discusses how eating disorders evolve and provides a self-test to determine if you have an eating disorder. Hollis says that eating disorders involve a physiological disorder and a psychological obsession with food. Further, she believes that most people with eating disorders are surrounded by 10 or 12 codependent people who, for reasons of their own, are enmeshed in trying to help or change the eating disorder but instead only perpetuate it. The reader is encouraged to attend or start an Overeaters Anonymous support group. Hollis includes many success stories of people who have followed her advice. Special attention is given to the family's role in eating disorders. This 3-star book promotes Overeaters Anonymous, which has helped many individuals learn to change their eating habits. But critics didn't like the preachy tone of the book and the codependency explanations.

★★★ *Why Weight? A Guide to Ending Compulsive Eating* (1989) by Geneen Roth. New York: Plume.

Geneen Roth founded the Breaking Free workshops that help people cope with eating disorders. She overcame her own compulsive overeating several years ago. First, she put an end to constant dieting that inevitably led to weight gain. She eliminated her compulsive overeating by developing seven eating guidelines that form the core of her Breaking Free program:

- Eat only when you are hungry.
- Eat only when sitting down.
- Eat without distractions.
- Eat only what you want.
- Eat until you are satisfied.
- Eat in full view of others.
- Eat with enjoyment.

The 16 chapters include written exercises that help compulsive overeaters become aware of what they are doing and information on the emotional basis of overeating, how it would feel to be thin, how it really felt to diet and binge all those years, and how the overeater can learn to eat only when physically hungry. Each chapter also contains charts and lists that focus on what is eaten, why, and when, and feelings associated with food. The 3-star book is full of helpful exercises for overeaters, is free of psychobabble, and provides insights about the nature of eating problems.

★★★   *When Food Is Love* (1991) by Geneen Roth. New York: Dutton.

This book explores the relation between eating disorders and close relationships. It was written by Geneen Roth, the author of *Why Weight?* The book focuses on how family experiences as we are growing up contribute to the development of eating disorders. Roth reveals her own childhood abuse, which led to compulsive overeating in adulthood and prevented her from having a successful intimate relationship with a man. According to Roth, similar patterns are found in people who are compulsive overeaters and lack intimacy in their life: excessive fantasizing, wanting what is forbidden, creating drama, needing to be in control, and the "one wrong move syndrome" (placing too much importance on doing the absolutely correct thing at this moment). This 3-star book does a good job of explaining how inadequate close relationships and eating disorders are linked. Critics say that Roth does not adequately consider biological and socio-cultural factors that determine eating disorders.

★★★   *Food for Thought* (1980) by the Hazelden Foundation. New York: Harper & Row.

Subtitled *Daily Meditations for Dieters*, this book presents a spiritually based approach to coping with eating disorders. The Hazelden Foundation is based near Minneapolis and is known primarily for its alcohol treatment program. Through short daily meditations, *Food for Thought* offers encouragement to anyone who has ever tried to diet, people who overeat or have an eating disorder, and members of Overeaters Anonymous. Each day's brief reading addresses the concerns of people with eating disorders. The book is especially designed for use by individuals who go to Overeaters Anonymous meetings, and it will have special appeal to individuals who want a spiritually based approach to coping with an eating problem.

Diamond in the Rough

♦   *The Body Betrayed: Women, Eating Disorders and Treatment* (1993) by
     Kathryn J. Zerbe. Washington, DC: American Psychiatric Press.

This book provides considerable information on the spectrum of eating disorders—the biological, social, and psychoanalytic aspects of these conditions as well as the dynamics of comorbidity (e.g., depression, abuse). In each chapter, Zerbe uses case studies to illuminate specific points. Chapters are devoted to the eating characteristics and dynamics of infants, children, athletes, and older women. Based on medical psychoanalytic theory, this book is geared more for the professional, although a well-read layperson may find it informative.

Not Recommended

★★   *You Can't Quit Eating until You Know What's Eating You* (1990) by
     Donna LeBlanc. Deerfield Beach, FL: Health Communications.

★   *Love Hunger: Recovery from Food Addiction* (1990) by Frank Minirth, Paul Meier,
     Robert Helmfelt, Sharon Sneed, and Don Hawkins. Nashville, TN: Thomas Nelson.

Strongly Not Recommended

†   *The Love-Powered Diet* (1992) by Victoria Moran. San Rafael, CA: New World Library.

AUTOBIOGRAPHIES

Recommended

★★★   *Am I Still Visible? A Woman's Triumph over Anorexia Nervosa* (1983) by
        Sandra Harvey Heater. White Hall, VT: Betterway.

The author, who teaches preschool reading, describes the development and treatment of her anorexia. She also provides a history of the disorder and theories and describes treatment options.

★★★   *Diary of a Fat Housewife: A True Story of Humor, Heartbreak, and Hope* (1995)
        by Rosemary Green. New York: Warner.

Now married with six children, this one-time beauty queen describes a 10-year battle with obesity. She began keeping a brutally honest journal at age 30 and tried various self-treatments. A good portrayal of what it means to be obese in America today.

★★★   *Starving for Attention* (1982) by Cherry Boone O'Neill. New York: Continuum.

A frank first-person account of the author's eating disorders; she had both anorexia and bulimia. Confronts the reader with the harsh realities and twisted perceptions of body image in both conditions. There is also a lengthy discussion of her personal life, career, and religious views.

Diamond in the Rough

◆   *Good Enough: When Losing Is Winning, Perfection becomes Obsession, and Thin
    Enough Can Never Be Achieved* (1998) by Cynthia N. Bitter. Penfield, NY:
    HopeLines Enterprises.

The author grew up in a difficult family situation. Her father had a bipolar disorder, and her mother was in denial about it. At age 14, she developed anorexia, binge-purge type, which almost resulted in her death, and this condition ended when she was 39. The book describes the numerous medical complications of the disorder, the self-destructive behaviors, the food obsessions, and the benefits of therapy, both inpatient and outpatient, that helped her finally overcome her disorder. Favorably but infrequently rated, probably owing to its recent publication; thus designated as a Diamond in the Rough.

MOVIES

Strongly Recommended

★★★★★   *The Karen Carpenter Story* (1989, made for TV) produced by
          Richard Carpenter III and directed by Richard Carpenter III and
          Joseph Sargent. 100 minutes.

Anorexia is portrayed as a family-based disorder that led singer Karen Carpenter to have little sense of control, except over the food she ate. Her brother Richard was designated the talented one of the family, and when Karen's voice overshadowed Richard's, she felt she had betrayed her parents' dream. The complexity and power of eating disorders come through effectively and accurately. This 5-star film biography of a contemporary pop star may serve as a valuable model for adolescent girls.

★★★★ *Best Little Girl in the World* (1981, made for TV) produced by Lynn Loving and directed by Sam O'Steen.

Being the second daughter and following a troublesome older sister sets Casey up for unrealistically high expectations of herself that place her on a trajectory toward self-starvation. When hospitalized, Casey meets two people, a fellow patient and a psychotherapist, who give her hope, support, and motivation. This story portrays the road to recovery and the need to confront longstanding familial conflicts.

★★★★ *Eating* (1990) directed and produced by Henry Jaglom. R Rating. 110 minutes.

A birthday party attended by women friends sets the stage for candid self-disclosures about relationships, food, money, food, loneliness, food, men, and food. In other words, many aspects of women's lives are revealed and shared, particularly women's love–hate relationship with eating. The characters are familiar and real people—people who make the subject seem ordinary, natural, and at times very funny. Subtitled *A Very Serious Comedy about Women and Food,* this movie is also rated under Women's Issues (Chapter 29).

Recommended

★★★ *For the Love of Nancy* (1994, made for TV) produced by Vin DiBona, Harry R. Sherman, Donna Stokes, and Lloyd Weintraub and directed by Paul Scheider.

Nancy is a very anxious high-school graduate whose social isolation, constant exercising, and sudden temper tantrums were clear signs of an addictive behavioral cycle, but no one heard. The familiar pattern of family attempts to force eating, resulting in further restraint from food, is well-illuminated. The story poignantly reveals that the family must experience healing and positive change before anorexia can be treated. This is a touching story with an overarching message that, in many cases, the family is the patient.

INTERNET RESOURCES

Metasites

★★★★★ *Something Fishy* http://www.something-fishy.org

A rich site well worth exploring; every therapist will learn something, and if a client reads even half the materials, he or she will understand the disorders very well. Old Fashioned Ideas is an excellent corrective to inaccuracies about eating disorders and sufferers. The *Eating Disorders Links* list is superb and enormous.

★★★★ *Anorexia Nervosa and Related Eating Disorders* http://www.anred.com

The factual materials here are numerous, detailed, and organized. They can be edited into handouts. They also deal with rarely addressed issues and disorders.

★★★★ *Mental Health Net, Eating Disorders* http://mentalhelp.net/guide/eating.htm

A superb and rich site for accessing information on all aspects of eating disorders.

★★★★ *The Mining Company* http://eatingdisorders.miningco.com

The Mining Company editors have found and evaluated hundreds of sites and keep them updated. Cultural Issues and Body Image are especially good.

Psychoeducational Materials for Clients and Families

★★★★ *Eating Disorders Awareness and Prevention* http://www.edap.org

A source of several dozen educational brochures (under ED Info) and curriculum materials for sale. For example, How to Help a Friend with an Eating Disorder could be a useful handout for school presentations.

★★★★ *Eating Disorders Articles* http://www.noah-health.org/english/illness/ mentalhealth/mental.html#Eating%20Disorders

About 20 readings from national sources. Each could serve as a handout and several would make a good introductory package.

★★★★ *National Eating Disorders Organization (NEDO)* http://www.kidsource.com/nedo/

Among the best educational materials with clear explanations of dynamics and causative factors, focused materials for families, information to use in school settings, and criteria for evaluating a treatment option.

★★★★ *Mirror, Mirror* http://www.mirror-mirror.org/eatdis.htm

Relapse prevention does not use the Marlatt model, but the Relapse Prevention Plan is a fill-in form that may be clinically useful, and Relapse Warning Signs is a good list.

★★★★ *Close to You* http://closetoyou.org/eatingdisorders

The sections on Medical Complications, Caffeine, Why Our Bodies Need Fats, Dehydration, Nutrition, Vitamin Deficiencies, Normal Eating, OTC Drug Use, and Diet Drugs contain educationally useful facts.

★★★ *Is Food a Problem? (Eating Disorders)* http://www.utexas.edu/student/cmhc/eating.html

There are three factual brochures here, each well-written and for college students, but more widely usable.

★★★ *Anorexia and Bulimia* http://www.rcpsych.ac.uk/public/help/anor/anor_frame.htm

A brief (five-page) but comprehensive overview of symptoms, causes, and treatment.

★★★　*Anorexia Nervosa General Information*
　　　　http://mentalhelp.net/factsfam/anorexia.htm

A good introductory text in six pages from the federal government.

★★★　*Peace, Love, and Hope*
　　　　http://www.healthyplace.com/Communities/Eating_Disorders/peacelovehope

Click on Body Views to access body dysmorphic disorder; this seems to be the only site with this information.

★★★　*Tips for Doctors*　http://www.something-fishy.org

Under Doctors and Patients, this offers well-articulated fears of patients to sensitize health care providers.

★★★　*The Road to an Eating Disorder Is Paved with Diet Rules*
　　　　http://closetoyou.org/eatingdisorders/road.htm

Simple and hard-hitting.

★★★　*Eating Disorders*
　　　　http://closetoyou.org/eatingdisorders/sitemap.htm

This site includes articles such as "The Road to an Eating Disorder Is Paved with Diet Rules" and "Eating Disorder Self Test and Perfectionism Scale." "How You Can Help Someone with an Eating Disorder" includes four pages of good ideas and advice for realtives and friends of the client and "15 Styles of Distorted Thinking" is a good reference for cognitive therapy including good explanations of each of the styles.

★★★　*15 Styles of Distorted Thinking*
　　　　http://closetoyou.org/eatingdisorders/disthink.htm

Each style is explained well in the eight pages. A good reference for cognitive therapy.

★★★　*Harvard Eating Disorders Center*　http://www.hedc.org/about.html

Do I Have a Problem? is a fine short summary.

Other Resources

★★★★★　*The Gurze Bookstore*　http://www.gurze.com/titlecat.htm

Hundreds of books about eating disorders, with brief reviews and ways to order online.

Online Support Groups

Support-Group.com
http://www.support-group.com/cgi-bin/sg/get_links?eating_disorders

This site allows reading of postings to the Bulletin Board, access to lists of local support groups, and government and national organizations' sites.

Something Fishy http://www.something-fishy.org/online/options.php

Besides massive amounts of information, this site offers both live chat and Chat Guest appearances, America Online's Instant Messenger discussion groups, and family and friends support access.

Alt.Support.Eating-Disord

A well-organized compilation of information for, by, and about anorexics as well as a bulletin board.

See also Weight Management (Chapter 28).

NATIONAL SUPPORT GROUPS

American Anorexia/Bulimia Association
293 Central Park West, #1R
New York, NY 10024
Phone: 212-891-8686

For persons with eating disorders.

Compulsive Eaters Anonymous
PO Box 4403
10016 Pioneer Boulevard, Suite 101
Santa Fe Springs, CA 90670
Phone: 310-942-8161
Fax: 310-948-3721

A 12-step recovery program.

Food Addicts Anonymous
Phone: 561-967-3871
http://www.foodadictsanonymous.org

To find a local group, visit the website or call the World Service Office. No materials are available at the website, but books, articles, and tapes can be ordered.

National Association of Anorexia Nervosa and Associated Disorders
PO Box 7
Highland Park, IL 60035
Phone: 847-831-3438

For persons with eating disorders.

National Eating Disorders Organization
6655 South Yale Avenue
Tulsa, OK 74136-3329
Phone: 918-481-4044

For persons with eating disorders, their families, and friends.

Overeaters Anonymous (OA)
PO Box 44020
Rio Rancho, NM 87174-4020
Phone: 505-891-2664
http://www.overeatersanonymous.org

A 12-step self-help fellowship. Free local and online meetings are listed on the website.

We Insist on Natural Shapes (WINS)
PO Box 19938
Sacramento, CA 95819
Phone: 800-600-WINS
http://www.winsnews.org

A nonprofit organization dedicated to educating adults and children about what normal, healthy shapes are.

CHAPTER 16

Families and Stepfamilies

"A friend loves you for your intelligence, a mistress for your charm, but your family's love is unreasoning; you were born into it and are of its flesh and blood. Nevertheless, it can irritate you more than any group in the world," observed French philosopher André Maurois. Families who do not function well together often foster maladjusted behavior on the part of one or more members.

In this chapter we limit our evaluation to general books on families and stepfamilies, especially those that examine how families or blending families can be a source of distress. Other chapters cover the family's role in a number of specific areas, such as abuse (Chapter 2), addictive disorders (Chapter 3), child development (Chapter 10), divorce (Chapter 16), love and intimacy (Chapter 17), marriage (Chapter 18), and teenagers (Chapter 27).

Children born in the United States today have a 40% chance of living at least part of their lives in a stepfamily before they are 18 years of age. Stepfamilies are a heterogeneous group—about 70% are stepfather families, about 20% are stepmother families, and about 10% are so-called blended families to which both partners bring children from previous marriages. And many stepfamilies produce children of their own. We review a number of self-help resources directed specifically at stepfamilies and blended families.

Following our summary of recommended self-help resources, we consider in detail books, movies, and Internet resources related to families and stepfamilies. A list of national support groups rounds out the chapter.

SELF-HELP BOOKS

Strongly Recommended

★★★★★ *Old Loyalties, New Ties: Therapeutic Strategies with Step-Families* (1988) by
Emily Visher and John Visher. New York: Brunner/Mazel.

This book covers a broad range of topics designed to help stepfamilies cope more effectively. Visher and Visher argue that remarried families are not imperfect copies of

RECOMMENDATION HIGHLIGHTS

Self-Help Books

- For a family systems therapy approach to solving family problems:

  ★★★★ *The Family Crucible* by Augustus Napier and Carl Whitaker

- For a wide variety of family and stepfamily circumstances:

  ★★★★ *Old Loyalties, New Ties* by Emily Visher and John Visher

  ★★★ *The Shelter of Each Other* by Mary Pipher

- For stepfathers:

  ★★★★ *Step-Fathering* by Mark Rosin

- For blended families:

  ★★★★ *Step by Step-Parenting* by James D. Eckler

  ◆ *Stepfamilies* by James H. Bray and John Kelly

Movies

- Transcendent film about victimized mothers wanting more for their children:

  ★★★★★ *The Joy Luck Club*

- On the enduring value of flawed love in mother–daughter relationships:

  ★★★★ *Terms of Endearment*

- Fraternal bonding and moral growth in caring for a mentally disordered sibling:

  ★★★★ *Rain Man*

- On healing a strained parental relationship by helping others:

  ★★★★ *Fly away Home*

- A family driven by disabilities discovers inner strength:

  ★★★★ *What's Eating Gilbert Grape?*

- The pain of parental abuse and the resilience of children:

  ★★★★ *Radio Flyer*

Internet Resources

- For information on the legal side of remarriage:

  ★★★★★ *Family Court and You: An Informational Guide to the Family Court* http://www.nysba.org/public/famcourtandu.html

- For infertility and adoption:

  ★★★★ *Shared Journey* http://www.sharedjourney.com

nuclear families but are rather family systems created from the integration of old loyalties and new ties. They outline special therapeutic strategies they believe are most effective with stepfamilies—such as helping stepfamily members gain or enhance their self-esteem, reducing a sense of helplessness, teaching negotiation, and encouraging mutually rewarding dyadic relationships—all designed to achieve greater integration and stability in the stepfamily. Concrete ways in which therapists can help stepfamilies with specific types of problems are also described. Among them are how to deal with the many changes and losses in their lives, identify realistic belief systems so that expectations are manageable, resolve loyalty conflicts, develop suitable and adequate boundaries, cope with life-cycle discrepancies and complexities, and create a more equal distribution of power. Many case study examples illustrate the authors' therapy strategies. This is a very good book about remarried families, but it was written primarily for a professional audience rather than a self-help audience. Nonetheless, it is well-written, and the self-help reader can gain considerable insight into the dynamics of remarried families and which therapy strategies are most effective.

★★★★ *The Family Crucible* (1978) by Augustus Napier and Carl Whitaker.
    New York: Harper & Row.

This book presents a family systems approach to solving family problems. In family systems therapy, the family unit is viewed as a system of interacting individuals with different subsystems (husband–wife, sibling–sibling, mother–daughter, father–sibling–sibling, and so on). A basic theme is that most problems that seem to be the property of a single individual evolved from relationships within the family. Therefore, the best way to solve problems is to work with the family rather than the individual. One person within a family may show some disturbing symptoms, but those symptoms are viewed as a function of family relationships. Napier and Whitaker say that problem families have in common certain general patterns: acute interpersonal or intrapersonal stress, polarization (family members at odds with each other) and escalation (the conflict intensifies), triangulation (one member is the scapegoat for other members who are in conflict but pretend not to be), blaming, diffusion of identity (no one is free to be autonomous), and fear of immobility, which Napier and Whitaker equate with fear of death (of the family). The authors describe in considerable detail how they used family systems therapy with a particular family—an angry adolescent and other angry and equally distressed family members. This book is widely considered to be one of the classics in family systems therapy. However, it is written mainly for a professional audience and may be perceived as somewhat dated.

★★★★ *Step by Step-Parenting: A Guide to Successful Living with a Blended Family* (2nd
    ed., 1993) by James D. Eckler. White Hall, VA: Betterway Publications.

This book, as is evident from its title, is about blended families, families to which each adult has brought children from a previous marriage. The book reflects both the adjustments that made author James Eckler's blended family a successful one and his years of experience as a minister and pastoral counselor. A wide array of issues are covered, including the games stepchildren play, the rights of the stepparent, name changes, the pros and cons of adoption, discipline, stepsibling rivalries, marital communication, grandparents, and dealing with children at different developmental levels (preschool, elementary school, and adolescence). Our mental health experts said that this is a good self-help book for blended families—it presents a balanced approach and includes detailed discussions of blended families' stressful experiences, the variations that exist in blended families, and wise strategies for successful living in a blended family.

★★★★ *Step-Fathering* (1987) by Mark Rosin. New York: Simon & Schuster.

This was among the first self-help books to describe the stepfather family experience from the stepfather's perspective. Rosin draws on his own experiences as a stepfather and in-depth interviews with more than 50 stepfathers to help men cope effectively in a stepfather family. Chapters take stepfathers through such topics as the adjustment involved in becoming a stepfather, the problems of combining families and some possible solutions, how to handle discipline and authority, communication with the wife/mother, dealing with the other father, money matters, adolescent stepchildren, and the rewards of stepfathering. The expert consensus is that this is a fine self-help book for stepfathers. It is well-written and includes insightful examples that most stepfathers will be able to relate to.

Recommended

★★★ *Families: Applications of Social Learning to Family Life* (rev. ed., 1975) by Gerald Patterson. Champaign, IL: Research Press.

This volume presents a behavioral approach to improving children's behavior. To begin, Patterson explains some important behavioral concepts like social reinforcers, aversive stimuli, and accidental training. Time-out procedures and behavioral contracts are integrated into a step-by-step reinforcement management program for parents to implement with their own children. Behavioral management strategies are also tailored to children with specific problems. This book was very favorably evaluated by our mental health experts, but by only 12 of them, thus leading to a lower rating. Mental health professionals of a behavioral persuasion described this book as exceptionally good for parents who want to improve a child's behavior, especially the behavior of a child who is aggressive and out of control.

★★★ *The Shelter of Each Other: Rebuilding Our Families* (1996) by Mary Pipher. New York: Grosset/Putnam.

This is not a how-to book but a how-to-think book that sensitively exposes the breadth of struggles and problems facing families today. Pipher brings us face to face with a culture in which parents sell girl scout cookies to colleagues because girl scouts can't go door to door anymore and with an electronic revolution that has resulted in making media personalities more recognizable than neighbors. Pipher organizes the stories of families who are struggling with the times around the three central themes of character, will, and commitment. Through these themes, she brings hope that we as families and as community can shelter each other and decide the future and the culture we want, now that we see what we have become. This book was highly rated in our national study (average rating of 1.43) but only evaluated by 14 experts, probably because the book was recently released.

★★★ *Back to the Family* (1990) by Ray Guarendi. New York: Basic Books.

Subtitled *How to Encourage Traditional Values in Complicated Times,* this book is the result of a study sponsored by the Children's Hospital in Akron, Ohio, to identify the characteristics of healthy, adaptive families. One hundred happy families were nominated by award-winning educators in the National/State Teachers of the Year organization. Guarendi distilled information from interviews with the families and developed a how-to manual for parents who want to build a happy home. The interviews reveal how families can mature through good and bad times and how parents in happy, competent families sifted through various types of child-rearing advice to arrive at the way they reared their own children. At times the book is inspirational, but families frequently need more than a pep talk to solve their problems.

★★★ *The Second Time Around: Why Some Second Marriages Fail* (1991) by Louis Janda and Ellen MacCormack. New York: Carol Publishing Group.

Janda and MacCormack conducted a study of more than a hundred people who were in second marriages, which furnished much of the material in this book. Readers learn that a majority of individuals in stepfamilies find the adjustment to be more difficult than they anticipated. Janda and MacCormack believe that many people have expectations that are too high when they enter a stepfamily. And they say that stepchildren make any second marriage a challenge. The book received a 3-star rating because it was positively reviewed, but by only 10 respondents. The few mental health professionals who knew about it opined that it included a number of good examples of stepfamily problems and how to solve them effectively.

★★★ *Love in the Blended Family: Stepfamilies* (1991) by Angela Clubb. Deerfield Beach, FL: Health Communications.

This self-help resource concerns stepmother families, not blended families in the accepted sense of the term. At the beginning of the book, Clubb tells readers that what they are reading is biased because it is written by a stepmother and second wife. Her husband brought two children to the newly formed stepmother family, and the Clubbs subsequently had two children of their own. Thus, the book is primarily about relationships and experiences in one stepmother family, although Clubb does occasionally bring in mental health experts' views on stepfamily issues. This 3-star effort clearly shows Clubb's professional background as a writer; the book reads in places like a finely tuned novel. Many of the problems and issues Clubb has experienced in her stepmother family are those that any stepmother has to face.

★★★ *Strengthening Your Stepfamily* (1986) by Elizabeth Einstein and Linda Albert. Circle Pines, MN: American Guidance Service.

This 133-page book contains five comprehensive chapters. Chapter 1 describes stepfamily structure and how it is different from previous family structure. The authors discuss common stepfamily myths and unrealistic expectations. Chapter 2 focuses on the couple relationship and how to communicate more effectively and share feelings. Chapter 3 examines the basic strategies for creating positive relationships between stepparents and stepchildren. Chapter 4 explores children's feelings and behaviors in stepfamilies along with guidelines for helping children cope more effectively. Chapter 5 discusses the developmental process of making a stepfamily function well, along with hints for dealing with issues that range from daily routines to holiday celebrations. The book was positively rated in our national studies, but by only 10 respondents. This is an extremely easy-to-read overview of stepfamily problems and ways to solve them. A number of exercises are included, and readers are asked many questions that will stimulate them to think about applying the knowledge.

★★★ *Blending Families: A Guide for Parents, Stepparents, Grandparents, and Everyone Building a Successful New Family* (1999) by Elaine F. Shimberg. New York: Berkley.

This self-help resource takes a unique approach in viewing stepfamily dynamics. Interviews, surveys, and discussion groups were conducted, and the resulting information and experiences were recorded in the book. The information is presented in a practical fashion, with ideas and perspectives offered directly by stepfamily members about what worked for them and what strengthened their families. The book contains reflective quotes from adult children of stepfamilies looking back on their experiences as well as contemporary quotes by stepfamily members on a variety of family problems and challenges. The author intended the book to be a practical guide based on actual successes and shortcomings of real people who have lived in a stepfamily system. The content of the book is not only directed at stepparents, but also at stepchildren and extended family members.

★★★ *Adult Children: The Secrets of Dysfunctional Families* (1988) by John Friel and Linda Friel. Deerfield Beach, FL: Health Communications.

This book is primarily intended for adults who grew up in dysfunctional families and suggests what they can do to improve their lives. Modeled after the Twelve-Step program of Alcoholics Anonymous, it tries to shed light on why adults who grew up in dysfunctional families developed problems as adults—problems such as addiction, depression, compulsion, unhealthy dependency, stress disorders, and unsatisfying relationships. Five sections discuss (1) who adult children are and what their symptoms are, (2) family systems and how dysfunctional families get off track, (3) how the dysfunctional family affects the child, (4) a model of codependency, and (5) recovery. *Adult Children* barely received a 3-star rating; many mental health experts frown on the codependency approach of the authors.

Diamond in the Rough

♦ *Stepfamilies: Love, Marriage, and Parenting in the First Decade* (1998) by James H. Bray and John Kelly. New York: Broadway.

The results of a major 9-year project on the development of stepfamilies are presented clearly and meaningfully through the emerging findings of three types of stepfamilies and the identification of three cycles through which stepfamilies move. Converting these findings into a book provides an insider's look at understanding these three stepfamily types and how the three developmental cycles of a stepfamily can positively and negatively affect each. The information is nicely woven into many scenarios and played out through the stories of these composite family members. Special focus is given to important aspects of the stepfamily structure, such as bridging the insider–outsider gap, the stepmother, the nonresidential parent, and adolescence. This Diamond in the Rough book was recently published but received very high ratings from our respondents.

Not Recommended

★★ *Bradshaw on the Family* (1988) by John Bradshaw. Deerfield Beach, FL: Health Communications.

MOVIES

Strongly Recommended

★★★★★ *The Joy Luck Club* (1994) produced by Wayne Wang, Amy Tan, Ronald Bass, and Patrick Markey and directed by Wayne Wang. R Rating. 138 minutes.

This is a film about neither joy nor luck, but about hope and triumph of the will. When one of a group of four Chinese immigrant women dies, the event prompts the recollections of great hardships, despair, and loss and, most importantly, the effect these experiences had on their relationships with their own daughters. Two of the dominant themes are the effects of feelings of self-worthlessness on women's lives and mothers' desire for a better life for their children. This heartwarming 5-star film transcends culture, race, and generations.

★★★★ *Terms of Endearment* (1983) produced and directed by James L. Brooks. PG Rating. 130 minutes.

This film dominated the Academy Awards in 1983, but its popular acclaim should not overshadow its therapeutic value and portrayal of characters who struggle with enmeshment, marital infidelity, and loss in a poignant and heartwrenching way. The mother, Aurora, is overprotective, dominant, and consumed by running her daughter's life, while the daughter is overattached and dependent. A midlife relationship changes Aurora, while infidelity and sickness change her daughter. The film's enduring messages are the value of (flawed) love, strength in (flawed) relationships, and familial survival through pain.

★★★★ *Rain Man* (1988) produced by Mark Johnson, Peter Guber, and Jon Peters and directed by Barry Levinson. R Rating. 130 minutes.

Twenty-something Charlie, disinherited by his deceased father, discovers that he has an autistic older brother, Raymond, who has inherited the father's $3 million. The real story, however, is about Charlie's learned selflessness, the brothers' fraternal bonding, and Charlie's moral growth as he learns to care for Raymond. Raymond is tragic and funny, a survivor and yet fragile; he has built a life of required predictability that Charlie can penetrate only momentarily. This film realistically portrays mental illness and what it means to the life of a family. *Rain Man* deservedly garnered four Academy Awards in 1988, including Best Picture.

★★★★ *Fly away Home* (1996) produced by John Veitch and Carol Baum and directed by Carroll Ballard. PG Rating. 107 minutes.

Adolescent Amy loses her mother in an auto accident and must move from her home in New Zealand to Canada to live with her father, with whom she has a strained relationship. When Amy finds a gaggle of geese that follow her around and will not fly on their own, she and her father join forces to nurture the geese and teach them how to fly. This is a classic story of the healer who is healed through caring for others. Amy and her father find common ground and common values in assisting others and in identifying with the desire to fly free.

★★★★ *What's Eating Gilbert Grape?* (1994) produced by Meir Teper, Bertil Ohlsson, and David Matalon and directed by Lasse Hallstrom. PG-13 Rating. 118 minutes.

The energy, the relationships, and the purpose of life for the members of the Grape family are driven by disabilities. The father committed suicide; the mother subsequently ballooned to 500 pounds and developed mild agoraphobia; and one son has severe mental retardation. The mother places herself squarely in the lives of the family, while the breadwinning son becomes responsible for all family members. This story is about family loyalty, community caring, fraternal caretaking, a mother's letting go, and most of all, the power of internal strength.

★★★★ *Radio Flyer* produced by Lauren Shuler-Donner and directed by Richard Donner. PG-13 Rating. 120 minutes.

Life becomes horrific for Mike and Bobby when their mother marries an alcoholic man who physically and verbally abuses them. They escape into their own world as they dream of turning their Radio Flyer wagon into an airplane in order to fly away. The film reveals the pain of physical abuse, living with substance abuse, the denial of the mother about what is happening, and the valiant attempts of young children to insulate their mother from pain. This is a story for everyone who has walked this path and for people who have experienced the resilience of children in an abusive home. Also reviewed in Abuse (Chapter 2).

Recommended

★★★ *The Father of the Bride* (1991) produced by Nancy Meyers, Carol Baum, and Howard Rosenman and directed by Charles Shyer. PG Rating. 114 minutes.

George and Nina are the parents of a daughter who has grown up when they weren't looking. The daughter has distressed her father by announcing her engagement. The film continues with the antics of wedding plans, costs, invitations, but underneath is the story of a father who sees himself losing his little girl and fighting it by complaining about expense, potential flaws in the fiancé, and the bossiness of the wedding coordinator. The film is touching and funny and speaks to all families moving through adult–child transitions.

INTERNET RESOURCES

Metasites

★★★★ *Flying Solo* http://www.flyingsolo.com

A fine site dedicated to single parenting. Click on Divorce and Separation on the left or in the text, and then on Remarriage and Stepfamilies. The 25 articles cover finances, law, prenuptual and other agreements, and research. SAA Article and Research Findings about Stepchildren leads to two articles for kids. This site could be a useful addition to a more focused set of readings.

Psychoeducational Materials for Clients and Families

Families (General)

★★★★ *Family Life Library*
          http://www.oznet.ksu.edu/library/famlf2/#Family%20Living

Numerous articles suitable as handouts and brochures from a Kansas State University program. They have to be downloaded and opened in Adobe's Acrobat Reader.

★★★★★ *Fathering Magazine* http://www.fathermag.com

Hundreds of articles are available online. The site might be ideal for expanding and validating a father's view of his role.

Blended Families/Stepfamilies

★★★★★ *Stepfamily in Formation* http://www.stepfamilyinfo.org/sitemap.htm

There are about 700 pages of information and ideas here, covering almost every family topic. There is a lot to read, but it is clearly written and well-arrayed. It does not espouse any exclusive perspective and is of use in any kind of family structure. Use the left column headings to navigate, but it will take a while to grasp the site's organization and which pages are of value. Under Mail Order are about 20 booklets, many with worksheets that could be used in workshops. Thank you, Peter Gerlach, MSW.

★★★★★ *Family Court and You: An Informational Guide to the Family Court*
          http://www.nysba.org/public/famcourtandu.html

All about the legal side of remarriage. Although from New York State, it offers a complete orientation to the procedures, roles, and functions of the Family Court in about 20 pages.

★★★★ *Supporting Stepfamilies: What Do the Children Feel?*
    http://www.ianr.unl.edu/pubs/NebFacts/nf223.htm

Focuses on the emotions of children during blending or combining families.

★★★★ *Divorce and the Family in America* by Christopher Lasch
    www.TheAtlantic.com/politics/family/divorce.htm

For those needing a historical perspective on family and divorce, this is superb, despite being from 1966. College education may be needed.

★★★★ *Parenting Apart: Patterns of Childrearing after Marital Disruption*
    by Frank Furstenberg, Jr., and Christine Winquist Nord
    http://www1.tpgi.com.au/users/resolve/ncpreport/Furstenberg(1985).html

A good national survey of the qualities of family relations. It clearly shows that a former spouse's remaining active with the kids is a very positive influence. Perhaps could be motivational for some clients.

★★★★ *Wicked Stepmothers, Fact or Fiction?*
    http://www.snowcrest.net/skiing/stepmom.htm

A seven-page paper that details the pervasiveness and harm done by culturally transmitted stereotypes of stepmothers. Thought-provoking materials for counseling. See also *The Evil Stepmother* by Marueen F. McHugh at http://www.en.com/users/mcq/stepmother.html.

★★★★ *Ten Steps for Steps*
    http://www.stepfamily.org/tensteps.html#forstepfath

Actually 80 steps because there are guidelines for all roles and relatives. These might be useful handouts to focus discussions on issues and practices.

★★★ *Blended Families* by Willard F. Harley, Jr., PhD
    http://www.parenthoodweb.com/parent_cfmfiles/pros.cfm/155

A two-page essay on resolving conflicts in blended families.

★★★ *Stepfamily Information* http://www.positive-way.com/step.htm

This site has four sections: an introduction with 11 good suggestions, Tips for Stepfathers, Tips for Stepmothers, and Tips for Remarried Parents. They are all very brief but could be useful.

★★★ *Stepfamilies on Television* by Marie Van Dam
    http://www.msu.edu/course/mc/111/journal/STEPFAMS.html

Only two pages, but it may help people differentiate media portrayals from reality.

★★★   *How to Succeed as a Stepfather* by Barbara F. Meltz
http://www.boston.com/globe/columns/meltz/061898.htm

Only four pages, but deals with important issues: discipline, closeness, rejection.

★★★   *Adjusting to the Stepfamily*
http://stepparenting.about.com/msubadj.htm?pid=2803&cob=home

Here you will find links to about 20 articles on the conflicts of entering and making blended families work.

Single-Parent Families

★★★★   *Single Rose: Article Database*   http://www.singlerose.com/articles/

About 60 articles on many aspects of being a single mom, such as Arts and Crafts, Child Development, Education, Family Concerns, Home Maintenance, and Time Management. A smaller-scale place to start exploring than the metasites.

★★★   *Facts about Single Parent Families*
http://www.parentswithoutpartners.org/Support1.htm

A two-page list of surprising facts; possibly useful for overcoming stereotypes and media illusions.

★★★   *Practical Parenting . . . Tips to Grow On*
http://www.parentswithoutpartners.org/Support2.htm

A six-page listing of practical advice on topics like Coping and Grieving, Talking to Children, Child Discipline, Visitation, and Never Married Parents. A useful quick guide for beginning discussions of single parenthood.

Adoption

★★★★   *Shared Journey*   http://www.sharedjourney.com

This site offer materials on infertility and adoption. There is a mini-textbook on infertility's medical aspects. Just keep clicking for a full education. The Adoption button leads to some basic readings.

★★★   *The Adopted Child*   http://www.aacap.org/publications/factsfam/adopted.htm

A brief essay on telling a child about his or her adoption.

★★★   *Adopt . . .*   http://www.adopting.org

The site is an adoption service, but under Library are many articles on this complex process and its outcomes. Look down the list for Professional Articles to give to clients.

See also Divorce (Chapter 14); Child Development and Parenting (Chapter 10); Men's Issues (Chapter 19); Women's Issues (Chapter 29).

NATIONAL SUPPORT GROUPS

Adoptive Families of America
3333 Highway 100 North
Minneapolis, MN 55422
Phone: 612-535-4829

For adoptive and prospective adoptive families.

Concerned United Birthparents (CUB)
2000 Walker Street
Des Moines, IA 50317
Phone: 800-822-2777

For adoption-affected people.

National Foster Parent Association
226 Kilts Drive
Houston, TX 77024
Phone: 713-467-1850

Support, education, and advocacy for foster parents and their children.

NCSAC (National Child Support Advocacy Coalition)
PO Box 4629
Alexandria, VA 22303-0629
Phone: 800-84-NCSAC

Advocates for child support enforcement and collection.

Parents without Partners
401 North Michigan Avenue
Chicago, IL 60611-4287
Phone: 800-637-7974

Stepfamily Association of America
215 Centennial Mall, #212
Lincoln, NE 68508-1814
Phone: 800-735-0329

Information and advocacy for stepfamilies.

CHAPTER 17

Love and Intimacy

For centuries, philosophers, songwriters, and poets have been intrigued by what love is. Only recently, though, have psychologists turned their attention to love and offered recommendations on how to improve your love life and your intimacy.

Love is a vast and complex territory of human behavior. Much of romantic love and physical intimacy has traditionally occurred in the context of marriage, a topic to which we devote the next chapter (Chapter 18). In this chapter, we cover self-help books, movies, and Internet resources devoted to love and intimacy, which admittedly overlaps with the following chapter. Indeed, simply because of the immense pool of resources, we chose not to review the thousands of autobiographies touching on the subject.

SELF-HELP BOOKS

Strongly Recommended

★★★★★ *Love Is Never Enough* (1988) by Aaron Beck. New York: Harper & Row.

This volume presents a cognitive therapy approach to love from one of the founders of cognitive therapy. Beck tells couples how to overcome misunderstandings, resolve conflicts, and improve their relationship by following cognitive therapy strategies. Beck first helps partners understand the specific self-defeating attitudes that plague their troubled relationships. Then he applies his cognitive therapy approach to what he labels the most common marital problems:

- How negative perceptions can overwhelm the positive aspects of marriage.
- The swing from idealization to disillusionment.
- The clash of differing perspectives.
- The imposition of rigid expectations and rules.
- How partners fail to hear what is said and often hear things that are not said.

RECOMMENDATION HIGHLIGHTS

Self-Help Books

- On improving loving relationships with cognitive therapy:

  ★★★★★ *Love Is Never Enough* by Aaron Beck

- On the nature of love and the forms of love:

  ★★★★ *The Art of Loving* by Erich Fromm

  ★★★★ *The Triangle of Love* by Robert Sternberg

- On improving intimate relationships by understanding yourself and previous relationships:

  ★★★★ *The Dance of Intimacy* by Harriet Lerner

  ◆ *In the Meantime* by Iyanla Vanzant

Movies

- Changing romantic partners as couples grow old together:

  ★★★ *The Four Seasons*

- The complexity and challenge of contemporary heterosexual relationships:

  ★★★ *When Harry Met Sally*

Internet Resources

- Useful sites on love:

  ★★★★★ *Love and Relationships* http://www.topchoice.com/~psyche/love

  ★★★★ *Love Is Great* http://loveisgreat.com

- An acceptable place to seek relationships:

  ★★★★ *Singlescoach* http://www.singlescoach.com/resources.html

---

- How personal bias disrupts a relationship.
- How automatic negative thinking leads to conflict.
- How partners cognitively distort a relationship that drives couples apart.

In the last half of the book, Beck presents a number of different cognitive therapy approaches to fit the specific needs of couples. The book was written primarily as a self-help guide to improve love relationships and it remains the highest-rated book in its category. Practical, inspiring, and clear.

★★★★ *The Dance of Intimacy: A Woman's Guide to Courageous Acts of Change in Key Relationships* (1989) by Harriet Lerner. New York: Harper Perennial.

Written for women and about women's intimate relationships, *The Dance of Intimacy* weaves a portrait of our current self and relationships that Lerner believes is derived from longstanding relationships with mothers, fathers, and siblings. Drawing on a combination of psychoanalytic and family systems theories, Lerner tells women that, if they are having problems in intimate relationships with a partner or their family of origin, they need to explore their upbringing to find clues to the current difficulties. Women learn how to avoid distancing themselves from their families of origin and overreacting to problems. Lerner intelligently tells women that they should balance the *I* and the *we* in their lives and be neither too self-absorbed nor too other-oriented. To explore unhealthy patterns that have been passed down from one generation to the next, Lerner helps women create a "genogram," a family diagram that goes back to the grandparents or earlier. This is an outstanding self-help book on understanding why close relationships are problematic and how to change them in positive ways. It does not give simple, quick-fix strategies. Lerner accurately avows that change is difficult, but she shows that it is possible. The extensive examples and case studies are well chosen.

★★★★ *The Art of Loving* (1956) by Erich Fromm. New York: Harper & Row.

This philosophical and psychological treatise on the nature of love was penned by Dr. Erich Fromm, a well-known psychoanalyst and social philosopher. He describes love in general, as well as different forms of love. In Fromm's view, love is an attitude that determines the relatedness of the person to the whole world, not just toward one love object. Love is an act of faith, a commitment, a complete giving of oneself. There are no quick fixes for developing love; rather Fromm argues that learning to love is a long and difficult process, requiring discipline, concentration, patience, sensitivity to self, and the productive use of skills. Fromm stresses that although the principle underlying capitalistic society and the principle of love are incompatible, love is the only sane and satisfactory solution to the human condition. As such, this book is very different from most of the books evaluated in our national studies; it doesn't include the usual exercises, case histories, and clinical examples. Rather, *The Art of Loving* tackles the complex question of what love is and how society can benefit if people learn how to love more effectively. Widely regarded as a classic, this is an intellectually challenging piece that is not written as clearly as most self-help books.

★★★★ *The Triangle of Love* (1987) by Robert Sternberg. New York: Basic Books.

The three sides of the triangle of love are the fire of sexual and romantic passion, the close emotional sharing of intimacy, and the enduring bond of commitment. The type and quality of a relationship depend on the strength of each side of the triangle in each partner and how closely the partners' triangles match. Sternberg argues that each side has its own timetable. For example, passion dominates the early part of a love relationship, while intimacy and commitment play more important roles as relationships progress. In the author's view, the ultimate form of love combines the passion, intimacy, and commitment. Sternberg gives specific guidelines for improving love relationships and includes a love scale for measuring the nature of one's own love. An insightful perspective on the nature of love, this book gives good advice about how to achieve perfect love, but it includes more academic discussion than is typical of self-help books. Nonetheless, Sternberg's analysis of love's nature is much easier reading than Fromm's *The Art of Loving*.

Recommended

★★★ *Obsessive Love* (1991) by Susan Forward. New York: Bantam.

This book is for people who are obsessive lovers and their targets. Obsessive love is not really love at all, according to Forward, but rather a pathological compulsion. She believes that obsessive love is caused by rejecting parents or separation problems in childhood. According to Forward, obsessive love occurs about equally in women and men and takes different forms: worshiping someone from afar, fantasizing about saving an addicted or troubled partner, or refusing to let go of a lover who has broken off a relationship. Forward intelligently tells obsessive lovers who are violence-prone to see a therapist immediately rather than simply relying on her self-help book. For obsessive lovers who are not violence-prone, she recommends detailed logging of emotions, a two-week vacation from contact with the target, and a probing self-evaluation in which obsessors ask themselves tough questions about whether anything in the relationship can be salvaged.

★★★ *Do I Have to Give Up Me to Be Loved by You?* (1983) by Jordan Paul and Margaret Paul. Minneapolis: CompCare.

This best-selling self-help book advocates probing and understanding the unspoken motivation behind what we do to solve our relationship problems. Using their intention therapy as a base, the authors tell readers how to become aware of self-created obstacles and develop more intimate relationships. A number of exercises help couples work on their power struggles, sexual expectations, and many other marital problems.

★★★ *Soul Mates: Honoring the Mysteries of Love and Relationship* (1994) by Thomas Moore. New York: HarperCollins.

Moore, a former Catholic monk turned best-selling author, reawakens the reader to discernment and nurturance of the soul in an effort to cultivate loving soulful relationships. He looks at relationships from a position of mystery, religion, and theology, believing it is a mistake to talk authoritatively about mysteries. Moore's objective is to help individuals change well-entrenched ideas of what it means to love and be one with others in friendship, marriage, and community. This 3-star book would probably be best received by religiously and spiritually oriented readers.

★★★ *Creating Love: The Next Great Stage of Growth* (1992) by John Bradshaw. New York: Bantam.

This best-selling author writes on the many dimensions of love and demystifies the belief that love is easy and a given among blood relatives. To paraphrase Bradshaw, love is difficult and requires hard work and honesty. The reader is forced to evaluate and perhaps surrender counterfeit love in exchange for the soul-building work of real love. Bradshaw addresses how to create love in various relationships (e.g., with God, parents, children, friends, spouses, work, and self). This 3-star book brings to the surface the mystical, spiritual, and soulful characteristics of love and will probably be useful to people who have struggled with painful relationships and uncertainty about love.

★★★ *A Return to Love* (1992) by Marianne Williamson. New York: HarperCollins.

This book is a spiritual journey back to our natural tendency to love. Best-selling author Williamson argues that we have frequently been taught to detach, to compete, and to dislike ourselves. Through this psychological, emotional, and spiritual journey, she encourages us to relinquish our social fears and accept back into our hearts the love we have been denying. A book about the practical application of love and its daily practice. An inspiring book for the spiritually minded and for those seeking a life based on the practice of love.

★★★ *Going the Distance: Secrets of Lifelong Love* (1991) by Lonnie Barbach and
        David Geisinger. New York: Doubleday.

The advice in *Going the Distance* is appropriate for a wide range of couples, from people just embarking on a close intimate relationship to people who want to renew their commitment to marital partners. According to Barbach and Geisinger, we bring the scars of old psychic wounds to any new relationship; a good close relationship is a healing one; and even individuals with a long history of troubled relationships can learn the skills needed to make a marriage work. The authors stress the importance of chemistry, courtship, trust, respect, acceptance, and shared values. They also suggest methods for overcoming commitment phobias, strategies to resolve power conflicts for control, and ways to improve a couple's sex life. A 50-item compatibility questionnaire helps couples evaluate how well-suited they are. Solid advice and well-written, even if standard fare for relationship books.

★★★ *Women Who Love Too Much* (1985) by Robin Norwood. New York: Pocket Books.

This volume was one of many best-selling self-help books in the 1980s that blame most of women's problems on a male-dominated society. Among the characteristics of a woman who loves too much are a childhood in which her emotional needs were not met, willingness to assume the majority of blame for a relationship's problems, low self-esteem, and a belief that she has no right to be happy. Such women choose men who need help, inevitably causing their marriage to become troubled. These women are addicted to pain, says Norwood, just as an alcoholic is addicted to liquor. The first step to recovering from a relationship addiction is to back off from the partner—quit nagging and stop making demands—and start focusing on her own problems instead of wasting energy on his problems. Norwood advocates finding a support group and leaving the relationship if necessary. *Women Who Love Too Much* headed the *New York Times* best-seller list for 37 weeks. It can inspire women who are trapped in bad relationships to evaluate their situations and chart better courses for their lives. On the other hand, critics say that it attributes women's problems disproportionately to men and doesn't adequately deal with what happens to a woman once she "recovers."

Diamonds in the Rough

◆ *In the Meantime: Finding Yourself and the Love That You Want* (1998) by Iyanla
    Vanzant. New York: Simon & Schuster.

The author focuses on the clarity of vision and purpose humans need to find their way through life. Vanzant asks, as you are working to achieve a state of love, what do you do in the meantime? Mental housekeeping is the answer—for example, repairing past hurts and painful memories along with addressing fears, self-doubts, and inaccurate information that stand in the way of finding true love. Vanzant states that love will come to us, but most of us won't recognize it since love rarely shows up in the place we expect or looks the way we expect it to look. She reinforces the point that true self-love needs to be in place in order to find the love that you want. Taking each experience and learning more about oneself is part of what to do in the meantime. But it's not easy. Reflection, evaluation, and unlearning require a willingness to do the grunge work. A highly but infrequently rated book for adults trying to understand themselves and willing to learn in the meantime.

♦ *Couples: Exploring and Understanding the Cycles of Intimate Relationships* (1993) by Barry Dym and Michael L. Glenn. New York: HarperCollins.

This book reviews stages of a relationship and how a couple changes over time, as does the couple's cultural narrative. The cultural narrative is the sum of a society's images and messages about how people should and do behave. Before trying to fix a couple, one should have a clear sense of how a couple functions and how the couple has developed. This book discusses normal couples, not psychopathology. This Diamond in the Rough is intended for the adult heterosexual couple. It is not a how-to-fix-troubled-relationships book, but more about how other normal couples have moved through such difficulties.

Not Recommended

★★ *Loving Each Other* (1984) by Leo Buscaglia. Thorofare, NJ: Slack.

★★ *Men Who Hate Women and the Women Who Love Them* (1986) by Susan Forward. New York: Bantam.

★★ *Men Who Can't Love: When a Man's Fear Makes Him Run from Commitment (and What a Smart Woman Can Do about It)* (1987) by Steven Carter. New York: Evans.

★ *When Someone You Love Is Someone You Hate* (1988) by Stephen Arterburn and David Stoop. Dallas: Word.

★ *What Smart Women Know* (1990) by Steven Carter and Julia Sokol. New York: Evans.

Strongly Not Recommended

† *Mars and Venus in the Bedroom: A Guide to Lasting Romance and Passion* (1995) by John Gray. New York: HarperCollins.

† *Women Men Love, Women Men Leave* (1987) by Connell Cowan and Melvyn Kinder. New York: Clarkson N. Potter.

† *What Every Woman Should Know about Men* (1981) by Joyce Brothers. New York: Simon & Schuster.

MOVIES

Recommended

★★★   *The Four Seasons* (1982) produced by Martin Bregman and directed by
       Alan Alda. PG Rating. 107 minutes.

This film provides a realistic view of small group dynamics—that is, the group members' relationship to each other and also the subset relationships of each person to his or her partner. Three couples have taken their vacations together for many years when one couple suddenly divorces. The man brings his new wife to the group's holiday, thereby challenging the nature of their relationships and the meaning of love. The film highlights the foibles of growing up and older together in very funny scenarios while also capturing the spirit of lifetime romantic changes. Also reviewed in the Divorce chapter (Chapter 14).

★★★   *When Harry Met Sally* (1990) produced by Rob Reiner and
       Andrew Scheinman and directed by Rob Reiner. R Rating. 95 minutes.

Harry and Sally run into each other every five years or so and find themselves at differing points in their romantic relationships. They repeatedly discuss the possibility of being friends, but Harry proclaims that men and women can't be friends because of the inevitability of sex. The uncertainty of their relationship and their commitment and caring for each other are the themes of this story. The complexity and challenge of contemporary relationships between men and women is revealed in funny, yet poignant ways.

★★★   *The Way We Were* (1973) produced by Ray Stark and directed by
       Sydney Pollack. PG Rating. 118 minutes.

Tearjerker in which a man and woman meet and fall in love years after their friendship in college. They find themselves with very different political and ideological perspectives that eventually drive them apart. The movie demonstrates the challenges of love and the difficulties of holding on to one's beliefs while accepting differences in a partner. The story is energetic, sad, and hopeful; in the end, it chronicles coping with interpersonal loss based on principles.

★★★   *Sleepless in Seattle* (1994) produced by Gary Foster and directed by
       Nora Ephron. PG Rating. 100 minutes.

The despair over a spouse's death and the search for a soulmate drive this heartwarming and funny story. Sam's wife died, leaving Sam and son Jonah adrift. Sam's initial abdication of a love life and his awkward attempts to console his son are realistic portrayals of families in turmoil. Holding out for the real thing so that love conquers all and the irrepressibility of a child's mission to make his family complete are the dual lessons of this story.

Not Recommended

★★   *Pretty in Pink* (1987) produced by John Hughes and Michael Chinich and
      directed by Howard Deutch. PG-13 Rating. 96 minutes.

Strongly Not Recommended

† *9½ Weeks* (1987) produced by Anthony Rufus Isaccs and Zalman King and directed by Adrian Lyne. R Rating. 113 minutes.

INTERNET RESOURCES

We review, in turn, websites devoted to love and romance in general, dating (both in person and on line), and specialized topics.

Love and Romance

★★★★★ *Love and Relationships* http://www.topchoice.com/~psyche/love

A full discussion of types of love (from the research) in about 20 pages; two neat online tests on the concept and experiences of love, with extensive verbal and graphic feedback; an article on expectations of sexuality and relationship level; articles on female courtship strategies; five essays on love and lust; and much more. This is the best site on love on the Internet: most materials are empirically based, it is written in a very accessible manner, and it offers insights that are positive and humane. Thank you Betty and Jim.

★★★★★ *Erotic Talk for Lovers and Performers* http://www.sexuality.org/talk.html

An unusual site: 46 pages of the best from seven books on how to talk sexy. This is a handout prepared for a workshop and is quite detailed, sex-positive, and, toward the end, instructive about setting up a phone sex-for-profit operation (so warn those you refer to this site). Ideal for the shy but eager client.

★★★★ *The Nature of Attraction and Love*
http://mentalhelp.net/psyhelp/chap10/chap10d.htm

Romantic and companionate love are different and must be understood. This is a wide-ranging introduction in eight pages.

★★★★ *Flirting* http://socpsych.lacollege.edu/flirting.html

This popular article explicates many flirting behaviors from interviews with two researchers.

★★★★ *Love Is Great* http://loveisgreat.com

There are thousands of sites about love and relationships. This is the most useful we have found about love: finding love, understanding and keeping love, and providing ways to show love. Lots of activities and ideas for those beginning to think about love and romance.

★★★★ *Some Great Advice on Reading Female Nonverbal Signals*
http://www.topchoice.com/~psyche/love/misc/signals9706.html

A useful essay for straight guys who seem to get rejected regularly.

★★★   *How to Kiss* http://www.kissingbooth.com/kiss.htm

Two pages on how to kiss.

★★★   *Romance 101* http://www.lovingyou.com/romance101/ideas.shtml

It says there are 1,161 romantic ideas (actually messages posted to a online group) here, so it might be useful site for those baffled by what *romantic* means these days.

★★★   *Rekindle Romance* http://www.positive-way.com/rekindle.htm

A very nice list of 14 brief and practical suggestions. Part of a larger marital communication project.

★★★   *Advice on Flirting* http://www.sexuality.org/flirtadv.html

A five-page collection of tips from a discussion group and a book on flirting.

★★★   *60 Starter Ideas for Having an Affair—with Your Spouse!*
         http://www.relationshipjourney.com

Click Marriage/Relationships, then the title above. Lists like this are often impossible, but these ideas are mostly doable, even for couples with some conflicts.

Dating: In Person and Online

★★★★★   *The Rebuttal from Uranus* http://ourworld.compuserve.com/homepages/
         women_rebuttal_from_uranus

John Gray's *Men Are from Mars, Women Are from Venus* and subsequent books have been popular. This site offers intelligent and devastating critiques. Thank you, Susan Hamson.

★★★★   *Singlescoach* http://www.singlescoach.com/resources.html

Although this is a commercial site, there are 80 columns written by psychotherapist and relationship coach Nina Atwood, which contain usable, nonrigid suggestions. The site is even searchable. An acceptable starting place for those seeking relationships.

★★★★   *Meeting Someone from On Line Safely*
         http://www.gloria-brame.com/meetsafe.htm

Designed for the kinky, this site offers 10 pages of detailed advice on going from ads to meetings safely. This site is not recommended for the inhibited, who will be distracted from the intelligent advice by the Dominant/Submissive details. See also the Tips for Posting Ads at http://www.gloria-brame.com/posttips.htm.

★★★   *Web-Based Matchmaking Services* http://www.sexuality.org/personal.html

A brief essay on the nature and uses of online personals ads.

★★★ *The Dating Doctor* http://www.datingdoctor.com

Although this is a commercial site, the FAQ could be useful to those with minor problems because it shows that others have the same kinds of problems. The advice is pretty solid and responsible.

★★★ *Guys Guide to Girls* by Philip Ovalsen http://www.philipov.com/guys1.htm

About 20 pages of musings on love, shyness, writing letters, and other social skills. The first four essays are gently written and supportive; the last two give good advice on using the Internet and finding a Russian woman as a mate. Useful as a starting point for those needing food for thought.

★★★ *Online Dating—Doing it Safely* http://www.datesafely.com

This page offers 16 brief rules to make online dating safer.

★★★ *Out of the Cave: Exploring Gray's Anatomy* by Kathleen Trigiani
        http://web2.airmail.net/ktrig246/out_of_cave

"This series of five essays takes a macroscopic look at the Mars and Venus phenomenon and concludes that we don't have to settle for Gray's worldview. This site is ideal for people who are interested in gender issues but don't have time to read the major literature."

Specialized Sites

★★★★ *HeartBeat—Relationship Advice with Flava!*
        http://www.askheartbeat.com/home.html

"Oriented towards the relationship issues of women of color." There are lots of advice sites; this one is both specialized and full of intelligent, usable, specific advice.

★★★ *Rainbowunions.com* http://www.rainbowunions.com/default.htm

The only ceremony-planning site for same sex couples.

★★★ *The Backrubs FAQ* http://www.ii.uib.no/~kjartan/backrubfaq

Lots of information, maybe too much, on how to do it.

★★ *Taller Women and Shorter Men* http://www.geocities.com/tallershorter

Unique and perfect for some. Support and advice.

See also Sexuality (Chapter 24).

CHAPTER 18

Marriage

The changes in American marital patterns have been revolutionary, not evolutionary. Not too long ago, people married in their teens and early twenties, had children, and stayed together for the rest of their lives. Men worked outside the home and were the breadwinners; women worked inside the home and cared for the children. In today's world, many people marry later or not at all. When they do get married, many couples postpone children until both partners have developed their careers. Or they choose to remain childless. Divorce captures 40% of all first marriages and 50% of subsequent marriages. Couples want their relationship to be deep and loving, and if it isn't, they increasingly see a psychologist or marriage counselor or consult a self-help resource that they hope will improve their marital relationship.

In this chapter we present the evaluative ratings and narrative descriptions of self-help resources on marriage. The content of this chapter obviously overlaps with the preceding chapter on love and intimacy, but if the thrust of the resource is marriage or couplehood, we placed it here.

SELF-HELP BOOKS

Strongly Recommended

★★★★★ *Why Marriages Succeed or Fail* (1994) by John Gottman. New York: Simon & Schuster.

Based on research conducted over a number of years with hundreds of couples, the principles presented in this book diagnose, interpret, and predict the success or failure of a marriage with a high degree of accuracy. Gottman, an internationally known researcher, effectively and systematically describes the three types of marriage styles and how healthy or unhealthy each may be depending on how interaction is played out. The four warning signs that a marriage is spiraling downward are described (i.e., criti-

---

RECOMMENDATION HIGHLIGHTS

Self-Help Books

- On healthy and unhealthy marriage styles:

    ★★★★★ *Why Marriages Succeed or Fail* by John Gottman

- On solving marital problems and improving the relationship:

    ★★★★ *Intimate Partners* by Maggie Scarf

    ★★★★ *Getting the Love You Want* by Harville Hendrix

    ★★★★ *Divorce Busting* by Michele Weiner-Davis

    ◆ *We Love Each Other but . . .* by Ellen Wachtel

- On pastoral marital counseling:

    ◆ *Love for a Lifetime* by James Dobson

Internet Resources

- For improving your relationship:

    ★★★★★ *Relationship Information for Couples*
        http://www.positive-way.com/relation.htm

- For rebuilding relationships after extramarital affairs:

    ★★★★★ *The Other Woman (TOW)* http://www.gloryb.com/index.html

    ★★★★ *Marriage Builders*
        http://www.marriagebuilders.com/graphic/mbi5051_qa.html

---

cism, contempt, defensiveness, and stonewalling) and in concluding chapters, the four keys to improving a marriage and reversing the spiral are discussed. The concepts hypothesized by Gottman are well-grounded in his research but are also logical and fit together. Quizzes allow couples to self-identify the status of their marriages. According to our mental health experts, a very valuable and research-based self-help book.

★★★★ *Intimate Partners: Patterns in Love and Marriage* (1986) by Maggie Scarf. New York: Random House.

This book tells readers how to solve their marital problems, especially by understanding the stages of development and how relationships with the family of origin influence the marital relationship. Scarf charts the lives of five married couples in depth, categorizing them according to their life stage: idealization, disenchantment, child-rearing and career-building, child-launching, and the retirement years. She starts with relative newlyweds and ends with a couple who have finished rearing their children and are free to focus on each other once again. Interviews with 32 couples are woven through the book. Like Harriet Lerner in *The Dance of Intimacy* (rated in Chapter 17), Scarf emphasizes the importance of a couple's birth families, configurations and genograms (diagrams of lines of attachment between marital partners and their parents, grandparents, and siblings) to illuminate how people often repeat the past. Unfulfilled needs are powerful, unconscious forces that shape a marriage from the beginning and continue to dominate it throughout the marriage stages. Scarf does an excellent job of encouraging marital partners to examine the stages of marriage and how longstanding relationships with parents continue to exert a strong influence.

★★★★ *Getting the Love You Want* (1988) by Harville Hendrix. New York: Henry Holt.

This book is based on workshop techniques that Hendrix has developed to help couples construct a conscious marriage—a relationship based on awareness of the unresolved childhood needs and conflicts that cause individuals to select particular spouses. The author tells readers how to conduct a 10-week course in marital therapy in the privacy of their homes. In a stepwise fashion, he helps readers learn how to communicate more clearly and sensitively, how to eliminate self-defeating behaviors, and how to focus attention on meeting their partners' needs. Hendrix's goal is to transform the downward spiral of the power struggle into a mutually beneficial relationship of emotional growth. This 4-star book is superb for marital partners engulfed in conflict. Hendrix does an excellent job of helping the reader become aware of longstanding family influences on current close relationships. The exercises for his 10-week in-home workshop are ingenious.

★★★★ *Divorce Busting* (1992) by Michele Weiner-Davis. New York: Summit.

This book advocates a brief, solution-oriented approach to keeping a marriage together. Author Weiner-Davis says that divorce is not the answer to an unhappy marriage. She says she came to this conclusion after observing that former spouses often continue to be unhappy after the divorce. Weiner-Davis's approach focuses on the present and the future and on actions rather than feelings. It is accomplished in brief rather than lengthy therapy or problem-solving sessions. (In her practice, she sees most couples for only four to five sessions.) *Divorce Busting* offers a step-by-step strategy that couples can follow to make their marriage loving again. Brief case histories show how couples have successfully used Weiner-Davis's approach to solve their marital difficulties. The steps can be followed alone or with a spouse. The therapeutic techniques are well-translated into everyday language that the reader will easily comprehend.

Recommended

★★★ *I Love You, Let's Work It Out* (1987) by David Viscott. New York: Simon & Schuster.

The cycle of working it out in Viscott's model begins with commitment and communication. Viscott shows the importance of assessing the obstacles to commitment and communication and how partners inhibit each other from attaining them as the foundation for their marriage. Accurately identifying the pattern of feelings and doubts of self and others sets the stage for the central focus of the book: a model for diagnosing and interpreting what couples argue about, how they argue, and what their individual and joint styles of interacting reveal about how to successfully work out problems. Protective styles (i.e., dependent, controlling, and competitive) are analyzed in relationship to couples styles (e.g., closed, open, analytic, emotional, affectionate), and an interaction is predicted and described for each. Working it out successfully means that once the dynamics and interactions that maintain conflict are understood, couples can break the cycle and make different choices. This text presents an interactive, organized system for understanding conflict patterns and lends itself to cognitive approaches toward solutions.

★★★ *Husbands and Wives: Exploring Marital Myths* (1989) by Melvyn Kinder and Connell Cowan. New York: Clarkson N. Potter.

The major problem in most marriages, the authors maintain, is that each partner tries to change the other instead of focusing on improving his or her own behavior. Kinder and Cowan call their approach self-directed marriage; it emphasizes the importance of each partner's taking responsibility for his or her own happiness and replacing other-directed blame with acceptance. The authors tell marital partners to accept their differences, become friends, and rediscover the enjoyment of marital life. *Husbands and Wives* barely received a 3-star rating in the national study. Mental health professionals who like the book said that its message can help individuals understand the importance of developing themselves instead of trying to change their partners. Critics said that the book's theme of self-development is too simplistic for today's world of complex marital relationships.

Diamonds in the Rough

♦ *We Love Each Other but . . .* (1999) by Ellen Wachtel. New York: Golden.

Intimate relationships are most often lost because of failure in basic, daily interactions, not because of major events. This self-help resource directs the reader to just those basics and tells how to maintain or regain the fundamental elements of the relationship that brought the two people together in the first place. There are no exercises, activities, or artificial interventions. Instead, Wachtel suggests how to think and act differently toward problems so that both partners will be heard and understood. She offers four basic truths about being in relationships and identifies seven areas of conflict that have emerged as most common in her work with couples. Very doable solutions are offered for each problem, accompanied by numerous examples from the author's experience with couples who successfully enhanced their relationships. Highly rated in our latest national study but not yet well-known, probably because of its recent publication. A wise and comforting book: Many couples have struggled through similar conflicts and have been able to successfully change.

♦ *Love for a Lifetime* (1998) by James Dobson. Sisters, OR: Multnomah.

James Dobson, a psychologist widely known for his many books on marriage and parenting, has written this book for adult singles, engaged couples, and those married less than 10 years. The author's intent is to identify the major pitfalls that undermine a relationship and make suggestions on how to avoid them. Christian principles frame the narrative, and his perspectives on relationships, money, sex, and family are consistent with Christian teachings. Topics addressed are controversial either in Christian teaching or in the general society, such as premarital sex, divorce, homosexuality, and gender differences. The teachings of this book will be helpful to people looking for guidance in relationship-building within conventional Christian beliefs. Diamond in the Rough status is given to this book because of the recent publication date and moderately high rating.

INTERNET RESOURCES

Psychoeducational Materials for Clients and Families

★★★★★ *Relationship Information for Couples*
http://www.positive-way.com/relation.htm

This site has 12 sections on improving a relationship, with good ideas about issues like Warning Signs, Hidden Issues and Expectations, Expressing Your Feelings, Who's The Boss, How to Love Your Mate, Create a New Beginning, Rekindle Romance, Relate to Create Happiness, Men, Housework, Better Sex, and Problem Solving. Each section has guidelines and suggestions, and often questionnaires, all of which seem eminently useful. This might be a good site to orient stuck couples.

★★★★★ *Parenting and Marriage Articles* by Kalman Heller, PhD
http://www.drheller.com/index.html

Under Parenting and Marriage, and then Marriage, are about a dozen very well-written one-page articles on aspects of married life, like conflict, gender, marital therapy, fair fighting, and so on. With permission to reprint, these might be handouts or useful in marketing.

★★★★★ *Marital Center* http://www.wholefamily.com/maritalcenter/index.html

In scripts and real audio, six realistic conflicts are played out and commented on by a therapist. The topics are Money, Cleaning, Sex and Romance, Discipline, In-Laws, and the Unemployed Son. These might be very useful for couples to read and see how typical their conflicts and relating styles are and how a therapist might see them. Therapy is not shown, only some comments by the therapists, which is an advantage for a therapist referring new clients to this site.

★★★★ *Marriage Mythology* by Many Laner
http://researchmag.asu.edu/stories/marriage.html

"When the reality of marriage doesn't meet our expectations, we tend to blame reality." Good for introducing marital therapy.

★★★★ *Marriage—A Many-Splendored, Sometimes Splintered, Thing* by Daniel Wayne Matthews, PhD http://www.ces.ncsu.edu/depts/fcs/pub/marriage.html

In only six pages, Matthews presents the challenges couples face when they marry, myths, financial and in-law issues, and more. An excellent premarital orientation.

★★★★ *Interfaith Relationships for Jews*
      http://www.shamash.org/cgi-bin/excite/AT-Complete_Searchsearch.cgi

There are a few dozen articles here which can be found by searching for "Interfaith marriage."

★★★★ *Tips on Using the Intentional Dialogue Developed by Harville Hendrix, PhD* by
      Dawn Lipthrott, MSW http://www.relationshipjourney.com

Click on Marriage/Relationships and then on this title. A handout of about seven pages describing how to use this tool.

★★★ *When the Answer Is "Not Tonight"* by Marlene M. Maheu, PhD
      http://mentalhelp.net/articles/sex1.htm

Maheu offers five possible causes and some interventions. This might be suitable for opening up discussions of this aspect of a couple's relationship.

★★★ *Marriage and Relationship Skills* http://www.pilot.infi.net/~susanf/marskl.htm

Here are rules for four skill exercises: Listening, Encouraging, Affirming, and Meeting. Some clients will find seeing these in print or on the Internet motivating.

★★★ *Traditional Family Values* by Peter McWilliams
      http://www.mcwilliams.com/books/aint/404.htm

Debunks the myths of perfect families of the 1950s. Useful to clear out assumptions of what marriage was and should be.

Affairs/Infidelity

★★★★★ *The Other Woman (TOW)* http://www.gloryb.com/index.html

This is a support and informational site for the partner of the married person having an affair. It presents all sides, offers personal stories, endings, and a large FAQ. The MM to English Dictionary is a painful read.

★★★★ *Marriage Builders* by Willard F. Harley, Jr., PhD
      http://www.marriagebuilders.com/graphic/mbi5051_qa.html

Harley is clearly against affairs but writes well about the emotional issues. Here are about a dozen articles he wrote in response to letters. *Coping with Infidelity: How Do Affairs Begin?* at http://www.parenthoodweb.com/parent_cfmfiles/pros.cfm/581 describes the elements of an affair as deposits and withdrawals in a love bank, stressful transitions, and broken rules. All of these may be useful to people who need to see all sides of an affair.

★★★★ *Marital Infidelity* by Robin Truhe http://www.umkc.edu/sites/hsw/affairs

In about eight pages (and lots of good links), almost all aspects are presented. This might be an excellent introductory handout.

★★★★ *Articles about Affairs* http://www.vaughan-vaughan.com/affairsmenu.html

Peggy Vaughn, author of book on affairs, offers good but brief essays on about 30 aspects of affairs. A very good orientation reading.

★★★ *Why Are People Unfaithful?* by John M. Grohol, PsyD
       http://mentalhelp.net/articles/grohol/rels2.htm

Grohol briefly suggests six reasons people are unfaithful. These might be useful for the wronged spouse to consider.

★★★ *Possible Good from an Affair?*
       http://www.divorcesource.com/info/affairs/good.shtml

A very brief list of six benefits—mainly knowing the truth. This might be useful to someone who has just discovered a spouse's affair.

Alternatives

★★★★ *Alternatives to Marriage Project* http://www.atmp.org/homepage.html

The FAQ of just five pages is enlightening and assertive about voluntary singlehood. The Resources list is very helpful. This is a wonderful site for those struggling to affirm the positives of relationships outside of marriage.

Other Resources

Marriage Encounter http://marriage-encounter.org

"National Marriage Encounter is a Judeo/Christian Based Ministry and Support Organization for Married Couples." It has programs all over the country and in every kind of church. It's purpose is to examine attitudes and improve good marriages.

PAIRS http://www.pairs.com/navigate.htm

This is the home page of a marital communication training program. The site might be useful to clients even if you do not use the PAIRS model to stimulate their thinking about their relationship's qualities and patterns. An outline of one of their basic techniques, *Process of the Fair Fight for Change,* is available at http://www.pairs.com/fair.htm. Also see http://www.pairs.com/dialogue-guide.htm for their PAIRS Dialogue Guide.

Retrouvaille http://www.retrouvaille.org/home.htm

Another marriage improvement program with a few articles to read. Oriented toward Roman Catholics.

Online Support Groups

Straight Spouse Network http://www.ssnetwk.org

"SSN is an international support network of heterosexual spouses and partners, current or former, of gay, lesbian, bisexual, or transgender mates. Members provide confidential personal support and resource information to spouses and partners nationwide and abroad. SSN is the only support network of its kind in the world."

The International Couples' Homepage
http://www.geocities.com/Heartland/4448/Couples.html

"This page is for those of you who are married (or planning to marry) with a person of a different nationality." See also the *United Front Japan* at http://www.ufj.gol.com for non-Japanese individuals with a Japanese spouses.

See also Families and Stepfamilies (Chapter 16); Love and Intimacy (Chapter 17); Sexuality (Chapter 24).

NATIONAL SUPPORT GROUPS

Association of Couples for Marriage Enrichment
PO Box 10596
Winston-Salem, NC 27108
Phone: 800-634-8325

No Kidding!
Box 27001
Vancouver, BC, Canada V5R 6A8
Phone: 604-538-7736

Mutual support and social activities for married and single people who either have decided not to have children, are postponing parenthood, are undecided, or are unable to have children.

Smart Marriages' Directory of Marriage Education Programs
http://www.smartmarriages.com/directory_browse.html

This is a searchable listing of about 150 local and national programs with annotations and complete addresses.

CHAPTER 19

Men's Issues

The male of the human species—what is he really like? What does he really want and need? At no other point in human history have males and females been placed under a psychological microscope the way they have been in the last 25 years. It began with the emergence of the women's movement and its attack on male bias and discrimination against women. As a result of the movement, women have been encouraged to value sensitive feelings and connectedness with others, to develop their own identity, and to resist men's attempts to dominate and enslave them.

In response to women's efforts to change what defines themselves, and to change men, men developed their own movement. The men's movement has not been as political or as activist as the women's movement. Rather it has been more of an emotional, spiritual movement that reasserts the importance of masculinity and urges men to resist women's efforts to turn them into "soft" males. Or it has been a psychological movement that recognizes that men need to be less violent and more nurturant but still retain their masculine identity. Many disciples of the men's movement argue that society's evolving gender arena has led men to question what being a man really means.

Self-help resources on men's issues traverse a large and heterogeneous group of materials. The early men's movement books broadly focus on coping with a society of fluctuating gender roles, while men's movement books in the early 1990s relied on mythological and spiritual accounts of man's recapturing his true masculinity. There are also resources on gay men discussed in Chapter 24 (Sexuality) and fathering discussed in Chapters 10 (Child Development and Parenting) and 16 (Families and Stepfamilies).

In what follows, we critically review self-help books, movies, and Internet resources on this expansive topic of men' issues.

RECOMMENDATION HIGHLIGHTS

Self-Help Books

- On rescuing sons from the destructive myths of boyhood:

    ★★★★ *Real Boys* by William Pollack

- On understanding the stages and transitions of men's life cycles:

    ★★★★ *Seasons of a Man's Life* by Daniel J. Levinson

- On improving the quality of men's identity and life:

    ★★★ *Being a Man* by Patrick Fanning and Matthew McKay

Movies

- A son caring for an aging father is able to dissolve their lifelong distance:

    ★★★★★ *I Never Sang for My Father*

    ★★★ *Nothing in Common*

- Story of the power of hope, identity development, and father–son rapprochement:

    ★★★★★ *October Sky*

- The magic of baseball for men and recapturing youth:

    ★★★★ *Field of Dreams*

Internet Resources

- On the men's movement:

    ★✳★★★ *Men's Stuff: The National Men's Resource Center*
    http://www.menstuff.org

- On domestic violence:

    ★★★ *Domestic Violence Resources*
    *http://*www.silcom.com/~paladin/madv

- On fathers coping with divorce and custody:

    ★★★★★ *Fathers Rights to Custody: Information to Assist Fathers in Gaining Custody* http://www.deltabravo.net/custody

SELF-HELP BOOKS

Strongly Recommended

★★★★   *Real Boys: Rescuing Our Sons from the Myths of Boyhood* (1998) by
        William Pollack. New York: Henry Holt.

The author explores this generation of boys' feelings of sadness, loneliness, and confusion while they try to appear tough, cheerful, and confident. Pollack takes the reader through the stages of childhood and adolescent development, ferreting out truth from myth, and recognizing the cultural and relational influences on male sexuality and behavior. Discussed is how to let real boys be real men by revising the "Boys' Code" and still feeling connected. Pollack writes about what boys are like, how to help them, and what happens if they aren't helped. Negative influences include early and harsh disconnection from family, mixed messages, and outdated models, rules, and assumptions that are making boys sick. Parents, teachers, and professionals actively connected with boys will find this book valuable and revealing. Although just published at the time of the study, it was very favorably evaluated by our mental health experts and received the highest ratings of any book in this category.

★★★★   *Seasons of a Man's Life* (1978) by Daniel J. Levinson. New York: Ballantine.

This national bestseller is reviewed in Chapter 4 (Adult Development and Aging) but merits a brief mention here. It outlines a number of stages men pass through, including the midlife crisis. Levinson describes the stages and transitions in the male life cycle from 17 to 65 years of age.

Recommended

★★★   *Being a Man: A Guide to the New Masculinity* (1993) by Patrick Fanning and
       Matthew McKay. Oakland, CA: New Harbinger.

This is a practical book written about men and what they can do to improve the quality and length of their lives. Filled with assurance, assistance, and information necessary for men to achieve their goals, the book addresses multiple topics, such as appreciating gender differences, relating to one's father, clarifying and acting on values, finding meaningful work, making and keeping male friends, and raising children. The authors convincingly argue that identity is strongly determined by whether an individual was born a boy or girl and by who the person's parents were. A person can't change these circumstances, but can ponder them and understand them better. For any man who wishes to reflect and evaluate the quality and context of his life, and for the woman wishing to understand man in context, this is an interesting and practical book. Indeed, its 3-star rating underestimates its value according to the 16 psychologists who evaluated it highly; had more known of it, this would surely be a 4-star or perhaps a 5-star resource.

★★★   *Man Enough: Fathers, Sons and the Search for Masculinity* (1993) by
       Frank S. Pittman. New York: Putnam.

In this book, masculinity is conceptualized as a group activity, as a cultural concept. Masculinity is different for each generation. It is supposed to be passed on from father to son. If a boy does not have men in his family, his need for mentors begins early. When children try to get close to their fathers, the practice of masculinity frequently gets in the way. Pittman writes tellingly of the plight of men who didn't get the fathering they needed to make them comfortable with their masculinity and of the healing of men who have rediscovered the forgotten profession of fatherhood. This book was rated favorably but relatively infrequently, resulting in its relegation to the 3-star category. It is an enlightening and helpful resource for adult males at any stage of their development.

★★★ *The Hazards of Being Male* (1976) by Herb Goldberg. New York: Signet.

Published in 1976, this was the first self-help book for men to come out after the woman's movement began to take hold in the 1970s. Goldberg became a central figure in the early development of the men's movement in the 1970s and early 1980s, mainly as a result of his writing about men's rights in *The Hazards of Being Male* and *The New Male*. Goldberg argues that a critical difference between men and women creates a precipitous gulf between them: Women can sense and articulate their feelings and problems; men—because of their masculine conditioning—can't. The result in men is an armor of masculinity that is defensive and powerfully maintains self-destructive patterns. Goldberg says that most men have been effective work machines and performers, but that about everything else in their lives suffers. Men live about 8 fewer years than women on the average, have higher hospitalization rates, and show more behavioral problems. Goldberg believes that millions of men are killing themselves by striving to be "true" men, a heavy price to pay for masculine privilege and power. Men need to determine what is critical for their survival and well-being. Goldberg especially encourages men to

- Recognize the suicidal success syndrome and evade it.
- Understand that occasional impotence is nothing serious.
- Become aware of their real needs and desires and get in touch with their own bodies.
- Elude the binds of masculine role-playing.
- Relate to women as equals rather than serving as women's guilty servant or hostile enemy.
- Develop male friendships.

This 3-star book is somewhat dated, but it still delivers important messages to men: Become more tuned into your inner self and emotional make-up, and work on developing more positive close relationships.

★★★ *The New Male: From Self-Destruction to Self-Care* (1980) by Herb Goldberg. New York: Signet.

The themes of Goldberg's second book on men's issues are similar to the first. Goldberg's purpose is to explore what the world of the traditional male has been like in the past, including relationships with women; what men's worlds are like in today's climate of changing gender roles; and what the future can hold in store for men if they examine, reshape, and expand their gender role behavior and self-awareness. In Part I,

He, Goldberg evaluates the traditional male role and its entrapments, and in Part II, He and She, he explores the traditional relationship between men and women. Part III, He and Her Changes, analyzes how the changes in roles of women brought about by the women's movement have affected men. Part IV, He and His Changes, provides hope for men by elaborating on how men can combine some of the strengths of traditional masculinity—such as assertiveness and independence—with increased exploration of the inner self, greater awareness of emotions, and more healthy close relationships with others to become more complete men. Occasionally dated in content and examples, this 3-star book expresses the timeless message of challenging men to explore their inner selves, get in touch with their feelings, and pay more attention to developing meaningful relationships.

★★★ *Fire in the Belly* (1991) by Sam Keen. New York: Bantam.

While Goldberg's books were the self-help bibles of the men's movement in the 1970s and 1980s, two authors ushered in a renewed interest in the men's movement in the 1990s—Sam Keen and Robert Bly. (Bly's book, *Iron John*, is listed in the Not Recommended category.) Keen's theme is that every man is on a spiritual journey to attain the grail of manhood. He strives to provide a road map for the journey, advising men on ways to avoid the dead ends of combative machismo and the blind alleys of romantic obsession. Keen says that he wrote *Fire in the Belly* because men have lost their vision of what masculinity is. Keen's answer is that men's true identity is fire in the belly and passion in the heart. Although this book was a *New York Times* best-seller, it received only a 3-star rating in our national studies. Virtually all books on men's issues—and women's issues—are controversial and stir up inflammatory feelings in the opposite sex. On the positive side, our experts applauded Keen's efforts to get men to reexamine their male identity, to incorporate more empathy into their relationships, and to reduce their hostility. On the other side, Keen's critics, especially female critics, didn't like his trashing of androgyny, his exaggeration of gender differences, and the mythology and mysticism that permeate the book. Keen adopts a Jungian perspective on man's inner journey to find himself, a perspective that is filled with symbols and metaphors that are not always clearly presented.

Not Recommended

★★ *Iron John: Straight Talk about Men* (1990) by Robert Bly. New York: Vintage.

★ *Why Men Don't Get Enough Sex and Women Don't Get Enough Love* (1990) by Jonathan Kramer and Diane Dunaway. New York: Pocket Books.

Strongly Not Recommended

† *What Men Really Want: Straight Talk from Men about Sex* (1990) by Susan Bakos. New York: St. Martin's.

† *Ten Stupid Things Men Do to Mess Up Their Lives* (1997) by Laura Schlessinger. New York: Cliff Street.

MOVIES

Strongly Recommended

★★★★★ *I Never Sang for My Father* (1969) produced and directed by Gilbert Cates. PG Rating. 92 minutes.

A son tries to care for an aging father, accepting his father's eccentricities and changing the quality of their relationship before its too late. The difficulties of disclosure, of admitting lifelong hurt, and of finding a way to dissolve the distance between them are the universal tasks undertaken by the father and son. The moving story is a realistic glimpse into the complexity and the fundamental challenges of father–son relationships. This 5-star resource is one of the most favorably rated of all movies in our national studies.

★★★★★ *October Sky* (1999) produced by Larry J. Franco and Charles Gordon and directed by Joe Johnston. PG Rating. 108 minutes.

An exhilarating story of the power of the human spirit conveyed through a young West Virginia boy whose life in the coal fields stands in stark contrast to his goal of launching a rocket. The boy's dream represents escape and triumph for the coal miners whose lives are painfully and realistically portrayed. They rally around the boy and support his science achievements and his attempt to go to the national science fair, but the father, who loves his son, does not believe science is a realistic out. The eventual success of the boy and his father's change of heart are characterized in this true story. The boy grew up to become a NASA scientist, as portrayed in his book *Rocket Boys*. This is a wonderful film for adolescents struggling with identity and for the approval of their fathers.

★★★★ *Field of Dreams* (1989) produced by Lawrence Gordon and Charles Gordon and directed by Phil Alden Robinson. PG Rating. 106 minutes.

Reminiscence about the glory days of baseball is its secondary theme, but the real story is the magic of baseball for boys and men. For them, baseball was another world, a cherished world. An Iowa farmer, Ray, builds a magical field in his cornfield, and the ghosts of professional ballplayers show up and compete in games. This is a warm and poignant film about men who connect to other men (and Ray to his father) through the special love of baseball.

Recommended

★★★ *Nothing in Common* (1986) produced by Alexandra Rose and directed by Garry Marshall. PG Rating. 118 minutes.

David is in his mid-30s and has been estranged from his critical, bitter, cynical father for many years. Suddenly, he learns that his mother is leaving his father. His father is scared but belligerent, lonely but angry, and his father needs him. Resentment, reconciliation, acceptance, and dealing with old pain are all part of the dynamics between David and his father. David learns that his unresolved problems with his father have to be faced in order to begin healing.

★★★ *Tootsie* (1983) produced by Sydney Pollack and Dick Richards and directed by Sydney Pollack. PG Rating. 116 minutes.

Michael, an out-of-work actor, takes on the identity of a female character, Dorothy, and wins a part in a daytime soap opera. He meets Julie on the set, and they become women friends, although Michael has strong romantic feelings for Julie. Living the life of Dorothy and having relationships as a female dramatically transforms Michael's perspective about women, men, and himself. This is a touching and funny story of gender roles and subsequent insights into the subtle but significant differences in how we relate as men and women.

★★★ *The Rape of Richard Beck* (1985, made for TV) produced by Robert A. Papazian, Jr., and directed by Karen Arthur.

Richard Beck is a big-city cop who is insensitive and uncaring, particularly to women. He rejects the trauma and violation of rape until he himself is raped. He is thrown into the same experience of humiliation and rage as the women he has known who have been victims of sexual assault. Although flawed, this film is one of the few that depicts the rape of a man; the reversal of a familiar story is eye-opening. The film conveys compassion and caring for all victims of rape.

Not Recommended

★★ *City Slickers* (1992) produced by Irby Smith and directed by Ron Underwood. PG-13 Rating. 110 minutes.

INTERNET RESOURCES

As is the case with Women's Issues in Chapter 29, the list of Internet sites on men's issues is long and heterogeneous. Thus, this section has more than the usual number of metasites and subsections.

Metasites

★★★★ *Men's Stuff: The National Men's Resource Center*
http://www.menstuff.org

A complexly rich but graphically simple site "with over 40 megs of information." Under the Issues link are an alphabetical list of 300 topics, or 42 major headings of hotlinked sites and pages. The depth and breadth is simply amazing. For example, abuse, aging, circumcision, divorce, fathers, health, isolation, mid-life, multicultural, prostrate, sexuality, spirituality, transition, Viagra, violence, work, divorce and custody, fathers, feelings, homophobia, and more. Under Resources on the left are about 50 headings of all kinds of resources that support "positive change in male roles and relationships." This directory includes over 2,600 listings.

★★★ *The Men's Issues Page* http://www.vix.com/pub/men/index.html

While there is much of value here, many sites are one-sided rants. We would not offer the whole site to a male client but for someone seeking some support and direction there are perspectives unique to this site.

Psychoeducational Materials for Clients and Families

★★★ *Menweb—Men's Voices Magazine*
http://www.vix.com/menmag/page1.htm

There are dozens of articles, some brief audiotapes, suggested books, advice on househusbanding, ideas about male violence, and so on. A good start toward awareness of the spiritual side of men's lives.

★★★ *Domestic Violence Resources* http://www.silcom.com/~paladin/madv

A good set of links to informative materials and readings, agency sites with more materials, and helplines.

Health and Sexuality

★★★★ *Prostate Cancer Program*
http://www.cancer.med.umich.edu/prostcan/prostcan.html

A medical site, but some of the articles are useful for background or current interpretations. Start with Staging Information.

★★★ *Stay Sexy Your Entire Life: Seven Simple Steps That Can Ensure Continued Sexual Satisfaction*
http://www.campuslife.utoronto.ca/services/sec/staysexy.html

Good general advice that may open a discussion of sexuality with middle-aged and older men.

Fathers and Child Support

These sites were created mainly to assert fathers' rights against the perceived overemphasis on mothers' rights and their political and legal manifestations. They are hostile to the generally accepted body of evidence in mental health.

★★★★★ *Fathers Rights to Custody: Information to Assist Fathers in Gaining Custody* http://www.deltabravo.net/custody

Here you can read a very complete *Guide to the Parenting Evaluation Process* and dozens of articles on coping with the divorce and custody processes, as well as download many forms and materials to help you make a case for father custody. High-quality and very complete.

★★★★ *American Coalition for Fathers and Children* http://www.acfc.org

This is a large site for political action and education. The Studies and Reports include many research articles on issues like custody, divorce, gender bias, posttraumatic stress disorder, and "parental alienation syndrome," so it can be a source of solid information. The Reading Room offers hundreds of (unfortunately unannotated) popular articles that can be thought-provoking.

★★★★ *ACFC Fathers Rights Citations Repository*
          http://www.acfc.org/html/study.htm

Here you will find links to about 50 large reports and documents, mainly from government sources, under headings like Access and Visitation; Child Abuse—False Allegations; Child Development: Importance of Paternal Presence; Custody; Dissertations by Fathers Rights Advocates; Gender Bias in Courts and Government; Parental Alienation; and Poverty and Father-Absence. This page is best for people who need factual information; brought to you by the American Coalition for Fathers and Children.

★★★ *Children's Justice* http://childrens-justice.org

Hostile to the current system (which is well-explained in their Facts and Myths and FAQ), the site offers a set of position papers, legislative agendas, and model child support formulas that would fix the system.

Men's Rights/Backlash

★★★★ *The Men's Defense Association* http://www.mensdefense.org

Online readings of magazine articles, the Men's Manifesto, Father Custody, and Fathers' Role in Society. Designed to counter antimale discrimination, especially in divorce.

★★★ *Men's Media Network* http://www.he.net/~menmedia

Dozens of documents that usually assert a positive view or a view antagonistic to the usual beliefs about domestic violence, rape, single fathers, and similar issues. If you or a client needs evidence for a nonstandard position there is a lot of it here.

★★★ *United Kingdom Men's Movement* http://www.ukmm.org.uk

Under Men's Issues, go to A Synopsis of Major Men's Issues for just that. Health, Domestic Violence, Family Issues, and the Media are the most relevant summaries.

★★★ *National Coalition of Free Men* http://www.ncfm.org/readroom.htm
About 20 articles to read, and many links.

★★ *The Fathers' Rights and Equality Exchange* http://dadsrights.org
The Legislation section is strong.

Pornography

★★★★★ *Men against Pornography* http://www.geocities.com/CapitolHill/1139

This site offers Quitting Pornography: Men Speak Out about How They Did It: An Online Anthology Edited by Men Against Pornography, which contains many suggestions and about eight personal stories. Ideal for men who are interested in giving up the distortions that pornography teaches.

★★★★ *Linnea's Playboy Site* http://www.talkintrash.com/playboy

About 30 pages that offer insightful and well-articulated paragraphs about the roles of pornography in lives and development. An excellent start to giving up pornography.

See also Child Development and Parenting (Chapter 10); Divorce (Chapter 14).

NATIONAL SUPPORT GROUPS

Several of these entries are based on a list by David R. Throop (throop@vix.com) and posted to *The World Wide Web Virtual Library* as Men's Organizations. The descriptions are from David R. Throop.

Association for Children for Enforcement of Support (ACES)
2260 Upton Avenue
Toledo, OH 43606
Phone: 800-537-7072

For custodial parents who are having difficulties collecting child support.

Coalition for the Preservation of Fatherhood
PO Box 8051
Boston, MA 02113
Phone: 617-649-1906
E-mail list:
cpf-l-request@stormy.salem.ma.us (in body of message type "SUBSCRIBE [your e-mail address]")

Fathers behind Bars
525 Superior Street
Niles, MI 49120

This group publishes a book, *Fathers behind Bars* by Arthur Hamilton, Jr. They are also a support group for incarcerated fathers.

Fathers' Resource Center
430 Oak Grove Street, Suite B3
Minneapolis, MN 55403
Phone: 612-874-1509
E-mail: frc@winternet.com

They publish *Father Times* and have a gopher.

**Fathers United for Equal Rights and
Women's Coalition**
PO Box 1032
Brick, NJ 08723
Phone: 800-537-7697
E-mail: jrinscheid@attmail.com

Focuses on rights of noncustodial parents.

Gay Fathers Unlimited
625 Post Street, Box 283
San Francisco, CA 94109

Joint Custody Association
10606 Wilkins Avenue
Los Angeles, CA 90024
Phone: 213-475-5352

M.A.D. D.A.D.S.
Phone: 402-451-3500
Fax: 402-451-3477

African American, antigang, counsels
delinquents.

**M.A.L.E. (Men Assisting, Leading,
and Educating)**
PO Box 460171
Aurora, CO 8004-01716
Phone: 303-693-9930 or 800-949-MALE
  (6253)
Fax: 303-693-6059
E-mail: male@malesurvivor.org

They publish a newsletter for male
sexual abuse survivors.

Men's Defense Association
17854 Lyons Street
Forest Lake, MN 55025-8107
E-mail: MensDefens@aol.com

Book distributors, nationwide attorney
referral, and newsletter publishing.

The National Center for Men
PO Box 555
Old Bethpage, NY 11804
Phone: 516-942-2020; activism/message
  line: 503-727-3686
E-mail: ncmen@teleport.com

Men's rights, male-choice, fathers'
rights.

**National Organization for Birthfathers
and Adoption Reform (NOBAR)**
PO Box 50
Punta Gorda, FL 33951
Phone: 813-637-7477

NOBAR supports birth fathers' rights
in adoption. Periodic newsletter for
members. Strong networking system.

National Organization for Men
11 Park Place
New York, NY 10007-2801
Phone: 212-686-MALE; 212-766-4030

For men seeking equal rights divorce,
custody, property, and visitation laws.

National Men's Resource Center
PO Box 800-SH
San Anselmo, CA 94979-0800
Phone: 415-453-2839

Promise Keepers
PO Box 18376
Boulder, CO 80308
Phone: 303-421-2800
Fax: 303-421-2918

Born-again Christian men's movement.

Real Men
PO Box 1769
Brookline, MA 02146
Phone: 617-422-1650
E-mail: treefrog@usa1.com or
  conejomiel@aol.com

Strongly pro-feminist.

**Society for the Preservation of Family
Relationships**
172 Berlin Drive
Knoxville, TN 37923
Phone: 423-694-8834
E-mail: S77@cosmail4.ctd.ornl.gov (Don
  Schaefferkoetter)

Family court reform, joint custody.

CHAPTER 20

Mood Disorders

Depression is a frequently used and abused term. When someone asks you what is wrong as they look at your gloomy face, you might respond, "I feel depressed about myself, about my life." Everyone is down in the dumps some of the time, but most people, after a few hours, days, or weeks, snap out of their despondent moods and again cope effectively with life's stresses. However, some people are not as fortunate. They have major depression, a mood disorder that involves feeling deeply unhappy, demoralized, self-derogatory, and apathetic. A person who has major depression often does not feel physically well, loses stamina, has a poor appetite, is listless, and experiences a sleep disorder. Major depression is so common in the United States that it has been called the flu of mental disorders.

While major depression is the most common mood disorder, some people also experience bipolar disorder, previously called manic–depression. Bipolar disorder is characterized by extreme mood swings between depression and mania. In the manic phase, people are exuberant, have tireless stamina, and tend toward excess.

Just as with anxiety, controversy swirls about the etiology and treatment of depression. Some experts believe that most depressions are psychologically and experientially determined and therefore best treated through psychotherapy. Other experts believe that depression is largely biologically determined and thus should be treated mainly with medication. But all experts acknowledge the reciprocal interaction of both psychology and physiology, and most believe in the superiority of a combination of medication and psychotherapy.

In this chapter we critically review the voluminous body of self-help books, autobiographies, movies, and Internet resources related to the mood disorders. These disorders primarily concern major depression and bipolar disorder but also seasonal affective disorder (SAD) and dysthymia as well.

RECOMMENDATION HIGHLIGHTS

Self-Help Books

- On alleviating depression through cognitive-behavioral methods:

  ★★★★★ *Feeling Good* by David Burns

  ★★★★★ *The Feeling Good Handbook* by David Burns

  ★★★★★ *Mind Over Mood* by Dennis Greenberger and Christine A. Padesky

  ★★★★★ *Control Your Depression* by Peter Lewinsohn and Associates

  ★★★★★ *Cognitive Therapy and the Emotional Disorders* by Aaron Beck

- On reducing depression by brief and practical directives:

  ★★★★ *When Living Hurts* by Michael D. Yapko

- On converting depression into new sources of growth:

  ★★★★ *When Feeling Bad Is Good* by Ellen McGrath

Autobiographies

- Best-selling accounts of bipolar disorder:

  ★★★★★ *An Unquiet Mind* by Kay R. Jamison

  ★★★★ *A Brilliant Madness* by Patty Duke and Gloria Hochman

- Sensitive descriptions of depression and near suicide:

  ★★★★★ *Darkness Visible* by William Styron

  ★★★★ *Undercurrents* by Martha Manning

- Adolescent's tale of probable depression and borderline personality:

  ★★★★ *Girl, Interrupted* by Susanna Kaysen

- Life with a manic–depressive mother:

  ◆ *Daughter of the Queen of Sheba* by Jacki Lyden

Movies

- Traumatic story of a girl who announces and then commits suicide:

  ★★★★ *'Night, Mother*

- Hotline volunteer tries to rescue a desperate caller who has overdosed:

  ★★★ *The Slender Thread*

Internet Resources

- Accurate and comprehensive information on depression:

  ★★★★★ *Depression* http://www.queendom.com/selfhelp/depression/depression.html

★★★★★ *Wing of Madness: A Depression Guide*
http://www.wingofmadness.com/index.htm

★★★★ *Psychology Information Online: Depression*
http://www.psychologyinfo.com/depression

- A terrific starting place for newly diagnosed bipolar disorder:

  ★★★ *Bipolar Disorder Frequently Asked Questions (FAQ)*
  http://www.moodswing.org/bdfaq.html

- Medication and/or psychotherapy for mood disorders:

  ★★★★★ *Are You Considering Medication for Depression?*
  http://www.utexas.edu/student/cmhc/meds.html

  ★★★★★ *Psychotherapy versus Medication for Depression: Challenging the Conventional Wisdom with Data*
  http://www.apaorg/journals/anton.html

- Guide for patients in cognitive-behavioral therapy:

  ★★★★★ *The Cognitive Therapy Pages*
  http://www.habitsmart.com/cogtitle.html

SELF-HELP BOOKS

Strongly Recommended

★★★★★ *Feeling Good: The New Mood Therapy* (rev. ed., 1999) by David Burns.
New York: Avon.

The cognitive therapy that Burns describes in this updated self-help classic is the most popular form of psychological treatment for depression. Cognitive therapists believe that people become depressed because of faulty thinking, which triggers self-destructive moods. Faulty thinking includes automatic negative thoughts, self-defeating statements that people often make when they encounter problems. Examples of automatic negative thoughts include all-or-nothing thinking (if a situation is anything less than perfect, it is a total failure), discounting the positive (positive experiences don't count), jumping to conclusions (making negative interpretations when there are no facts to support them), magnification (exaggerating the importance of problems and shortcomings), and personalization and blame (taking personal responsibility for events that aren't entirely under one's control). In *Feeling Good*, Burns outlines techniques people can use to identify and combat the false assumptions that underlie faulty thinking. These techniques have been extensively tested in published research studies; indeed, this is one of the few books in the entire self-help literature that can boast about its demonstrated effectiveness (Ackerson et al., 1998; Cuijpers, 1997). It is peppered with self-assessment tests, self-help forms, and charts. The self-assessment techniques include the widely used Beck Depression Inventory, an anger scale, and a dysfunctional attitude scale. The self-help forms and charts include a daily record of dysfunctional thoughts, an anti-procrastination sheet, a pleasure-predicting sheet, an anger cost/benefit analysis, and an antiperfection sheet. Updated in 1999 with a new section on antidepressant medications, this was the highest-rated book in the depression category of our national studies. It is an outstanding self-help book that has sold more than two million copies since its original publication in 1980. Burns's easy-to-read writing style, extensive use of examples and charts, and enthusiasm give readers a clear understanding of cognitive therapy and the confidence to try out its techniques.

★★★★★   *The Feeling Good Handbook* (rev. ed., 1999) by David Burns. New York: Plume.

In this sequel to *Feeling Good,* Burns says that one of the most exciting recent developments is the discovery that cognitive therapy, which he calls the new mood therapy, can help people with the entire range of mood problems they encounter in their everyday lives. These include feelings of insecurity and inferiority, procrastination, guilt, stress, frustration, and irritability. In this handbook, Burns explains why we are plagued by irrational worries and how to conquer our worst fears without having to rely on addictive tranquilizers or alcohol. Burns also describes the important application of cognitive therapy in recent years to problems in personal relationships, especially marital and couple relationships. *The Feeling Good Handbook* asks readers to complete a number of self-assessment tests once a week, just as patients do, to monitor progress. The tests ask about thoughts, feelings, and actions in a variety of circumstances that typically make people feel angry, sad, frustrated, or anxious. There are two main differences in *The Feeling Good Handbook* compared to the original edition: It covers a wider array of problems (anxiety and relationships as well as depression), and it includes daily logs to fill out. This 5-star resource can be used as an adjunct to *Feeling Good* or independent of it. In either case, it is a very valuable and prized self-help book.

★★★★★   *Mind Over Mood: Change How You Feel by Changing the Way You Think* (1995) by Dennis Greenberger and Christine A. Padesky. New York: Guilford Press.

The authors have taken the nuts and bolts of cognitive therapy and spelled out in a step-by-step fashion how a layperson can utilize these methods in dealing with depression, anxiety, anger, panic, jealousy, guilt, and shame. Strategies described in this book can also help solve relationship problems, handle stress better, improve self-esteem, and become less fearful and more confident. The book helps identify, understand, and make necessary changes in the relationship among thoughts, perceptions, beliefs, emotions, behavior, body changes, and events in one's life. Each chapter contains practice exercises. This 5-star cognitive therapy manual can be truly helpful for adults suffering from depressive complaints—truly a matter of "mind over mood."

★★★★★   *Control Your Depression* (1996) by Peter Lewinsohn, Ricardo Munoz, Mary Ann Youngren, and Antonette Zeiss. Englewood Cliffs, NJ: Prentice-Hall.

This book, also in the cognitive-behavioral tradition, is intended to teach a way of thinking about depression as well as controlling it. The book is divided into three parts: Part I explains how depressed people think; Part II provides step-by-step procedures to control depression; and Part III is about ensuring success. Examples of techniques used in the book are self-control, relaxation, pleasant activities planning, and modifying self-defeating thinking patterns. There are illustrations of how to gauge progress, maintain gains, and determine the need for further help. *Control Your Depression* has been shown in controlled research to work effectively in many cases (Cuijpers, 1998). This 5-star resource is a solid, research-based self-help book for treating depression.

★★★★★ *Cognitive Therapy and the Emotional Disorders* (1976) by Aaron Beck.
New York: International Universities Press.

This text, as the title implies, presents a cognitive therapy approach to depression and other emotional disorders. Aaron Beck pioneered the cognitive therapy approach to depression. He describes the cognitive triad that consists of negative thoughts about the self, ongoing experience, and the future. Depressive individuals' negative thoughts about the self are beliefs that they are defective, worthless, and inadequate. Negative thoughts about ongoing experience are interpretations that what happens is bad. Negative thoughts about the future view the future as hopeless. Beck believes that systematic errors in thinking, each of which darkens the person's experiences, produce depression. These errors include drawing a conclusion when there is little or no evidence to support it; focusing on an insignificant detail while ignoring the more important features of a situation; drawing global conclusions about worth, ability, or performance on the basis of a single fact; magnifying small bad events and minimizing large good events; and incorrectly engaging in self-blame for bad events. Cognitive therapy attempts to counter these distorted thoughts. People are taught to identify and correct the flawed thinking and are trained to conquer problems and master situations they previously thought were insurmountable. This valuable 5-star book was written primarily for professionals rather than a self-help audience. Many of the ideas in Beck's book are presented in a much easier-to-read fashion in Burns's *Feeling Good* and Greenberger and Padesky's *Mind Over Mood*. Beck's book will thus appeal primarily to the clinical community and to the very knowledgeable layperson.

★★★★ *When Living Hurts: Directives for Treating Depression* (1994) by
Michael D. Yapko. New York: Brunner/Mazel.

This volume addresses brief and practical methods for treating depression. The author states that just as stress is inevitable, so is depression. Yapko believes that depression, too, can be managed, and when it is well-managed, it doesn't hurt as much or as long. Given are directives and strategies intended to help the clinician intervene actively and provide catalysts for learning to interrupt the cycle of depression. The first part of the book provides a theoretical overview; the second part describes 91 directives; and the third part presents case narratives that illustrate applications of the directives. This excellent 4-star book is largely a reference book for clinicians; if a client were to use it as a self-help resource, it should probably be used in conjunction with a professional.

★★★★ *When Feeling Bad Is Good* (1994) by Ellen McGrath. New York: Bantam.

This book provides a program for women to convert "healthy depression" into new sources of growth. McGrath challenges the cultural myth that feeling bad must necessarily be negative and introduces a new perspective on women's depression. A woman's healthy depression may be a realistic and appropriate emotional response to the unhealthy culture in which she lives. McGrath identifies six types of healthy depression: victimization depression, relationship depression, age-range depression, depletion depression, body image depression, and mind–body depression. This valuable 4-star book is appropriate for women of all ages, ethnicities, and socioeconomic strata.

Recommended

★★★ *You Can Beat Depression: A Guide to Prevention and Recovery* (2nd ed., 1996) by John Preston. San Luis Obispo, CA: Impact.

In the second edition of this valuable book, the author helps readers appreciate that all depression is not alike (i.e., chronic and recurrent depression). After providing a clearer understanding of depression, Preston guides readers through various treatment choices, such as brief therapy, self-help approaches, family therapy, use of medication, and cognitive changes. Relapse-prevention programs are also addressed for the person who is working to maintain or improve gains. This 3-star book would actually be a 4-star selection if not for the fact that relatively few mental health professionals rated it. A very useful resource for people trying to understand and make choices about treating their depression or concerned about a significant other who may be experiencing depression.

★★★ *Getting Un-Depressed: How a Woman Can Change Her Life through Cognitive Therapy* (rev. ed., 1988) by Gary Emery. New York: Touchstone.

The cognitive therapy approach of this book is designed to help women cope effectively with depression. The risk for women of developing depression is about double of that of men; in fact, the most common mental diagnosis for both black and white women is depression. Emery explains what depression is and how cognitive therapy can help. He describes how women can get immediate relief from their symptoms (inactivity, negative feelings, thinking problems, and physical problems) and improve their state of mind. Next, the author focuses on ways to overcome common complications of depression (weight gain, alcohol and drug dependency, and relationship problems). After this, women learn that they can avoid future depression by working on the psychological causes of depression, which according to Emery are underlying negative beliefs and ineffective ways of handling stress. Finally, Emery outlines how women can lead more self-reliant and self-directed lives. This 3-star book, just missing the 4-star rating, is a popular and practical application of cognitive therapy to depression for women.

★★★ *How to Stubbornly Refuse to Make Yourself Miserable about Anything, Yes Anything!* (1988) by Albert Ellis. New York: Lyle Stuart.

This internationally respected psychologist, the originator of rational-emotive behavioral therapy (REBT), contends that we create our own feelings and choose to think and feel in self-harming ways. Ellis's goals here are to show people how to express and control their emotional destinies, how to stubbornly refuse to make themselves miserable, how to use scientific thoughts and reason, how to effectively change their personality, and how they create their present emotional and behavioral problems. The book certainly covers depression and misery, but it a broader in its coverage. This 3-star book can be helpful for laypersons who are self-motivated or who are already involved in cognitive-behavior therapy.

★★★ *How to Cope with Depression* (1989) by Raymond DePaulo and Keith Ablow. New York: McGraw Hill.

Subtitled *A Complete Guide for You and Your Family*, this book is primarily about the biological causes of depression and the treatment of depression through drug therapy. Part I, Depression: What We Know, defines depression and bipolar disorder (the authors call it manic–depressive illness) and describes the causes of depression as biological. Part II, The Experience of Depression, portrays the nature of depression from the perspective of the patient, the family, and the physician. Part III, The Four Perspectives of Depression, evaluates the disease perspective, the personality perspective, the behavior perspective, and the life-story perspective, and Part IV, Current Treatments, presents the authors' view of how depression should be treated. This 3-star book was not widely known in our studies (only 20 respondents evaluated it), and its title notwithstanding, it is less a guide to coping with depression than a primer on possible causes, treatments, and professional perspectives. The authors make clear their own view: Depression is a physical disease with genetic and biological causes that can be successfully treated only through drug therapy. Other therapies are given token discussion and are said to be useful only as supplements to drug therapy.

★★★ *When the Blues Won't Go Away* (1991) by Robert Hirschfeld. New York: Macmillan.

This book concerns one form of depression—dysthymic disorder—that is long-lasting and relatively mild. In the first several chapters, Hirschfeld describes the rut that people with dysthymic disorder (DD) get themselves into and what they do to stay in that rut. Many characteristics of DD resemble those of major depression, but DD's symptoms are less severe and usually last longer. Most DD sufferers have difficulty pinpointing why they are down in the dumps all the time. DD involves the way people think, feel, act, and relate to other people. People with DD continue to function at home and work, but not at the level they once did. Most of the book is devoted to getting rid of dysthymic disorder, and Hirschfeld does an excellent job of presenting a variety of strategies to help people overcome the blues. The author outlines self-help strategies and therapies that are tailor-made for such problems. He also discusses helpful antidepressant medications, and he shows how a combination of drug therapy and psychotherapy can be effective. This 3-star resource came out just before one of our studies was conducted, so only a small number of mental health professionals rated it. We believe that *When the Blues Won't Go Away* provides a well-balanced analysis of a specific type of depression—long-lasting, relatively mild depression.

★★★ *Listening to Prozac* (1997) by Peter D. Kramer. New York: Penguin.

This best-selling author guides us into the scientific study of biology and personality. Kramer explains the historical debate over what drives us as human beings—nature versus nurture. He then shares his psychiatric and philosophical observations about the influence of a medication like Prozac on a patient's outlook and self-image. His focus is limited mainly to explaining the impact of mood-altering drugs on the modern sense of self: What is Prozac's influence on personality, work performance, memory, dexterity? Does it affect character rather than illness? For the professional and layperson interested in the ongoing debates about mind versus body and nature versus nurture, this is a stimulating read.

Not Recommended

★★ *You Mean I Don't Have to Feel This Way?* (1991) by Colette Dowling. New York: Scribner.

★ *The Good News about Depression: Cures and Treatments in the New Age of Psychiatry* (1986) by Mark Gold. New York: Villard.

AUTOBIOGRAPHIES

Strongly Recommended

★★★★★ *An Unquiet Mind* (1997) by Kay R. Jamison. New York: Random House.

A psychologist known for her research on the relationship between bipolar disorder and creativity, Jamison discusses in this frank autobiography her own history of bipolar disorder, which started in adolescence and is now controlled by lithium. Jamison acknowledges the risks of going public with her disorder while still working professionally in a medical school. A sensitive and compelling autobiography and deservedly rated with 5 stars.

★★★★★ *Darkness Visible: A Memoir of Madness* (1992) by William Styron. New York: Vintage.

In beautifully written prose, novelist William Styron describes his gradual recognition of debilitating depression, his suicidal impulses, hospitalization, and recovery. One of the best portrayals of the loneliness and despair of major depression ever written. Widely known and very positively evaluated in our national studies.

★★★★ *Girl, Interrupted* (1993) by Susanna Kaysen. New York: Random House.

Written 25 years after her hospitalization with probable diagnoses of depression and borderline personality disorder, the author describes her self-mutilation and suicide attempts, problems at school and work, where she was chronically afflicted with boredom and ennui, and her 18-month hospital stay. A perennial favorite of our college students, both male and female. Made into a movie in 2000.

★★★★ *Undercurrents: A Therapist's Reckoning with Her Own Depression* (1994) by Martha Manning. San Francisco CA: HarperSanFrancisco.

In her late thirties, psychotherapist Manning experienced a severe unipolar depression. Symptoms included sleep disturbance, lack of energy, and suicidal impulses. Neither psychotherapy nor drugs seemed to help. Reluctantly, she underwent electric shock therapy (EST), described in detail, which lifted the depression. Afterwards, she learns that it is difficult to convince her colleagues and her friends that EST was a beneficial treatment. A very sensitive account by a therapist who was compelled to switch roles and become a client.

★★★★ *A Brilliant Madness* (1993) by Patty Duke and Gloria Hochman. New York: Bantam.

Cowritten by actress Duke and medical writer Hochman, the book details the disastrous effects of untreated bipolar disorder on the young actress' life and career. Duke suffered through periods of wild euphoria and crippling depression for almost 20 years before being properly diagnosed and treated with lithium, to which she attributes her recovery. Duke has become a public spokesperson on mental health issues. Hochman describes the different forms of affective disorder, treatments, and support groups available.

★★★★ *Leaves from Many Seasons: Selected Papers* (1983) by O. Hobart Mowrer. New York: Praeger.

As a psychologist, the author is best known for his research on learning. This book is a collection of his essays, one of which describes his history of depressive episodes. The first occurred when he was a freshman in high school, the next when he graduated from college and entered graduate school (where he tried psychoanalysis), as a post-graduate fellow when he began teaching at Yale, and again in Washington DC (again he tried psychoanalysis). And the last occurred when he was at the pinnacle of his career as president-elect of the American Psychological Association. He became a voluntary patient at a small Chicago psychiatric hospital. This last episode was the beginning of Mowrer's interest in the relation between religion and psychopathology.

Recommended

★★★ *Pain: The Essence of Mental Illness* (1980) by Anna Eisenhart Anderson. Hicksville, NY: Exposition.

This repetitive, rambling book describes the author's life in and out of mental hospitals with a diagnosis of bipolar disorder. There were numerous separate admissions. Anderson describes herself as "a highly cultivated intellectual somewhat frail of body and very frail of mind." A recurring theme is that she was most happy when she was in hospital.

★★★ *The Beast: A Journey through Depression* (1996) by Tracy Thompson. New York: Plume.

Drawing on notes in a personal journal she kept from adolescence onward and her considerable research skills as a reporter for the *Washington Post*, Thompson writes of her struggles with the depression, suicidal thoughts, and inner demons that have been with her since adolescence. She was treated with psychotherapy and various drugs, including Prozac and Imipramine. A very compassionate and well-written account told with openness and candor that captures the emotional depths of depression.

★★★   *The Bell Jar* (1995) by Sylvia Plath. Cutchogue, NY: Buccaneer.

Plath was a prize-winning poet who received much acclaim during her lifetime and afterward. This autobiographical novel, published only a month before her suicide in 1963, recounts the young woman's hospitalization for severe depression while she was a summer intern at a New York City magazine. She is given shock treatments and spends time in private psychiatric hospitals. The book is regarded as a literary classic in its sensitive description of inner pain so great it leads to suicide.

★★★   *Call Me Anna: The Autobiography of Patty Duke* (1988) by Patty Duke with Kenneth Turan. New York: Bantam.

Patty Duke was a successful child actress, but at the cost of normal contact with her family and with other children. She became a show business legend, but was an unfulfilled disturbed individual still searching for her lost childhood. She won three Emmy Awards and divorced three husbands and became notorious for tantrums, wild spending sprees, and promiscuous behavior. When her bipolar disorder was diagnosed, she began receiving treatment with lithium that enabled her to become a successful wife, mother, political activist, and fulfilled in her life. She also coauthored *A Brilliant Madness* reviewed earlier in this chapter.

★★★   *Breakdown: A Personal Crisis and a Medical Dilemma* (rev. ed., 1987) by Stuart Sutherland. New York: Oxford University Press.

In this update of a 1976 account, psychology professor Sutherland describes his bipolar episodes (including a description of hypomania), experiences with both psychodynamic and behavioral therapists, drug treatments, and two hospitalizations. This edition also presents the author's views on the way society treats the mentally ill, including ethical aspects of treatment. Simon Gray's book and play were based on *Breakdown*.

Diamond in the Rough

♦   *Daughter of the Queen of Sheba* (1998) by Jacki Lyden. New York: Viking Penguin.

Foreign correspondent Jacki Lyden describes her childhood in a dysfunctional family with a manic–depressive mother and a controlling stepfather who committed her mother and beat his stepdaughter. As a child, Lyden would find her mother wrapped in bedsheets with hieroglyphics drawn on her arms, convinced that she was the Queen of Sheba. Lyden and her sisters attempted to find treatment for their mother, who now functions on lithium. This book, though positively rated, was recently published at the time of the national study and is thus designated a Diamond in the Rough.

Not Recommended

★★   *Prozac Nation: Young and Depressed in America* (1997) by Elizabeth Wurtzel. New York: Riverhead.

★   *The Loony-Bin Trip* (1990) by Kate Millett. New York: Simon & Schuster.

MOVIES

Strongly Recommended

★★★★ *'Night, Mother* (1987) produced by Alan Greisman and Aaron Spelling and directed by Tom Moore. PG-13 Rating. 96 minutes.

A traumatic story of a daughter who announces to her mother that she is going to commit suicide. The mother tries to dissuade her as they stay up late together laughing and reminiscing. Then the daughter, in fact, takes her life. The daughter's painful struggle is revealed through their storytelling that night, and we see that the daughter is living with a lifetime accumulation of challenges with which she can no longer cope. The compelling message is to deal with life problems on a manageable scale rather than turning away and allowing the reserve of heartache to triumph. This 4-star resource also reveals that suicide is the daughter's desperate way of taking charge after years of being dominated by others and being devalued as a person. The film is an adaptation of a Broadway play that received a Pulitzer Prize in 1983.

Recommended

★★★ *The Slender Thread* (1965) produced by Stephen Alexander and directed by Sydney Pollack. 98 minutes.

This film is based on the true story of a college student working on a crisis hotline who finds himself on the phone with a woman who has taken an overdose of sleeping pills and doesn't know where she is. She has reached despair because her husband has discovered that he is not the father of their son; she is deeply depressed and does not have the strength to go on. His frantic attempts to keep her on the phone while the police track her location is a story of caring about the life of a stranger and the desperate state that people reach before they reach out.

INTERNET RESOURCES

Metasites

★★★★★ *Depression* http://www.queendom.com/selfhelp/depression/depression.html

Click on Depression in the left column. A rich site offering eight depression measures, articles, medication information, online support groups, case studies, links to reources, FAQs, and the like. Everything is here.

★★★★★ *Wing of Madness: A Depression Guide* http://www.wingofmadness.com

Sensible and accurate information, with many clearly organized sections and links, designed for laypersons. A pleasure to explore. Support, personal experiences, advice, links, and so on. This may be all you will need for clients.

★★★★★ *Dr. Ivan's Depression Central*
http://www.psycom.net/depression.central.html

Offers about a million links, papers, and other materials under about 70 headings. Many are by Ivan K. Goldberg, MD, an expert on psychopharmacology. While the site is medication-oriented, some subjects are free of this (e.g., Grief and Bereavement, Psychotherapy for People with Depression). Most materials are aimed at professionals and the sophisticated, but some can be used as introductory materials. Dr. Goldberg keeps the site updated, but the materials are not clearly organized.

★★★★★ *Bipolar Planet* http://www.tcnj.edu/~ellisles/BipolarPlanet

Hundreds of links to both formal and personal sites about mood disorders, anxiety, support, search engines, researchers, and humor.

★★★★ *Psychology Information Online: Depression*
http://www.psychologyinfo.com/depression

A very large site organized by psychologists full of accurate information about diagnosis, cognitive therapy, SAD, medication, and many other topics. Most sections are quite small but may be useful for people needing an overview. This is a product of Donald J. Franklin, PhD, and offers his *National Directory of Psychologists*.

Psychoeducational Materials for Clients and Families

General Sites on Depression

★★★★★ *Depression* http://www.nimh.nih.gov/publicat/depressionmenu.cfm

From the National Institute of Mental Health, this page offers about a dozen brochures organized by audience (adolescents, employers, senior citizens, and women) and by topic (bipolar, suicide, comorbidity, etc.).

★★★★★ *Depression in Children and Adolescents: What It Is and What to Do about It*
by Jim Chandler, MD
http://www.klis.com/chandler/pamphlet/dep/depressionpamphlet.htm

About 20 pages of solid information and some vignettes written for the public and teens. The section What Can be Done? is about behavioral interventions.

★★★★★ *Construction of Your Own Life Chart: The NIMH Life Chart Method™*
(the LCMTM-S) http://www.bpso.org/ourfavs.htm#charting

These two articles describe a way to collect data to improve diagnostic accuracy of mood disorders. You may have to register, but it is free and useful.

★★★★ *BPSO-Bipolar Significant Others* http://www.bpso.org

Hundred of linked, high quality, articles, clearly and pragmatically organized. Lots to offer clients.

★★★★ *So You Don't Want to Go to a Psychiatrist!* by Internet Mental Health
http://www.mentalhealth.com/fr20.html

Look under Major Depressive Disorder, then Stories of Recovery followed by this title. Although it never mentions nonpsychiatrists, this three-pager addresses all the anxieties of clients. Perhaps use this for an ambivalent patient.

★★★★ *Just a Mood . . . or Something Else?* http://www.ndmda.org/justmood.htm

A five-page brochure for teens about depressive illnesses. The parallel *Is My Adolescent Depressed?* can be found at http://www.ndmda.org/myteen.htm.

★★★★ *People with Depression Tend to Seek Negative Feedback*
http://www.shpm.com/articles/depress/negfeed.html

A brief but useful handout because it addresses and teaches this important point.

★★★★ *Understanding and Treating Depression*
http://www.couns.uiuc.edu/depression.htm

A brief, balanced, and complete overview.

★★★★ *Have a Heart's Depression Home*
http://www.geocities.com/HotSprings/3628/index.html

Stephen L. Bernhardt, PhD, offers several fine essays: Depression: Understanding Suicidal Thoughts (he covers seven triggers for suicide in about five pages); Helping a Depressed Friend; Emotional Thought Stopping (an exercise); and others. Very clear and useful for therapy.

★★★★ *How to Help a Person with Depression*
http://www.mentalhealth.com/story/p52-dps2.html

Two pages of explicit guidelines. Very valuable family education.

★★★★ *Steven Thos's Mental Health Resources—Depression and Bipolar Disorder*
http://www.mhsource.com/wb/thow9903.html

About 40 questions very likely to be asked by patients or families and annotated links to multiple answers.

★★★★ *Andrew's Depression Page* http://www.blarg.net/~charlatn/Depression.html

Many articles and links on all aspects: Poems and autobiographies, treatment, suicide, mood scales.

★★★ *(23) Best Things to Say to Someone Who Is Depressed*
http://www.pendulum.org/articles/best_to_say.html

★★★ *(99) Worst Things to Say to Someone Who Is Depressed*
http://www.pendulum.org/articles/worst_to_say.html

Perhaps useful for family members to consider.

Bipolar Disorder

★★★★★   *Manic–Depressive Illness: An Information Book for Patients, Their Families and Friends* by Erika Bukkfalvi Hillard, MSW
http://www.mentalhealth.com/fr20.html

Click on Bipolar in the left column and then, under Booklets, on this title. In 25 pages, Hillard covers theory, treatments (with short shrift given to psychotherapy in general and cognitive-behavior theory in particular), hospitalization, and especially Family Considerations, which make a good family support handout, especially after a hospitalization.

★★★★★   *Bipolar Affective Disorder in Children and Adolescents* by James Chandler, MD
http://www.klis.com/chandler/pamphlet/bipolar/bipolarpamphlet.html

About 20 pages of solid information and three cases written for the public and teens. While nonmedical treatments are only briefly addressed, the rest would be a very good introduction for families.

★★★★   *Bipolar Disorder* http://www.healthguide.com/english/brain/bipolar

A series of short but well-written informative pages providing symptoms and diagnoses and reinforcing medications.

★★★★   *Expert Consensus Treatment Guidelines for Bipolar Disorder: A Guide for Patients and Families* http://www.psychguides.com/bphe.html

A large (16-page) overview of bipolar disorder with almost no attention paid to psychotherapy.

★★★★   *How to Avoid a Manic Episode* by Julia Mayo, PhD http://www.bpso.org

Look under Information, then Our Favorites, then the title. A list of triggering circumstances and advice in three pages.

★★★★   *Bipolar Kids Homepage* http://www.geocities.com/EnchantedForest/1068

A large set of links, but the Articles for Families of Bipolar Kids and the School Issues sections contain much of use to families. Written for an educated audience.

★★★   *Bipolar Planet* http://www.tcnj.edu/~ellisles/BipolarPlanet

Beside the good links, if you would like some lightness about bipolar disorder, check out Shop for That Special Bipolar Home, The WebART Gallery (poetry), Brother John's Online Bipolar Church, Home of the Sacred Turtle Story, and Play the Bipolar Jukebox.

★★★   *Bipolar Disorder Frequently Asked Questions (FAQ)*
http://www.moodswing.org/bdfaq.html

About 30 pages of very complete information—symptoms and diagnosis, therapies, insurance, rights, helping others, medications, coping. An excellent starting place for the newly diagnosed. It contains personal and expressive materials as well as scientific information. Last revised September 1996.

★★★ *Alternative Approaches to the Treatment of Manic–Depression*
　　　http://www.pendulum.org/alternatives/lisa_alternative.htm

A 10-page overview suitable as an introduction to the uses of nutrients and the like.

Medication Treatment

★★★★★ *Are You Considering Medication for Depression?*
　　　　http://www.utexas.edu/student/cmhc/meds.html

About eight pages in a question and answer format on medications. Very relevant questions and well-written, so it would make a useful handout before a medication evaluation.

★★★★ *Pharmacological Treatment of Mood Disorders* by David M. Goldstein, MD
　　　　http://www.med.jhu.edu/drada/ref/goldstein.html

A rather sophisticated six-page review of medications.

Against a Solely Medical Formulation and Treatment

★★★★★ *Psychotherapy versus Medication for Depression: Challenging the Conventional Wisdom with Data* by David O. Antonuccio, PhD, William G. Danton, PhD, and Garland Y. DeNelsky, PhD
　　　　http://www.apa.org/journals/anton.html

"This article reviews a wide range of well-controlled studies comparing psychological and pharmacological treatments for depression. The evidence suggests that the psychological interventions, particularly cognitive-behavioral therapy, are at least as effective as medication in the treatment of depression, even if severe. These conclusions hold for both vegetative and social adjustment symptoms, especially when patient-rated measures are used and long-term follow-up is considered." Written for the reading level and sophistication of professionals.

★★★ *Placebo Effect Accounts for Fifty Percent of Improvement in Depressed Patients Taking Antidepressants* http://www.shpm.com/articles/depress/antidprs.html

Written for the public.

Cognitive Therapy

★★★★★ *Cognitive Therapy*
　　　　http://www.depression.com/health_library/treatments/cognitive.html

An explanation in eight pages with descriptions of twisted thinking and how to untwist it. Rather complete for an introduction. Based on David Burns's book.

★★★★★   *The Cognitive Therapy Pages* by Robert Westermeyer, PhD
            http://www.habitsmart.com/cogtitle.html

In six sections of two to four pages each, Westermeyer offers complete and accessible explanations. Suitable for introducing almost all patients to cognitive-behavior therapy.

★★★★   *Basics of Cognitive Therapy*   http://mindstreet.com/mindstreet/cbt.html

Only three pages, but useful because it is so positive. Suitable for the better-educated.

★★★   *Cognitive Therapy: A Multimedia Learning Program*
            http://mindstreet.com/synopsis.html

In a series of 11 brief excerpts (downloadable as QuickTime movies), the basics of the cognitive therapy of depression are presented. They are from a commercial CD-ROM that is a sophisticated training program in cognitive-behavior therapy for patients. This could serve as an introduction to treatment for the less-skilled reader or those who like computerized presentations.

Self-Injury

★★★★★   *Secret Shame: Self-Injury Information and Support*
            http://www.palace.net/~llama/psych/injury.html

An excellent page, with Self-Injury: A Quick Guide to the Basics, Self Help (for stopping), First Aid, Coping Ideas, and more. Absolutely comprehensive, sensitive, and well-organized.

Suicide

★★★★★   *A Comprehensive Approach to Suicide Prevention*
            http://www.lollie.com/suicide.html

About eight intense pages of straight-from-the-shoulder information, perspectives, and metaphors. The best readings for someone contemplating suicide.

★★★★★   *If You Are Thinking about Suicide . . . Read This First* by Martha Ainsworth
            http://www.metanoia.org/suicide/

Excellent suggestions, seven informational pages, three books, and links to resources for the actively suicidal.

★★★★★   *Suicide Prevention Help*
            http://members.tripod.com/~suicideprevention/index.html

This personal site of about 14 pages contains some of the best advice on coping with suicidal thoughts or friends. Realistic, practical, and sensitive, the site might be given to a client to bring to the surface hidden thoughts or to family members to provoke discussions.

★★★★★ *Suicide and Suicide Prevention*
  http://www.psycom.net/depression.central.suicide.html

A comprehensive list of about 60 links to all kinds of materials on suicide. Many can be used for patient education and support as well as clinician improvement.

★★★★ *SA/VE—Suicide Awareness/Voices of Education* http://www.save.org

The site offers, besides support, a dozen well-written and helpful brochures on thoughts of suicide, telling children, misconceptions, and the like.

★★★★ *Signs of Suicide Risk* http://vcc.mit.edu/comm/samaritans/warning.html

A very good but short list for a quick evaluation of one's fears for another person that can be used with concerned family.

★★★★ *How to Help Someone You Care About*
  http://vcc.mit.edu/comm/samaritans/brochure.html

Very solid and well-phrased guidelines for family.

★★★ *Now Is Not Forever: A Survival Guide* by J. Kent Griffiths, DSW
  http://members.aol.com/dswgriff/suicide.html

A series of about 75 pages with a sentence or suggestion or two on each, customized with your name and age. Print out a simple no-suicide contract, write some notes, do some problem solving, reach out, and explore other exercises. The ads are very distracting from what are generally good ideas (especially for adolescents). The ideas have to be worked on and not just clicked through.

Seasonal Affective Disorder (SAD)

★★★★ *Seasonal Light/SAD*
  http://www.geocities.com/HotSprings/7061/sadhome.html

This site is only about SAD. It offers many links, bibliographies, organizations, and lists of products. Similar is *Outside In* at http://www.outsidein.co.uk/sadinfo.htm.

Biographical and Autobiographical Vignettes

★★★★ *A Primer on Depression and Bipolar Disorder* by Dimitri Mihalas
  http://chandra.astro.indiana.edu/bipolar/physical.html

Touching and informative, this biographical sketch in about 20 pages can be most useful for those still struggling over commitment to treatment. Although Mihalas speaks mostly about medications, he does indicate the value of psychotherapy.

★★★ *A Compilation of Writings by People Suffering from Depression*
  http://www.blarg.net/~charlatn/voices/voices.html

About 75 essays and poems.

★★★ *Creativity and Depression and Manic-Depression*
    http://www.med.jhu.edu/drada/creativity.html

Talks by Kay Redfield Jamison on four famous writers with mood disorders.

★★★ *First Person Experiences* http://www.med.jhu.edu/drada/firstperson.html

Five stories, 3 from famous persons and 2 from family members. Excellent

★★★ *Poetry from People Living with Depression*
    http://www.something-fishy.com/cry.htm

About 50 or more poems.

Online Support Groups

Pendulum

"The Pendulum mailing list is a support group for people who have a cyclical affective disorder (either bipolar or unipolar depression)." To subscribe to Pendulum, send a message to majordomo@ucar.edu containing this command: SUBSCRIBE PENDULUM (your e-mail address).

Walkers-in-Darkness

"Walkers-in-Darkness is a list for people diagnosed with various depressive disorders (unipolar, atypical, and bipolar depression, SAD, related disorders). The list also includes sufferers of panic attacks and Borderline Personality Disorder." To subscribe to Walkers or Walkers-Digest, send a message to majordomo@world.std.com containing one of the following lines: "SUBSCRIBE WALKERS (your e-mail address)" for the mailing list, or "SUBSCRIBE WALKERS-DIGEST (your e-mail address)" for the digest.

MADNESS

"An electronic action and information letter for people who experience moods swings, fright, voices, and visions." To subscribe, send a message to listserv@sjuvm.stjohns.edu with this command in the body of the message: SUBSCRIBE MADNESS (first name) (last name).

Befrienders International http://www.befrienders.org/mainindex.htm

Support, information, self and other help advice, helplines, and more.

BiPolar Children and Teens Homepage
http://hometown.aol.com/DrgnKpr1/BPCAT.html

A site with links to perhaps hundreds of home pages of families with a bipolar child.

NATIONAL SUPPORT GROUPS

American Suicide Foundation
1045 Park Avenue, Suite 3C
New York, NY 10028
Phone: 800-ASF-4042; 212-210-1111

Provides referrals to national support groups for suicide survivors.

Depressive and Related Affective Disorders Association
Johns Hopkins Hospital
600 North Wolfe Street
Baltimore, MD 21205
Fax: 410-614-3241
Email: drada@welchlink.welch.jhu.edu
http://infonet.welch.jhu.edu/
   departments/drada/default

Emotional Health Anonymous
PO Box 429
Glendale, CA 91202-0429

Fellowship of people who meet to share experiences, strengths, and hopes with each other so they may solve common problems of mental health.

Emotions Anonymous
PO Box 4245
St. Paul, MN 55104
Phone: 612-647-9712

Fellowship for people experiencing emotional difficulties.

Friends for Survival
PO Box 214463
Sacramento, CA 95821
Phone: 916-392-0664; 800-646-7322

For family, friends, and professionals after a suicide death.

National Alliance for the Mentally Ill
200 North Glebe Road, Suite 1015
Arlington, VA 2203-3754
Phone: 703-524-7600
http://www.nami.org

National Depressive and Manic Depressive Association
730 North Franklin
Chicago, IL 60610
Phone: 800-82N-DMDA
Fax: 312-642-7243
http://www.ndmda.org.

National Organization for Seasonal Affective Disorder (NOSAD)
PO Box 40133
Washington, DC 20016

For SAD patients and their families.

Prozac Survivors Support Group
2212 Woodbourne Avenue
Louisville, KY 40205
Phone: 502-459-2086

Postpartum Support International
927 North Kellogg Avenue
Santa Barbara, CA 93111
Phone: 805-967-7636

To increase the awareness of the emotional changes women often experience during pregnancy and after the birth of a baby.

Recovery
802 North Dearborn Street
Chicago, IL 60610
Phone: 312-337-5661

A community mental health organization that offers a self-help method of will training: a system of techniques for controlling temperamental behavior and changing attitudes toward nervous symptoms, anxiety, anger, and fears.

SOLOS—Survivors of Loved Ones' Suicides
PO Box 1716
Springfield, VA 22151-0716
http://www.1000deaths.com

Support and testimony.

CHAPTER 21

Pregnancy

Although Sara and Jim did not plan to have a baby right away, they did not take any precautions to prevent it, and it was not long before Sara was pregnant. They found a nurse–midwife they liked and invented a pet name—Bibinello—for the fetus. They signed up for birth preparation classes, and each Friday night for 8 weeks they faithfully practiced for contractions. They drew up a birth plan that included the type of care provider they wanted to use, the birth setting they desired, and other aspects of labor and birth. They moved into a larger apartment so that the baby could have its own room and spent weekends browsing through garage sales and secondhand stores to find good prices on baby furniture—a crib, a high chair, a stroller, a changing table, a crib mobile, a swing, a car seat.

Jim and Sara also spent a lot of time talking about what kind of parents they wanted to be, what their child might be like, and what changes the baby would make in their lives. One of their concerns was that Sara's maternity leave would last only 6 weeks. If she wanted to stay home longer, she would have to quit her job, something she and Jim were not sure they could afford.

These are among the many scripts and questions expectant couples have about pregnancy. And there have been many resources created to help expectant parents like Sara and Jim better understand pregnancy and make more informed decisions about their offspring's health and well-being, as well as their own. We review, in this chapter, the most useful self-help books, movies, and Internet resources for doing so.

SELF-HELP BOOKS

Strongly Recommended

★★★★★ *What to Expect When You're Expecting* (rev. ed., 1996) by Arlene Eisenberg, Heidi Eisenberg Murkoff, and Sandee E. Hathaway. New York: Workman.

This revision of the best-selling first edition reflects advances in obstetrical practice but just as importantly incorporates new or expanded areas suggested by the readers: sec-

RECOMMENDATION HIGHLIGHTS

Self-Help Books

- A month-by-month, step-by-step guide to pregnancy:

    ★★★★★ *What to Expect When You're Expecting* by Arlene Eisenberg and Associates

- An excellent overview of pregnancy:

    ★★★★★ *The Complete Book of Pregnancy and Childbirth* by Sheila Kitzinger

    ◆ *The Girlfriends' Guide to Pregnancy* by Vicki Iovine

- For expectant fathers:

    ◆ *The Expectant Father* by Armin A. Brott and Jennifer Ash

Movies

- A diabetic woman makes a life-threatening decision to maintain her pregnancy:

    ★★★ *Steel Magnolias*

Internet Resources

- On pregnancy:

    ★★★★★ *Ask NOAH about: Pregnancy*
    http://www.noah-health.org/english/pregnancy/pregnancy.html

    ★★★★★ *Sabrina's Pregnancy Page*
    http://www.fensende.com/Users/swnymph

- On infertility:

    ★★★★ *Infertility* http://infertility.miningco.com

- On teen pregnancy and abortion:

    ★★★★★ *Planned Parenthood* http://www.plannedparenthood.org

- On adoption:

    ★★★★ *Adoption.com* http://www.adoption.com/index.shtml

ond pregnancies, chronic medical conditions, what to do if you get sick, more on common pregnancy symptoms, and more on complications. This is a month-by-month, step-by-step guide to pregnancy and childbirth. The authors are a mother–daughters team, and their book was the result of the unnecessarily worry-filled pregnancy of the second author (Heidi Murkoff). The book tries to put expectant parents' normal fears into perspective by giving them comprehensive information and helping them enjoy this transition in their lives. *What to Expect When You're Expecting* is an excellent self-help book for expectant parents. It is reassuring and thorough. The authors do an outstanding job of walking expectant parents through the 9 months of pregnancy and childbirth.

★★★★★   *The Complete Book of Pregnancy and Childbirth* (1996) by Sheila Kitzinger.
          New York: Knopf.

This comprehensive guide to pregnancy and childbirth emphasizes an active and informed stance to giving birth. The expectant mother prepares for an active role in childbirth by learning about the changes that are occurring in her body, pregnancy and childbirth options, and who does what to her and why. In this book, expectant mothers learn about the early weeks of pregnancy and the emotional and physical changes they are likely to experience at this time. Kitzinger educates expectant mothers about prenatal care and how to understand medical charts. She describes common worries and problems of expectant mothers, lovemaking during pregnancy, and the father's role. The author recommends relaxation and breathing exercises and provides advice about medical checkups. She covers what happens during the stages of labor, support during labor, coping with pain, the option of gentle birth, and what to expect in the first few hours and days after birth. The book has numerous charts, drawings, and photographs. The book's enthusiasts especially liked Kitzinger's holistic approach to pregnancy, her emphasis on women's choices, and her ideas about relaxation and breathing techniques.

Recommended

★★★   *What to Eat When You're Expecting* (1986) by Arlene Eisenberg, Heidi Murkoff, and Sandee Hathaway. New York: Workman.

The book, written by the authors of *What to Expect When You're Expecting*, is based on 20 years of practical application in the Eisenberg family. They present the "best odds" diet, which they believe increases the probability of having a healthy baby by controlling the factors that can be influenced and minimizing the risk and worry about factors that cannot be controlled. The book describes the mother's nutritional needs during pregnancy and how they affect the baby. Daily recommended portions are given. The expectant mother learns how to assess her current eating habits and how to alter them if they are not good. Also described are practical solutions for cooking and enlisting the whole family in the eating plan. Almost 100 pages of recipes and a lengthy appendix of nutritional charts are also included. The book is well-written and easy to read, and the nutritional plan for expectant mothers is sound, albeit perhaps dated.

★★★   *Pregnancy after 35* (1976) by Carole McCauley. New York: Pocket Books.

The older mother faces unique medical and emotional problems during pregnancy. This book is based on medical journal articles and interviews with physicians, psychologists, midwives, and older couples to address the special concerns of pregnancy in older women. Women over 35 learn about genetic counseling, risk factors, and psychological issues that arise throughout pregnancy. The book was published in 1976 and is dated, especially in terms of nutritional advice. And, of course, it does not cover a number of tests that have been developed in recent years to assess the likelihood of having a healthy baby.

★★★ *The Well Pregnancy Book* (rev. ed., 1996) by Mike Samuels and Nancy Samuels. New York: Summit.

This guide to pregnancy and childbirth emphasizes a holistic approach. It provides an overview of childbirth practices in different cultures and serves as an expectant parents' guide to pregnancy, childbirth, and the postpartum period. It covers nutrition and fitness, physical changes in the expectant mother and the offspring, and the medical aspects of hormonal and bodily changes in pregnant women. This book is better used in cases of uncomplicated pregnancies rather than high-risk ones. Critics also said that the book is too simplistic and is poorly organized.

★★★ *From Here to Maternity* (1986) by Connie Marshall. Citrus Heights, CA: Conmar.

This self-help book is a general guide to pregnancy that emphasizes childbirth preparation and selection of a health care team. Its purpose is to improve the expectant couple's ability to communicate knowledgeably with their health care team. The book's three parts deal with (1) emotions during pregnancy, the expectant mother's body and prenatal growth, drug use, and choosing breast or bottle feeding; (2) selecting a doctor; and (3) labor and delivery. *From Here to Maternity* received a 3-star rating, but some critics said that the book is superficial and poorly illustrated.

Diamonds in the Rough

◆ *The Girlfriends' Guide to Pregnancy* (1995) by Vicki Iovine. New York: Pocket Books.

The author recounts that during her four pregnancies, she bought and read every pregnancy book available and found in the end that 90% of the good information she received came from girlfriends, not the experts. This is the backdrop for the hilarious *Girlfriend's Guide* that does in fact discuss every phase of pregnancy and certainly answers many questions most women would never ask their physicians. The conversational style of the book gives the sense of lunch with a particularly candid best friend. Much factual information is offered here; myths are dispelled or upheld; rumors are confirmed or denied; and lies about pregnancy are revealed. This book takes a funny, bold, realistic, but also sensitive and knowledgeable view of pregnancy, which contributes, along with its strong ratings (but few raters), to Diamond in the Rough status.

◆ *The Expectant Father* (1995) by Armin A. Brott and Jennifer Ash. New York: Abbeville Press.

Information for expectant mothers is readily available; however, Brott and Ash maintain that the expectant father has been overlooked in the pregnancy and preparation for birth literature. The purpose of this book is to recognize and validate the experiences of expectant fathers and to offer ways for them to remain equally involved in the pregnancy and birth. Each of the first nine chapters characterizes that month's development of the baby, what's going on with the mother (physically and emotionally), what the expectant father is going through, and how he can stay involved. Very practical suggestions as well as thoughtful ideas are offered, ranging from prenatal communication, medical leave, and childbirth classes to financial planning and Cesarean section. The expectant father is encouraged to be a full participant in his child's development and birth and to reject the stereotypical role assigned to fathers. This book merits the Diamond in the Rough designation because of its very strong ratings by a handful of our mental health experts.

MOVIES

Recommended

★★★ *Steel Magnolias* (1990) produced by Ray Stark and directed by Herbert Ross. PG Rating. 118 minutes.

This movie spans several years in the lives of a group of women whose central meeting place is a beauty salon. One of the central characters, a diabetic woman, gives birth to a child her physician warned her not to have and subsequently lapses into a terminal coma. More generally, the film is about the support of good friends, accepting loss, and learning to grow beyond differences. Through troubling times, there is a rebirth of relationship and newfound support.

Not Recommended

★ *Father of the Bride II* (1995) produced by Sandy Gallin and Nancy Meyers and directed by Charles Shyer. PG Rating. 106 minutes.

★ *Nine Months* (1995) produced by Anne Francois, Chris Columbus, Mark Radcliffe, and Michael Barnathan and directed by Chris Columbus. PG-13 Rating. 102 minutes.

★ *Baby M* (1988, made for TV) produced by Gordon L. Freedman and directed by James Stephen Sadwith. PG Rating. 128 minutes.

INTERNET RESOURCES

Metasites

★★★★★ *Ask NOAH about: Pregnancy*
http://www.noah-health.org/english/pregnancy/pregnancy.html

A superbly organized site with literally thousands of links to papers and other sites under headings like Family Planning, Prenatal Care and Birth, Problems and Risks, Postnatal Care, and Pregnancy Resources. This could be a place to start because of its clear organization or the only place because of its encyclopedic scope.

★★★★★ *Pregnancy/Birth* http://pregnancy.miningco.com

Under headings like Cesarean Section, Fetal Development, and Episiotomy are perhaps a thousand sites with comments, but no ratings.

★★★★ *Infertility* http://infertility.miningco.com

Under headings like Infertility 101, Counseling, Child-free, Fertile World, Causes, Holidays, and others are hundreds of links with brief comments. It is very unlikely that you will fail to find what you seek or need in this massive collection.

Psychoeducational Materials for Clients and Families

General Sites

★★★★★ *Childbirth.org* http://www.childbirth.org

A very large and comprehensive site with lots to read and do on every aspect. Thank you, Robin Elise Weiss. About 25 *FAQs* at http://www.childbirth.org/articles/faqs.html are well done and cover some unusual areas, like Low Tech Fertility Methods and Amniotomy.

★★★★ *The Dad Zone* http://www.babycenter.com/dads

This commercial site offers about 25 fine articles from preconception to baby's first year.

★★★ *ParenthoodWeb*
http://www.parenthoodweb.com/parent_cfmfiles/pregnancy_labor.cfm

This site has dozens of short articles on every topic imaginable.

★★★ *OBGYN.net: The Universe of Women's Health* http://www.obgyn.net

"This site, with original content by obstetrics and gynecology practitioners, is also an annotated subject directory of Web resources. Some of the topics covered in the For Women and Patients section are: contraceptives, medications, infertility, grief, pregnancy and birth, raising children, sexuality and reproductive health, and fitness. There's also an acronym glossary and it's searchable." The layout is complex, so the search engine is appreciated. There are industry and commercial sections. Patients who still have medical questions after looking elsewhere and do not consult their physician can probably find the answer here.

Medical Aspects

★★★★★ *Sabrina's Pregnancy Page* http://www.fensende.com/Users/swnymph

The gift of a very knowledgeable midwife, this site has personal items as well as dozens of well-considered links on pregnancy, parenting, breast-feeding, references (indexed pages), and good FAQs. The FAQ page also offers WebRings that change often and are more focused, so they should not be pursued until the stronger sites have been read.

★★★★★ *BabyZone* http://babyzone.com

An enormous site for any kind of question related to medication, diseases, symptoms, procedures, and so on. Go to http://babyzone.com/drnathan/glossary.htm to search by term.

★★★★ *Pregnancy Calendar* http://www.pregnancycalendar.com

This site "will build a day-by-day customized calendar detailing the development of a baby from before conception to birth." The larger site (ParentsPlace.com) also offers interactive ways to create a plan for birth, and has much material on nutrition, newborn care, and breast-feeding as well as chat and bulletin boards.

★★★ *StorkNet's Week-by-Week Guide to Your Pregnancy!*
     http://www.pregnancyguideonline.com

Similar to the *Pregnancy Calendar* (above) but also includes Fetal Development, Maternal Changes, Checkups, Readings, and Ideas for Dad.

Getting Pregnant and Infertility

★★★★★ *OnHealth: Baby Channel*
     http://onhealth.webmd.com/baby/home/index,4.asp

This site seems to have everything for pregnant parents or those trying to conceive; testing, calculators, contraception, postpartum, dictionaries, safe medications, alternative medications, and more.

★★★★★ *Getting Pregnant and Infertility*
     http://www.noah-health.org/english/pregnancy/fertility.html

Perhaps a hundred links to pages and sites, all selected with NOAH's usual high quality standards by their professional judes and editors.

★★★★★ *Plus-Size Pregnancy Website* http://www.vireday.com/plus

Here are 20 very informative articles on preparing for and being pregnant, complications, clothing, and breast-feeding, and superb links and support for the large woman. A wonderful gift from Kmom. See also *FertilityPlus* at http://www.pinelandpress.com which has a Infertility FAQ for Women of Size, which is unique.

★★★★ *Infertility FAQ* http://www.fertilityplus.org/faq/infertility.html

Totalling about 40 pages, this is a well-organized and superbly complete overview of the medical aspects that should be understood before exploring the psychological ones. It also covers online news groups, books and readings, and how to join online groups. The FAQs in section 12 are extremely informative about the more complex medical issues.

★★★★ *Preconception* http://www.babycenter.com/preconception

Although a commercial site, this offers about 100 short pieces on the issues, with specific information and some reporting of myths and errors.

★★★ *Infertility Resources* http://www.ihr.com/infertility/index.html

Under Educational are hundreds of articles. The most relevant are under Male Factor and four of the articles under Psychological and Social Issues.

Twins, Triplets, and Multiple Births

★★★   *Cool Sites for Twins and Triplets*
        http://www.geocities.com/Heartland/Hills/7920/twinlink.htm
A good set of links to various sites.

★★   *National Organization of Mothers of Twins Clubs*   http://www.nomotc.org
This site offers a few online brochures of tips under Nursery, but it is mainly a collection of local support groups.

Pregnancy Loss

See Death and Grieving (Chapter 12) and Online Support, below, for Compassionate Friends and HAND.

★★★★   *A Heartbreaking Choice*   http://www.erichad.com/ahc
There are two short but useful articles here: What Makes This Loss So Different and Difficult? by Irving G. Leon, PhD, a sensitive introduction; and It Happened Once—Will It Happen Again? by Helga V. Toriello, PhD, which is for those in need of a three-page introduction to genetic risks.

★★★   *Hygeia*   http://hygeia.org/poems0.htm
Volume 1 contains 12 professional articles, of which numbers 9 and 10 are on the emotional impact of pregnancy loss. They are first-person essays by a nurse and a social worker, both with a lot of experience. The articles are well-written but may be too intense for the average client. Volume 2's essays 2 and 7 are similar.

★★★   *Waiting with Love*   http://www.erichad.com/wwl
"For parents who choose to continue a pregnancy knowing their unborn baby will die before or shortly after birth and for families who learn their newborn will die."

★★★   *Center for Loss in Multiple Birth (CLIMB)*   http://www.climb-support.org
Just a description and ways to order their newsletter here.

Untoward Pregnancies

★★★★★   *Planned Parenthood*   http://www.plannedparenthood.org
The authoritative *Fact Sheets* at http://www.plannedparenthood.org/library/factsheets. htm include those on Birth Control and on Teen Pregnancy and Abortion. The nine publications under Abortion provide solid facts to counter fears.

★★★★   *Adoption.com*   http://www.adoption.com
This site seeks to connect children (and pregnancies) with people seeking to adopt, and it offers commercial products. However, their Adoption Library is a searchable collec-

tion of thousands of articles on the literature, poetry, law, statistics, foster parenting, special needs kids, birthparents, and more. Probably the best starting site for those considering adoption.

★★★ *Pregnancy Centers Online* http://www.pregnancycenters.org
Offering addresses of local groups, this site is for women who have a crisis (unwanted) pregnancy, do not want to abort, and want support. It is vigorously antiabortion.

Other Resources

★★★★ *ProMoM* http://www.promom.org
If a woman needs information or support, this site is enthusiastically in favor of breast-feeding.

★★★★ *Breastfeeding Resources on the Internet*
        http://www.prairienet.org/laleche/other.html
An organized and annotated listing of hundreds of sites. Comprehensive and authoritative. Thank you, Sue Ann Kendall.

★★★★ *A Social Support Network, Information Center, and Research Guide*
        http://www.postpartum.net
A unique site with a good overview essay, a guide to prevention.

Online Support Groups

All the general sites and many of the others make available chat, bulletin boards, personal stories, or other forms of support.

Online Post Partum Depression Support Group
http://www.geocities.com/Wellesley/4665
A mail group and chat room with a very large FAQ.

The Infertility FAQ http://www.fertilityplus.org/faq/infertility.html
Explains how to join online groups.

MISS: Mothers in Sympathy and Support http://www.misschildren.org
"The mission of Mothers in Sympathy and Support is to allow a safe haven for parents to share their grief after the death of a child."

Center for Loss in Multiple Birth (CLIMB) http://www.climb-support.org

Maribeth's Pregnancy after Loss Support Site http://www.erichad.com/pal
"Pregnancy after loss is never the same, read the author's experiences."

NATIONAL SUPPORT GROUPS

Pregnancy

Fetal Alcohol Network
158 Rosemont Avenue
Coatesville, PA 19320
Phone: 610-384-1133

Mutual support for parents of persons with fetal alcohol syndrome.

Fetal Alcohol Syndrome Adolescent Task Force
PO Box 2525
Lynnwood, WA 98070
Phone: 206-778-4048

Grassroots coalition of families and professionals concerned with fetal alcohol syndrome.

Pregnancy Hotline
Phone: 800-848-5683
Fax: 609-848-2380

Free, confidential information for pregnant women, shelters for women, baby clothes, adoption referrals.

Planned Parenthood
Phone: 800-230-7526 (referrals)
  or 800-829-7732 (administration)
http://www.plannedparenthood.org

Referrals to neighborhood Planned Parenthood clinics nationwide.

Pregnancy Hotline
Phone: 800-238-4269
http://www.bethany.org

Information and counseling for pregnant women. Referrals to free pregnancy test facilities, foster care, and adoption centers. Sponsored by Bethany Christian Services.

National Abortion Federation
Phone: 800-772-9100
http://www.prochoice.org

Provides information and referrals regarding abortions; financial aid.

National Adoption Center
Phone: 800-TO-ADOPT
Fax: 215-735-9410
http://www.adopt.org/adopt

Information on adoption agencies and support groups. Network for matching parents and children with special needs.

Losses

Compassionate Friends
http://www.compassionatefriends.org

The mission of the Compassionate Friends is to assist families in the positive resolution of grief following the death of a child and to provide information to help others be supportive. The Compassionate Friends is a national nonprofit, self-help support organization that offers friendship and understanding to families who are grieving over the death of a child of any age, from any cause. There is no religious affiliation.

Helping after Neonatal Death (HAND)
http://www.h-a-n-d.org

"HAND . . . is a non-profit, volunteer group founded in the early 1980's to provide support and information to bereaved parents, their families and friends following a miscarriage, stillbirth, or newborn death." They have many local chapters.

Resolve
1310 Broadway
Somerville, MA 02144-1779
http://www.resolve.org

For those coping with infertility, this is the oldest and largest organization.

CHAPTER 22

Schizophrenia

Schizophrenia is a serious mental disorder afflicting about 1% of the population and characterized by disorganized thinking, impairment in reality testing, hallucinations, delusions, and other symptoms of psychotic disorders. Many scientific and academic books are available describing this disorder; however, the resources reviewed in this chapter were explicitly chosen for their usefulness and applicability to individuals who deal with schizophrenia in their daily lives.

In recent years, mental health professionals have come to realize what laypersons touched by schizophrenia have known all along, namely that schizophrenia can have as devastating an effect on family and friends as on the mentally ill individuals themselves. Because the onset is typically during the late teens for males and the mid-20s for females, family and friends experience a deterioration of a loved one for whom the early years were normal. The person they had come to know is experiencing a metamorphosis before their very eyes. Parents and caretakers of schizophrenic children suffer enormous emotional upheaval while also being responsible for seeking medical and psychological assistance, dealing with emotional trauma within the family, and attending to financial, social, educational, and employment changes. Siblings of the mentally ill find their worlds turned upside down with nowhere to seek help because their fears and their needs have suddenly become low priority. Extended family and friends are at loss, not knowing what to do or not to do. Often, estrangement ensues.

The self-help resources reviewed here are primarily directed to patients, family, friends, and professionals who desperately need direction that is often not provided by systems or individuals with whom they consult. We consider, in turn, the evaluative ratings and descriptions of self-help books, autobiographies, movies, and Internet resources, followed by an alphabetical listing of national support organizations.

RECOMMENDATION HIGHLIGHTS

Self-Help Books
- For the families:

  ★★★★★ *Surviving Schizophrenia* by E. Fuller Torrey

  ★★★ *How to Cope with Mental Illness in Your Family* by Diane T. Marsh and Rex M. Dickens

  ♦ *Coping with Schizophrenia* by Kim T. Mueser and Susan Gingerich

- For understanding the disorder and patient advocacy:

  ♦ *Understanding Schizophrenia* by Richard S. E. Keefe and Philip D. Harvey

  ♦ *Schizophrenia Simplified* by John F. Thornton and Mary V. Seeman

Autobiographies
- On schizophrenic breakdown and subsequent spiritual quest:

  ★★★★ *Out of the Depths* by Anton T. Boisen

- Critical look at treatment:

  ★★★★ *Too Much Anger, Too Many Tears* by Janet Gotkin and Paul Gotkin

- Classic memoir of schizophrenic episode among 1960s turbulence:

  ★★★ *The Eden Express* by Mark Vonnegut

Movies
- Enduring male friendship despite catatonic schizophrenia:

  ★★★★ *Birdy*

- True and inspiring story of brilliant and probably schizophrenic pianist:

  ★★★★ *Shine*

- Successful search for the Holy Grail and healing despite mental disarray:

  ★★★★ *The Fisher King*

Internet Resources
- Informative and comprehensive sites:

  ★★★★★ *Schizophrenia.com* http://www.schizophrenia.com

  ★★★★ *Internet Mental Health* http://www.mentalhealth.com/dis/p20-ps01.html

  ★★★★ *Schizophrenia: Youth's Greatest Disabler* www.mentalhealth.com/book/p40-sc02.html#Head_2

- Biographies and advice:

  ★★★★★ *The Experience of Schizophrenia* www.mgl.ca/~chovil

SELF-HELP BOOKS

Strongly Recommended

★★★★★ *Surviving Schizophrenia: A Manual for Families, Consumers, and Providers* (1995) by E. Fuller Torrey. New York: HarperPerennial.

The author, a renowned expert on schizophrenia, is both a psychiatrist and the brother of a person diagnosed with schizophrenia. As a result, this book is written with a personal perspective and also with thorough and accurate medical information. The important aspects of this disease are addressed factually and also with encouragement to hope and to become an advocate. View from the inside, view from the outside, what the disease is not, and questions asked are examples of topics discussed in an understandable and respectful way. The decline in outpatient services, rehabilitation, housing, and other needed assistance leads to a closing section on how to be an effective advocate. This 5-star resource is widely regarded as the best self-help book on the subject.

Recommended

★★★ *How to Cope with Mental Illness in Your Family: A Self Care Guide for Siblings, Offspring, and Parents* (1998) by Diane T. Marsh and Rex M. Dickens. New York: Jeremy P. Tarcher/Putnam.

This book is written from the point of view of a family affected by mental disorder. One of the authors is a psychologist who works with families of the mentally ill, and the other author is an adult who grew up with a mentally ill sibling. The book is therefore directed to family members, particularly the siblings and adult children of the mentally ill. It describes the effect of the illness on the childhood and adolescence of the siblings and the effect that living with this disease may have on a person's world view. Experiences of siblings are cited as illustrative of how they learned to cope and how they managed losses and challenges. Chapters are devoted to such topics as how the illness disrupts the family, the emotional burden of daily problems, peer relationships, vulnerability, and adaptation across developmental stages. The concluding focus is on strengths, coping skills, and hopefulness for family members developed through support groups and other resources.

Diamonds in the Rough

◆ *Coping with Schizophrenia: A Guide for Families* (1994) by Kim T. Mueser and Susan Gingerich. Oakland, CA: New Harbinger.

Until recent years, the families of the mentally ill have been denied explanations of symptoms and diagnoses and have been shut out of treatment information and planning by mental health professionals. Movement toward family education has begun, and this text is a significant contribution to helping family members improve the quality of life of the family and the mentally ill member. The authors comprehensively present all aspects of the disease and offer recommendations for coping and making decisions. The text provides an overview of the disease, diagnosis, symptoms, medication and side-effects, and early warning signs of relapse. Other sections focus on solving problems, managing stress, establishing household rules, and dealing with depression, anxiety, and alcohol and drugs. The strengths of the book are writing style, content, currency, and practical aspects, such as the numerous checklists and exercises (e.g., coping methods, household rules worksheet, early warning signs questionnaire, and stress checklist) that allow family members to gauge progress and status of the mentally ill member. Because of the thoroughness and moderately high evaluations by nine raters, this book is considered a Diamond in the Rough.

♦ *Understanding Schizophrenia: A Guide to the New Research on Causes and Treatment* (1994) by Richard S. E. Keefe and Philip D. Harvey. New York: Free Press.

A special feature of this text is that it effectively serves as a handbook for ongoing reference during the course of the illness and selection of treatments. It provides a description of the nature of schizophrenia, the impact on self and families, and state-of-the-art treatments and presents recent scientific and clinical advances. This book is useful tool to help families gauge the knowledge and ability of the medical professionals with whom they are working. The key areas of focus are symptoms and characteristics, related problems, genetic and biochemical factors, and drug and behavioral treatments. Families are the audience of this book, and the authors' optimism on improved treatments will provide encouragement and support to the mentally ill and their families. For the special focus of this text and the moderately high ratings by the few mental health experts familiar with it, this book is designated a Diamond in the Rough.

♦ *Schizophrenia Simplified: A Field Guide to Schizophrenia for Frontline Workers, Families, and Professionals* (1995) by John F. Thornton and Mary V. Seeman. Toronto: Hogrefe & Huber.

Even though everyone who deals directly with schizophrenia has had experiences with the systems described here, *Schizophrenia Simplified* is one of the very few sources that clearly explains the relationship between symptoms, the family, the medical and rehabilitation systems, and the legal system. Well-organized flowcharts characterize each section (color coded for convenience), and each of four sections focuses on one of the four systems (i.e., symptoms, family, medical, legal). A number of tables that summarize section topics are provided for efficiency and convenience. This book is a road map for decision making and action that allows the reader to cross-reference material and better understand where any given person would be in the system and what the next step should be. The underlying purpose is to integrate, explain, and simplify in a useful way the systems involved in the journey of a person with schizophrenia. Although not included in our national studies, the unique organizational perspective of this text gives it Diamond in the Rough status.

AUTOBIOGRAPHIES

Strongly Recommended

★★★★ *Out of the Depths: An Autobiographical Study of Mental Disorder and Religious Experience* (1960) by Anton T. Boisen. New York: Harper.

This older book briefly describes the author's breakdown when he was a young theology student. He found a cause in his illness and dedicated himself to the mental health movement. An interesting account of the relationship between mental illness and religious experience. Boisen believed that many religious leaders, including George Fox, Swedenborg, and John Bunyan, went through a psychotic experience. In his research, he assessed religious factors in 173 schizophrenic patients at Worcester State Hospital. He published several books on religion and was active in the mental health movement.

★★★★   *Too Much Anger, Too Many Tears: A Personal Triumph over Psychiatry* (1992)
　　　by Janet Gotkin and Paul Gotkin. New York: HarperPerennial.

Janet exhibits many symptoms of schizophrenia, tries suicide on several occasions, is hospitalized numerous times, and receives drug treatment, ECT, and individual psychotherapy. Janet's recollections of her hospitalizations and treatment are interesting and often insightful. However, she rejects the diagnosis of schizophrenia and maintains that the treatments were not helpful. Both authors are active in the Mental Patients Liberation Movement. The book will provide further support for those disenchanted with parts of the mental health system.

Recommended

★★★   *Welcome, Silence: My Triumph over Schizophrenia* (1987) by Carol S. North.
　　　New York: Simon & Schuster.

The author is a psychiatrist who was chronically psychotic for almost 8 years. She experienced auditory hallucinations and was hospitalized, receiving drug and megavitamin therapies. An interesting book, but disconcerting to many clinicians in that North attributes her recovery to dialysis.

★★★   *Nobody's Child* (1992) by Marie Balter and Richard Katz. New York: Addison
　　　Wesley Longman.

Following a 20-year hospitalization on chronic wards, Balter went on to graduate from Harvard and become a vocal advocate for mental health consumers. The book has a very hopeful message in showing that there can be potential for achievement and career enhancement among long-term mental health clients.

★★★   *The Eden Express* (1988) by Mark Vonnegut. New York: Dell.

Now a pediatrician, Mark Vonnegut, a child of the 1960s and the son of a famous novelist, eloquently describes his hippie life in a British Columbia commune, his breakdown and diagnosis of schizophrenia, and the precarious road to recovery. In an note for this reprinting, Vonnegut believes that using today's definitions, he would probably be diagnosed as having an affective disorder. An engaging story of madness and eventual recovery.

★★★   *When the Music's Over: My Journey into Schizophrenia* (1996) edited by
　　　Richard Gates and Robin Hammond. New York: Plume.

This disorganized, semifictional account documents the brief life of David Burke, a young Australian who, before he committed suicide, asked his former psychology instructor, Richard Gates, to edit his notes for publication. Much of the manuscript was written while Burke was in a variety of jails, mental hospitals, and halfway houses. Both the disjointed format and the text illustrate the bizarre thinking characteristic of paranoid schizophrenia.

★★★ *Father, Have I Kept My Promise?: Madness as Seen from Within* (1988) by Edith Weisskopf-Joelson. West Lafayette, IN: Purdue University Press.

A psychology professor describes in diary form her episode of paranoid schizophrenia, admission to a state hospital for a year, and life afterward as a teacher at Purdue University. The author is a very inspiring person who positively views her breakdown as leading to constructive changes in her life.

★★★ *Beyond All Reason* (1965) by Morag Coate. Philadelphia: Lippincott.

A well-educated woman with a career in writing and various white-collar jobs describes a history of acute schizophrenia with numerous hospital admissions. She was treated with drugs and with individual, group, and insulin coma therapy. Many descriptions of her religious life and insights.

★★★ *An Angel at My Table: An Autobiography, Volume Two* (1984) by Janet Frame. New York: George Braziller.

An Angel at My Table is a sequel to *Faces in the Water*, a fictional account of life in a mental hospital, which was published almost 30 years after the author was discharged from the last of her five hospitalizations. Frame is an accomplished New Zealand writer with an international reputation for fiction. The first volume of her autobiography traces her difficult childhood; this second volume covers her life at college and her treatment for schizophrenia; and the third volume covers her subsequent literary career.

★★★ *Autobiography of a Schizophrenic Girl: An Astonishing Memoir of Reality Lost and Regained* (1984) by Frank Conroy. New York: Dutton.

A reprint of a classic account of a young girl's schizophrenia compiled from case materials by her therapist Marguerite Sechehaye.

★★★ *The Quiet Room: A Journey out of the Torment of Madness* (1996) by Lori Schiller and Amanda Bennett. New York: Warner.

Expanded from an article in the *Wall Street Journal*, this gripping account of Schiller's descent into schizophrenia and recovery, based on diary notes, is accompanied by interviews with family members and mental health practitioners.

MOVIES

Strongly Recommended

★★★★ *Birdy* (1985) produced by Alan Marshall and directed by Alan Parker. R Rating. 120 minutes.

A powerful story about friendship and helping others survive the effects of the Vietnam War. One of the veterans suffers from catatonic schizophrenia, probably arising from both life and war experiences. These friends are fighting not only to overcome the ravages of war but also to rise above their lower socioeconomic existence in South Philadelphia. They refuse to abandon each other, and they celebrate their male bonding. This self-help resource is enthusiastically recommended by psychologists in our national studies as well as by movie critics.

★★★★   *Shine* (1996) produced by Jane Scott and directed by Scott Hicks. PG-13 Rating. 105 minutes.

A true and inspiring story of David Helfgott, an Australian piano prodigy whose brilliant career is interrupted by an unspecified mental illness, probably schizophrenia or bipolar disorder. As a child and then as an adult, he struggles to separate and individuate from his domineering father. The movie is described as glorious, powerful, and extraordinary. It takes you from David's childhood to his adulthood and shows all the joys and sorrows of this brilliant man's complex disorder.

★★★★   *The Fisher King* (1991) produced by Debra Hill and Lynda Obst and directed by Terry Gilliam. R Rating. 137 minutes.

A substance-abusing talk-show host finds himself on the outs. His life is dramatically turned around when he meets a man who has been traumatized by witnessing the death of his wife. In what appears to be a psychotic state (or severe posttraumatic stress disorder), this man attempts to rediscover the meaning in life by searching for the Holy Grail. Both men struggle with their own demons, but together they secure the Grail and find healing. The movie is funny and inspiring but at times quite confusing.

Recommended

★★★   *Benny and Joon* (1994) produced by Susan Arnold and Donna Roth and directed by Jeremiah Chechik. PG Rating. 100 minutes.

The predominant themes here are accepting people and their limitations, struggling with mental illness, and learning to let go in a relationship. Benny and Joon is a love story; it reminds us that there is someone in the world for everyone. It reinforces the myth that love will conquer all. The movie creators walk a thin line between comedy and tragedy in their efforts to demonstrate the plight of a woman with schizophrenia. Overall, it emerges as a likable and effective comedy/drama.

Not Recommended

★   *Mad Love* (1995) produced by David Manson and directed by Antonia Bird. PG-13 Rating.

INTERNET RESOURCES

Metasites

★★★★★   *Schizophrenia.com* http://www.schizophrenia.com

This site offers basic information, more in-depth information, and discussion and chat areas as well as a search engine with a time- and effort-saving Most Common Searches list. This labor of love is the most complete and rich site for any and all aspects of schizophrenia. No matter what you seek, you will find it here. Thank you, Brian Chiko.

★★★★ *Mentalhelp* http://mentalhelp.net/guide/schizo.htm

Mentalhelp has a large collection of articles from many sources as well as links to other sites.

★★★★ *Internet Mental Health* http://www.mentalhealth.com/dis/p20-ps01.html

Hundreds of links and articles on all aspects of schizophrenia. This is one part of Phillip W. Long's vast high-quality site. He is a Canadian and so can see both the American and European perspectives.

★★ *New York NAMI (National Alliance for the Mentally Ill)*
     http://www.nami-nyc-metro.org

This site has hundreds of articles under such headings as Diagnosis, Medicines and Treatment, Rehabilitation and Day Treatment, Coping and Managing Tips, First Person Accounts and Advice, Policy and Advocacy Papers, and writings of Dr. E. Fuller Torrey. NAMI policy is that schizophrenia is to be understood as almost exclusively a neurobiological disorder.

Psychoeducational Materials for Clients and Families

★★★★ *Schizophrenia.com* http://www.schizophrenia.com/newsletter

This site has many branches containing articles suitable for handouts. It is the most complete psychoeducational site for schizophrenia. At http://www.schizophrenia.com/newsletter/buckets/coping.html are articles on what parents or spouses can and can't do, symptom management, avoiding relapses, and rehabilitation. Frederick J. Frese's *Coping with Schizophrenia* is particularly informative and meaningful. At http://www.schizophrenia.com/newsletter/buckets/intro.html are introductory materials, popular news stories, and some materials in Spanish. The Early Psychosis Identification Training Pack is a presentation-quality program suitable for teaching non-mental health professionals about the dynamics, diagnosis, and treatment of schizophrenia. *Information for Families and Friends* (http://www.schizophrenia.com/newsletter/newpages/family.html) seems to cover all aspects and is an excellent starting place for families or for materials for families; topics include Causes, Housing and Homelessness, Health Insurance, Genetics Research, and Violence and Crime. *Information for People Who Have Schizophrenia* (http://www.schizophrenia.com/newsletter/newpages/consumer.htm) is similar.

★★★★ *Schizophrenia* http://www.nimh.nih.gov/publicat/schizoph.htm#schiz1

These well-written 15 pages are from the National Institute of Mental Health.

★★★★ *Schizophrenia: Youth's Greatest Disabler*
     http://www.mentalhealth.com/book/p40-sc02.html#Head_2

These 40 pages cover almost all aspects of schizophrenia. The site is from a Canadian source, but the information is universal. The material is very realistic and may be too intense or complex for introducing clients or families. The FAQ is very good, as is the material on stigma and the Glossary.

★★★★ *Schizophrenia: A Handbook For Families*
        http://www.mentalhealth.com/book/p40-sc01.html

About 50 pages. Similar in format to the above, but with mostly unique information.

★★★ *Understanding Schizophrenia: A Guide for People with Schizophrenia and Their Families* http://www.mhsource.com/narsad/schiz.html

This 10-page brochure is also available in Spanish.

★★★ *Schizophrenia*
        http://www.health-center.com/mentalhealth/schizophrenia/default.htm

Good for basic information in small doses for beginners; well-illustrated and very biological.

★★★ *Schizophrenia*
        http://www.mentalhealth.com/dis/p20-ps01.html

These are about 15 booklets here, such as excerpts from *Surviving Schizophrenia* by E. Fuller Torrey, MD; Schizophrenia: A Handbook for Families; Useful Information on . . . Paranoia; and Expert Consensus Guideline for the Treatment of Schizophrenia.

★★★ *Recovery, Inc.* http://www.recovery-inc.com

The site offers about 10 readings describing the approach of Recovery, Inc.

Biographical and Autobiographical Vignettes

★★★★★ *The Experience of Schizophrenia* http://www.mgl.ca/~chovil

Ian Chovil's home page contains a biography, resources, advice, and diagrams from which to teach.

★★★ *Schizophrenia.com*
        http://www.schizophrenia.com/newsletter/buckets/success.html

Here you will find success stories—16 short biographical accounts, sites with links to the stories of famous people with schizophrenia, and the personal web pages of people with schizophrenia.

Online Support Groups

Schizophrenia.com Home Page http://www.schizophrenia.com/discuss/Disc3.html

Besides the Main Message Board, there are areas for People Diagnosed with Schizophrenia, Parents, Spouses, Siblings, Children/Offspring of Parents with Schizophrenia, Childhood Schizophrenia, Financial/Resources, Dual Diagnosis, and so on.

Schizophrenia Support Organizations http://members.aol.com/leonardjk/USA.htm

J. K. Leonard provides both the mail and linked online addresses of local branches of national organizations.

NATIONAL SUPPORT GROUPS

National Alliance for the Mentally Ill (NAMI)
200 North Glebe Road, Suite 1015
Arlington, VA 22203-3754
Phone: 800-950-NAMI or 703-524-7600
http://www.nami.org

   NAMI construes schizophrenia as a brain disease.

National Alliance for Research on Schizophrenia and Depression (NARSAD)
60 Cutter Mill Road, Suite 404
Great Neck, NY 11021
Phone: 516-829-0091
http://www.narsad.org

National Mental Health Association (NMHA)
1021 Prince Street
Alexandria, VA 22314-2971
Phone: 800-969-6942 or 703-684-7722
http://www.nmha.org

National Mental Health Consumers' Self-Help Clearinghouse
1211 Chestnut Street, Suite 1000
Philadelphia, PA 19107
Phone: 800-553-4539 or 215-751-1810
http://www.mhselfhelp.org

Recovery Inc.
802 North Dearborn Street
Chicago IL 60610
Phone: 312-337-5661
Fax: 312-337-5756
http://www.recovery-inc.com

Schizophrenics Anonymous
15920 West Twelve Mile Road
Southfield, MI 48076
Phone: 810-557-6777

   For people with a schizophrenia-related disorder.

Schizophrenia Society of Canada
75 The Donway West #814
Don Mills, Ontario, Canada M3C 2E9
Phone: 416-445-8204

Tardive Dyskinesia/Tardive Dystonia National Association
PO Box 45732
Seattle, WA 98145-0732
Phone: 206-623-7279

CHAPTER 23

Self-Management and Self-Enhancement

"Don't worry, be happy!" are the words of a popular tune by Bobby McFerrin, " 'Cause when you worry, your face will frown, and that will bring everybody down.... " Is McFerrin's cheerful optimism an effective self-management strategy?

Starting with the earliest human writings, self-help resources have advanced strategies to cope more successfully and manage undesirable behaviors. Some self-help writers suggest avoiding negative people; some preach trust in God; some teach positive thinking; and some advocate perceiving reality as accurately as possible. In the early 1990s, a number of psychologists began recommending "positive illusions"—that is, happy people often entertain falsely high opinions of themselves, give self-serving explanations for events, and have exaggerated beliefs about their ability to control the world around them. In the late 1990s, the pendulum had swung to encouraging acceptance of life's inevitable travails and returning to spirituality, a topic considered in Chapter 25.

In a way, all self-help resources are about self-improvement. But in this chapter, we critically consider a multitude of self-help books and Internet resources devoted to general strategies of self-management and self-enhancement. This is admittedly a broad topic; indeed, so broad and inclusive that we purposefully excluded movies and autobiographies because they number in the hundreds.

SELF-HELP BOOKS

Strongly Recommended

★★★★★ *The 7 Habits of Highly Effective People* (1989) by Steven Covey. New York: Simon & Schuster.

Covey's best-selling and influential book provides an in-depth examination of how people's perspectives and values determine how competently they perform in their busi-

RECOMMENDATION HIGHLIGHTS

Self-Help Books

- For a general approach to self-improvement, especially in business:

  ★★★★★ *The 7 Habits of Highly Effective People* by Steven Covey

- On the success—and limitations—of changing behaviors:

  ★★★★★ *What You Can Change and What You Can't* by Martin Seligman

- On improving life with optimistic thinking:

  ★★★★★ *Learned Optimism* by Martin Seligman

- On doing the right thing at the right time (stages) in order to change:

  ★★★★ *Changing for Good* by James O. Prochaska and Associates

- For a cognitive self-talk approach to self-management:

  ★★★★ *A New Guide to Rational Living* by Albert Ellis and Robert Harper

  ★★★★ *Feel the Fear and Do It Anyway* by Susan Jeffers

  ★★★★ *What to Say When You Talk to Yourself* by Shad Helmstetter

- To optimize natural healing and bodily functioning:

  ★★★★ *Spontaneous Healing* by Andrew Weil

- On learning to respond to life with ease:

  ★★★★ *Don't Sweat the Small Stuff . . . and It's All Small Stuff* by Richard Carlson

- On conquering procrastination:

  ★★★★ *Overcoming Procrastination* by Albert Ellis and William Knaus

- On women's self-enhancement and why they should not blame their mothers:

  ★★★★ *Don't Blame Mother* by Paula Caplan

Internet Resources

- On emotional intelligence:

  ★★★★★ *Emotional Intelligence, etc.* http://eqi.org

  ★★★★★ *Emotional Intelligence Test* http://www.queendom.com/emotionaliq.html

- On self-esteem:

  ★★★★★ *Self-Esteem—What Is It?* http://www.positive-way.com/self-esteem%20what%20is%20it.htm

ness and personal lives. Covey argues that in order to be quality leaders in an organization, people must first become quality-oriented, identifying the underlying principles that are important in their lives and evaluating whether they are living up to those standards. Covey lists seven basic habits that are fundamental to anyone's efforts to become quality-oriented:

- Be proactive instead of reactive.
- Begin with the end in mind.
- Put first things first.
- Think win/win.
- Seek first to understand, then to be understood.
- Synergize.
- Sharpen the saw (renewal).

This 5-star resource is a breath of fresh air among the superficial quick-fix books that populate the checkout counters across the nation. Covey's choices of personal, family, educational, and professional examples to illustrate the habits of highly effective people are excellent. Critics said that no research has been conducted to confirm that these are the seven core habits of competent individuals.

★★★★★ *Learned Optimism: The Skill to Conquer Life's Obstacles, Large and Small* (1990) by Martin Seligman. New York: Pocket Books.

This psychological approach to positive thinking was authored by Martin Seligman, a professor of psychology at the University of Pennsylvania. *Learned Optimism* is based on psychological research rather than spiritual belief. Seligman argues that optimism and pessimism are not fixed, inborn psychological traits but rather are learned explanatory styles—habitual ways we explain things that happen to us. Pessimists, says Seligman, perceive a defeat as permanent, catastrophic, and evidence of personal inadequacy; optimists, in contrast, perceive the same mishap as a temporary setback, something that can be controlled, and rooted in circumstances or luck. Seligman's positive message is that since pessimism is learned, it can be unlearned. Included are self-tests to determine the reader's levels of optimism, pessimism, and depression. Seligman reviews a great deal of research on explanatory styles, concluding that optimists do better in school, in athletics, and at work because they persist at attaining success even in the face of setbacks, while equally talented pessimists are more likely not to stay the course. Seligman also reviews research to demonstrate that pessimists have weaker immune systems, have more health problems, and are more likely to be depressed. This 5-star resource is an excellent self-help book on positive thinking. It is well-documented but not overly academic and is psychobabble-free.

★★★★★ *What You Can Change and What You Can't* (1993) by Martin Seligman. New York: Knopf.

Seligman, one of the world's leading authorities on depression and motivation, also authored this 5-star self-help resource. This book provides a wealth of scientific thought and scholarly opinions about the effect of biology, genetics, heredity, environment, and self-motivation on how we think and change. What we can change has definite limitations, but Seligman repeatedly reminds us that there is much we can do within the boundaries to influence our quality of life. In several chapters, Seligman gives his own evaluation of treatments for various disorders (e.g., anxiety, anger, depression). This book is written at a higher level than most self-help manuals but will be very informative for the interested general public.

★★★★ *Feel the Fear and Do It Anyway* (1987) by Susan Jeffers. San Diego, CA: Harcourt Brace Jovanovich.

This book applies a cognitive approach, much of it based on Ellis's rational–emotive therapy, to coping with fear. Jeffers believes that most inaction, whether it involves changing jobs, breaking off a relationship, starting a relationship, and so on, stems from the fear of not being able to handle whatever comes along. She says that fear never completely goes away. Fear should be a sign to us that we are being challenged, and we should confront the fear by taking reasonable risks. Jeffers does a good job of showing how faulty thinking is the source of most people's unreasonable fears, and she gives valuable advice about how to modify such irrational thinking.

★★★★ *Changing for Good* (1995) by James O. Prochaska, John C. Norcross, and Carlo C. DiClemente. New York: Avon.

Prochaska, Norcross, and DiClemente bring their 20 years of federally-funded research and 50 years of collective knowledge to bear on behavior change. The book is organized around the stages of change: precontemplation, contemplation, preparation, action, and maintenance. This scientific approach to self-change helps identify the stage of change for a particular problem and then reviews the common obstacles, best change methods, and interpersonal support for that particular stage. One of the few self-change books to be based on and backed by scientific research; this 4-star resource will be helpful to laypersons who wish to understand the stages of change and valuable to the professionals working with them. (In the interest of full disclosure, *Changing for Good* was coauthored by one of the coauthors of this *Authoritative Guide to Self-Help Resources in Mental Health*.)

★★★★ *A New Guide to Rational Living* (1975) by Albert Ellis and Robert Harper. Englewood Cliffs, NJ: Prentice-Hall.

This cognitive approach to self-enhancement is coauthored by Albert Ellis, a well-known psychologist and prolific author of self-help books. His rational–emotive therapy states that people develop psychological problems because they use irrational beliefs to interpret what happens to them and their world. In this view, people disturb themselves by thinking in self-defeating, illogical, and unrealistic ways. According to Ellis and Harper, years of lengthy psychotherapy are not needed to attack the root of emotional problems. They believe that rational–emotive therapy can quickly help people learn how to detect their irrational thinking, overcome the influence of the past, erase dire fears of failure, conquer anxiety, and acquire self-discipline. The book is filled with conversations between irrational thinkers and therapists and the subsequent interchanges that led to successful living. This valued 4-star book is widely known (evaluated by 238 psychologists) and came close to making a 5-star rating. The book's enthusiasts say that Ellis's approach is very effective in motivating people to restructure their thinking and rid themselves of harmful irrational beliefs.

★★★★ *Spontaneous Healing: How to Discover and Enhance Your Body's Natural Ability to Maintain and Heal Itself* (1995) by Andrew Weil. New York: Knopf.

This author and physician describes the mechanisms of the body's healing system; simply put, the body can heal itself because it has a healing system. Weil delineates the ways an individual can optimize the functioning of his or her own system and incorporate alternative medicines and treatments to enhance the healing system. Using clear and concise language, this best-seller explains how the healing system operates (e.g., its interaction with the mind, system of self-diagnoses, self-repair) and provides information on how foods, environments, and lifestyles can maintain well-being. Included is an 8-week program that can help the body's natural healing powers. Weil cleverly combines current western medical practice with alternative treatments (e.g., acupuncture, biofeedback, guided imagery, and herbal medicine). For the general public interested in the study of the internal healing system, this book provides a wealth of knowledge.

★★★★ *What to Say When You Talk to Yourself* (1986) by Shad Helmstetter. Scottsdale, AZ: Fine.

The author examines the literature on success and concludes that in the many recommendations there are some missing ingredients: permanent solutions, knowledge of mind–brain functions, and word-for-word directions for programming the unconscious mind. Helmstetter concludes that the only solution that includes all three ingredients is self-talk and goes on to outline five levels of self-talk, the highest being the level of universal affirmation. The author spells out the self-talk strategies of silent self-talk, self-speak, self-conversation, self-write, tape-talk, and creating self-talk tapes. He covers a number of other ideas about self-talk problem-solving strategies for changing attitudes, changing behaviors, and dealing with different situations. Favorably evaluated but not particularly well-known, this book presents some very helpful strategies for coping with stressful circumstances, especially for negative thinkers and people low in motivation. Helmstetter spells out what to say to yourself to improve your life instead of just being a cheerleader like so many motivational self-help book authors. Critics contend that the material about the nonconscious mind is fuzzy.

★★★★ *Don't Sweat the Small Stuff . . . and It's All Small Stuff* (1997) by Richard Carlson. New York: Hyperion.

A small best-selling book about simple ways to keep the little things from taking over your life. Carlson argues that when you learn the habit of responding to life with more ease, problems that seem insurmountable will begin to seem more manageable, and even the biggies won't throw you off track as much as they once did. The book consists of 100 strategies, covered in one page each, to replace old habits of reaction with new habits of perspective. Many of the strategies apply not only to isolated events but also to many of life's most difficult challenges. For teens and adults who wish to live life more reflectively and fully.

★★★★ *Overcoming Procrastination* (1977) by Albert Ellis and William Knaus.
New York: Institute for Rational Living.

Subtitled *How to Think and Act Rationally in Spite of Life's Inevitable Hassles*, the book applies rational–emotive therapy to the task of combating procrastination. Ellis and Knaus begin by explaining what procrastination means and then turn to its main causes—self-downing, low frustration tolerance, and hostility. They recommend a cognitive approach to overcoming procrastination and outline the basic ideas of Ellis's rational–emotive therapy. The last chapter includes a psychotherapy transcript of a therapist and procrastinator and shows how rational–emotive therapy helped the client. *Overcoming Procrastination* just barely received a 4-star rating, but it presents a creative, practical approach to solving procrastination in many areas of life.

★★★★ *Don't Blame Mother: Mending the Mother–Daughter Relationship* (1989) by
Paula Caplan. New York: Harper & Row.

The thesis here is that society and psychology have shortchanged mothers, blaming them far too often and too much for their children's problems. Caplan argues that daughters are taught to criticize the work of mothering and to make their mothers the scapegoats for any problems the daughters have as adults. Caplan believes that myths of idealization give rise to impossible expectations and set mothers up for failure. However, Caplan says, mothers and daughters can move beyond these troublesome stereotypes and negative perceptions and gain a new appreciation for each other and their relationship. She gives advice on identifying conflicting messages and myths that weaken the mother–daughter bond. Caplan also underscores the value of women sharing experiences with other women as a means of personal change and self-improvement. Just making the 4-star rating, this book rejects the notion, especially popular among those with a codependency perspective, that blaming mother is a means of psychological growth. *Don't Blame Mother* is a much-needed antidote. This is an excellent self-help book on mother–daughter relationships, especially how to improve them in the adult years.

Recommended

★★★ *Positive Illusions: Creative Self-Discipline and the Healthy Mind* (1989) by
Shelley Taylor. New York: Basic Books.

Taylor's main themes are similar to Seligman's (reviewed above): Facing the complete truth about ourselves is often not the best mental health strategy. The healthy human mind has a tendency to block out negative information; positive illusions help us cope. Taylor believes that creative deceptions are especially beneficial when we are threatened by adversity. Taylor describes research on cancer patients, disaster victims, and other people facing crises to portray how mental and physical well-being can be improved by having an unrealistically positive view of one's self and abilities. This book was positively rated but by too few respondents (only 13) to make the 4-star or 5-star categories. It is a good book on positive thinking, but one that becomes too formal and academic in places. However, the quality of Taylor's documentation is outstanding, and intellectual readers will enjoy the book.

★★★   *Emotional Intelligence* (1994) by Daniel Goleman. New York: Bantam.

This best-selling book reviews the importance of social and emotional competencies (e.g., self-awareness, self-discipline, and empathy) that can determine the quality of life. A *New York Times* reporter and social psychologist, Goleman gives equal weight to one's emotional quotient (EQ) and intelligence quotient (IQ). Goleman discusses how to understand and bolster emotional intelligence, which can be nurtured and strengthened throughout life. Heavy on science reporting at times, this book has a more scholarly flare than most but appeals widely to educated laypersons. The book is written about EQ and has little how to. Frequently rated in our national studies, it almost made the 4-star listing.

★★★   *The 60-Second Shrink* (1997) by Arnold A. Lazarus and Clifford N. Lazarus. San Luis Obispo, CA: Impact.

The internationally known psychologist Arnold Lazarus and son distill 100 complex mental health topics into a back-pocket reference book for those who desire to cope more effectively with life's stressors. Depending on need, this book lends itself to time-efficient selective reading. It is a technically eclectic, scientifically based, problem-solving self-help book, usable by professionals and laypersons alike. Topics traverse the mental health landscape: healthy thinking, action steps, relationship-building, effective communication, handling emotions, stress reduction, weight management, and choosing various psychotherapies, for example. This valuable 3-star resource just missed making the 4-star category.

★★★   *Staying Rational in an Irrational World* (1991) by Michael Bernard. New York: Carol.

This book applies cognitive therapist Albert Ellis's rational–emotive therapy to a number of different life domains—love, dating, sex, work, children, parents, women's issues, homosexuality, and death and dying. The basic theme of rational–emotive therapy is that to cope effectively, we need to replace irrational thinking with rational thinking. The book includes many examples in which individuals learn to talk to themselves more effectively and think in more rational ways. Two final chapters include an interview with Ellis about rational–emotive therapy and a long list of Ellis's books, tapes, and talks.

★★★   *Positive Addiction* (1985) by William Glasser. New York: HarperCollins.

William Glasser became famous in the 1960s and 1970s for founding a school of therapy known as reality therapy—a results-oriented therapy designed to help people cope with their immediate environment. In *Positive Addiction*, Glasser turns from therapy to the problems virtually all of us have in developing our potential. Glasser argues that every person can overcome self-imposed weaknesses by engaging in positive addictions or activities, such as running and meditation, that help people to lose their consciousness. Glasser says that when people do this, they "spin free" and almost mystically arrive at new strategies for coping with life. By contrast, negative addictions are escapes from the pain of striving for things people want but doubt they can accomplish, such as career or athletic achievements. Glasser's list of negative addictions includes drinking, gambling, overwork, overeating, and smoking. This 3-star resource contains ideas much more popular in the 1970s than today. *Positive Addiction* was written in 1976, and frequent references to well-known people of that time—Jimmy the Greek and Tim Galloway (*Inner Tennis*), for example—seriously date the book. Critics also say that in places the book regresses into mystical explanations.

★★★ *Talking to Yourself: Learning the Language of Self-Affirmation* (1981) by
      Pamela Butler. New York: Stein and Day.

Butler says that each of us experiences an inner self as a distinct person speaking to us. Each of us engages this inner person in a dialogue throughout our lives. Through this inner dialogue with ourselves, we make decisions, set goals, and feel satisfied or dejected. Butler believes that our behavior, thoughts, feelings, and self-esteem are strongly influenced by such inner speech. In this book, Butler provides a number of specific strategies for changing our self-talk and making it work better. Topics include anger and self-talk, sex and self-talk, and gender and self-talk. A 3-star resource, this book provides good advice about how to improve the way we talk to ourselves and consequently improve our ability to cope with difficult circumstances

★★★ *Life's Little Instruction Book* (1991) by H. Jackson Brown. Nashville, TN:
      Rutledge Hill.

This book of instruction was inspired by a father's love for his son and his desire to guide his son along life's many paths. The instructions start with (1) compliment three people every day and ends with (511) call your mother. A compact booklet filled with 511 one-liners that can be helpful for an adolescent or adult looking for good advice or recalling consensual wisdom of the ages.

★★★ *Self-Defeating Behaviors* (1991) by Milton Cudney and Robert Hardy.
      San Francisco: Harper.

This is a cognitive and behavioral approach to eliminating a wide range of self-defeating behaviors, such as procrastination, defensiveness, alcohol and drug abuse, shyness, and smoking. While not the healthiest means of coping, these behaviors provide comfort and protection and thus function well enough to become entrenched in our behavior patterns. Cudney and Hardy argue that people can free themselves from these self-destructive patterns by doing the following:

- Identifying the problem-causing behavior.
- Specifying when, where, and with whom the behavior comes into play.
- Intercepting the behavior while it is being practiced.
- Developing replacement techniques.
- Facing fears.
- Overcoming setbacks.

The book received a 3-star rating in our national study but was evaluated by only 10 respondents, probably because it was published shortly before one of studies was conducted. It provides valuable steps for eliminating self-defeating behaviors, though it is difficult reading for a self-help book.

★★★ *All I Really Need to Know I Learned in Kindergarten: Uncommon Thought on Common Things* (1998) by Robert Fulghum. New York: Ivy.

This best-selling author's approach to finding wonderment and meaning in the smallest of life's experiences is presented with wit and humor. Fulgum's book is one that you can read a little, put down, pick up later, and put it down again without worrying about the plot resolution or missing the overarching theme. His simple rules of life gleaned from early years in kindergarten—for example, share, play fair, clean up, say you're sorry, don't take things that aren't yours—are extrapolated into adult life at home, in the office, in government, or wherever one may be at the moment. When you go out into the world, it is best to hold hands and stick together. The author concludes the book with, "Peace is not something you wish for; it's something you make, something you do, something you are, and something you give away." A valued, insightful, perhaps overly simplistic book that received a 3-star evaluation in one of our national studies.

★★★ *Making Life Right When It Feels All Wrong* (1988) by Herbert Fensterheim. New York: Rawlins.

Fensterheim recommends an eclectic mix of strategies for self-enhancement that combines changing actions with conquering long-standing, buried problems. This unusual approach to self-improvement actually combines behavioral and psychoanalytic strategies. Fensterheim says that you may not be able to control what happens to you, but you can control your reaction to it. The author applies his ideas to many different domains of life: love, assertiveness, work, friendships, and sports. The book includes many vignettes, anecdotes, and case studies. This 3-star resource creatively integrates behavior therapy principles and psychoanalytic concepts of needs and blocks.

★★★ *Chicken Soup for the Soul* (1991) by Jack Canfield and Mark Victor Hansen. Deerfield Beach, FL: Health Communications.

These best-selling authors have selected a number of stories to illuminate life paths and motivate us to pursue a fulfilling lifestyle. Each of the 101 stories is designed to open our minds and hearts to our potential. The stories are divided into seven sections: love, learning to love yourself, parenting, learning, living your dream, overcoming obstacles, and eclectic wisdom. This 3-star, entertaining book can be read at length or for 15 minutes and will leave one feeling inspired.

★★★ *Gentle Roads to Survival* (1991) by Andrew Auw. Boulder Creek, CO: Asian.

This book, in the humanistic tradition, is a guide to making self-healing choices in difficult circumstances. Auw explains how to become a survivor. He believes that while some people may be born survivors, most of us have to learn survival skills. Auw addresses personal crises in religion, morality, parenting, marriage, cross-cultural adaptation, and many other stressful life circumstances. He especially advocates that each person has to discover his or her own unique path of adaptation and coping. This 3-star book is an effective self-help resource for people facing highly stressful circumstances in their lives. Auw's tone is warm and compassionate throughout.

★★★ *I'm OK, You're OK* (1967) by Thomas Harris. New York: Harper & Row.

This best-seller presents a transactional analysis approach to self-management. Transactional analysis maintains that people are responsible for their behavior in the present and future regardless of what has happened to them in the past. It distinguishes three main components in each person's makeup: the Parent, the Adult, and the Child. The Parent involves the many dont's and a few do's of our early years. The Child represents spontaneous emotion. Both Parent and Child have to be kept in proper relation to the Adult, whose function is maintaining reality through decision making. The goal of transactional analysis is strengthening and emancipating the Adult from the Parent and the Child. Harris identifies four life positions that underlie people's behavior: (1) I'm not OK—You're OK, the anxious dependency of an insecure person; (2) I'm not OK—You're not OK, a position of despair or giving up; (3) I'm OK—You're not OK, the criminal position; and (4) I'm OK—You're OK, the response of mature adults who are at peace with themselves and others. Harris believes that most people unconsciously operate from the I'm not OK—You're OK position. The 3-star book is extremely well-known and was immensely successful when it was published. Despite its popularity, it receives a tepid evaluation from mental health professionals. Some experts still praise the book and some are glad that it has lost much of its luster due to its superficiality, but all agree that its popularity has waned dramatically.

★★★ *How to Live 365 Days a Year* (1975) by John Schindler. Englewood Cliffs, NJ: Prentice-Hall.

This book takes the stance that illnesses and problems in life arise out of emotions. The book is divided into two main parts. In Part I, How Your Emotions Make You Ill, readers learn that emotions produce most physical diseases and also about the good emotions and the bad emotions. Part II, How to Cure Your Emotionally Induced Illness, describes how to attain emotional maturity in many different areas of life—family, sexually, and at work, for example. *How to Live 365 Days a Year* received a 3-star rating. On the positive side, it presents some important ideas about how emotional difficulties cause illness and how to take control of emotional life, but on the negative side, it is dated and inferior to more modern books.

★★★ *Unlimited Power* (1986) by Anthony Robbins. New York: Fawcett Columbine.

This book is based on the theory of neurolinguistic programming that claims that people can be programmed in ways that will make and keep them highly successful. Robbins advocates a host of mental, emotional, and physiological programming strategies, especially developing confidence in the mind's power. To convince people of their mental powers, Robbins strongly recommends firewalking, a barefoot jaunt over hot coals. A basic step in becoming successful, he says, is selecting a successful person as a model and learning about how the person became successful and how they conduct their lives. Essential to Robbins's "ultimate success formula" are clarity of desired goals, energy, passion, persistence of action, effective communication skills, and altruistic motives. *Unlimited Power* barely received a mixed 3-star rating: Mental health professionals said that this book has some good points mixed with some bad points. A good point is that

Robbins's enthusiastic approach can motivate people to develop their talents and to select a competent model to emulate. The bad points are that research has generally not supported the postulates of neurolinguistic programming, that the mind-over-matter firewalking demonstrations are misleading (scientists have demonstrated that people can walk across hot coals without getting burned if they move quickly enough), and that Robbins's claims that just about anyone can develop "unlimited power" are unsubstantiated and outlandish.

Diamond in the Rough

◆ *Success Is a Choice: Ten Steps to Overachieving in Business and Life* (1997) by Rick Pitino with Bill Reynolds. New York: Broadway.

Pitino, a highly respected and successful basketball coach, believes that success is not about shortcuts. He maintains the need to aim higher and work harder then ever before in order to succeed. His 10-step program teaches people to build self-esteem, identify goals, and use a positive attitude to accomplish what they want. Being better comes in many forms. Pitino speaks to the importance of communication, role models, and turning adversity into advantage. Before working on this 10-step program, a plan of attack, a sense of direction, needs to be formalized. Pitino ends his book: "Your real journey begins now." This book, a Diamond in the Rough because of its favorable but infrequent ratings, is for adolescents and adults who are willing to study and work hard to achieve their goals.

Not Recommended

★★ *Your Maximum Mind* (1987) by Herbert Benson. New York: Random House.

★★ *Tough Times Never Last, but Tough People Do!* (1983) by Robert Schuller. New York: Bantam.

★★ *Your Erroneous Zones* (1976) by Wayne Dyer. New York: Funk & Wagnalls.

★★ *The Power of Optimism* (1990) by Alan McGinnis. San Francisco: Harper & Row.

★ *The Power of Positive Thinking* (1952) by Norman Vincent Peale. New York: Ballantine.

★ *How to Stop Worrying and Start Living* (1944) by Dale Carnegie. New York: Simon & Schuster.

★ *Steps to the Top* (1985) by Zig Zigler. Gretna, LA: Pelican.

★ *Awaken the Giant Within* (1991) by Anthony Robbins. New York: Fireside.

INTERNET RESOURCES

On this broad topic, the Internet is full of absolute junk. For example, Self-Growth.com (http://www.selfgrowth.com) offers, among others, Aging and Longevity, Aromatherapy, Body Language, Brain Enhancement, Feng Shui, Gurus, Happiness and Self

Improvement, Herbal Remedies, Memory Training, New Age, Spiritual Development, Subliminal Learning, Success Coaching, and Television Programming. In reviewing some of these sites, Ed Zuckerman, our computer whiz, could find nothing with empirical basis or noncommercial content. Therefore, reported here are only the sites with materials that he considered to have some research support or widespread agreement on the value of the ideas.

Metasites

★★★★★ *Emotional Intelligence, etc.* http://eqi.org

An enormously rich site by Steven Hein, PhD. Hein offers reviews of other emotional intelligence sites, Signs of High and Low EQ, an enormous list of Feeling Words, and the like. EQ and Romantic Relationships might be useful for couples in some conflicts.

Psychoeducational Materials for Clients and Families

★★★★★ *Emotional Intelligence Test* http://www.queendom.com/emotionaliq.html

Long, with 70 items, but a well-designed interactive test with multiple choices that really teach about emotional intelligence.

★★★★★ *Self-Esteem—What Is It?*
http://www.positive-way.com/self-esteem%20what%20is%20it.htm

After a good introduction, this site offers three more sections: a self-esteem questionnaire; Stopping Your Inner Critic from *Self-Esteem*, by Matthew McKay, PhD and Patrick Fanning; and 25 ideas to develop self-esteem. This site is a mini-course and worth exploring.

★★★★ *Self-Esteem: What It Is, Where It Comes from, and Why We Need It* by
Steven Hein, PhD http://eqi.org/sebook.htm

In just 4 pages, Hein covers the development and definition of self-esteem.

★★★ *What's Your Emotional Intelligence Quotient?* http://www.utne.com/azEq2.tmpl
Only 10 questions.

—————— CHAPTER 24 ——————

Sexuality

Sex has its magnificent moments throughout the animal kingdom. Insects mate in mid-air, peacocks display their plumage, and male elephant seals have prolific sex lives. These are all instinctive behaviors. Experience plays an important role in human sexual behavior. We can talk about sex with each other, read about it in books, and watch it on television and in the movies.

But although we can talk about sex with each other, we often don't. Sex in America still comes cloaked in mystery, and as a nation we are neither knowledgeable about sex nor comfortable talking about it. While many people manage to develop a mature sexuality, even those who do handle sex maturely have periods of vulnerability and confusion. Many people wonder and worry about their sexual attractiveness, their ability to satisfy their sexual partner, and whether they will be able to experience their ultimate sexual fantasies. Our worries are fueled by media stereotypes of sexual potency and superhuman sexual exploits. Sexual concerns also prevail because of our inability to communicate about sex directly with one another.

In this chapter, we critically examine self-help books, movies, and websites devoted to sexuality in its many manifestations.

SELF-HELP BOOKS

Strongly Recommended

★★★★ *For Each Other: Sharing Sexual Intimacy* (1982) by Lonnie Barbach. Garden City, NY: Anchor.

For Each Other, like its precursor, *For Yourself*, is written for and about women who wish to improve their sexual fulfillment. This book focuses on sexual concerns within the sexual relationship with a partner. Basic aspects of sexuality and the cultural context in which women learn about sexuality are reviewed; orgasmic problems and recommenda-

RECOMMENDATION HIGHLIGHTS

Self-Help Books

- For improving sexual relationships and communication:
    - ★★★★ *For Each Other* by Lonnie Barbach
    - ★★★★ *Illustrated Manual of Sexual Therapy* by Helen Kaplan
    - ★★★ *Sexual Awareness* by Barry McCarthy and Emily McCarthy

- For men:
    - ★★★ *Male Sexuality* by Bernie Zilbergeld

- For women:
    - ★★★ *For Yourself* by Lonnie Barbach
    - ◆ *Becoming Orgasmic* by Julia Heiman and Joseph LoPiccolo

- For gays and lesbians:
    - ◆ *Permanent Partners* by Betty Berzon

Movies

- Powerful story of accepting homosexuality and then loss:
    - ★★★★ *Torch Song Trilogy*

- Intriguing look at underground lifestyle of gay men:
    - ★★★ *Paris Is Burning*

- Gay men struggling with sexual identity and personal relationships:
    - ★★★ *The Boys in the Band*

Internet Resources

- For premier sexuality information:
    - ★★★★★ *Society for Human Sexuality*
      http://www.sexuality.org/index.html
    - ★★★★ *SIECUS: Sexuality Information and Education Council of the United States* http://www.siecus.org

- For sexually active teens:
    - ★★★★★ *Coalition for Positive Sexuality*
      http://www.positive.org/Home
    - ★★★★★ *Teenwire* http://www.teenwire.com

- For self-pleasuring methods:
    - ★★★★★ *Bianca's Good Vibration Masturbation Guide*
      www2.bianca.com/shack/goodvibe/masturbate

- For information on STDs:

  ★★★★★ *Facts and Answers about STDs*
            http://www.ashastd.org/stdfaqs/index.html

- For birth control:

  ★★★★★ *Birth Control Methods*
            http://www.plannedparenthood.org/BIRTHCONTROL/index.htm

tions are described; and general level of sexual interest is discussed. Various exercises that the author has found effective in her practice are suggested for each problem area. The subject of female sexuality is approached candidly and in support of the women for whom this book is written. One of the few books on sexuality that receives a favorable evaluation from mental health experts.

★★★★ *Illustrated Manual of Sexual Therapy* (1987) by Helen Kaplan. New York: Brunner/Mazel.

Kaplan espouses an integrated approach to improved sexual experience through couples therapy and use of specific sexual techniques and exercises, which are outlined in this book. She does not incorporate psychotherapeutic strategies with the sexual exercises; however, an important context for the sexual aspects is an understanding of how the activities promote the relationship and what the resulting emotional impact is. Strategies are offered to counteract the difficulty some couples may have actually trying out these therapeutic exercises. Specific techniques are targeted for specific dysfunctions (e.g., orgasmic problems, premature ejaculation). The narrative is accompanied by numerous drawings that show couples or therapists using this manual how to carry out the exercises. A favorite of sex therapists for training, it might be a bit too academic and graphic for some couples.

Recommended

★★★ *Male Sexuality: A Guide to Sexual Fulfillment* (1978) by Bernie Zilbergeld. Boston: Little, Brown.

Male Sexuality presents a number of ideas about ways to improve male sexuality and effectively disposes of a number of myths that have victimized men and contributed to unhappy relationships. One common myth Zilbergeld attacks is that all that men really want is sexual intercourse. When men want something else, such as love and sensitivity, they are inhibited by the stereotype. Zilbergeld believes that men have gotten themselves into a losing situation by adopting superhuman standards by which to measure their genitals, sexual performance, and satisfaction. Zilbergeld's book is not a sex guide full of gimmicks or gymnastics; it does not try to impose a lifestyle on anyone; and it doesn't accept the premise that all men are the same. Instead, Zilbergeld draws on his extensive background as a sex therapist to portray the real experiences, problems, and needs of men (and women as well). He describes and explains the most common sex problems, the importance of touching, how to relax in sexual situations, how to be sensitive to your sexual partner, and sex for older adults and disabled individuals. A series of exercises—verbal and physical—encourages men to recognize and understand their sexual values, feelings, and preferences. Although rated by only 18 of our experts, its rating was one of the highest ever obtained in our national studies. Far above the crowd of how-to sex books, it is a literate, thoughtful analysis of male sexuality that can enhance the sexual lives of many men.

★★★ *The New Joy of Sex* (1991) by Alex Comfort. New York: Crown.

This book is the revision and expansion of *The Joy of Sex,* published in 1973, that sold more than eight million copies. It was a manual of uninhibited sexual techniques with boldly explicit illustrations. *The New Joy of Sex* continues the uninhibited approach to sexual expression and explicit illustrations that characterized its predecessor, along with new material on AIDS and other sexually transmitted diseases (including a stern lecture on the importance of using condoms). It contains six main sections, including several with unlikely titles. The first, Ingredients, covers topics such as love, fidelity, breasts, buttocks, lubrication, and penis. Appetizers examines exercises, kisses, and bites, among other topics. Main Courses includes mouth music, rear entry, standing positions, and the like. Sauces covers such topics as playtime, Chinese style, G-string, leather, vibrators, and bondage. Venues describes locations, such as beds, bathtubs, rocking chairs, railways, and motorcycles. Health and Other issues explores such topics as AIDS, frigidity, age, bisexuality, fetishes, and transvestitism. This well-known book (rated by 173 psychologists) is educational and can be beneficial in helping people rid themselves of sexual anxieties and achieve greater sexual satisfaction. However, it's definitely more for liberal thinkers than conservative ones.

★★★ *Making Love: A Man's Guide* (1984) by Barry White. New York: Signet.

As its title implies, this book is designed to help men improve their lovemaking and sexual skills. *Making Love* advises men about what they can give women, the role of appearance in sex, women's sexual hang-ups, how to make women feel like making love, foreplay, intercourse, women's sexual anatomy, what to do after having sex, how to keep sex exciting, and what to do about sexual problems. This is mainly a how-to book with specific recommendations to help men become better lovers. Although the book provides some good suggestions in places, too often it regresses to pop-psych descriptions of sexuality. The consensus of the mental health professionals is that Zilbergeld's *Male Sexuality* is a much better choice.

★★★ *Making Love: A Woman's Guide* (1983) by Judith Davis. New York: Signet.

Davis points out that at one time the woman was supposed to be the passive partner in making love, always waiting for the man to make the move and following his lead after that. She says that the rules have changed in today's world—that women can now take a more active, assertive role and can enjoy sex. This sexual how-to guide for women provides explicit instructions on how to become better lovers and attract men sexually. The book includes a number of recommendations, such as 20 sure-fire turn-ons, 7 come-love-me hints, and 9 "please-touch" erogenous zone tips. Some mental health professionals consider this to be a helpful guide for women who are too inhibited sexually, but others complain that the book contains too many sensationalist comments.

★★★ *Sexual Awareness: Enhancing Sexual Pleasure* (1993) by Barry McCarthy and
        Emily McCarthy. New York: Carroll & Graf.

This book is written for couples who want to improve their sexual communication, feelings, and functioning. Basis skills and techniques are presented within major book sections about comfort and pleasure, enhancing sexual satisfaction, and overcoming sexual
problems. The approach utilizes both the research findings of Masters and Johnson and
strategies consistent with social-learning theory. A variety of exercises are proposed
with each set of presenting concerns. The exercises are meant to provide choices and
alternatives to couples as well as ways they can explore, learn, and improve their sexual
relationships. *Sexual Awareness* received very favorable ratings but relatively few evaluations, thus resulting in a 3-star designation.

★★★ *The Soul of Sex* (1998) by Thomas Moore. New York: HarperCollins

The author describes *The Soul of Sex* as a book about sexuality that contains no information on biology, anatomy, or health and little about techniques and relationships. He says
that the human soul is a composite of meanings: emotions, dreams, wishes, fears, a past,
culture, thought, and fantasy. Therefore, he directs the reader to the soul of sex, meaning
not the physical only, but a more spiritual and complex integration of all aspects of self.
This book is written in a poetic, narrative form that draws on Greek mythology, English literature, and other sources that allow symbolic representation in expressing meaning and
interpretation. The author is a psychotherapist who intends this book to be read by psychotherapists, clients, and others who are drawn to his broader perspective of sex.

★★★ *What Really Happens in Bed* (1989) by Steven Carter and Julia Sokol
        Coopersmith. New York: M. Evans.

This self-help book presents a broad-based approach to improving sexual competence and
relationships for both women and men. It represents an effort to cut through sexual expectations that too often are based on myths and romantic fantasies. The authors interviewed
several hundred women and men to provide a profile of what people are really doing and
saying in their sexual lives. The book is divided into two main sections. Section 1, Talking
about Sex, explodes a number of sexual myths and unrealistic expectations and explores
why people are reluctant to talk about what really happens in bed. Section II, Sexual Life
Patterns and Stages, examines the single life and temporary sexual solutions, sexual fantasies and experimentation, marriage and sex, extramarital affairs, and what people can
learn to improve their sex lives. The book includes a number of excerpts from the interviews the authors conducted. On the positive side, it cuts through many sexual myths and
includes extensive material about communication and relationships. On the negative
side, critics faulted the authors for the unscientific nature of their interviews.

★★★ *For Yourself: The Fulfillment of Female Sexuality* (1975) by Lonnie Barbach.
        New York: Doubleday.

Barbach addresses the worries that often distress nonorgasmic women and tells them
how they can achieve orgasm. Barbach attacks the negative cultural belief that women
should not enjoy sex. A number of exercises that will enable women to achieve orgasm
are presented, and each exercise is accompanied by an explanation of why it can be
effective as well as pitfalls to avoid. The book also includes many examples from the

sexual lives of women the author has counseled in her sex therapy groups. How to achieve an orgasm through masturbation and the eventual transference to orgasms with a partner are covered. This book was very positively rated, but by only 17 respondents. The book's enthusiasts said that Barbach sensitively and clearly explains to women how they can achieve a more satisfactory sex life. The book is a bit dated, however.

Strongly Not Recommended

† *Dr. Ruth's Guide to Good Sex* (1983) by Ruth Westheimer. New York: Warner.

† *Dr. Ruth's Guide to Erotic and Sensuous Pleasures* (1991) by Ruth Westheimer and Louis Lieberman. New York: Warner.

Diamonds in the Rough

◆ *Becoming Orgasmic: A Sexual Growth Program for Women* (rev. ed., 1988) by Julia Heiman and Joseph LoPiccolo. New York: Prentice-Hall.

This resource offers women permission, encouragement, and specific behavioral exercises to become more sexually fulfilled. The book leads women through a personal sex history to understand their own sexual feelings and experiences, includes self-touch exercises for learning how to relax and gain sexual pleasure, and presents advice for sharing pleasures with a partner. Among the topics that are addressed include looking at oneself, vaginal exercises, erotic literature, fantasizing, using a vibrator, and intercourse. *Becoming Orgasmic* received a high positive rating but was evaluated by only nine respondents; for these reasons, it is in the Diamonds in the Rough category. The mental health professionals who evaluated the book said that it presents extraordinarily good sexual advice for preorgasmic women.

◆ *Permanent Partners: Building Gay and Lesbian Relationships* (1988) by Betty Berzon. New York: Dutton.

This resource presents knowledge and understanding that will help gay and lesbian couples make their relationships work, satisfy, and last. Berzon examines the obstacles that same-sex couples face as they try to create a life together. Among the obstacles she explores are the lack of visible long-term same-sex couples as role models; absence of support from society—from employers to landlords to insurers—and from the couple's families; a tradition of failure; and the guidance gap that has not provided adequate advice for how to effectively build a life with another man or another woman. *Permanent Partners* received a high positive rating in the national survey but was evaluated by fewer than 10 respondents, hence its placement in the Diamonds in the Rough category. This is an excellent book for gays and lesbians who are thinking about becoming coupled or are perplexed about their current relationship, and for others who want to improve their understanding of gay and lesbian couples.

◆ *The Family Book about Sexuality* (1989) by Mary S. Calderone and Eric W. Johnson. New York: Harper & Row.

The authors cite the proliferation of misinformation and myth about sexuality as an important reason to write this book. They want people to understand the sexual part of their lives, the role sex plays in all lives, and the new information learned from research about sexuality and human behavior. The topic is thoroughly and comprehensively discussed—from the human sexual response, reproduction, and family planning, to the family and its role, people with special problems, and sexually transmitted diseases. The second half of the book is what the authors call the Concise A–Z Encyclopedia, which defines and describes approximately 100 words related to sexuality. This combination of encyclopedia and information guide makes this book unique and useful for families or individuals who want to understand this subject more accurately. This book is included as a Diamond in the Rough because of its strong rating, albeit by a small number of respondents.

◆ *Seven Weeks to Better Sex* (1995) by Domeena Renshaw. New York: Random House.

The audience for this book is couples who have serious concerns and those who are interested in sexual enrichment. This text was written to help committed couples overcome roadblocks in their sexual relationship. The author is founder of the Loyola Sex Therapy Clinic, where more than 1,500 couples have been treated with the same principles, exercises, and recommendations that are found here. Renshaw declares the relationship the patient and treats only the whole person: mind, body, and feelings. Causal problems (e.g., body image, anxiety, earlier trauma) are acknowledged, and the six most common sexual problems are described, accompanied by specific treatment suggestions. Useful questionnaires are included with each stage of exercises. There is a section about working with special needs, including disability and illness. Positively received by the handful of mental health experts in our national surveys who knew the book.

MOVIES

Strongly Recommended

★★★★ *Torch Song Trilogy* (1989) produced by Howard Gottfried and directed by Paul Bogart. R Rating. 117 minutes.

A story of two gay men struggling to tell their families and friends about their mutual love. Tragedy strikes when one is murdered in a senseless killing. The theme is more about love and relationship struggles than about homosexuality. The movie shows the importance of being loved for who we are versus being loved conditionally. A highly regarded and rated film, it is a celebration of the tenacity of the human spirit with its often-thwarted search for love and acceptance.

Recommended

★★★ *Paris Is Burning* (1992) produced by Jennie Livingston and Barry Swimar and directed by Jennie Livingston. No Rating. 78 minutes.

This film depicts an underground lifestyle in Manhattan where gay men work in fashion and dance shows to earn money. During the day they prepare for the shows, and in the evening they perform. There are multiple story lines with different endings. More of a documentary than a commercial film, but it is effective in reminding clients of the centrality of accepting people for who they are.

★★★ *The Boys in the Band* (1970) produced by Matt Crowley and Kenneth Utt and directed by William Friedkin. R Rating. 120 minutes.

A gathering of gay men at a birthday party turns into a sharing of intimate feelings and needs. At the end of the party, two of the men struggle with their personal relationships. A movie that can be comforting for those who struggle with their sexual identity. Discovering oneself in any relationship is never easy, but it is worth the journey.

★★★ *Carnal Knowledge* (1971) produced and directed by Mike Nichols. R Rating. 97 minutes.

A story about two college friends whose main mission in life is to meet women and have sex. As time passes, they both struggle to fill the emotional void in an intimate relationship. *Carnal Knowledge* has become a cult classic; whether teen or adult, you will get the messages woven throughout.

Strongly Not Recommended

† *9½ Weeks* (1987) produced by Anthony Rufus Isaacs and directed by Adrian Lyne. R Rating. 113 minutes.

INTERNET RESOURCES

Metasites

★★★★★ *Society for Human Sexuality* http://www.sexuality.org/index.html

This is likely the premier sexuality information site on the Internet. Clients may benefit from readings under Learning More, such as Erotic Massage, Erotic Talk, Sex Toys, and G-Spot Play. Other topics and areas may too intense for some, such as BDSM (Bondage, Discipline, Slave, Master), Hosting Erotic Events, and Polyamory.

★★★★ *SIECUS: Sexuality Information and Education Council of the United States* http://www.siecus.org

"SIECUS is a 35 year old nonprofit organization, dedicated to affirming that sexuality is a natural and healthy part of life. SIECUS develops, collects, and disseminates information, promotes comprehensive education, and advocates the right of individuals to make responsible sexual choices." The Publications/Resources button leads to the following that may be of use with clients: How to Talk to Your Children about AIDS (6 pages); fact sheets (typically 2 to 3 pages) including Sexually Transmitted Diseases in the United States; Sexual Orientation and Identity; Gay, Lesbian, and Bisexual Adolescents; and Adolescence and Abstinence.

★★★★ *Health Oasis: Mayo Clinic* http://www.mayohealth.org/mayo/library/htm/sexual.htm

Here are about 25 brief articles on medical aspects of sexuality such as sexually transmitted diseases (STDs), dysfunctions, and infertility. Well-written information on several topics not found elsewhere.

Psychoeducational Materials for Clients and Families

General Sites

★★★★★   *The Society for the Scientific Study of Sexuality*
            http://www.ssc.wisc.edu/ssss/wssk1.htm

Here are three brochures of about three pages each: What Sexual Scientists Know about
. . . Compulsive Sexual Behavior, Rape, and Pornography. The contents are empirically
based and may be used to counteract clients' hysterical reactions to these hot topics.

★★★★★   *Coalition for Positive Sexuality* http://www.positive.org/Home

This site offers an online tour (called Just Say Yes) with about 12 topics of special concern to sexually active teens (Should I have sex? safe sex, birth control, homosexuality,
pregnancy, and STDs) presented without preaching or moralizing. The site is prochoice
and in favor of needle exchange. The FAQ has about 10 questions and answers about
HIV and others on heavy topics like abortion, sin, and abstinence.

★★★★★   *Sexuality Database* http://www.sexualitydata.com

There is information on hundreds of topics, and it tends to be fuller than information
presented elsewhere and of high quality. The site offers a search function and an index
of topics.

★★★★★   *Facts of Life Netline*
            http://www.telesouth1.com/~avatar/sexinfo/ppfasexi.html

Totaling about 70 pages, this site offers quality information in an easily searchable format on sexual development, sexually transmitted diseases, birth control, pregnancy,
abortion, and more. It is best used as an overview for clients who are curious but don't
know where to start.

★★★★★   *Guide to Sex for Large Couples* http://www.sexuality.org/l/sex/fatsex.html

Examines negative attitudes toward the sexuality of fat people and offers clear advice
on suitable positions. See also *Guide to Sexual Positions for Large People* at http://
www.sexuality.org/l/sex/fatposit.html.

★★★★   *Alt.sex FAQ Index* http://www.halcyon.com/elf/altsex/shortdex.html

This is a series of FAQs (of perhaps 20 pages each) with information on terms, vulvas,
penises, intercourse, cunnilingus, fellatio, anal intercourse, toys, legal issues, STDs, and
safer sex. It is authoritative and comprehensive, although dated 1994, so some information may no longer be accurate.

★★★★   *Advanced Fellatio Techniques*
            http://www.sexuality.org/l/incoming/afell.html

Just what it says in six pages.

★★★★ *Sexual Disorders* by B. Green, MB, ChB http://www.priory.com/sex.htm
A seven-page overview of diagnoses and treatments, suitable as an introduction.

Self-Pleasuring

★★★★★ *Bianca's Good Vibration Masturbation Guide*
    http://www2.bianca.com/shack/goodvibe/masturbate

Advice; directions; encouragement on clitoral, vaginal, G-spot, and anal masturbation for women; penile, anal, and prostate masturbation for men. Toys, hang-ups, and positive values of masturbation are addressed briefly. A good site to refer the unsure and ambivalent or those with little experience.

Sexually Transmitted Diseases (STDs)

★★★★★ *Facts and Answers about STDs* http://www.ashastd.org/stdfaqs/index.html
The best site for STD information. Here are 10 FAQs with complete information on specific STDs. The section on *STD Information* at http://www.ashastd.org/std/std.html is very complete because it addresses both the medical and social aspects of STDs—for example, A Practical Guide for the Tongue-Tied: How to Talk with Your Health Care Provider about HPV and Other STDs. Under the heading ASHA Programs are links to hotlines and materials about STDs from major sources for any follow-up information needed. At http://www.ashastd.org/abc/ is a thorough *Glossary* of terms to help the reader understand sexually transmitted diseases.

★★★★ *AVERT: AIDS Education and Research Trust*
    http://www.avert.org/yngindx.htm

This Young People's Section is a set of linked pages with good-quality information for teenagers on puberty, AIDS, homosexuality, relationships, and so on. Quite liberal and very complete. The home page at http://www.avert.org offers more information on AIDS.

Gay and Lesbian Issues

★★★★ *Queer Resources Directory* http://www.qrd.org
The Internet offers thousands of pages on homosexuality, and this is the best site for finding information on families, religion, the workplace, youth, and more.

★★★★ *Valuing a Gay or Lesbian Self-Identity* http://www.ksu.edu/ucs/gay.html
This set of seven linked pages from a university counseling center might be the best place to start for someone who has just recognized a homosexual identity.

★★★★ *Coming Out* http://www.couns.uiuc.edu/comout.htm
A two-page brochure on the process and experience of coming out from a college counseling center. Similar are *The Self-Discovery of Being Queer* at http://www.unhcc.unh.edu/

queer.html, *Sexual Identity* at http://www.soa.uc.edu/psc/SH_Sexual_Identity.htm, and *What Are Your Beliefs about Gays and Lesbians?* at http://ub-counseling.buffalo.edu/Relationships/Lgb/orient.html.

Birth Control

★★★★★   *Birth Control*
          http://womensissues.miningco.com/msub15.htm?pid=2771&cob=home

Links to about 20 sites with complete, independent, and accurate information on birth control.

★★★★★   *Ann Rose's Ultimate Birth Control Links*
          http://gynpages.com/ultimate

Everything is here—all methods, decisions, and resources.

★★★★★   *Birth Control Methods*
          http://www.plannedparenthood.org/BIRTHCONTROL/index.htm

As you might expect from Planned Parenthood, this is comprehensive, accurate, detailed, timely, and well-organized. If a client need any information to assist with making decisions about birth control methods, it is here.

★★★★★   *Emergency Contraception* http://ec.princeton.edu

For those who need to prevent pregnancy after unprotected sexual intercourse, all the methods and information are here.

★★★★   *Hoboken Family Planning: Sex Ed 101*
          http://www.sex-ed101.com

Some clients are ignorant about sexual health issues. Here they can find current but brief coverage of the facts of contraception, STDs, breast self-examination, mammography, testicular self-examination, and common vaginal infections.

★★★★   *Ask NOAH About: Family Planning and Contraception*
          http://www.noah-health.org/english/pregnancy/contraception.html

Everything is here and comes from authoritative, up-to-date sources.

Sexual Addiction

★★★★   *Sex Addiction* http://www.sexhelp.com

This is the home page for Patrick Carnes's books and has materials about sexual addiction such as tests, bibliographies, reading lists and FAQs. Sex Addiction Q&A (eight pages) and the Introduction to Out of the Shadows (six pages) provide all you want to know about this perspective on the behavior.

★★ *Sex Addicts Anonymous* http://www.sexaa.org

A 12-step approach with online readings. See also *Sexual Compulsives Anonymous* at http://www.sca-recovery.org.

Aging and Sexuality

★★★★ *Sexual Issues for Aging Adults* by Charette A. Dersch, Steven M. Harris, Thomas Kimball, James P. Marshall, and Michael A. Negretti
http://www.hs.ttu.edu/sexuality&aging

This site offers only introductory information, so it may be suitable as introductory reading to orient or disinhibit a client.

★★★ *Sexuality and Aging: Myths, Attitudes, and Barriers* by Marilyne Scott
http://socserv2.mcmaster.ca/soc/courses/soc3k3e/stuweb/scott/scottm4.htm

An overview in about eight pages. There is a link at the end for another summary. See also *Sex and Aging* at http://www.sexhealth.org/infocenter/SexAging/sexaging.htm which offers short pages of information. *Sexuality in Later Life* at http://www.agepage. com/sex1.htm is four pages from the National Institute on Aging.

For Teens

★★★★★ *Teenwire* http://www.teenwire.com

Addressing teen sexuality issues in an attractive and inviting format, this site from the Planned Parenthood Federation of America can be an source of solid social and medical information for the curious teen.

★★★★★ *All about Sex* http://www.AllAboutSex.org

The Topics for Teens and Topics for Pre-Teens buttons lead to areas with about 20 articles. One example is First Sexual Intercourse, which offers about 12 pages of information and assistance in deciding and preparing. The Sex for One button goes to a very informative set of pages. The site is progressive and sex-positive and has several articles criticizing statements by the far religious right.

★★★★★ *Puberty 101* http://www.virtualkid.com/p101/p101_menu.shtml

Using a question and answer format, this site offers clear and complete information on difficult and important questions. The information on stages of development is unavailable elsewhere on the Internet. Thank you, J. Geoff Malta, MA.

★★★★ *Sex, Etc.* http://www.sxetc.org

Described as "a website by teens for teens," it offers a lot of information and answers. There are back issues of a newsletter here, and the site is searchable. It is sponsored by the Network for Family Life Education at Rutgers. This could be the first place to refer curious teens for accurate information on gender, harassment, relationships, and other topics.

Other Resources

★★★★★ *Kegel Exercises*
             http://dir.yahoo.com/Health/Women_s_Health/Kegel_Exercises

If you want clients to learn to do Kegel exercises (for erotic or continence reasons), the five working sites listed here are comprehensive and balanced.

See also Love and Intimacy (Chapter 17); Marriage (Chapter 18); Teenagers and Parenting (Chapter 27).

Hotlines

National AIDS Hotline

Phone: 800-342-AIDS; 1-800-344-7432 Español; 800-243-7889 Deaf Access (TTY)

National Gay and Lesbian Hotline

Phone: 888-843-4564

Teens and AIDS Hotline

Phone: 800-440-TEEN

NATIONAL SUPPORT GROUPS

This is a heterogeneous listing of groups. Some are support groups, some are consciousness raising groups, and some are political activism groups.

ACT UP (AIDS Coalition to Unleash Power)
New York office: 212-966-4873
http://www.actup.org

Augustine Fellowship, Sex and Love Addicts Anonymous
PO Box 119
New Town Branch
Boston, MA 02258
Phone: 617-332-1845

12-step fellowship based on AA for those who desire to stop living out a pattern of sex addiction, obsessive–compulsive sexual behavior, or emotional attachment.

Codependents of Sex Addicts (COSA)
PO Box 14537
Minneapolis, MN 55414
Phone: 612-537-6904

A 12-step program for those in relationships with people who have compulsive sexual behavior.

Dignity/USA
1500 Massachusetts Avenue NW, #11
Washington, DC 20005
Phone: 800-877-8797

Organization of lesbian, bisexual, and gay Catholics and their families and friends.

Gay Men's Health Crisis
119 West 24th Street
New York, NY 10011
Phone: 212-807-6655

Information is available in Spanish and Creole.

Family Pride Coalition
PO Box 34337
San Diego, CA 92163
Phone: 619-296-0199
http://www.familypride.org

Herpes Resource Center
PO Box 13827
Research Triangle Park, NC 27709
Phone: 919-361-8488

LLEGO (National Latino/a Lesbian and Gay Organization)
1612 K Street NW, Suite 500
Washington, DC 20006
Phone: 202-466-8240

Lesbian Avengers
Phone: 202-861-1393
http://www.lesbian.org/chicago-avengers

NARAL (National Abortion and Reproductive Rights Action League)
1156 15th Street NW
Washington, DC 20005
Phone: 202-973-3000
http://www.naral.org

National Advocacy Coalition on Youth and Sexual Orientation
1711 Connecticut Avenue NW, Suite 206
Washington, DC 20009
Phone: 202-319-7596

National Association of People with AIDS
1413 K Street NW, #7
Washington, DC 20005-3405
Phone: 202-898-0414

NOW (National Organization for Women)
1000 16th Street NW, #700
Washington, DC 20036
Phone: 202-331-0066

!OUTPROUD! (The National Coalition for Gay, Lesbian and Bisexual Youth)
369 Third Street, Suite B-362
San Rafael, CA 94901
Phone: 415-460-5452

PFLAG (Parents and Friends of Lesbians and Gays)
1101 14th Street NW, #1030
Washington, DC 20005
Phone: 202-638-4200
http://www.pflag.org

Planned Parenthood
810 Seventh Ave
New York, NY 10019
Phone: 800-230-PLAN
http://www.plannedparenthood.org

Sex Addicts Anonymous
PO Box 70949
Houston, TX 77270
Phone: 713-869-4902

A 12-step program of recovery from compulsive sexual behavior.

Sexual Compulsives Anonymous
PO Box 1585
New York, NY 10113-0935
Phone: 800-977-4325

The Society for the Scientific Study of Sexuality
PO Box 208
Mount Vernon, IA 52314-0208
Phone: 319-895-8407
Fax: 319-895-6203
TheSociety@worldnet.att.net

CHAPTER 25

Spiritual and Existential Concerns

Spirituality is far more than formalized religion. Its not simply a prayer we say on the Sabbath, but a prayerful life we live with our family and neighbors. Spirituality resides within our intellect, our emotions, our physical existence, and our daily lives. The mental health professions and self-help authors have recently rediscovered the centrality of spirituality in our personal lives. But understanding spirituality is not new. More than 400 years ago, St. Ignatius compiled his notes into what today is known as the *Spiritual Exercises*, a practical guide on discernment and living a life of spirituality.

Spirituality is inevitably concerned with the elusive search for the purpose and meaning of life. These existential concerns focus on life's ultimate questions—freedom, existence, meaning, authenticity, and death. Life, existence itself, is in a constant state of becoming; to live in the moment is a dynamic process of person and environment experiencing life.

In this chapter, we critically consider self-help books and Internet resources devoted to an assortment of spiritual and existential concerns.

SELF-HELP BOOKS

Strongly Recommended

★★★★★ *Man's Search for Meaning* (rev. and updated ed., 1998) by Viktor Frankl. New York: Pocket Books.

Viktor Frankl, a professor of psychiatry at the University of Vienna Medical School, takes an existential approach to the pursuit of self-fulfillment. After Frankl survived the German concentration camp at Auschwitz, he founded a school of psychotherapy he called

---

RECOMMENDATION HIGHLIGHTS

Self-Help Books

- For an existential approach to life and self-fulfillment:

  ★★★★★ *Man's Search for Meaning* by Viktor Frankl

- For rediscovering the joy of everyday life:

  ★★★★ *Finding Flow* by Mihaly Csikszentmihalyi

- For a spiritual approach to meaning and self-fulfillment:

  ★★★★ *The Road Less Traveled* by M. Scott Peck

  ★★★★ *When All You Ever Wanted Isn't Enough* by Harold Kushner

- For an inner-healing mind–body approach to self-improvement:

  ★★★★ *Peace, Love, and Healing* by Bernie Siegel

- For prayer and a religious approach to self-fulfillment:

  ◆ *Illuminata* by Marianne Williamson

  ◆ *The Search for Significance* by Robert McGee

Internet Resources

- On depression and the effect of spiritual life:

  ★★★★★ *Depression and Spiritual Growth* by Dimitri Mihalas
  http://chandra.astro.indiana.edu/bipolar/spirit.html

---

logotherapy, which maintains that the desire to find a meaning in life is the primary motive of human beings. Frankl's mother, father, brother, and wife died in the concentration camps. Frankl emphasizes each person's uniqueness and the finiteness of life. He thinks that examining the finiteness of existence and the certainty of death adds meaning to life. Frankl believes that the three most distinct human qualities are spirituality, freedom, and responsibility. Spirituality, in his system, does not have a religious underpinning. Rather, it refers to a human being's uniqueness—to spirit, philosophy, and mind. Freedom is the freedom to make decisions. With the freedom to make decisions is responsibility for those decisions. Logotherapists often ask clients such questions as why they exist, what they want from life, and what the meaning of their life is. Originally published in 1946, *Man's Search for Meaning* is a 5-star classic that still commands a great deal of respect among mental health professionals. This book challenges readers to think about the meaning of their lives. The reading is rough going at times, but for those who persist and probe Frankl's remarkable insights, the rewards are well worth the effort.

★★★★ *Finding Flow: The Psychology of Engagement with Everyday Life* (1997) by
Mihaly Csikszentmihalyi. New York: Basic Books.

Csikszentmihalyi (pronounced "chik-sent-mee-high-yee") has been investigating the concept he calls "flow" for more than two decades. Flow is the state of deep enjoyment and happiness that people feel when they have a sense of mastering something. Supported by a number of research studies, this self-help resource addresses how people can better structure their everyday lives in joyful ways. What we do in our day can largely determine what kind of life we live, and how we emotionally experience what we do is even more important. When in flow, what we feel, what we wish, and what we think are in harmony. This excellent 4-star book offers engaging, research-supported information on creating and discovering flow in everyday life. The quality of life depends on what we do with what we have.

★★★★   *When All You Ever Wanted Isn't Enough* (1986) by Harold Kushner. New York: Summit.

Harold Kushner, rabbi and author of *When Bad Things Happen to Good People* (evaluated in Chapter 12), here offers a spiritual message of self-fulfillment. Subtitled *The Search for a Life That Matters*, the book maintains that material rewards create almost as many problems as they solve. Kushner believes that sooner or later we come face to face with a big question: What am I supposed to do with my life? We want to be more than just brief biological flashes in the universe that disappear forever. Kushner argues that there is no one big answer to the meaning of life, but that there are answers. And the answers are found in filling day-to-day existence with meaning, with the love of friends and family, and with striving for integrity, instead of just reaching for the pot of gold. Kushner spends considerable time analyzing the book of Ecclesiastes in the Bible because it asks us to think about life. Kushner believes, like Ecclesiastes, that life is its own reward.

★★★★   *Peace, Love, and Healing* (1989) by Bernie Siegel. New York: Harper & Row.

Bernie Siegel, a surgeon and the best-selling author of *Love, Medicine and Miracles,* offers an inner-resource self-healing approach to self-improvement. Siegel believes that the medical field has ignored the power of self-healing for too long. He argues that modern medicine and self-healing are not mutually exclusive. Among the self-healing techniques he recommends are meditation, visualization, relaxation, and developing peace of mind. Siegel describes a number of exceptional patients who used self-healing to improve physical and mental well-being. Although *Peace, Love, and Healing* received a 4-star rating, it is controversial in the medical field. Some physicians feel that Siegel overexaggerates the power of self-healing and that his ideas may keep some people from getting adequate medical treatment. Siegel's supporters among the mental health professionals said that he has inspired many patients, nurses, medical students, and even some doctors to look at healing in a larger context and to look at illnesses in new ways.

★★★★   *The Road Less Traveled* (1978) by M. Scott Peck. New York: Simon & Schuster.

This spiritual and psychological approach to life has been on best-seller lists for more than 10 years. M. Scott Peck, a psychiatrist, begins the book by stating that life is difficult and that we all suffer pain and disappointment. He counsels us to face up to life's difficulties and not be lazy. Indeed, Peck equates laziness with original sin, going on to say that people's tendency to avoid problems and emotional suffering is the root of mental disorders. Peck also believes that people are thirsting for integrity in their lives. They are not happy with a country that has "In God We Trust" as a motto and at the same time leads the world in the arms race. They also can't tolerate being only Sunday-morning Christians. To achieve integrity, says Peck, people need to move spirituality into all aspects of their daily lives. Peck speaks of four important tools to use in life's journey: delayed gratification, acceptance of responsibility, dedication to the truth, and balance. After a thorough analysis of each, Peck explores the will to use them, which he calls love. Then he probes further and analyzes the relationship of growth and religion, which leads him to examine the final step of the road less traveled: grace. By grace, Peck means the whole range of human activities that support the human spirit. This immensely popular 4-star resource has developed a cultlike following, especially among young people. Peck has obviously recognized important voids in many people's lives, especially the need for an integrated, spiritually oriented existence. While many of Peck's ideas are not new, he has succeeded in packaging them in contemporary American language that has enormous appeal. Some mental health professionals fault Peck for the fuzziness of his ideas, especially when he arrives at the meeting point between God and man and between conscious and unconscious worlds.

Recommended

★★★ *Further Along the Road Less Traveled* (2nd ed., 1998) by M. Scott Peck. New York: Touchstone.

Peck, a psychiatrist and the best-selling author of *The Road Less Traveled* (reviewed above), starts this book with the phrase "Life is complex." He describes the road each person has to travel as a rocky wilderness through which we must carve out our own individual paths. Searching for individual meaning and the center of spirituality is woven throughout this book. The author encourages us to glory in the mystery of life and not to be dismayed. Peck's book is interesting for the self-motivated layperson and the mental health professional. The author applauds the scientific advances of medicine but cautions of the danger of losing the centrality of psychological and social wisdom and of neglecting our spirituality.

★★★ *Care of the Soul* (1992) by Thomas Moore. New York: HarperCollins.

Moore, a former Catholic monk and presently a psychotherapist, makes a case for the loss of soul as the great malady of the 20th century. The soul is embodied in genuineness and depth and is revealed in attachment, love, and community. This best-selling book is about living a soulful life. Moore repeatedly distinguishes between spirituality and soul. Those interested in the influence of philosophy and religion coupled with a modern view of spirituality and soulfulness will find this book both challenging and enlightening.

★★★ *The Seven Spiritual Laws of Success: A Practical Guide to the Fulfillment of Your Dreams* (1994) by Deepak Chopra. San Rafael, CA: Amber-Allen.

This book shatters the myth that success is the result of hard work, planning, and driving ambition. Chopra, a best-selling author, distills the way to create a successful and fulfilling personal life into seven principles. Essentially, personal understanding and harmony help promote fulfilling relationships. The overriding message is that once we understand our true nature and live in harmony with natural law, a sense of well-being, health, fulfilling relationships, enthusiasm for life, and mental satisfaction will flow effortlessly. This is a book you can reference time and again. It is for anyone looking for a spiritual, mature, and human perspective on living a successful life.

★★★ *Flow: The Psychology of Optimal Experience* (1990) by Mihaly Csikszentmihalyi. New York: Harper & Row.

Flow is a state of enjoyable concentration in which a person becomes absorbed while engaging in an activity. The author says that flow can be controlled and should not be left to chance. We can develop flow by setting challenges for ourselves, by stretching ourselves to the limit to achieve something worthwhile, by developing competent coping skills, and by combining life's many experiences into a meaningful pattern. Flow can be found in many different experiences and walks of life. Rock climbers can become so absorbed that they feel at one with the cliff face. Chess masters play in a trancelike state. Artists dab paint on a canvas for hour after hour in a state of immersed concentration. The famous humanistic psychologist Abraham Maslow described a similar sense of euphoria in the early 1960s. What distinguishes Csikszentmihalyi's concept of flow from Maslow's peak experiences is the frequency of flow experiences. Maslow thought people were fortunate if they caught a peak experience several times in their entire lives; Csikszentmihalyi, by contrast, says that if people cultivate flow experiences, they can have them several times a day. This 3-star resource documents that the path to happiness does not lie in mindless hedonism but rather in mindful challenges. It is a serious, thoroughly documented, and well-researched book, but our mental health experts preferred Csikszentmihalyi's newer book, *Finding Flow*, reviewed earlier in this chapter.

Diamonds in the Rough

♦ *Illuminata: Thoughts, Prayers, Rites of Passage* (1994) by Marianne Williamson. New York: Random House.

This best-selling author attempts to bring prayer into our daily life. The prayers are designed for people of all ages in all types of relationships and traverse the human experience—prayers to release anger, find forgiveness, discover great love, and achieve intimacy. Williamson gives us prayers to heal our souls, hearts, body, and country. Another section includes rites of passage, ceremonies of light for the signal events in our lives, blessing of the newborn, coming of age, marriage, and death. The author concludes that through prayer, we find what we cannot find elsewhere: a peace that is not of this world. This book is an effort to create a context for the observation of God, that we might see Him more clearly and call forth His power more perfectly in our lives. Highly rated by our mental health experts, but not frequently, thus receiving the designation of Diamond in the Rough. A book for the young and old who find prayer an important part of their lives.

♦ *The Search for Significance* (1990) by Robert McGee. Houston, TX: Rapha.

The Christian spiritual approach taken by this book suggests that self-fulfillment comes not from the ability to please others, but from the love and forgiveness of Jesus Christ.

In Part I, McGee discusses the search for significance, good and evil, the process of hope and healing, and how a Christ-based approach is the only path to self-fulfillment and happiness in life. Part II is an extensive workbook with many religiously based exercises. In two of our studies, *The Search for Significance* was positively rated, but by only 11 and 9 psychologists respectively, thus receiving the designation of Diamond in the Rough. This is a much stronger religious approach to life's meaning than the other spiritually based books in this category—for example, M. Scott Peck's *The Road Less Traveled* and Harold Kushner's *When All You've Ever Wanted Isn't Enough.* It will appeal mainly to Christians who seek self-fulfillment through religious commitment.

Not Recommended

★★ *The Celestine Prophecy: An Adventure* (1993) by James Redfield. New York: Warner.

★ *The Be (Happy) Attitudes* (1985) by Robert Schuller. Waco, TX: Word.

Strongly Not Recommended

† *The Way of the Wizard: Twenty Spiritual Lessons in Creating the Life You Want* (1995) by Deepak Chopra. New York: Harmony.

† *Clear Body, Clear Mind* (1990) by L. Ron Hubbard. Los Angeles: Bridge.

† *Dianetics: The Modern Science of Mental Health* (1950) by L. Ron Hubbard. Los Angeles: The Church of Scientology of California.

† *Scientology: The Fundamentals of Thought* (1988) by L. Ron Hubbard. Los Angeles: Bridge.

INTERNET RESOURCES

The Internet has exploded of late with a burgeoning interest in the intersection of religion and psychology, especially in therapy, healing, and growth. In truth, all the concerns in this book contain existential and spiritual components. Yet, of the dozens of mental health sites we reviewed, only one had entries under religion or spirituality.

Of course, there are an enormous numbers of links to specific religious traditions, especially Asian, and to complementary and alternative medicine. Sites in this area range from flaky (e.g., channeling, out-of-body experiences, lightwork), to part psychological (e.g., transcendental meditation) and to actively hostile (e.g., Scientology). We have excluded the sites of specific religions, science versus religion, and schools of existential psychotherapy.

Psychoeducational Materials for Clients and Families

★★★ *Transcendental Meditation* http://www.tm.org

The site offers briefly annotated citations to 508 research studies of the value of transcendental meditation for increasing intelligence, creativity and productivity, and reducing anxiety, medical care, stress, drug use, crime, and violence. There are no readings or training available on the site.

★★★ *Religion and Spirituality*
        http://www.pastoralcounseling.net/religionandspirituality.html

A short page from a book by Jean G. Fitzpatrick on the differences between religion and spirituality and suggesting the need to live a spiritual life beyond the religious one.

★★★ *Psychotherapy and Spirituality Institute* http://www.mindspirit.org

Although sponsored by an organization of therapists in New York, this site offers some essays (under Articles) that address various aspects of living and relating.

★★ *Psychology of Religion Pages* by Michael Nielsen, PhD
        http://psychwww.com/psyrelig/index.htm

"This is a general introduction to the psychology of religion, for example, as it is studied by scientists in Division 36 of the American Psychological Association. Here you will find a description of what psychologists have learned about how religion influences people's lives." This may be useful for people who are struggling with social and psychological (but not spiritual) aspects of their faith.

Biographical and Autobiographical Vignettes

★★★★★ *Depression and Spiritual Growth* by Dimitri Mihalas
          http://chandra.astro.indiana.edu/bipolar/spirit.html

"The main purpose of this essay to discuss how a struggle with major depression can lead, seemingly paradoxically, to significant spiritual growth by the victim of the illness." This 15-page personal essay is an absolutely superb presentation on the interaction of depression with spiritual life, spiritual healing, and related issues. For the college-level reader.

Other Resources

★★★ *Religion and Philosophy Resources on the Internet*
        http://www.bu.edu/sth/library/resources.html

Boston University offers this excellent starting point about specific religions and philosophies. It is not devoted to mental health issues.

★★★ *John Templeton Foundation* http://www.templeton.org

After having made millions in international investing, Templeton set up a foundation to fund writing and research on forgiveness, optimism, spirituality, and health and to annually award a large monetary prize for progress in religion.

CHAPTER 26

Stress Management and Relaxation

We live in a stress-filled world. According to the American Academy of Family Physicians, two-thirds of all office visits to family doctors are for stress-related symptoms. Stress is also thought to be a major contributor to coronary disease, accidental injuries, cirrhosis of the liver, and suicide—four of the leading causes of death in the United States. Several of the best-selling drugs in the United States are antianxiety (Xanax, Klonopin) and ulcer (Tagamet, Zantac) medications.

There are many ways to cope effectively with stress, just as there are many ways to cope ineffectively with stress. Converging research suggests that the most effective approach is to employ a variety of strategies instead of relying on a single method. For example, people who have had heart attacks are usually advised to change more than one aspect of their lives. The advice might go something like this: Practice relaxation; lose weight; confide in good friends; quit smoking; begin to exercise several times a week; reduce your anger; and take vacations on a regular basis. One of these alone may not turn the tide against stress, but a combination will maximize success.

In this chapter, we evaluate self-help books and Internet resources that deal directly with relaxation and stress management. Many other self-help resources reviewed in this book also provide advice on coping with stress; consult in particular Chapters 5 (Anger), 6 (Anxiety Disorders), 7 (Assertiveness), 11 (Communication and People Skills), and 23 (Self-Management and Self-Enhancement). In addition, for stress stemming from a particular source, such as career problems, the death of a loved one, divorce, or loneliness, the recommended resources in those chapters may be appropriate.

RECOMMENDATION HIGHLIGHTS

Self-Help Books

- For comprehensive strategies to reduce stress:

  ★★★★★ *The Relaxation and Stress Reduction Workbook* by Martha Davis and Associates

  ★★★★★ *The Stress and Relaxation Handbook* by James Madders

- For learning meditation and mindfulness:

  ★★★★★ *Wherever You Go, There You Are* by Jon Kabat-Zinn

- For mind–body, behavioral medicine approach to combating stress:

  ★★★★★ *The Wellness Book* by Herbert Benson and Eileen M. Stuart

  ★★★★ *Why Zebras Don't Get Ulcers* by Robert M. Sapolsky

- For learning relaxation to cope with stress:

  ★★★★★ *The Relaxation Response* by Herbert Benson

  ★★★★ *Beyond the Relaxation Response* by Herbert Benson

- For a spiritually based approach to coping with stress:

  ★★★★ *Each Day a New Beginning* by the Hazelden Foundation

  ★★★ *Touchstones* by the Hazelden Foundation

Internet Resources

- On alleviating headaches:

  ★★★★ *The Excedrin Headache Resource Center* http://www.excedrin.com

- On learning relaxation:

  ★★★★ *Basic Guided Relaxation: Advanced Technique* http://www.dstress.com/guided.htm

SELF-HELP BOOKS

Strongly Recommended

★★★★★ *The Relaxation and Stress Reduction Workbook* (1995) by Martha Davis, Elizabeth Robbins Eschelman, and Matthew McKay. Oakland, CA: New Harbinger.

This 5-star workbook can be used as a general reference book and valuable resource to learn how to relax and manage stress in a number of environmental settings. There are a variety of stress management and relaxation techniques to choose from. The first two chapters are designed to help examine personal reactions to stress and understand the dynamics of stress and stressors. The book is easy to read and is accompanied by pictures of proper body positioning for specific techniques. The highest rated book in this category and among the most favorably evaluated in all our national studies, it can be useful for laypersons reducing stress and for professionals as a reference guide when using homework assignments with their clients. A very popular and apparently effective resource.

★★★★★ *Wherever You Go, There You Are* (1994) by Jon Kabat-Zinn. New York: Hyperion.

This book is a practical guide to meditation—in essence, a book about mindfulness/ wakefulness. Psychologist Kabat-Zinn repeatedly reminds us that the moment is all we really have to work with. To allow ourselves to be in the moment, we have to pause in our experience long enough to let the present moment sink in. Meditation is simply about being oneself and knowing something about who that is. Mindfulness has to do, above all, with attention and awareness. This engaging 5-star resource will be of value to both the beginning and the experienced practitioner of meditation.

★★★★★ *The Stress and Relaxation Handbook: A Practical Guide to Self-Help Techniques* (1997) by James Madders. London, UK: Vermilion.

Fully illustrated throughout, this book contains relaxation exercises to apply throughout the day. There are specific techniques designed for children, adults, and older adults. Some exercises are designed to help manage the pain and tension found in such problems as migraine, insomnia, digestive disorders, and the menstrual cycle. The message here is that we all suffer emotionally and physically from the stress and strain of life, but that our reactions can be modified and controlled by training. Chapters begin with factual information about stress, our reactions to stress, and how we can reduce the negative effect of stress with proper relaxation techniques. Rated favorably in our national studies, earning a 5-star rating.

★★★★★ *The Relaxation Response* (1975) by Herbert Benson. New York: Morrow.

This influential book presents a specific strategy for reducing stress—learning how to relax. Benson believes that the relaxation response can significantly improve a person's ability to cope with stressful circumstances and can reduce the likelihood of a number of diseases, especially heart attacks and strokes. He points out that the relaxation response has been used for centuries in the context of religious teachings, usually in Eastern cultures, where it often is practiced on a daily basis. Benson developed a simple method of attaining the relaxation response and explains how to incorporate it into daily life. The relaxation response consists of four essential elements: (1) locating a quiet context; (2) developing a mental device, such as a word or phrase (e.g., *om*) that is repeated in a precise way over and over again; (3) adopting a passive attitude, which involves letting go of thoughts and distractions; and (4) assuming a comfortable position. Practicing the relaxation response 10 to 20 minutes one or two times a day improves well-being, according to the research. This important 5-star book was published at a time when Americans were skeptical about the spiritual and psychological practices of Eastern cultures. Through his research and translation, Benson demystified the strategies that helped people in these cultures cope effectively with stress. Many mental health professionals recommend Benson's approach to their clients because they have found that it works. The relaxation response is a simple, effective, self-healing technique for reducing the negative effects of stress.

★★★★★   *The Wellness Book: A Comprehensive Guide to Maintaining Health and Treating Stress Related Illness* (1992) by Herbert Benson and Eileen M. Stuart. New York: Fireside.

This book, coauthored by Benson of *The Relaxation Response* fame (reviewed above), is a comprehensive guide to the successful implementation of behavioral medicine and to maintaining health and treating stress-related diseases. Behavioral medicine combines the talents of mind and body and uses psychological approaches to prevent illness and improve health. This book covers numerous wellness topics, principally the relaxation response, nutrition, exercise, body awareness, cognitive restructuring, stress management, coping, problem solving, and humor. This 5-star book is highly rated by the experts in our national studies as an excellent and practical guide to mind–body interaction, but many advised that people should undertake major lifestyle changes under the supervision of a health-care professional. The book provides sound advice for preventing disease and improving health, presents up-to-date material on the role of stress in disease, and is especially good at describing the powerful role of relaxation and other techniques that help people reduce their chances of incurring life-threatening diseases such as heart disease and cancer.

★★★★   *Beyond the Relaxation Response* (1984) by Herbert Benson. New York: Times Books.

This is Herbert Benson's sequel to *The Relaxation Response* (reviewed above). A decade after Benson coined the term *relaxation response,* he concluded that combining it with another strategy is even more powerful in combating stress. The other strategy is faith in a healing power either inside or outside the self. Benson arrived at this conclusion because of his own clinical observations and studies of Tibetan monks in the Himalayas, which are described in detail in this book. The healing power can be belief in a certain dogma or a traditional religious system, or it can be faith in oneself, in the state attained while exercising, or in the relaxation response itself. Benson explains how to harness the power of faith in a number of different situations—while jogging, walking, swimming, lying in bed, or praying. *Beyond the Relaxation Response* is a 4-star book that clearly conveys the power of mental strategies in influencing health and the healing process.

★★★★   *Minding the Body, Mending the Mind* (1987) by Joan Borysenko. New York: Bantam.

This book is mainly about the positive effects of relaxation on the mind and body. The author discusses how deep relaxation and meditation can shift disease-promoting physiological mechanisms into a healing mode. The focus of the book is on reducing anxiety and stress and developing control over one's life. It also serves as a guide for conditioning the mind to function as a healer and health enhancer. The general public can use this book as a guide to coping with stress and disease more effectively. For those interested in the mind–body relationship to healing, this will be an informative resource. A solid book and a solid message.

★★★★ *Why Zebras Don't Get Ulcers: A Guide to Stress, Stress-Related Diseases and Coping* (1994) by Robert M. Sapolsky. New York: Freeman.

Drawing on current scientific research, this book is provocative and often amusing as it looks at the interconnections between emotion and physical well-being. Sapolsky discusses the interactions between the body and the mind and the ways in which emotions and personality can have an effect on the health of virtually every cell in the body. Stress and our vulnerability to disease are best understood in the context of the person who is suffering from that disease. Links are made between stress and increased risk for certain diseases, with specific chapters on the circulatory system, energy storage, growth, reproduction, the immune system, depression, and the aging process. The last chapter describes how to manage stress. For the interested reader or professional working with stressed clients, this is a very informative 4-star book. It is also a scientific book for the nonscientist.

★★★★ *Each Day a New Beginning* (1982) by the Hazelden Foundation. New York: HarperCollins.

This book of daily meditations for women follows the same format of *One Day at a Time in Al-Anon* and *A Day at a Time*, the daily meditative books described in Chapter 3. Each page of the book is devoted to one day—from January 1 through December 31—and has three elements: a beginning quotation, a paragraph or two about a daily thought and meditation, and an ending self-affirmation. The book is a spiritually oriented approach for women coping with a wide array of difficulties in life, not only addictions. Each day is perceived as a new opportunity for growth and successful coping. *Each Day a New Beginning* is well-conceived and presents thought-provoking ideas in a warm, personal tone. The book is especially appealing to women with a spiritual orientation.

Recommended

★★★ *Touchstones* (1986) by the Hazelden Foundation. New York: HarperCollins.

This is the male counterpart of *Each Day a New Beginning* (described above). It is a spiritually based approach to coping with stress for men, with each page devoted to a day of the year—from January 1 through December 31—and containing a quotation, a meditative commentary, and a self-affirming statement. The breadth of the quotations is extensive, ranging from comments by former New York Yankees baseball manager Billy Martin to passages from D. H. Lawrence and poems by Emily Dickinson. The meditative thoughts also are broad, from awareness of one's problems, to letting go, to confession. The meditative commentary is warm, sensitive, and supportive, and the self-affirmations are motivating. This book will especially appeal to men with a spiritual orientation who are having difficulty coping with life's stress.

★★★ *The Male Stress Syndrome* (1986) by Georgia Witkin-Lanoil. New York: Berkley.

This self-help resource was written by a woman for men and presents strategies for helping men cope effectively with stress. Combining the results of a survey administered to more than 500 men and the women closest to them with examples from her own clinical practice, Witkin-Lanoil isolates the key stress factors common to most men. She also provides suggestions on how to recognize these factors and manage them. Relaxation exercises are among the suggested stress management strategies for males. Some stress-reduction strategies are tailored to specific male problems, such as sex therapy for sex-related problems. This 3-star book provides a good understanding of male-related stress factors and ways to reduce them.

Diamond in the Rough

♦ *Inner and Outer Peace through Meditation* (1996) by Rajinder Singh. Rockport, MA: Element.

The author has codified simple exercise techniques, coupled with spiritual guidance and his own experience with meditation, to help people achieve freedom from fear and achieve a personal state of contentment. Singh explains how peace can be created by meditation and inner reflection. He connects the workings of inner (self) and outer (world) peace. The key to genuine world peace is inner peace founded on interpersonal respect and love. To create inner peace, it is necessary to calm the mind; hence the importance of meditation. Highly but infrequently rated, thus earning Diamond in the Rough classification. This is a book for young and old alike who are already meditating or seeking to learn the art of meditation.

INTERNET RESOURCES

Psychoeducational Materials for Clients and Families

★★★★　*The Excedrin Headache Resource Center*　http://www.excedrin.com

Although you cannot avoid the commercial aspects of this site, there are many educational materials on the types, causes, nonmedical treatment, and effects of headaches.

★★★★　*Basic Guided Relaxation: Advanced Technique* by L. John Mason, PhD
　　　　http://www.dstress.com/guided.htm

A very good four-page script.

★★★★　*Stress* by Scott Wallace, PhD
　　　　http://www.virtualpsych.com/stress/stressframeset.htm

This site offers about a dozen well-written pages of information with a casual style, a self-test, tips, and more, emphasizing cognitive change.

★★★　*Progressive Muscle Relaxation* by R. Richmond, PhD
　　　http://members.aol.com/avpsyrich/pmr.htm

A five-page brochure on how to do progressive muscle relaxation. See also his superb presentation on stress at http://members.aol.com/avpsyrich/stress.htm.

★★★   *Stress Management* http://www.couns.uiuc.edu/stress.htm

Look under Self Help Brochures for a clear two-page handout from a university counseling center.

★★   *Mastering Your Stress Demons* by Joseph Napora
   http://www.intelihealth.com

At the Intellihealth.com site, search for this title or for "stress." About 10 pages of a general talk Napora gave on what he calls "centering" to manage stress.

★★   *Meditation, Guided Fantasies, and Other Stress Reducers*
   http://www.shpm.com/articles/stress

At *Self-Help and Psychology Magazine*, there are some relaxing nature pictures, inspiring thoughts, and fifteen one- to two-page essays on stress topics.

Other Resources

★★★★★   *Car Accident Family Web Site* http://www.stresspress.com/car

General coping and assessment information in a lively format for people who have been in an automobile accident.

★★   *Job Stress Help* http://www.jobstresshelp.com

The Tips to Reduce Job Stress and the FAQ are brief sets of ideas.

★★   *Coping with Racial Stress* http://www.omhrc.gov/ctg/mhm-02.htm

There is only a brief statement here, but the page offers an 800 number for further information from the federal government.

See also Anxiety Disorders (Chapter 6).

———— CHAPTER 27 ————

Teenagers
and Parenting

Growing up has never been easy. It wasn't easy for the parents of today's adolescents when they were teenagers. It isn't easy for today's youth. What will become of today's younger generation? It will grow up and start worrying about the younger generation.

In matters of taste and manners, the youth of every generation seem radical, unnerving, and different from adults—different in how they behave, the music they enjoy, hairstyles, and the clothing they choose. Acting-out and boundary-testing are time-honored ways in which teenagers move toward accepting, rather than rejecting, parental values. Many parents have a difficult time coping with the acting-out and boundary-testing of their adolescents. They want to know why their adolescents talk back to them and challenge their rules and values. They want to know if they should be authoritarian or permissive. They want to know why adolescents have such mercurial moods—happy one moment, sad the next. And they want to keep their adolescents from drinking alcohol, taking drugs, delinquency, dropping out of school, becoming depressed, getting involved with the wrong peer group, choosing the wrong career, and being sexually permissive.

As parents worry about these treacherous roads, adolescents have their own concerns. For them, the transition from childhood to adulthood is a time of evaluation, of decision making, of commitment, and of carving out a place in the world. They try on one face after another, trying to find an identity of their own. They want to find out who they are, what they are all about, and where they are going in life. They move through a seemingly endless preparation for life. They want their parents to understand them, but often feel they don't. And in the end, there are two paradoxical gifts they hope parents will give them—one is roots, the other is wings.

Self-help resources on teenagers and parenting fall into three main categories:

RECOMMENDATION HIGHLIGHTS

Self-Help Books

- For adolescent girls, their parents, and psychotherapists:

    ★★★★★ *Reviving Ophelia* by Mary Pipher

- For improving parent–adolescent relationships:

    ★★★★★ *Between Parent and Teenager* by Haim Ginott

    ★★★ *Positive Parenting Your Teens* by Karen Renshaw Joslin and Mary Bunting Decher

    ★★★ *You and Your Adolescent* by Laurence Steinberg and Ann Levine

- For teens:

    ★★★★ *All Grown Up and No Place to Go* by David Elkind

    ★★★ *When Living Hurts* by Sol Gordon

    ♦ *Bringing Up Parents* by Alex J. Packer

Movies

- Superb film on friendship and the rites of adolescent passage:

    ★★★★★ *Stand by Me*

- Inspirational film on adolescent identity development and authority conflicts:

    ★★★★ *Dead Poets Society*

- Five diverse teenagers genuinely encounter each other and themselves:

    ★★★★ *The Breakfast Club*

- Good, old-fashioned coming of age flick:

    ★★★★ *Circle of Friends*

- Classic film on teenage sisters moving from childhood to adult pleasures:

    ★★★★ *Little Women*

- Young man struggling with giftedness and buried child abuse:

    ★★★★ *Good Will Hunting*

Internet Resources

- On the social, emotional, and sexual development of adolescents:

    ★★★★★ *Adolescence Directory On-Line (ADOL)*
        http://education.indiana.edu/cas/adol/adol.html

    ★★★★★ *Teenwire* http://www.teenwire.com/index.asp

resources written to help adolescents navigate the muddle of the middle years; those that provide an overview of adolescence and cover parenting recommendations; and those that focus exclusively on parent–adolescent relationships, with recommendations for how to parent more effectively. Let us now consider self-help books, movies, and Internet resources for adolescents and their parents.

SELF-HELP BOOKS

Strongly Recommended

★★★★★ *Reviving Ophelia: Saving the Selves of Adolescent Girls* (1994) by
       Mary Pipher. New York: Grosset/Putnam.

This is a sensitive, insightful journey into the torn lives of adolescent girls who as children were alive, eager, confident, and curious, and who upon the arrival of adolescence lose their way and their selves. Mary Pipher observes the dark turn of culture in which adolescent girls are pressured to conform, compete, and be superficially physically attractive. She tells moving, challenging, and successful stories of many adolescent girl clients and her experiences with them in therapy. Chapters on families, mothers, fathers, divorce, depression, and other forces that touch adolescent girls discuss ways parents can support their daughters and also identify ways parents become agents of culture and unknowingly steer girls toward rejection and self-doubt. The author discusses healthy directions that she takes in therapy, including teaching skills on centering, separating thinking and feeling, making conscious choices, holding boundaries, managing pain, modulating emotions, and enjoying altruism. The highest rated book in its category.

★★★★★ *Between Parent and Teenager* (1969) by Haim Ginott. New York: Avon.

Despite the fact that this valuable book is well past adolescence itself (it was published more than 30 years ago), it continues to be one of the most widely read and recommended books for parents who want to communicate more effectively with their teenagers. It has sold several million copies. Ginott describes a number of commonsense solutions and strategies for parents who are having difficulty understanding and communicating with their teenagers. At the same time parents are trying to shape up their teenagers, the teenagers are fighting to be the masters of their own destiny. For Ginott, parents' greatest challenge is to let go when they want to hold on; only by letting go can parents reach a peaceful and meaningful coexistence with teenager. This is an easy and enjoyable book to read. Throughout, Ginott connects with parents through catchy phrases such as "Don't collect thorns" and "Don't step on corns"; "Don't talk in chapters," that is, don't lecture, but rather be a good listener and discuss issues with the adolescent; "Accept teenagers' restlessness and discontent," which reminds parents that normal adolescents experience a great deal of uncertainty and difficulty; and "Don't put down their wishes and fantasies," which underscores that normal adolescents are idealists and dreamers. Ginott's nontechnical, easy-to-read writing style and many examples of interchanges between parents and adolescents give parents a sense of what to say (and how and when to say it) when conflict begins to build. His strategies can make the life of parents and teenagers a kinder, gentler world.

★★★★ *All Grown Up and No Place to Go: Teenagers in Crisis* (rev. ed., 1997) by David Elkind. Reading, MA: Addison-Wesley.

Elkind believes that raising teenagers is more difficult than ever. He argues that today's teens are expected to confront adult challenges too early in their development. By being pressured into adult roles too soon, they are all grown up with no place to go—hence the title of his book. The book is divided into three main parts. Part I, Needed: A Time to Grow, describes today's teenagers as in the midst of a crisis, informs parents about how adolescents think, outlines the perils of puberty, and provides details about peer shock. Part II, Given: A Premature Adulthood, analyzes American society and informs parents that adolescents don't have any rites of passage to guide them, how the hodge-podge of American family structures has made adolescence a difficult transition, and how bad secondary schools really are. Part III, Results: Stress and Its Aftermath, examines the effects of these family and societal problems on teenagers' identity and ability to cope with stress and other problems. A very helpful appendix provides a list of services for troubled teenagers. This 4-star book provides important recommendations for how parents, teachers, and other adults could communicate and interact more effectively with teenagers. Elkind does an especially good job of showing how adolescents develop and how our society has neglected their needs. Parenting recommendations are scattered through the book, embedded in discussions of different areas of adolescents' lives. *All Grown Up and No Place to Go* provides more up-to-date discussion of adolescent problems than Ginott's *Between Parent and Teenager* (discussed above). Elkind's book also presents more information about the nature of adolescent development in different areas (such as cognitive development, puberty and physical changes, schools, and so on).

Recommended

★★★ *You and Your Adolescent: A Parent's Guide for Ages 10–20* (2nd ed., 1997) by Laurence Steinberg and Ann Levine. New York: HarperCollins.

This book presents an excellent overview of many areas of adolescent development and mixes in wise parenting strategies along the way. Steinberg and Levine tackle the dual task of giving parents a solid understanding of adolescent development and prescribing parenting strategies. Part I, The Basics, paints a picture of what makes a good parent, the nature of family communication, and what today's families are like. Part II, The Pre-teens: From 10 to 13, discusses the nature of physical health and development (puberty, sexual awakening, and drugs), psychological health and development (how young teenagers think and feel), and the social world of the young adolescent (peers, dating, middle schools and junior high, and achievement). Part III, The Teens: From 14 to 17, focuses on sex and the high-school student, drug and alcohol use in high school, the search for identity, a number of problem behaviors such as delinquency and running away, friends and social life, school, and work. Part IV, Toward Adulthood: From 18 to 20, explores the transition from adolescence to adulthood and how parents can ease this transition for themselves and their offspring. Two aspects of Steinberg and Levine's book especially set it apart from other self-help books on teenagers and parenting. First, Steinberg and Levine accurately tell readers that some of the horror stories they have heard about adolescents are false. They believe that boundary-testing and acting-out are time-honored traditions that, if not taken to extremes, are a normal part of adolescent development. Second, Steinberg and Levine's book is organized developmentally. Adolescent experts increasingly recognize that the 12-year-old is different in many ways from the 17-year-old. Our mental health experts opined that *You and Your Adolescent* presents a good balance between educating parents about the nature of adolescence and giving insightful parenting recommendations.

★★★ *Positive Parenting Your Teens* (1997) by Karen Renshaw Joslin and
      Mary Bunting Decher. New York: Fawcett Columbine.

The organizational style of this book is unique. The book is intended to be a sequel for parents of teens to the book *Positive Discipline A–Z* (reviewed in Chapter 10). Several short sections describe the goal of creating an atmosphere of cooperation and responsibility and explain how to have discussions, engender trust, and accomplish follow-through. The major focus of the book is describing and teaching how to solve the 100 common concerns that parents and teens have. For each common concern, the authors offer an example, explain how to understand the situation, tell what to say and do, suggest preventative measures, and indicate how to know when to seek help. The list is thorough (e.g., rebelliousness, friends, depression, clothes, swearing) and succinctly but effectively addresses each concern. Our mental health experts consistently rated this book very favorably, but not enough rated it to move it to the 4-star or 5-star category.

★★★ *When Living Hurts: For Teenagers and Young Adults* (rev. ed., 1994) by
      Sol Gordon. New York: Union of American Hebrew Congregations.

The table of contents of this book is labeled "A table of wisdom, worry, and what to do," which gives the reader a sense of the book's style, sincerity, and good old-fashioned advice. The topics are timely (e.g., suicide, depression, sex, religion, parents, purpose of life). More important, however, is the person-to-person approach and the format, which includes thoughts for the day, slogans, advice, short writings of teenagers, hopeful and funny poems, photos, and short narratives, such as "What's a mensch?" This book reads as if the teenager is having a confidential conversation with a favorite uncle. It is written for teenagers, but it is applicable for parents of all cultures, genders, and races. Highly regarded but not particularly well-known by the psychologists in our national studies.

★★★ *Surviving Adolescence: Helping Your Child through the Struggle* (1991) by
      Larry Dumont. New York: Villard.

This book is especially geared toward educating parents about the early-warning signs of adolescent disorders, ranging from substance abuse and eating disorders to learning disabilities, depression, and suicidal behavior. In addition, Dumont describes a number of treatment strategies for troubled teens, including inpatient and outpatient hospital sessions, psychotherapy, group therapy, behavior therapy, and drug therapy. He spends considerable time explaining to parents how to make a decision about whether to hospitalize an adolescent. This 3-star book is especially good for helping parents make a decision about hospitalizing a teenager with a serious behavioral problem and provides excellent coverage of a number of adolescent disorders. Critics argue that *Surviving*

Adolescence may cause some parents to overreact to adolescent misbehaviors that are not serious but are rather part of the normal course of adolescent development.

★★★   *Toughlove* (reissue ed., 1996) by Phyllis York, David York, and Ted Wachtel. New York: Bantam.

This book squarely places the blame for adolescents' problems on the adolescents, not the parents. The book communicates that many parents are victimized by the guilt caused by their teenagers' behavior. According to the authors, many parents are too hard on themselves instead of on the teenager and the peer group when their adolescent takes drugs, fails at school, engages in promiscuous sex, or commits delinquent acts. *Toughlove* teaches parents how to face crises, take stands, demand cooperation, and meet challenges by getting tough with teenagers. Although tough love may in the short run cause the gulf between parents and teenagers to widen, in the long run it is the only way the teenager will develop maturity, according to tough love advocates. This book barely received a 3-star rating in one of our national studies. Most of the mental health experts preferred the gentler, more balanced approach of Pipher, Ginott, and Elkind to the harsh approach of *Toughlove*. Its problem, in addition to its punitive approach, is that controlled research has not been conducted on the method; it may lead parents to exaggerate their teenagers' problems; it may inadvertently blame individual adolescents for societal or family problems; and it may cause even more serious problems in some youth.

Diamonds in the Rough

◆   *What Teenagers Want to Know about Sex: Questions and Answers* (1988) by Boston Children's Hospital, Robert P. Masland, and David Estridge. Boston: Little, Brown.

This book is written for teenagers to provide truthful information about human development and sexuality and help them understand the physical and emotional changes that occur during adolescence. The Boston Children's Hospital visited many schools asking students to share questions and concerns and asking teachers and educators to recount their most frequently asked questions. The results are the comprehensive questions that appear as the various topics in this book (e.g., hygiene, human reproduction, thoughts and feelings, puberty, STD, alcohol and drugs). The authors respond objectively to the questions by answering factually but with sensitivity. The questions and answers are well-formed, accurately geared to teenagers, and are not judgmental or patronizing. The scientific aspects and the positive ratings by study participants merit a Diamond in the Rough rating.

◆   *Bringing Up Parents: The Teenager's Handbook* (1992) by Alex J. Packer. Minneapolis: Free Spirit.

The humorous slant of this book is a unique approach to giving advice to teenagers. The informality, matter-of-factness, and air of collaboration with the teenage reader are consistent with the principles of the text. The book targets 12- to 17-year-old readers and is not written from an "us against them" perspective, but rather as "how to take the first step in making the relationship better." Chapter titles include "Taking Charge of the Fight Brigade," "Tricks and Treats," and "Close Encounters of the Worst Kind." The book focuses on the perennial conflicts and developmental tensions between parents and teenagers. Parents will not feel ganged up on by this book, but would agree with the author on the identified problems and solutions. The strong albeit infrequent ratings and interesting slant of this text gives it Diamond in the Rough status.

Not Recommended

★★ *Preparing for Adolescence* (1978) by James Dobson. Santa Ana, CA: Vision House.

MOVIES

Strongly Recommended

★★★★★ *Stand by Me* (1987) produced by Bruce A. Evans, Raynold Gideon, and Andrew Scheinman and directed by Rob Reiner. R Rating. 89 minutes.

An excellent film about the rites of passage of four adolescents who grow toward manhood through a series of events ignited by the accidental death of a young boy. The boys learn the importance of friendship and loyalty. During their two-day journey, they encounter a number of adventures that further clarify for each what kind of a person he is becoming. As their journey progresses, each boy is put to the test, and each responds with a mixture of childish fear or grief within his evolving person. One of the highest-rated movies in our national studies.

★★★★ *Dead Poets Society* (1990) produced by Steven Haft, Paul Junger Witt, and Tony Thomas and directed by Peter Weir. PG Rating. 129 minutes.

An English teacher struggles to fit into a conservative prep school. His passion for poetry and his charismatic personality help establish a strong bond with his male students. Several of the boys revive a secret society. Conflict ensues between the boys and adults, with tragedy befalling one of the boys as his father tries to pull him out of the theater society. The teacher's inspirational motto is "seize the day." A powerful and uneasy movie that received four Academy Award nominations.

★★★★ *The Breakfast Club* (1986) produced by Ned Tanen and John Hughes and directed by John Hughes. R Rating. 95 minutes.

Five high-school students from different walks of life in suburban Chicago serve Saturday detention together. As the day progresses, they delve into each other's private worlds and struggle to be honest with themselves and one another. The realistic diversity and separation of roles among the five students is likely to resonate with many adolescents. A valuable lesson on how misleading first impressions and preconceived ideas often get in the way of nurturing relationships.

★★★★ *Circle of Friends* (1995) produced by Frank Price, Arlene Sellers, and
         Alex Ninitsky and directed by Pat O'Connor. PG-13 Rating. 112 minutes.

This roommate comedy set in Ireland in 1957 is a good old-fashioned coming-of-age
story about three friends who confront their changing lives in unique ways. The combined and complex forces of church, economics, social class, and sex weigh heavily on
their choices.

★★★★ *Little Women* (1933) produced by David O. Selznick, Merian C. Cooper, and
         Kenneth MacGowan and directed by George Cukor. 117 minutes.

A timepiece; a movie about transition to adulthood during the Civil War era, detailing
the ups and downs of teenage sisters. A humorous story of how four sisters learn moral
lessons and grow from childish pleasures to adult joys. Received three Academy Award
nominations. Based on the Louisa May Alcott novel of the same title.

★★★★ *Good Will Hunting* (1997) produced by Lawrence Bender and directed by
         Gus Van Sant. R Rating. 126 minutes.

Will Hunting, a brilliant 20-year-old man, is acting out his conflicts through fighting
and oppositional behavior, which lands him in a life-altering relationship with a psychologist played by Robin Williams. Will is a college janitor who is discovered to be a mathe-
matical genius and is mentored by a math professor who sees a great future for Will.
There is no future, however, until Will is able to resolve several dilemmas in his turbu-
lent therapy. He must accept that his intellectual gift will lead him away from his blue-
collar culture and the friends who have been his mainstay; he must heal his rage and
shame from unacknowledged early childhood abuse; and he must recognize that his
intellect and his secret have squelched his ability to feel. This is a powerful story that
illuminates class struggle, the responsibility of giftedness, and the centrality of human
connection. This film won an Academy Award for Best Original Screenplay in 1997,
and Robin Williams won the Best Supporting Actor award.

Recommended

★★★ *My Bodyguard* (1980) produced by Melvin Simon and directed by
        Michael Hayes. PG Rating. 96 minutes.

The son of a hotel manager finds himself the target of a school bully, then employs a
school outcast, the biggest kid in class, to be his bodyguard. The adolescents struggle
with communication and conflict resolution, friends and support systems, and parent–
child relationships. Filmed in and around Chicago, this comedy/drama is entertainment with an enduring message.

★★★ *Powder* (1995) produced by Roger Birnbaum and Daniel Grodnik and
        directed by Victor Salva. PG-13 Rating. 111 minutes.

On her way to the delivery room, a mother is struck by lightening and dies. Her child is
born an albino, and the distraught father calls him Powder because of his white skin.
Left to be raised by his grandparents, Powder lives in basement. He possesses a photo-

graphic memory, an exceptionally high IQ, and telepathic powers. All of these qualities provide Powder with his greatest ability: compassion. A well-meaning film that goes to supernatural heights to demonstrate acceptance and rejection, love and hate, and identity development.

★★★ *Pretty in Pink* (1987) produced by John Hughes and Michael Chinich and
         directed by Howard Deutch. PG-13 Rating. 96 minutes.

A high-school girl lives with her loving father who must budget their money wisely. Accompanied by her insecure best friend, she feels threatened when a wealthy and well-meaning boy asks her out on a date. An entertaining and sensitive movie about growing pains and the meaning of money.

★★★ *Sixteen Candles* (1985) produced by Universal and directed by John Hughes.
         PG Rating. 93 minutes.

A fresh comedy about a 16th birthday party that turns out to be anything but sweet. The parents forget the girl's birthday party, and she doesn't receive an invitation to the big dance. The story focuses on the feelings of a 16-year-old girl who dreams of finding Mr. Right, who already has his eye on her.

Not Recommended

★★ *St. Elmo's Fire* (1986) produced by Lauren Shuler and directed by
        Joel Schumacher. R Rating. 110 minutes.

INTERNET RESOURCES

Metasites

★★★★★ *Adolescence Directory On-Line (ADOL)*
              http://education.indiana.edu/cas/adol/adol.html

This "is a collection of World-Wide-Web (WWW) documents that focus on the social and emotional growth and development needs of adolescents. . . . ADOL exists as a way to help educators, parents, health practitioners, researchers, and teens access the many resources available on the WWW." Although we have not visited all the linked sites, they are very impressive, and appear to be of very high quality and well-chosen. Clients could be safely referred to relevant sections to find much useful information. The sections are Conflict and Violence (resources about violence prevention and peer mediation); Mental Health Issues (attention-deficit/hyperactivity disorder, eating disorders, depression, adolescent development, and other issues related to the psychological well-being of teens); Health and Health Risk Issues (alcohol and other drugs, obesity, AIDS, sexuality, acne, and other health related concerns); Counselor Resources (resources to help counselors find information fast, including information on professional organizations and links to other resources); and Teens Only (teen zines, help with homework, sports information, pen pals, and games—a teen haven).

★★★★ *About Teens Now* http://www.wholefamily.com/kidteencenter/index.html

An intriguing site. It offers dramas, newsletters, comments by professionals, and other current and popular formats for addressing many important issues in the lives of teens. I expect that a teen who likes to read and explore will find many perspectives of value here.

Psychoeducational Materials for Clients and Families

★★★★★ *Teen Dramas* http://www.aboutteensnow.com/dramas

In scripts (and real audio), 26 realistic conflicts are played out and commented on by a therapist. The topics include Divorce, Affairs, Eating Disorders, Sexuality, School, Feelings, Loneliness, Suicide, Dating, Pregnancy, Family Fights, and more. These might be useful for teens and their parents to read so that they can see how typical their conflicts and relating styles are and how a therapist might view them. The therapy is not shown, but there are comments by the therapists—which is an advantage for a therapist referring clients to this site.

★★★★★ *Teenwire* http://www.teenwire.com/index.asp

A large, high-quality, and rich site, as would be expected from Planned Parenthood. It offers information written for adolescents on issues like relationships, sexuality, and pregnancy. The Warehouse has articles about dating, love, sex, birth control, infections, diseases, abortion, sexual orientation, parents and friends, feelings, and more. World Views presents teen issues from other parts of the world. Hothouse is a teen-written zine.

★★★★ *The Teenager's Guide to the Real World!*
http://www.bygpub.com/books/tg2rw/tg2rwtoc.htm

Sections from the book of the same name include essays on dating and relationships, sexuality, studying, volunteering, jobs, cars, college, and others.

★★★★ *Teenshealth*
http://www.teenshealth.org

There are about 150 readings of value here. For example, under Body Basics is Compulsive Exercise and under Sexual Health are Sexually Transmitted Diseases: What They Are, What Causes Them, How to Prevent Them, and More. Many of these can be of use to teens on depression, suicide, body image, conflict with parents, and other topics. It is like a text on teens.

★★★★ *Self-Help Brochures* http://www.couns.uiuc.edu

The Counseling Center at the University of Illinois has posted online brochures for their students, which address issues many teens deal with. Here are the titles of those available that are not listed elsewhere in this book: Addictive Relationships; Coming

Out; Committed Relationships and School; Understanding Dysfunctional Relationship Patterns in Your Family; and When Your Parent Has a Mental Illness.

★★★   *Friends First* http://www.friendsfirst.org

This program "asks kids to begin to reason through the tough choices and consequences of being sexually involved before marriage and stresses monogamy as the safest and best choice in marriage." Abstinence means no genital contact here. The site emphasizes decision making and assertiveness and provides research findings showing less divorce among those who have not been sexually intimate before marriage. Only bibliographies are available online, and materials are for sale, but we include this site because it is almost the only one available for this perspective. For readings on a similar topic see *All about Cohabiting Before Marriage* at http://members.aol.com/cohabiting.

★★★   *What To Do When Your Kids Discover Sexuality on the Net*
       http://www.topchoice.com/~psyche/love/misc/parenting1.html

A short response to a parent's dilemma, which essentially says to use this for opening discussions with your child about sexuality.

Hotlines

Boys Town National Hotline (bilingual)
Phone: 800-448-3000
http://www.boystown.org/home.htm

   They provide crisis intervention, information, and referrals for the general public. Free, confidential, short-term crisis intervention. They work with children and families.

Kid Save
Phone: 800-543-7283
http://www.kidspeace.org

   They offer information and referrals to public and private services for children and adolescents in crisis. They make referrals to shelters, mental health services, sexual abuse treatment, substance abuse treatment, family counseling, residential care, and adoption or foster care.

NineLine
Phone: 800-999-9999

   A nationwide crisis/suicide hotline. Referrals are made for youth or parents for drugs, domestic violence, homelessness, runaways, and so on. They offer message relays, report abuse, and help parents with problems with their kids.

National Youth Crisis Hotline
Phone: 800-HIT-HOME

   A crisis hotline and information and referral service for runaways or youth (17 and younger) with other problems and their parents. Sponsored by Youth Development International.

See also Child Development and Parenting (Chapter 10); Families and Stepfamilies (Chapter 16).

NATIONAL SUPPORT GROUPS

International Youth Council
401 North Michigan Avenue
Chicago, IL 60611-4212
Phone: 800-637-7974

Brings teens from single-parent homes together to share ideas and problems, develop leadership skills, and plan fun activities.

"Just Say No" International
2101 Webster Street
Oakland, CA 94612-3027
Phone: 800-258-2766

Through its Youth Power program, provides materials, technical assistance, and training to help youth lead healthy, productive lives by developing the skills they need to avoid destructive behavior.

S.A.D.D. (Students Against Drunk Driving)
PO Box 800
Marlboro, MA 01752
Phone: 508-481-3568

CHAPTER 28

Weight Management

Even ancient Romans were known to starve themselves, but never before have so many people, especially women, spent so much time, energy, and money on their weight. Since its inception in 1963, Weight Watchers alone has enrolled more than 22 million members. And understandably so: about half of the U.S. population is considered overweight. The number of Americans considered clinically obese—defined as more than 30% over their ideal body weight—has soared to 18%.

The hundreds of self-help resources that recommend strategies for losing weight reflect our national obsession with being thin, or at least thinner than we are. Some materials that encourage dietary modifications combined with exercise are based on sound nutritional and health principles. However, many materials aimed directly at weight loss itself are based on a gimmick, some quick fix for obesity, that is either nutritionally unsound or impossible to follow for any length of time, or both. The quick-fix books received neutral or downright negative evaluations in our studies. In fact, there are more negative ratings—and thus daggers—for weight loss books than in any other category.

The weight management resources in this chapter revolve around three interrelated topics: weight loss programs; comprehensive weight management plans that involve changes in eating, exercise, and spirituality; and weight acceptance messages. As you read about the ratings of weight management resources, keep in mind that they were made by mental health professionals who frequently treat individuals who want to lose weight, not by nutritionists or physicians who specialize in weight loss.

SELF-HELP BOOKS

Strongly Recommended

★★★★ *Eight Weeks to Optimum Health* (1997) by Andrew Weil. New York: Knopf.

In this book, Weil translates the information contained in his best-seller *Spontaneous Healing* into a practical plan. The program takes full advantage of the body's natural

RECOMMENDATION HIGHLIGHTS

Self-Help Books

- On an eight-week program to manage weight and enhance your healing system:

    ★★★★ *Eight Weeks to Optimum Health* by Andrew Weil

- On the cultural and psychological underpinnings of women's weight loss:

    ★★★★ *Fat Is a Feminist Issue* by Susie Orbach

- On losing weight and maintaining it by changing your lifestyle:

    ★★★ *The LEARN Program for Weight Control* by Kelly Brownell

Autobiographies

- A personal tale of overeating, semistarvation, and inspiring recovery:

    ★★★★★ *Feeding the Hungry Heart* by Geneen Roth

- Meaningful stories and advice on overcoming compulsive overeating:

    ★★★★ *Breaking Free from Compulsive Eating* by Geneen Roth

Internet Resources

- A guide to cultural influences on weight, health, and body image:

    ★★★★★ *Weight Loss* http://weightloss.about.com

- A guide to size acceptance:

    ★★★★★ *Size Wise* http://www.sizewise.com

- A guide to brochures on many aspects of eating and food:

    ★★★★★ *NAAFA: National Association to Advance Fat Acceptance*
    http://naafa.org/documents/brochures

---

healing power. Weil fine-tunes current eating habits, incorporates antioxidant supplements, and adds walking and stretching into the weekly regimen. He provides five basic breathing exercises that create greater relaxation and energy, explains the techniques of visualization, and shows how to avoid environmental hazards. Weil suggests making art, music, and the natural world a greater part of life. The book has a dozen additional customized plans for specific ages, genders, lifestyles, and medical needs. This informative 4-star book is roundly recommended to the layperson willing to commit to an 8-week program that works with the body's own healing system.

★★★★ *Fat Is a Feminist Issue: The Anti-Diet Guide for Women* (1997) by
    Susie Orbach. New York: Galahad.

This book is a compilation of two international best-sellers, *Fat Is a Feminist Issue* and *Fat Is a Feminist Issue II* and is a psychological exploration of why so many women are compulsive overeaters. It is not a diet book per se. Orbach states that because compulsive overeating is primarily a woman's problem, it may have something to do with being a female in today's society. Examining compulsive overeating from feminist and psychoanalytic perspectives, Orbach believes that being fat serves a number of purposes for women: It prevents them from being perceived as sex objects, expresses anger they have been conditioned to deny, or reflects problems of separation from their mothers. Orbach presents a program to help women learn the difference between hunger and boredom or loneliness and to show them how to use food to satisfy only their hunger rather than more profound longings. These ideas are then presented in a workbook fashion to facilitate behavior change. The book deals with food, fat, thin, compulsive eating, bulimia, anorexia, and body image. *Fat Is a Feminist Issue* is favorably evaluated for its important insights into the nature of obesity and the psychological underpinnings of compulsive overeating. It is one of the few self-help books in this category that received a positive rating.

Recommended

★★★   *The LEARN Program for Weight Control* (1990) by Kelly Brownell. Dallas: American Health Publications/Brownell & Hager.

The LEARN Program for Weight Control advocates a change in lifestyle in order to lose weight. LEARN stands for lifestyle, exercise, attitudes, relationships, and nutrition. The book includes 16 lessons that guide effective, medically sound weight loss. The LEARN program promises an average weight loss of 20 to 25 pounds, translating into a 1- to 2-pound weight loss each week for the 1 to 20 weeks the program usually lasts. Self-assessment questionnaires and homework assignments accompany each of the 16 lessons. These exercises show which techniques are working and how much progress has been made. Brownell teaches when, how, and why habits occur and how to change them. In two of our studies, the *LEARN Program for Weight Control* was rated very positively, but by relatively few mental health professionals. In both studies, its average rating would have placed it as a 5-star book had more psychologists been aware of it. This book presents an excellent strategy for weight loss that has a much better chance of helping people lose weight and maintain the loss than quick-fix diet books. It contains no gimmicks, no quick fixes, and no false promises; rather, readers are encouraged to alter their exercises, lifestyles, and eating patterns in order to lose weight and keep it off. The book is clear, well-written, and nicely organized. Its only problem is that it is not widely available.

★★★   *Make the Connection: Ten Steps to a Better Body—and a Better Life* (1996) by Bob Green and Oprah Winfrey. New York: Hyperion.

In this book, Green, a professional trainer, and Winfrey, a national television host, show what to do physically and mentally to lose weight and feel good about oneself. The book starts with Oprah's personal stories about her own work to get into shape. Oprah's inspiring journey and Green's professional knowledge combine for a realistic model of a healthy lifestyle. The authors cover reasons we eat, methods of enhancing self-awareness, the purpose of body fat, the physics of body weight, and their 10-step program on physical, emotional, and dieting changes. People looking for inspiration and usable information will find this 3-star book helpful.

★★★ *Eat More, Weigh Less* (1993) by Dean Ornish. New York: HarperCollins.

Cardiologist Ornish discusses what really motivates people to make and maintain lifestyle changes, based on three research studies conducted during the past 16 years. He believes that being overweight is not solely a physical problem; it needs to be addressed in a broader context. On his Life Choice program, meals are so low in fat that you get full before you consume too many calories. Your metabolism doesn't slow down, so you can eat more frequently, eat a greater quantity of food, and still lose weight. The author notes that the Life Choice program is an adjunct to, not a substitute for, conventional medical therapy. In the process of making this lifestyle change and losing weight, you may want to share this book with your physician. The latter section of the book presents 250 gourmet recipes containing less than 10 percent fat. This is an educated and helpful book for people looking for a lifestyle change and not just weight loss.

★★★ *The New Fit or Fat* (rev. ed., 1991) by Covert Bailey. Boston: Houghton Mifflin.

This book describes ways to become healthy by developing better diet and exercise routines. Bailey argues that the basic problem for overweight people is not losing weight, which fat people do periodically, but gaining weight, which fat people do more easily than those with different body chemistry. He explores the way our body stores fat and analyzes why crash diets don't work. He explains the relation between fat metabolism and weight, concluding that the ultimate cure for obesity is aerobic exercise coupled with a sensible low-fat diet. Originally published in 1977, the 1991 edition is greatly expanded with new information on fitness lifestyles and recent scientific advances. A new chapter answers readers' most frequently asked questions about Bailey's views on diet and exercise. A new section suggests strategies for getting started. This 3-star book offers solid, no-nonsense advice about how to lose weight and become more physically fit.

★★★ *Sugar Busters: Cut Sugar to Trim Fat* (1995) by H. Leighton Steward, Morrison C. Bethea, Samuel S. Andrews, and Luis A. Balart. New York: Ballantine.

This book takes the position that low-fat foods are full of sugar, which is related to the production of insulin, which in large amounts keeps you from losing weight, no matter how strictly you diet or how often you exercise. The authors show you how to reduce the sugar in your daily menu. You develop a diet plan, determine the glycemic levels of foods, decide which foods to eat at what time of the day, avoid certain food combinations, and learn various myths about calories, fats, cholesterol, and weight gain. Also included is a 14-day meal plan. The book provides a history of refined sugar and the biological and metabolic usage of sugars in our body. Included is a useful glossary to assist understanding some of the technical terms. In consultation with a physician, this best-seller could be a helpful book for individuals with sugar-related concerns or those willing to follow this diet plan.

Not Recommended

★★ *Diet for a Small Planet* (20th anniversary ed., 1991) by Frances Lappe. New York: Ballantine.

★★ *The Zone* (1995) by Barry Sears. New York: HarperCollins.

★ *The Pritikin Program for Diet and Exercise* (1979) by Nathan Pritikin. New York: Bantam.

★ *One Meal at a Time: Step-By-Step to a Low-Fat Diet for a Happier, Healthier, Longer Life* (1991) by Martin Katahn. New York: Norton.

★ *Dr. Atkins' New Diet Revolution* (1992) by Robert C. Atkins. New York: M. Evans.

Strongly Not Recommended

† *The T-Factor Diet* (1989) by Martin Katahn. New York: Norton.

† *The Rotation Diet* (1986) by Martin Katahn. New York: Norton.

† *The Diet Center Program: Lose Weight Fast and Keep It Off Forever* (rev. ed., 1990) by Sybil Ferguson. Boston: Little, Brown.

† *The 35-Plus Diet for Women* (1987) by Jean Spodnik and Barbara Gibbons. New York: Harper & Row.

† *Dr. Atkins' Diet Revolution* (1972) by Robert Atkins. New York: M. Evans.

† *Dr. Abravanel's Anti-Craving Weight-Loss Diet* (1990) by Elliot Abravanel and Elizabeth King. New York: Bantam.

† *The Carbohydrate Addict's Diet* (1991) by Rachael Heller and Richard Heller. New York: Dutton.

† *The 5-Day Miracle Diet* (1997) by Adele Puhn. New York: Ballentine.

† *The Beverly Hills Diet* (1981) by Judy Mazel. New York: Macmillan.

AUTOBIOGRAPHIES

Strongly Recommended

★★★★★ *Feeding the Hungry Heart: The Experience of Compulsive Eating* (1993) by Geneen Roth. New York: NAL/Dutton.

The author discusses her personal history of overeating followed by semistarvation and her recovery as she learned to control her eating. She includes stories from other people in the weight management seminars that she conducts. Many overeaters find this 5-star autobiography to be a very inspiring and realistic account that motivates them to change their destructive eating habits.

★★★★ *Breaking Free from Compulsive Eating* (1993) by Geneen Roth. New York: NAL/Dutton.

Speaking from personal experience, the author of numerous books about eating and dieting (*Why Weight? When You Eat at the Refrigerator, Pull Up a Chair;* and *Feeding the Hungry Heart*) advises readers about how they can free themselves from compulsive eating. She outlines the techniques developed in her weight loss workshops. She has helped many women get off the dietary roller coaster.

INTERNET RESOURCES

Metasites

★★★★★ *Weight Loss* http://weightloss.about.com/library/weekly

Jennifer R. Schott maintains this site and offers 29 subsites about the cultural aspects of weight, health, and body image and about the facts of weight loss. There are several hundred pages here covering anything one might want to know or explore.

★★★★★ *Size Wise* http://www.sizewise.com

"This site serves as an on-line companion to the book *Size Wise—A Catalog of More Than 1000 Resources for Living with Confidence and Comfort at Any Size.*" A searchable and well-organized guide to all aspects of size acceptance, including clothing, medical care, kids, fitness, and groups.

★★★★ *Calorie Control Council* http://www.caloriecontrol.org

Centered on minding calories, this site offers abundant information on exercise, different eating, and other materials for supporting healthy eating.

Psychoeducational Materials for Clients and Families

★★★★★ *NAAFA: National Association to Advance Fat Acceptance*
　　　　http://naafa.org/documents/brochures

A dozen brochures offer facts and guidelines about dieting, hypertension, eating disorders, and rights. Under Official Documents are policy statements based on research related to drugs, surgery, fitness, and those who admire fat people. Very enlightening.

★★★★★ *About-Face* http://www.about-face.org/index.html

Designed to combat negative and distorted images of women in the media. This might be a good referral for a woman too concerned with her appearance and too controlled by the consumer culture.

★★★★ *Fat!So!* http://www.fatso.com/index.html

A site with attitude. The readings at Greatest Hits offer facts and stories that are very helpful for acceptance. Click on the exclamation points on the pages to go on.

★★★ *Big Folks Health FAQ*
　　　http://www.cis.ohio-state.edu/hypertext/faq/usenet/fat-acceptance-faq/
　　　health/faq.html

This document contains information about often-exaggerated health costs for fat people.

★★★ *Largesse, the Network for Size Esteem* http://www.eskimo.com/~largesse

A very comprehensive list of books, links, and organizations. The section on Size-Positive Support and Educational Materials offers affirmations and help with using them.

Online Support Groups

The Council on Size and Weight Discrimination
PO Box 305
Mt. Marion, NY 12456
Phone: 914-679-1209
E-mail: councilswd@aol.com

   Information, referrals, advocacy.

Hugs International
Box 102 A, RR #3
Portage La Prairie, MB, Canada R1N 3A3
Phone: 204-428-3432
Fax: 204-428-5072
E-mail: linda@hugs.com
http://www.hugs.com

   A support network for getting off the diet roller coaster. Hugs Club News, material and workshops for teens.

Largesse: The Network for Size Esteem
E-mail: largesse@eskimo.com
http://www.eskimo.com/~largesse

   Some online resources, information, affirmations, and educational handouts.

See also Eating Disorders (Chapter 15).

NATIONAL SUPPORT GROUPS

Food Addicts Anonymous
4623 Forest Hill Boulevard, #111-4
West Palm Beach, FL 33415
Phone: 407-967-3871

   A 12-step fellowship to recover from the disease of food addiction.

Healthy Weight Network
402 South 14th Street
Hettinger, ND 58639
Phone: 701-567-2646
Fax: 701-567-2602
E-mail: fmberg@healthyweight.net
http://www.healthyweight.net

   Obesity research watchdog organization, advocate for healthy eating and fitness.

ISAA (International Size-Acceptance Association)
PO Box 82126
Austin, TX 78758
E-mail: Director@size-acceptance.org
http://www.size-acceptance.org

   Advocacy, activism, chapters, posters and brochures, newsletter.

Largely Positive
PO Box 17223
Glendale, WI 53217
Phone: 414-299-9295
E-mail: positive@execpc.com

   Promotes health and self-esteem for larger people through a newsletter, workshops, and local support groups.

NAAFA: National Association to Advance Fat Acceptance
PO Box 188620
Sacramento, CA 95818
Phone: 800-442-1214
http://www.naafa.org

One of the original and still one of the best advocacy groups. Their Book Service has excellent materials. Membership newsletter, educational materials, regional chapters, annual convention, pen-pal program.

National Center for Overcoming Overeating
PO Box 1257
Old Chelsea Station
New York, NY 10113-0920
Phone: 212-875-0442
http://www.OvercomingOvereating.com

Home of the Women's Campaign to End Body Hatred and Dieting.

Overeaters Anonymous
PO Box 44020
Rio Rancho, NM 87174-4020
Phone: 505-891-2664

A 12-step program of recovery from compulsive eating disorders.

Shape Up America!
6707 Democracy Boulevard, Suite 306
Bethesda, MD 20817
http://www.shpaeup.org

A nonprofit organization started by former Surgeon General C. Everett Koop to advance the benefits of keeping active and maintaining a healthy weight.

Take Off Pounds Sensibly (TOPS)
PO Box 07360
4575 South 5th Street
Milwaukee, WI 53207-0360
Phone: 800-932-8677

For overweight people who wish to attain and maintain their goal weight.

CHAPTER 29

Women's Issues

The mental health professions have historically portrayed human behavior in male-dominant themes. While much progress has been made in recent decades, sexism is still evident in society, and women continue to be discriminated against in the workplace, in politics, at home, and perhaps in self-help resources.

Critics argue that self-help books have perpetuated many stereotypes and myths harmful to women. What are some of these stereotypes and myths? We can journey through the chapters of the *Authoritative Guide to Self-Help Resources in Mental Health* and find books that characterize women as having dysfunctional personalities and that treat codependency as a woman's disease, eating disorders as uniquely female problems, and mothers as responsible for children's problems. We find books that overdramatize sex differences, with the differences invariably favoring men (women are described as overly invested in romantic love, dependent on others, and incapable of controlling their emotions), and that consistently undervalue women's strengths. Few authors bother to write about the positive features of being female, and fewer still give credence or respectability to many of the daily responsibilities women have traditionally performed and continue to manage.

The best self-help resources on women's issues address such concerns and try to help women become aware that what have been labeled as character defects in the past are actually strengths that should be nurtured, rewarded, and cherished. Of course, many resources in other categories address women's issues and provide self-help advice for women. In other chapters, we recommend a number of excellent self-help books on specific aspects of women's lives, such as recovery from sexual abuse, assertion, communication, parenting, intimacy, pregnancy, and sexuality.

In this chapter, we describe and evaluate self-help resources—books, autobiographies, movies, and websites—that address quintessentially women's issues. These include work and parental roles, gender stereotypes, sex differences, feminist concerns, and women's bodies and health.

RECOMMENDATION HIGHLIGHTS

Self-Help Books

- On women's health and well-being:

    ★★★★★ *The New Our Bodies, Ourselves* by the Boston Women's Health Book Collective

- On women's work and parenting roles:

    ★★★★ *The Second Shift* by Arlie Hochschild

- On women's life stages and transitions:

    ★★★★ *The Seasons of a Woman's Life* by Daniel J. Levinson and Judy D. Levinson

- On inspiring and nurturing women:

    ★★★★ *Chicken Soup for the Woman's Soul* by Jack Canfield and Associates

- On gender stereotypes, myths, and sex differences:

    ♦ *The Mismeasure of Women* by Carol Tavris

- On women's bodies and their self-image traps:

    ★★★ *Body Traps* by Judith Rodin

Autobiographies

- Inside look at the women's movement:

    ★★★ *Deborah, Golda, and Me* by Letty Cottin Pogrebin

- Women and mothering experiences that influenced the author's life:

    ♦ *Mothers* by Alexandra Stoddard

Movies

- Depicting women bonding on the baseball field:

    ★★★★ *A League of Their Own*

- Quilting as a metaphor for women sharing experiences with love and life:

    ★★★★ *How to Make an American Quilt*

- Women insightfully conversing about food and life:

    ★★★★ *Eating*

- Complex Gothic story of mother, daughter, music, and physical abuse:

    ★★★ *The Piano*

Internet Resources

- A guide to solid information on a broad topic:

  ★★★★★ *WWWomen* http://www.wwwomen.com

  ★★★★ *Femina: Web Search for Women* http://femina.cybergrrl.com

- A guide to the medical aspects of menopause:

  ★★★★★ *North American Menopause Society*
  http://www.menopause.org/faq.htm

- A guide to employment discrimination:

  ★★★★★ *Equal Employment Opportunity Commission* http://www.eeoc.gov

---

SELF-HELP BOOKS

Strongly Recommended

★★★★★ *The New Our Bodies, Ourselves* (25th anniversary ed., 1996) by
the Boston Women's Health Book Collective. New York: Touchstone.

This highly rated book updates an earlier edition with new information on AIDS, older women, birth control methods, and disorders that primarily affect women, to name a few topics. The new edition keeps women updated on physical and mental health, along with legal, political, and social organizational realities of women's identity and roles. A mission for the authors is to encourage women to get together—to meet, talk to, and listen to each other. Women interested in women's passions and potentialities will thoroughly enjoy this resource. This 5-star book will probably leave women feeling, to use one of the most overused words of the decade, empowered. One of the most highly regarded self-help resources in any of our studies, and deservedly so.

★★★★ *The Second Shift* (1989) by Arlie Hochschild. New York: Viking.

This self-help resource focuses on the inequality of gender roles in two-career couples with children. Hochschild conducted extensive interviews and home observations of 50 two-career couples with children under the age of 6 to discover how they allotted their time and responsibility to careers, child-rearing, and household chores. Not surprisingly, she found that women handled the bulk of child care and housework in addition to holding down full-time jobs outside the home. Hochschild labels married couples as traditional (the husband works and the wife stays at home), transitional (both work, and he does less than she thinks he should around the house), or egalitarian (both spend equal time on work and home responsibilities). In her study, all the families were in the last two categories, and the majority were transitional. Hochschild believes that men and women use gender strategies that are based on deep-seated emotional beliefs about manhood and womanhood as they try to define how to juggle jobs, child-rearing, and household responsibilities. The married partners may not even be aware that they are using gender strategies. One of Hochschild's main goals in *The Second Shift* is to bring these gender strategies out into the open so that married couples can discuss and benefit from them. Multiple solutions—from the personal to the societal—are presented to rectify the inequalities. What separates *The Second Shift* from standard feminist fare is the texture of the reporting and the subtlety of the insights. A valuable, if disconcerting, book.

★★★★ *The Seasons of a Woman's Life* (1996) by Daniel J. Levinson and
　　　Judy D. Levinson. New York: Knopf.

This book, the counterpart to Levinson's *Seasons of a Man's Life* (reviewed in Chapter 4), traces the developmental themes and stages of women's adulthood. It is based on lengthy interviews conducted in the 1980s of 55 randomly selected women from various professions and at various stages in their lives. This study confirms that in every woman's life, there is a mixture of joy and sorrow, success and failure, and self-fulfillment and self-defeat. This 4-star book is favorably regarded and compellingly addresses women's development throughout the life cycle.

★★★★ *Chicken Soup for the Woman's Soul* (1996) by Jack Canfield, Mark Victor
　　　Hansen, Jennifer Read Hawthorne, and Marci Shimoff. Deerfield Beach,
　　　FL: Health Communication.

These best-selling *Chicken Soup* authors have written another nurturing and inspiring book, this time specifically for women. The book is designed to reinforce the bond between women using 101 stories describing the unique and the common life experiences that reflect historical and current lifestyles of girls and women. Some of the experiences shared in this book address goals, relationships, giving birth, job responsibilities, family, and friendships. This is a book you can pick up for two minutes or two hours that will make you feel moved and guided. It is informative and moving.

Recommended

★★★ *Too Good for Her Own Good: Breaking Free from the Burden of Female Responsibility*
　　(1990) by Claudia Bepko and Jo-Ann Krestan. New York: Harper & Row.

The authors sensitively examine low self-esteem in women that results from feeling that they are not good enough. The Goodness Code requires women to be attractive, ladylike (low-keyed, controlled), unselfish, of service to others, the moving force in making relationships work, and competent—all without complaining. The authors argue that goodness comes to most women almost instinctively; they feel they must be competent in virtually everything they do while remaining responsible for the happiness of others around them. Yet no matter how hard women work to please others, they often feel inadequate, because part of being good is knowing that they are never good enough. The results: Far too many women have a low self-image, feel insecure, and are overworked. The authors then discuss how to break free from all of this goodness by changing the balance of various factors. A number of case histories are described to buttress the authors' points. The book's enthusiasts said that many women with low self-esteem who have lived their lives in the service of others while not paying enough attention to their own needs will find themselves described on almost every page of this book.

★★★   *Body Traps* (1992) by Judith Rodin. New York: Morrow.

This book addresses how society has constructed a negative and destructive perception of female bodies and how women can free themselves from this trap. Rodin argues that good looks, appearance, and fitness have become the measures women use to evaluate their self-worth. A number of the traps described and discussed by Rodin are the variety trap, the shame trap, the competition trap, the food trap, the dieting rituals trap, the fitness trap, and the success trap. Mental health experts in our studies consistently rated the book favorably, but it was not frequently rated. The book is a thoughtful, penetrating look at society's preoccupation with women's appearance and the unrealistic expectations and harmful effects the preoccupation has produced. *Body Traps* is informative and well-written, and it is a very helpful guide to what women's bodies mean to them.

★★★   *The Silent Passage* (rev. ed., 1998) by Gail Sheehy. New York: Random House.

As reviewed in Chapter 4, this best-seller addresses menopause. Sheehy's objectives are to erase the stigma of menopause, normalize the process, and direct women to medical and psychological resources. An engaging and easy read on a neglected topic.

★★★   *Women Who Run with the Wolves: Myths and Stories of the Wild Women Archetype* (1992) by Clarissa Pinkola Estes. New York: Ballantine.

Estes's work as a Jungian analyst influences her psychic-archeological portrait of the female archetype. She draws a parallel between healthy wolves and healthy women in two ways: (1) They share certain psychic characteristics, keen sensing, a playful spirit, and a heightened capacity for devotion; and (2) both have been hounded, harassed, and falsely imputed to be devouring, devious, and overly aggressive by their detractors. Estes maintains that once women reassert their relationship with their wild nature, they will be gifted with a permanent and internal watcher, a visionary, who will guide them through the inner and outer workings of the world. In this book, *wild* means to live a natural life, one in which a creature has innate integrity and healthy boundaries. On the positive side, this 3-star (almost 4-star) resource can be deeply inspiring and insightful. On the negative side, some mental health experts contend that it can be easily misinterpreted and misapplied and complain that the Jungian orientation has no scientific support.

★★★   *Backlash: The Undeclared War against American Women* (1991) by Susan Faludi. New York: Crown.

This book concerns the way women and feminism are portrayed by the media. Faludi uncovers a growing backlash against women and feminism in the United States. This backlash has hurt women in two main ways: first, by convincing women that their feelings of dissatisfaction and distress are the result of too much feminism and independence; and second, by simultaneously undermining the minimal progress that women have made at work, in politics, and in their own minds. She cites the (in)famous Harvard–Yale study, which in 1988 reported that a single, college-educated woman over the age of 30 has only a 20% chance of ever getting married, and that by the time she is 40, she will have only a 1.3% chance. Faludi says that the man shortage is only one of the myths propagated by the media (another is the infertility epidemic) and finds evidence of other antifeminist orientations in movies, television, and fashion advertising. The result is that feminism declined in the 1980s and early 1990s. *Backlash* received a 3-star rating, and though a best-seller when published, it has received mixed reviews. Some of the book's supporters say that it makes a brilliantly argued case for feminist backlash in the media. However, several critics argue that it is another 1980s-type bashing book that, while well-written and scholarly, makes stick-figure stereotypes of relationships between women and men. Clearly, it is a controversial book about which people rarely feel neutral.

★★★ *We Are Our Mother's Daughters* (1998) by Cokie Roberts. New York: Morrow.

This chief congressional analyst for ABC News discusses significant concerns facing women today. She explores the diverse roles women have assumed as they have traveled the personal and political pathways of American history. Each essay is an introduction to several of the fascinating women the author has encountered during her career and of significant women in her life. This book celebrates the diversity of choice and perspective available to women today. Roberts' position is that women are connected throughout time and, in turn, are their mother's daughters. A 3-star book that helps women experience the great conversation all women have shared throughout history.

★★★ *My Mother/Myself* (1977) by Nancy Friday. New York: Delacorte.

Nancy Friday has authored a number of best-selling books on women's sexuality, including this one and *My Secret Garden*, about women's sexual fantasies. *My Mother/Myself* was based on more than 200 interviews with women (most were mothers and, of course, all were daughters) as well as consultations with a number of mental health experts. Its basic premise is psychoanalytic in nature: Daughters identify with their mothers while becoming their mothers' rivals, and the influence of this complex relationship is felt throughout a daughter's life. Friday also describes the conflicting messages daughters receive from their mothers about their body and sexuality, as well as unconscious introjection of the mothers' bad qualities. She describes the mother–daughter relationship in early childhood, then moves through a number of women's milestones, such as loss of virginity and menopause. One of her basic themes is that society's denial of women's sexuality often conflicts with their role as mothers. This book was easily the most widely rated book in the Women's Issues category, evaluated by 187 psychologists. The book's supporters said that it broke new ground when it was published in the late 1970s by providing a probing, insightful analysis of mother–daughter relationships and society's negative portrayal of women's sexuality. However, critics argued that Friday overdramatizes and stereotypes the body inferiority and sexual difficulties of women. All told, an interesting if dated resource on women's sexuality.

Diamonds in the Rough

♦ *Life Preservers: Good Advice When You Need It Most* (1996) by Harriet Lerner. New York: HarperCollins.

Lerner, a nationally recognized author of several best-sellers, offers a collection of the monthly advice columns she writes for a national women's magazine. This book covers interpersonal relationships, self-growth for women, social issues, and employment concerns for women in the 1990s. Positively but infrequently rated by mental health experts in our national studies, this book received the Diamond in the Rough designation. A thoughtful book written for women based on the experience of women.

♦ *The Mismeasure of Women* (1992) by Carol Tavris. New York: Simon & Schuster.

This book, unfortunately missed in our national studies, explores the stereotyping of women and similarities and differences between women and men. Author Carol Tavris also wrote *Anger: The Misunderstood Emotion*, which received a 4-star rating (Chapter 5). *The Mismeasure of Women* explores the following main topics: why women are not inferior to men; why women are not superior to men; premenstrual syndrome, postmenstrual syndrome, and other normal "diseases"; why women are sick but men have problems; fables of female sexuality; and how women cornered the love market. Tavris believes that no matter how hard women try, they can't measure up. They are criticized for being too female or not female enough, but they are always judged and measured by how well they fit into a male world. The book contains a thorough review of research that documents how women continue to be ignored, misrepresented, and even harmed by the (still) male-dominated health professions, which base their standards of normality on male anatomy, physiology, and psychology. Tavris believes that more evidence exists for similarities between the sexes than for differences between them. She explores how society pathologizes women through psychiatric diagnoses, sexist divorce rulings, and images of women as moody, self-defeating, and unstable. This is an excellent analysis of gender stereotyping, similarities and differences between the sexes, and how women should be measured by their own standards, not men's. It is well-documented and captivating, presenting a witty feminist portrayal of women's dilemmas and what can be done about them.

Strongly Not Recommended

† *Secrets about Men Every Woman Should Know* (1990) by Barbara DeAngelis. New York: Delacorte.

AUTOBIOGRAPHIES

Recommended

★★★ *Deborah, Golda, and Me: Being Female and Jewish in America* (1992) by Letty Cottin Pogrebin. New York: Doubleday.

A founding member of *Ms* magazine and a noted feminist thinker, Pogrebin uses this book to reconcile her Jewish faith, which she rejected for much of her life, with her feminism. The book touches on a variety of related issues, including anti-Semitism within the women's movement and the sometimes strained relations between blacks and Jews. A very helpful book for those interested in women's studies and Jewish studies.

Diamonds in the Rough

♦ *Mothers: A Celebration* (1997) by Alexandra Stoddard. New York: Avon.

In this color-illustrated book, the popular author Alexandra Stoddard (*Grace Notes, Living a Beautiful Life; Living in Love*) recounts her experiences as a mother and step-mother and writes about the women who influenced her life. Many poignant anecdotes and stirring personal recollections about what it means to be a mother. Favorably evaluated by just a few respondents in our national studies, thus earning a Diamond in the Rough designation.

♦ *Telling: A Memoir of Rape and Recovery* (1999) by Patricia Weaver Francisco. New York: HarperCollins.

In 1981, while her husband was away, an intruder broke into Francisco's home and raped her. She went into counseling, but it was unable to relieve her pain. Eventually her marriage broke up, which she attributes to the rape. She carried the story inside her for more than 15 years before writing this frank memoir. She describes the horror of the assault as well as its aftermath. Francisco attended rape and domestic violence trials to collect additional material for the book. This well-researched and moving account was brand new at the time of the latest national study and thus not yet widely known, leading to a rating of Diamond in the Rough.

MOVIES

Strongly Recommended

★★★★ *A League of Their Own* (1993) produced by Robert Greenhut and Elliot Abbott and directed by Penny Marshall. PG Rating. 124 minutes.

An excellent film depicting the formation of the All American Girl's Professional Baseball League. The film starts out in the 1990s at the Baseball Hall of Fame and then flashes backs to the 1943 season, a time the female players cherish forever. This feminist film shows team sports building character and binding women together. It also effectively demonstrates women's societal struggles during World War II and the attendant changes in gender roles. Widely known and favorably evaluated in our national studies.

★★★★ *How to Make an American Quilt* (1995) produced by Sarah Pilsbury and Midge Sanford and directed by Jocelyn Moorhouse. PG-13 Rating. 116 minutes.

A gathering of women to make a wedding quilt turns into a social support network. The quilt serves as a metaphor for their varied experiences with life and love. Although not an uplifting film, it refreshingly shows strong women alive and doing well. It deservedly received a bevy of awards.

★★★★ *Eating* (1990) directed and produced by Henry Jaglom. R Rating. 110 minutes.

A group of women attending a birthday party sit and talk about food and life. Their conversations are realistic, fascinating, and often hilarious. Not as well known as other movies in this category, but a valuable and entertaining flick.

Recommended

★★★ *The Piano* (1993) produced by Jan Chapman and directed by Jane Campion. R Rating. 121 minutes.

This complex film is, among other things, a gothic romance dressed in Victorian clothes. A mute mother with modern and unconventional sensibilities travels with her daughter to New Zealand, where the mother meets her new husband. The bond among mother, daughter, and music (the piano) provides them with a mutual security and vehicle for expression during some dark times, which include physical abuse. A beautiful and haunting picture nominated for multiple Academy Awards, *The Piano* effectively demonstrates women's struggles for emotional and physical survival.

★★★ *My Breast* (1994) produced by Meredith Baxter, Judy Frisch, and Diane Kerew and directed by Betty Thomas. 90 minutes.

A New York journalist has an unsatisfying relationship with her boyfriend. The diagnosis of breast cancer leads her to dramatically change her life. This television movie received modest and mixed reviews by our mental health experts, but it is one of the few that addresses breast cancer forthrightly.

★★★ *Thelma and Louise* (1992) produced by Ridley Scott and Mimi Polk and directed by Ridley Scott. R Rating. 129 minutes.

Two women find each other when all seems hopeless in their lives. This controversial movie follows their cross-country jaunt. Searching for freedom and fighting for survival, the women ride into a tragic ending. The movie is unsettling, with easy justification of murder, rape, and escape. It is bound to precipitate heated discussions about women's power and choices.

INTERNET RESOURCES

What is a woman's issue, or better yet, what part of human behavior is not? Everything has a women's angle, so the number of topics and therefore Internet sites is enormous. As a result, this section offers a larger-than-usual number of metasites—places from which you can find many sites on just about any topic of relevance to women.

Metasites

★★★★★ *WWWomen* http://www.wwwomen.com

Links to thousands of sites, each with a brief and accurate description. The site is noncommercial, positive, and offers solid information; it is the best metasite we have located on this broad topic.

★★★★★　*Women's Guide—Body and Spirit*
　　　　http://www.netguide.com/Women/Body

This metasite offers links to psychological topics like Aging, Flirting, Infertility, Menopause, and other health topics. Each site is well-described and linked. The home page covers Money, Kids, Career, Education, Travel, and more.

★★★★★　*Women's Issues—Home Page*　http://home.about.com/index.htm

Because this site is always changing, enter "Women" in the search box and follow your interest. Thousands of links under about 25 headings like Discrimination, Domestic Violence, Self-Defense, Self-Image, Sexual Assault, Sexual Harassment, and Workplace Rights.

★★★★　*WWWomen: Mothers*
　　　　http://www.wwwomen.com/category/mother/general.html

Many interesting sections, each with dozens of sites for MOMs (makers of memories) and about motherhood. Support, chat, inspiration, tips, kid-safe materials. Lots of local or state sites offering support and information for new mothers, stay-at-home moms, work-at-home mothers, employed moms, single parents, older parents, and so on.

★★★★　*Femina: Web Search for Women*　http://femina.cybergrrl.com

This site offers thousands of links that are well-organized under the headings most useful to clients: Girls, Health, Computers, Family, and so on, and a good search engine. To start a woman exploring the Internet and to seek specific information, this is an excellent place for exploring.

★★★　*Black Stump Women Page: Girls Guide*
　　　　http://werple.net.au/~lions/women.htm

They claim to list 16,128 sites under 22 headings, such as artists, history childbirth, politics, sports, travel.

★★★　*Women's Health*
　　　　http://www.go.com/Center/Health/Family/Womens_health

A magazine with articles under the headings of Aging, Cancer, Fitness and Nutirition, General Health, Looking Good, Menopause, Pregnancy, and a feature story.

Psychoeducational Materials for Clients and Families

Health

★★★★　*Alcohol and Women*　http://silk.nih.gov/silk/niaaa1/publication/aa10.htm

About four pages of research information still valuable, though written in 1990. "Drinking behavior differs with the age, life role, and marital status of women." A good introduction to the differences gender makes from the National Institute on Alcohol Abuse and Alcoholism.

★★★★ *How Stress Affects the Body* by Jeanne Spurlock, MD
http://www.amwa-doc.org/publications/WCHealthbook/
stressamwa-ch09.html

In eight pages, "information on why women are vulnerable to stress, how to cope, how to change behavior, and the psychological signs of stress" from the American Women's Medical Association.

★★★ *Women's Health Issues* http://feminist.com/health.htm

Here are about a hundred site links under the headings of General Health, Breast Cancer/Cancer, Reproductive Health, and Women and AIDS. The last two have unique and valuable links. It is a good place to start but does not have a search engine.

Feminism

★★★★★ *On the Issues* http://www.echonyc.com/~onissues/about.htm

This is a progressive woman's magazine with articles (under Features) offering well-written, sometimes hard-hitting feminist perspectives on contemporary issues.

★★★★ *Feminist Utopia* http://www.AmazonCastle.com/feminism/feminism.htm

A good starting place because of its breadth; everyone will find something of value from statistics on health and work to nonsexist language, from suffragettes and Herstory to definitions and wise quotations. Thank you, Colleen McEnearny.

★★★★ *Feminist Activist Internet Resources* http://www.igc.org/women/feminist.html

A site designed to connect feminists to each other and to sites concerned with large issues. An ideal site for those eager to take action and make a difference.

★★★ *Feminista* http://www.feminista.com

Readings for the more sophisticated feminist on "art, literature, social commentary, philosophy, wit, humor, and respect."

Menopause

★★★★★ *North American Menopause Society*
http://www.menopause.org/aboutm/index.html

A complete presentation of all medical aspects of menopause in about 50 pages. The FAQs are quite informative but very medical.

★★★★ *Menopause* http://fbhc.org/modules/menopause.cfm

A six-part primer on menopause, simply written with good links for more information.

★★★★ *Menopause Information and Resources*
http://www.pslgroup.com/MENOPAUSE.HTM

Current medical information designed for physicians.

★★★   *Menopause* http://www.nih.gov/health/chip/nia/menop/men1.htm

A booklet of about 30 pages from the National Institute on Aging addressing most aspects of menopause. Good for basic information, but written in 1992, so it is not entirely current.

Lesbian Issues

★★★★★   *Gay/Lesbian Issues*
            http://gaylesissues.about.com/index.htm?COB=home&PID=2771

A metasite with many subsites on mental health issues, such as Families/Parenting, Out and Outing, Hate Crimes, Religion and Bible Abuse, Work Issues, and Marriage.

★★★   *Lesbians* http://www.wwwomen.com/category/lesbia1.html

Hundreds of sites under 10 headings, like arts, business, personal, publications, and so on. See also Lesbian and Bisexual under the Society and Culture set of links at http://femina.cybergrrl.com.

Workplace Rights

★★★★★   *Equal Employment Opportunity Commission*
            http://www.eeoc.gov

If you have concerns about employment discrimination, this is the place to start. The Quick Start sections are excellent, and all the laws and policies are here.

★★★   *Employment Discrimination: An Overview*
            http://www.law.cornell.edu/topics/employment_discrimination.html

The site is very legal and offers links to all the important documents and decisions. It is likely to be of use to sophisticated readers needing legal support before contacting a lawyer.

★★★   *National Committee on Pay Equity*
            http://www.feminist.com/fairpay

Lots of information on the wage gap between the sexes and what to do about it. See also *Working Women: Equal Pay* at http://www.aflcio.org/women/equalpay.htm.

Other Resources

★★★   *Women's Sports* http://www.wwwomen.com/category/sports1.html

Sections of links for each of 14 sports. See also *Sports—Women's Issues* at http://womensissues.miningco.com/msub20.htm?pid=2771&cob=home.

See also Abuse (Chapter 1); Pregnancy (Chapter 21); Sexuality (Chapter 24); Weight Management (Chapter 28).

NATIONAL SUPPORT GROUPS

Business and Professional Women
2021 Massachusetts Avenue NW
Washington, DC 20036
Phone: 202-293-1100

Organization comprised of working women to promote workplace equity and provide networking opportunities.

Love-N-Addiction
PO Box 759
Willimantic, CT 06226
Phone: 203-423-2344

Explores how loving can become an addiction.

National Black Women's Health Project/Self-Help Division
1237 Abernathy Boulevard, SW
Atlanta, GA 30310-1731
Phone: 800-ADK-BWHP

Committed to the empowerment of all women through wellness.

National Organization for Women
1000 16th Street NW, #700
Washington, DC 20036
Phone: 202-331-0066

Women Employed
22 West Monroe Street, Suite 1400
Chicago, IL 60603
Phone: 312-782-3902

CHAPTER 30

Strategies for Selecting Self-Help Resources

A massive and systemic revolution is occurring in mental health today and is gathering steam for tomorrow: self-help efforts with or without professional treatment. This self-help revolution entails diverse activities: changing behavior by oneself, reading and applying self-help books, attending support and 12-step groups, watching movies and incorporating their cinematic lessons, surfing the Internet for advice and treatments, and participating in alternative health care. All these and many other examples compellingly indicate that people are making concerted efforts to change themselves on their own in addition to, or without, professional treatment.

When you select or recommend self-help materials, you obviously want those that will help the most. You visit a bookstore, Internet site, or video store and begin to look through the dozens that address your particular problem—maybe addiction, or depression, or divorce, or weight management, or sexuality, or something else. And you wish you had some guidelines to help you pick the best.

As the volume and accessibility of self-help information soar, the question of quality assumes urgency. Of the thousands of websites launched yearly and of the estimated 2,000 self-help books published annually, more than 95% are published without any controlled research documenting their accuracy or effectiveness. The self-help market resembles a Persian bazaar with proliferating choices and without clear answers: Should you nurture others or nurture your inner child; seek success or simplicity; just say no or just do it; confront your fears or honor them (Albom, 1997)? Sorely needed are trustworthy means of determining the utility and quality of self-help resources.

In the preceding chapters, we have tried to provide just that. The expert ratings and descriptions of self-help books, autobiographies, movies, and Internet resources are designed to guide mental health professionals' recommendations to patients as well as consumers' selection of meritorious resources.

There is no magic key to the self-help kingdom, but several strategies can help you select the best resource and avoid the clunkers. By analyzing the mental health experts' comments in our five national studies and by reviewing the professional literature on self-help, we have arrived at nine strategies for selecting an effective self-help resource.

1. Don't select a self-help resource because of its cover, its title, or its glitzy advertising campaign. The old saying, "You can't tell a book by its cover," probably applies to self-help books more than to any other type of book. Self-help has become big business. Publishers spend huge sums of money to create splashy covers with sensational titles and to put together glitzy, Madison Avenue advertising campaigns. They describe each year's new crop of self-help books as "phenomenal breakthroughs" and "scientific revolutions" in understanding life's problems. Some good self-help books have fancy covers and catchy titles, but so do some bad ones. The same is true with expensive advertisements—the bad books are just as likely to have huge advertising outlays as the good books.

One category with especially flashy titles, huge advertising outlays, good fodder for talk shows, and an abundance of new books virtually every year is love, intimacy, and marriage. Several of our Not Recommended books were, in fact, national best-sellers, had huge advertising budgets, and have very catchy titles. Based on what you hear and see on talk shows, book covers, and advertising, there isn't any way people can sort through titles in this category and tell that these books aren't good self-help books.

Publishers and bookstores influence self-help book purchases by how many books they display and where the books are located. However, this year's top-selling book that is stacked from floor to ceiling often finds its way to next year's wastebasket. Or something worse happens: Lavish advertising, expensive promotional campaigns, and support by national book chains enable some bad self-help books to sell extremely well. With no guidelines, consumers don't know that these books are bad. It is not unusual for bookstores to have only one or two copies of some of the best self-help books hidden on the bottom shelves or to not carry them at all.

When one area of self-help becomes popular, many authors jump on the bandwagon and quickly pump out books in rapid succession, hoping to cash in on the latest "in" topic or movement. In the early 1990s, codependency, the inner child, and dieting were especially hot topics, and authors whipped out books on them at an astonishing pace. In the late 1990s, spirituality was in the ascendancy. Yet most of the books in these hot categories were not rated favorably by mental health experts.

In sum, be an intelligent consumer of psychological knowledge by going beyond the cover, the testimonies by celebrities, the fancy ads, the author's appearance on talk shows, and the bookstore's elaborate display. Instead, make your choices based on the next eight strategies.

2. Select a resource that makes realistic rather than grandiose claims. If you have a problem, you want to cope with it as effectively and painlessly as possible. The quicker you can fix the problem, the better. Unfortunately, the self-help resources that make extravagant claims are the most alluring and thus sell better than books that are more realistic. Most problems do not arise overnight, and most can't be solved overnight. Books that promise magical, wondrous insights that can immediately solve problems should be avoided.

If a resource states that a "miraculous" new diet has been discovered that will help you lose one pound a day and keep the weight off permanently, don't buy it. The largest number of low-rated books in our national studies were in the weight management category. Most of these books tend to make extravagant claims and take a very narrow approach to weight loss. More reasonable books are not as eye-catching and not as sensational, but they present a much more balanced approach to weight loss—and tend not to sell as well, even though they are far better self-help books.

Try to make a realistic judgment about the book's claims. Be skeptical of anything that sounds easy, magical, and wondrous. Overcoming depression, losing weight, improving relationships, and becoming more self-fulfilled are not easy tasks. They all take a lot of effort. Coping effectively with any of life's tasks and problems—anxiety, parenting, divorce, addiction, or career development—is a lifelong project.

3. Examine the evidence reported in the self-help resource. Unfortunately, many self-help resources are not based on reliable scientific evidence but rather on the author's anecdotal experiences or personal testimonials of people who say that the author's ideas worked for them. In some instances, evidence is gleaned from interviews with a narrow range of people or a few clients seen in therapy. Too much of what you read in the self-help literature is based on speculative intuitions.

Most of the self-help resources highly rated by the mental health professionals were based on reliable research or clinical evidence. The cognitive therapy of depression advocated by David Burns in *Feeling Good* (Chapter 20) has undergone careful scrutiny by the clinical and research community and been found to be effective for many people. The same is true for Herbert Benson's *The Relaxation Response* (Chapter 26), *Learned Optimism* by Martin Seligman, and *Changing for Good* by James O. Prochaska and Associates (Chapter 23). These books are not based on the subjective opinions of the authors or the testimonials of others. They are based on years of sound research and clinical results.

Hardly any self-help resource contains elaborate research citations. This is by design because lengthy citations make the books difficult to read. However, authors of the most effective resources typically describe the research evidence, the clinical evidence, or both on which the book is based. And the good books often have a list of sources in an appendix.

4. Select self-help materials that recognize that problems are caused by a number of factors and have alternative solutions. It's not just your imagination. You are a complex being living in a complex world. Your problems are not so simple that they have a simple cause and a single solution. Yet the human mind is biased toward simple answers to complex problems. After all, solving a problem is easier if there is one simple solution than if you have to modify a number of factors in your life.

Consider stress and anxiety. Thinking positively may well help you cope more effectively with stress, but self-help resources that deal only with positive thinking often oversimplify the coping process. Stress and anxiety reduction can be facilitated by optimistic thinking, rearranging your life, practicing relaxation, exercising regularly, learning assertion skills, training your breathing, knowing your personality, and cultivating more interpersonal support.

Counter the "single trick" mentality by examining self-help materials for multiple causes and multiple sources of assistance. A variety of self-change methods in your armamentarium will assuredly be more successful than a solitary technique.

5. Self-help resources that focus on a particular problem are better than those that claim to be a general approach to solving all of your problems. Effective self-help materials tend to concentrate on a specific problem rather than promising to cure all of life's ills. Materials that try to solve all problems are shallow and lack the precise, detailed recommendations that are needed to improve a particular problem. When authors claim that their methods will solve all of your problems and will help everybody, don't buy it, figuratively and literally.

The more authors can convince the public that their books are for everyone, the greater their chances of selling millions of copies. And that is exactly what far too many self-help authors try to do—write books that are so broad in scope that they will appeal to a huge audience. The concept of codependency (Chapter 3) initially applied to the specific problems of people married to alcoholics, especially women married to male alcoholics. But the concept spread rapidly to a host of other circumstances, and codependency authors now claim that codependency is anything and that everything is codependent. That is far too broad and all-encompassing for most mental health experts.

Most of the leading self-help resources in our studies tackle specific disorders. Davis and Associates' *The Relaxation and Stress Reduction Workbook* is a perfect illustration. As the title indicates, it is specific and detailed; it does not promise a panacea for all conditions. Bourne's *The Anxiety and Phobia Workbook* does likewise. *The Courage to Heal* addresses recovery from child sexual abuse, and Brazelton's *Infants and Mothers* focuses on a specific age—infants from birth to 1 year of age—and how parents should respond to active, average, or quiet infants. These books don't try to reel everyone in and don't pretend to be all things to all people. They focus on specific types of problems and offer specific solutions to those problems.

6. Don't be conned by psychobabble and slick writing. In 1977, R. D. Rosen wrote *Psychobabble*, a sizzling attack on the psychological jargon that fills the space between the covers of many self-help resources. Unfortunately, two decades later psychobabble is still alive and well. Psychobabble is a hip and vague language that will not improve your ability to cope with a problem. Too many self-help authors write in psychobabble, saying things like "You've got to get in touch with your feelings"; "Get with the program"; "You've got to get it"; "the real you"; "To solve your problem you need some high-energy experiences"; "You are sending off the wrong vibes," and on and on. In a number of chapters, we specifically criticized some books for having too much psychobabble and praised others for being free of it.

Psychobabble is not the only semantic problem of poor self-help materials. Some disguise their inadequacies with slick writing that is so friendly that it seems as if the author is personally talking to you. After you have read only a few pages of the book or website, you say to yourself, "Wow! This can really help me." All too often such slick books offer little more than one or two basic ideas that could be communicated in two or three pages. The rest of the book is filled with polished writing that provides little additional knowledge. Such books lack the extensive, detailed recommendations and sound strategies needed to cope more effectively with life's problems.

Self-help resources characterized by psychobabble and slick writing frequently regress into motivational cheerleading and inspirational sermons. This approach can get you pumped up to solve your problem, but then it lets you down by giving you no precise strategies for coping with life's ills. After a few weeks or months, the buzz wears off because the author's recommendations lack depth. Examples of books characterized by this approach are Zig Zigler's *Steps to the Top* (in contrast to Steven Covey's *The 7 Habits of Highly Effective People*, which has detailed, effective strategies; Chapter 23) and Leo Buscaglia's *Loving Each Other* (in contrast to Aaron Beck's *Love Is Never Enough*, which examines the complexity of love and its many different avenues; Chapter 17).

We are not opposed to personal and fluid writing. However, it takes a lot more than an author's slick language to help you cope effectively. Select self-help materials that are clearly written in language you can understand and that include detailed recommendations for how to cope with a specific problem.

7. Check out the author's educational and professional credentials. Not all authors of self-help resources are mental health professionals who have gone through rigorous educational training at respected universities and who have spent years rendering professional treatment. Just about anyone can get their self-help ideas onto the web if they have a modicum of computer skills, and most can get those ideas into print if they can convince an agent or publisher that they will make money. But most of the best self-help books and internet sites (excluding autobiographies) are written by mental health professionals, not professional writers laypersons.

In our national studies, the authors of 80 to 90% of the top self-help books have PhDs or MDs and have done extensive research or have had clinical training. Aaron Beck and David Burns, the authors of excellent books on depression and relationships, are highly respected psychiatrists and professors at medical schools. T. Berry Brazelton, author of three highly touted books, is an esteemed pediatrician who has experience working with parents and babies; he is affiliated with the Harvard Medical School. Harriet Lerner, author of *The Dance of Anger* and *The Dance of Intimacy* has a PhD and is a psychologist on the staff of the famous Menninger Clinic.

Of course, the reverse can also happen. A PhD or an MD does not guarantee a wonderful self-help book. The consensus of the mental health experts in the national studies was that Joyce Brothers, Ruth Westheimer, and Wayne Dyer, all of whom have PhDs, and a large number of authors with PhDs or MDs in the weight management category, have written self-help books that should be avoided.

8. Be wary of authors who reject the conventional knowledge of mental health professionals. Mental health professionals—such as psychologists and psychiatrists—don't have the answers to all of life's problems, and if they tell you they do, they are being intellectually dishonest.

Some self-help authors attack the mental health professions as being too conservative and overly concerned with scientific evidence. Consider such attacks a red flag, and avoid these authors. These antiestablishment, antiscience mavericks avow that their ideas are way ahead of their time and that it will take years for mental health professionals to catch up with their avant garde thinking and insight. Many New Age and Scientology authors, such as L. Ron Hubbard, fall into this category.

There is nothing wrong with new ideas, of course. But there is something seriously wrong with new ideas uncritically promulgated in the absence of reliable evidence of their effectiveness and safety. For the most part, the materials of self-help authors who condemn the mental health establishment will not meaningfully assist you.

9. Use the *Authoritative Guide to Self-Help Resources in Mental Health* as a guide. Even armed with the first eight strategies for selecting an effective self-help resource, you may still experience difficulty in sorting through the jungle and picking the best one. With practice in using the strategies, you will become a more knowledgeable consumer.

For us, the most trustworthy strategy for selecting good self-help materials and avoiding the lemons is accessing the knowledge of the most highly trained and experienced mental health professionals in the United States. We have compiled and shared their knowledge in this book. As explained in Chapter 1, our five national studies have involved more than 2,500 psychologists in evaluating self-help books, autobiographies, and movies. Professional consensus is no absolute guarantee, but it is superior to individual judgements, random selection, or best-seller lists. We trust and value the collective ratings of thousands of experts. Use their knowledge to help select effective self-help materials.

The Five
National Studies

Over the past 7 years, we have conducted a series of national studies to determine the most useful and most frequently recommended self-help resources for a number of diverse problems. The resources we evaluated are self-help books, autobiographies, and, most recently, movies. In each case, the methodology and the samples were very similar: a lengthy survey mailed to clinical and counseling psychologists residing in the United States. The responding psychologists rated self-help resources with which they were sufficiently familiar on the same 5-point scale:

+2	Extremely good	Outstanding; highly recommended book, best or among best in category
+1	Moderately good	Provides good advice, can be helpful; worth purchasing
0	Average	An average self-help book
–1	Moderately bad	Not a good self-help book; may provide misleading or inaccurate information
–2	Extremely bad	This book exemplifies the worst of the self-help books; worst, or among worst in its category

The precise wording was slightly altered, of course, for ratings of autobiographies and movies. For example, the wording read "An average autobiographical account," "Outstanding; highly recommended movie," and so on.

As authors of this book and lead researchers on the five studies, we strove to avoid theoretical bias. Our theoretical orientations are explicitly eclectic or integrative; that is, we believe that a number of treatment approaches can be used to help people overcome disorders and cope effectively with life transitions. Something of value can be found among the dizzying diversity of treatment alternatives ranging from A to Z—analytical, behavioral, cognitive, all the way to Zen Buddhism.

Overall, the mental health experts were far more likely to rate the self-help resources positively than negatively. The stars (1 to 5) and the dagger assigned to the various resources were based primarily on the average rating of the resource and secondarily on its frequency of rating. After extensive discussions and data analyses, we selected the cutoff points for 1 to 5 stars described in Chapter 1 and presented below:

★★★★★ Average rating of 1.25 or higher; the resource was rated by 30 or more mental health professionals

★★★★ Average rating of 1.00 or higher; rated by 20 or more mental health professionals

★★★ Average rating of .50 through .99; rated 10 or more times

★★ Average rating of .25 through .49; rated 10 or more times

★ Average rating of .00 through .24; rated 10 or more times

† Average negative rating; rated by 10 or more mental health professionals

The sole exception to this rating system was the autobiographies. There, we used a cutoff of 8 or more ratings, as opposed to 10, simply because fewer psychologists were sufficiently familiar with autobiographies than with self-help books or movies and because in one of our investigations (Study 2) we had previously used 8 as the minimum number of raters. Thus, the rating systems for autobiographies was:

★★★★★ Average rating of 1.25 or higher; rated by 24 or more mental health professionals

★★★★ Average rating of 1.00 or higher; rated by 16 or more mental health professionals

★★★ Average rating of .50 through .99; rated 8 or more times

★★ Average rating of .25 through .49; rated 8 or more times

★ Average rating of .00 through .24; rated 8 or more times

† Average negative rating; rated by 8 or more mental health professionals

Our recommendations in each chapter are guided by the collective judgment of the mental health experts in our studies. The Strongly Recommended self-help resources are those receiving 5 or 4 stars. The 3-star resources receive the more modest designation of Recommended. Although the 1-star and 2-star books were in the positive range, they were low positive and received large number of 0 and even some negative ratings. Thus, we opted not to recommend them. And, as described in Chapter 1, the worst rating—the dagger (†)—was reserved for books, autobiographies, and movies receiving a negative rating. This rating, it should be noted, was given to only 5% of all the self-help resources in our studies.

The individual ratings for all the self-help resources canvassed in the five studies are detailed in Appendix B (self-help books), Appendix C (autobiographies), and Appendix D (movies).

Across the five studies, more than 2,500 psychologists contributed their expertise and judgment to evaluate self-help resources. Below we briefly review the survey methodology and sample composition of each study.

STUDY 1: SELF-HELP BOOKS

The first study entailed mailing a questionnaire to 4,000 members of the clinical and counseling divisions of the American Psychological Association (APA), almost one-half of all members in those divisions. Almost 800 psychologists returned the questionnaires, but full ratings of the books were completed by just under 600. Some of the members had died, and their spouses returned the unanswered questionnaires with a note; more than 100 respondents filled out the first part of the questionnaire (demographic information and general items about self-help books) but did not rate individual books; and some respondents returned the forms unanswered. In many such studies, a follow-up mailing is conducted to increase the sample size. We considered this alternative but did not exercise it for a simple reason: inadequate funds. The results of the first national study formed the basis for *The Authoritative Guide to Self-Help Books* by John W. Santrock, Ann M. Minnett, and Barbara D. Campbell (1994).

The responding mental health professionals all held doctorates. They lived in every state and represented a broad cross-section of clinical and counseling psychologists in the United States. While the respondents were members of the clinical and counseling divisions of the American Psychological Association, their evaluations of self-help books in the study and in this book are not in any way endorsed by the APA itself.

STUDY 2: AUTOBIOGRAPHIES

A few years later, we expanded our focus to embrace autobiographies of people suffering from a behavioral or mental disorder. Our inclusion criteria were that they be first-person narrative accounts that dealt primarily or substantially with the author's disorder or treatment in book-length works. Excluded were fictional and second-person accounts. Brief articles, poetry collections, and film accounts were also excluded. Our aim was to obtain solid, national data on the published autobiographies that psychologists recommend to their clients.

We mailed a cover letter, a four-page questionnaire, and a stamped return envelope to 1,000 randomly selected members of the APA's Division of Psychotherapy living in the United States. Of these, 379 questionnaires (38%) were returned; however 17 were not usable because the psychologists were retired or did not wish to participate. The final sample consisted of 362 psychologists who were demographically and geographically representative of the entire Division of Psychotherapy membership. Thirty-five percent of the psychologists were women, and 94% were Caucasian. Primary employment settings were private practice (66% of sample), universities (10%), hospitals (5%), and outpatient clinics (5%). Portions of these results were reported in a *Professional Psychology* article authored by Jennifer S. Clifford, John C. Norcross, and Robert Sommer (1999).

STUDY 3: SELF-HELP BOOKS

In preparation for the present book, we conducted three new studies. Study 3 canvassed self-help books published since Study 1 was performed and included self-help books on three additional disorders—schizophrenia, attention-deficit/hyperactivity disorder (ADHD), and dementia/alzheimer's. Study 4 assessed psychologists' knowledge and evaluations of autobiographies not covered

TABLE A1. Descriptive Summary of Responding Psychologists in Three Studies

Characteristic	Study 3		Study 4		Study 5	
	N	%	N	%	N	%
Gender						
Male	384	57	181	59	222	56
Female	291	43	124	41	177	44
Ethnic/racial background						
Native American	8	1	2	1	3	1
African American/Black	18	3	7	2	6	1
Caucasian/White	628	93	290	95	371	94
Hispanic/Latino	13	2	3	1	11	3
Asian American	7	1	2	1	6	1
Theoretical orientation						
Behavioral	67	10	28	9	35	9
Cognitive	192	28	75	24	98	25
Eclectic/integrative	188	28	93	30	125	31
Humanistic/existential	36	5	17	6	29	7
Interpersonal	39	6	23	7	24	6
Psychodynamic/analytic	107	16	48	16	57	14
Systems/family systems	22	3	8	3	16	4
Other	25	4	15	5	17	4
Employment setting						
Private practice	284	42	124	41	165	41
General hospital	35	5	15	5	10	2
Outpatient clinic	30	4	17	6	27	7
Psychiatric hospital	22	3	12	4	18	5
University	166	25	65	22	105	26
Medical school	45	7	22	7	19	5
Other	94	14	47	15	55	14

in our earlier study. And Study 5 entered new territory: psychologists' evaluations of movies as self-help resources.

For Study 3, two separate surveys were mailed to a total of 3,000 randomly selected members of the APA's clinical psychology and counseling psychology divisions. The first questionnaire was sent to 1,500 psychologists soliciting quality ratings on self-help books for 14 problem areas; the second questionnaire was sent to another 1,500 psychologists requesting ratings on self-help books on a different set of 15 problems. The first questionnaire was returned by 336 psychologists, and full ratings of the books were completed by 324. The total response rate was 22%. The second questionnaire was completed and returned by 376 psychologists; of these, 357 provided usable data. This yielded a total response rate of 25%.

Table A1 summarizes the demographic and professional characteristics of the psychologists participating in Study 3, as well as those participating in Study 4 and Study 5 (described below).

The responding psychologists constituted a broad sample of mental health experts. Hailing from every state in the union, they all held doctoral degrees and averaged 15 years of postdoctoral experience. As shown in the table, the psychologists represented diverse theoretical orientations and a variety of employment sites, largely private practice and academia.

STUDY 4: AUTOBIOGRAPHIES

A lengthy questionnaire was mailed to 1,500 members of APA's clinical psychology division and counseling psychology division seeking their ratings on the value of autobiographies concerning 13 different problems. Of these, 328 were returned, but 21 were incomplete, leaving 307 usable questionnaires. As in the other studies, the primary reasons for returning an incomplete questionnaire were that the psychologists were not in clinical practice or had recently retired. The total response rate for this study was 22%.

STUDY 5: MOVIES

Our final study involved a lengthy questionnaire concerning the value of specific movies, sent to 1,500 members of the APA's clinical and counseling psychology divisions. Psychologists were asked to rate the quality of listed movies with which they were sufficiently familiar for 20 problem areas. A total of 417 surveys were returned, with usable data provided by 401 of the respondents, a 28% total response rate. As in the previous studies, the participating mental health experts were all doctoral-level psychologists of various genders, ethnicities, theoretical orientations, and work settings (see Table A1 for details).

Ratings of Self-Help Books in the National Studies

Only those self-help books rated five or more times in our national studies are included in this list. Some books appear on this list but were not included in the text because they were rated by fewer than 10 mental health experts. Please consult Appendix A for details on the methodology of the national studies and the meaning of the guide ratings.

Category and title	Author(s)	Study no.	Avg. rating	No. of raters	Guide rating
Abuse					
Abused No More	Ackerman & Pickering	1	0.48	57	★★
Allies in Healing	Davis	3	1.24	33	★★★★
Battered Wives	Martin	1	0.85	56	★★★
Battered Woman, The	Walker	1	1.22	121	★★★★
Beginning to Heal	Bass & Davis	3	0.84	43	★★★
Breaking Violence in a Relationship	Blue	3	1.00	6	–
Courage to Heal, The	Bass & Davis	1	1.53	244	★★★★★
Getting Free	NiCarthy	1	1.00	38	★★★★
Healing the Shame That Binds You	Bradshaw	1	0.56	192	★★★
I Never Called It Rape	Warshaw	3	1.53	17	★★★
Reclaiming the Inner Child	Abrams	1	0.20	97	★
Toxic Parents	Forward	1	0.47	119	★★
Victims No Longer	Lew	3	1.19	21	★★★★
Verbally Abusive Relationship, The	Evans	3	1.61	13	★★★

Category and title	Author(s)	Study no.	Avg. rating	No. of raters	Guide rating
Waking the Tiger: Healing Trauma	Levine & Frederick	3	0.83	6	—
Wounded Boys, Heroic Men	Sonkin	3	0.80	10	★★★
You Can't Say That to Me!	Elgin	3	1.00	9	◆

Addictive Disorders and Codependency

Category and title	Author(s)	Study no.	Avg. rating	No. of raters	Guide rating
Addiction and Grace	May	1	0.67	26	★★★
Adult Children of Alcoholics	Woititz	1	0.52	220	★★★
Alcoholic Man, The	Carey	1	0.35	17	★★
Alcoholics Anonymous	Alcoholics Anonymous	1	1.13	179	★★★★
Beyond Codependency	Beattie	3	0.90	61	★★★
Co-Dependence	Whitfield	1	0.04	52	★
Codependent No More	Beattie	1	0.84	197	★★★
Day at a Time, A	CompCare	1	0.72	52	★★★
Healing the Addictive Mind	Jampolsky	1	−1.05	20	†
How to Break Your Addiction to a Person	Halpern	1	0.49	72	★★
It Will Never Happen to Me	Black	1	1.61	14	★★★
Love Is a Choice	Helmfelt et al.	1	0.05	41	★
Miracle Method, The	Miller & Berg	3	−0.08	12	†
One Day at a Time in Al-Anon	Al-Anon Family Group	1	0.93	110	★★★
Out of the Shadows	Carnes	3	0.67	39	★★★
Recovery Book, The	Mooney et al.	3	0.86	21	★★★
Resisting 12-Step Coercion	Peele et al.	3	0.17	6	—
Sober and Free	Kettelhack	3	0.86	14	★★★
Time to Heal, A	Cermak	3	1.14	22	★★★★
Truth about Addiction and Recovery, The	Peele et al.	3	0.73	11	★★★
Twelve Steps and Twelve Traditions	Alcoholics Anonymous	1	1.02	180	★★★★
When AA Doesn't Work for You	Ellis & Velton	3	0.88	33	★★★

Adult Development and Aging

Category and title	Author(s)	Study no.	Avg. rating	No. of raters	Guide rating
Ageless Body, Timeless Mind	Chopra	3	0.77	43	★★★
Aging Well	Fries	1	0.84	16	★★★
Complete Guide to Health and Well-Being after 50	Weiss & Subak-Sharpe	1	0.88	24	★★★
Enjoy Old Age	Skinner & Vaughan	3	1.75	8	◆
50+ Wellness Program, The	McIlwain et al.	1	0.24	17	★
Fly Fishing through the Midlife Crisis	Raines	3	1.00	5	—
Fountain of Age, The	Friedan	3	0.69	16	★★★
How to Deal with Your Parents	Osterkamp	1	0.50	24	★★★
How to Live Longer and Feel Better	Pauling	1	0.53	46	★★★
It's Better to be over the Hill Than under It	LeShan	3	1.18	11	★★★
Making Peace with Your Parents	Bloomfield	1	0.99	69	★★★
Necessary Losses	Viorst	1	1.10	182	★★★★

Category and title	Author(s)	Study no.	Avg. rating	No. of raters	Guide rating
Adult Development and Aging *(cont.)*					
Old Folks Going Strong	York	1	0.61	7	—
Passages	Sheehy	1	0.72	356	★★★
Seasons of a Man's Life	Levinson	1	1.05	222	★★★★
Silent Passage, The	Sheehy	3	0.81	73	★★★
When You and Your Mother Can't Be Friends	Secunda	1	0.60	30	★★★
Your Renaissance Years	Veninga	3	1.00	5	◆
Anger					
Anger at Work	Weisinger	3	1.33	6	◆
Anger: Deal with It, Heal with It, Stop It From Killing You	Defoore	1	0.38	24	★★
Anger: How to Live with and without It	Ellis	1	0.85	24	★★★
Anger Kills	Williams & Williams	3	1.44	9	◆
Anger: The Misunderstood Emotion	Tavris	1	1.18	83	★★★★
Anger Workbook, The	Bilodeau	3	1.13	31	★★★★
Angry All the Time	Potter-Efron	3	1.21	14	★★★
Angry Book, The	Rubin	1	0.52	95	★★★
Angry Men and the Women Who Love Them	Hegstrom	3	0.71	7	—
Dance of Anger, The	Lerner	1	1.39	211	★★★★★
How to Control Your Anger before It Controls You	Ellis & Tafrate	3	1.14	35	★★★★
Letting Go of Anger	Potter-Efron & Potter-Efron	3	1.30	23	★★★★
Volcano in My Tummy, A	Whitehouse & Pudney	3	1.33	6	◆
When Anger Hurts	McKay et al.	1	0.92	36	★★★
Anxiety Disorders					
Anxiety and Panic Attacks	Handly	1	0.81	27	★★★
Anxiety and Phobia Workbook, The	Bourne	3	1.58	117	★★★★★
Anxiety Disease, The	Sheehan	1	0.64	59	★★★
Anxiety Disorders and Phobias	Beck & Emery	1	1.18	172	★★★★
Don't Panic	Wilson	1	1.04	82	★★★★
End to Panic, An	Luerchen-White	3	1.42	12	★★★
Feel the Fear and Do it Anyway	Jeffers	3	1.15	34	★★★★
Good News about Panic, Anxiety, and Phobias, The	Gold	1	0.59	45	★★★
How to Control Your Anxiety before It Controls You	Ellis	3	0.95	59	★★★
Life without Fear	Wolpe & Wolpe	3	0.85	33	★★★★
Mastery of Your Anxiety and Panic II	Barlow & Craske	3	1.53	58	★★★★★
Obsessive–Compulsive Disorders	Levenkron	1	1.00	31	★★★★
Panic Disorder	Rachman & de Silva	3	0.93	29	★★★
Peace from Nervous Suffering	Weekes	1	0.88	57	★★★
Sky Is Falling, The	Dumont	3	1.33	9	◆
S.T.O.P. Obsessing	Foa & Wilson	3	1.36	50	★★★★★

Category and title	Author(s)	Study no.	Avg. rating	No. of raters	Guide rating
Assertiveness					
Asserting Yourself	Bower & Bower	3	1.10	20	★★★★
Assertive Woman, The	Phelps & Austin	3	1.35	43	★★★★★
Control Freaks	Piaget	1	0.00	11	★
Creative Aggression	Bach & Goldberg	1	0.43	72	★★
Don't Say Yes When You Want to Say No	Fensterheim & Baer	1	0.91	150	★★★
Gentle Art of Verbal Self-Defense, The	Elgin	1	0.66	61	★★★
Good-Bye to Guilt	Jampolsky	1	0.77	31	★★★
Looking Out for Number One	Ringer	1	−0.73	67	†
Pulling Your Own Strings	Dyer	1	0.19	148	★
Stand Up, Speak Out, Talk Back	Alberti & Emmons	1	1.11	75	★★★★
Stick Up for Yourself	Kaufman & Raphael	3	0.67	3	◆
When I Say No, I Feel Guilty	Smith	1	1.00	223	★★★★
Winning through Intimidation	Ringer	1	−1.11	83	†
Your Perfect Right	Alberti & Emmons	1	1.37	283	★★★★★
Attention-Deficit/Hyperactivity Disorder					
ADHD and Teens	Alexander-Roberts	3	1.17	12	★★★
Distant Drums, Different Drummers	Ingersoll	3	1.00	8	◆
Driven to Distraction	Hallowell & Ratey	3	1.26	73	★★★★★
Learning to Slow Down and Pay Attention	Nadeau & Dixon	3	1.13	15	★★★
Living with ADHD Children	Buntman	3	1.00	13	★★★
Ritalin Nation	DeGrandpre	3	0.00	6	—
Running on Ritalin	Diller	3	0.60	5	—
Taking Charge of ADHD	Barkley	3	1.41	65	★★★★★
Career Development					
Career Anchors	Schein	3	1.20	5	◆
Career Mastery	Levinson	3	0.80	5	◆
Diversity and Women's Career Development	Farmer et al.	3	1.28	7	◆
Do What You Love, the Money Will Follow	Sinetar	1	0.57	38	★★★
Knock 'Em Dead	Yate	1	0.74	15	★★★
100 Best Companies to Work for in America, The	Levering et al.	1	0.27	33	★★
Portable MBA, The	Collins & Devanna	1	0.40	15	★★
Shifting Gears	Hyatt	1	0.85	20	★★★
Staying the Course	Weiss	1	1.06	33	★★★★
Upward Nobility	Edwards	1	0.00	6	—
What Color Is Your Parachute?	Bolles	1	1.32	324	★★★★★
Win–Win Negotiating	Jandt	1	1.02	47	★★★★

Category and title	Author(s)	Study no.	Avg. rating	No. of raters	Guide rating
Child Development and Parenting					
Between Parent and Child	Ginott	1	1.30	261	★★★★★
Childhood	Konner	1	0.67	9	—
Children: The Challenge	Dreikurs	1	1.27	126	★★★★★
Common Sense Parenting	Burke & Herron	3	1.43	7	◆
Drama of the Gifted Child, The	Miller	1	1.90	5	◆
Dr. Spock on Parenting	Spock	1	1.05	114	★★★★
Dr. Spock's Baby and Child Care	Spock & Rothenberg	1	1.43	187	★★★★★
Father's Almanac, The	Sullivan	1	0.90	16	★★★
First Three Years of Life, The	White	1	1.34	102	★★★★★
First Twelve Months of Life, The	Caplan		1.33	60	★★★★★
Helping the Child Who Doesn't Fit In	Nowicki & Duke	3	1.00	7	◆
How to Discipline Your 6- to 12-Year-Old without Losing Your Mind	Wyckoff & Unell	1	0.57	22	★★★
How to Talk So Kids Will Listen and Listen So Kids Will Talk	Faber & Mazlish	3	1.35	63	★★★★★
Hurried Child, The	Elkind	1	1.17	114	★★★★
Infants and Mothers	Brazelton	1	1.47	114	★★★★★
Living with Children	Patterson	1	1.83	11	★★★
1-2-3 Magic	Phelan	3	1.27	33	★★★★★
Parent Effectiveness Training	Gordon	1	1.15	259	★★★★
Parenting the Strong-Willed Child	Forehand & Long	3	1.45	20	★★★★
Parent Power!	Rosemond	3	0.27	11	★★
Positive Discipline A–Z	Nelson et al.	3	0.94	16	★★★
Systematic Training for Effective Parenting	Dinkmeyer & McKay	1	1.96	8	◆
Tips for Toddlers	Beebe	1	0.71	7	—
Toddlers and Parents	Brazelton	1	1.37	101	★★★★★
To Listen to a Child	Brazelton	1	1.41	89	★★★★★
What Every Baby Knows	Brazelton	1	1.44	105	★★★★★
What to Expect the First Year	Eisenberg et al.	1	1.44	37	★★★★★
Your Baby and Child	Leach	1	1.32	32	★★★★★
Communication and People Skills					
Are You the One for Me?	DeAngelis	3	0.11	18	★
Body Language	Fast	1	0.20	113	★
Boundaries	Cloud & Townsend	3	1.44	23	★★★★
Coping with Difficult People	Bramson	1	0.87	62	★★★
Difficult People	Cava	3	0.91	22	★★★
Games People Play	Berne	1	0.62	350	★★★
Getting to Yes	Fisher & Ury	1	1.03	69	★★★★
How to Argue and Win Every Time	Spence	3	0.29	14	★★
How to Communicate	McKay et al.	3	1.17	23	★★★★
How to Start a Conversation and Make Friends	Gabor	1	0.42	12	★★
How to Win Friends and Influence People	Carnegie	1	0.24	161	★
Intimate Connections	Burns	1	1.08	46	★★★★
Intimate Strangers	Rubin	1	1.18	82	★★★★

Category and title	Author(s)	Study no.	Avg. rating	No. of raters	Guide rating
Just Friends	Rubin	1	1.07	31	★★★★
Mars and Venus on a Date	Gray	3	−0.31	32	†
Men Are from Mars, Women Are from Venus	Gray	3	0.32	167	★★
Opening Up	Pennebaker	1	0.91	18	★★★
Peoplemaking	Satir	1	1.47	7	♦
People Skills	Bolton	1	1.03	32	★★★★
Shyness	Zimbardo	1	1.14	164	★★★★
Stop! You're Driving Me Crazy	Bach & Deutsch	1	0.50	46	★★★
Talk Book, The	Goodman & Esterly	3	1.11	9	♦
That's Not What I Meant!	Tannen	1	0.99	61	★★★
You Just Don't Understand	Tannen	1	1.24	148	★★★★

Death and Grieving

Bereaved Parent, The	Schiff	1	2.00	5	—
Coming Back	Stern	1	0.78	9	—
Final Exit	Humphrey	1	−0.33	61	†
Grief Recovery Handbook, The	James & Cherry	3	1.46	26	★★★★
Helping Children Grieve	Huntley	1	1.08	25	★★★★
How to Go on Living When Someone You Love Dies	Rando	1	1.25	31	★★★★★
How to Survive the Loss of a Love	Colgrove et al.	1	1.41	100	★★★★★
How We Die	Nuland	3	0.58	19	★★★
Learning to Say Good-By	LeShan	1	1.22	52	★★★★
Life After Loss	Volkan & Zintl	3	0.78	9	—
Living through Personal Crisis	Stearns	1	1.06	18	★★★
On Children and Death	Kübler-Ross	3	1.28	61	★★★★★
On Death and Dying	Kübler-Ross	1	0.99	355	★★★
Recovering from the Loss of a Child	Donnelly	1	1.15	27	★★★★
Sudden Infant Death	DeFrain et al.	1	1.00	16	★★★
Talking about Death	Grollman	1	1.23	40	★★★★
Time to Say Good-bye, A	Goulding	3	1.20	10	★★★
When Bad Things Happen to Good People	Kushner	3	1.29	150	★★★★★
Widowed	Brothers	1	−0.02	34	†
Widow's Handbook, The	Foehner & Cozart	1	0.54	13	★★★
Working It Through	Kübler-Ross	3	1.19	36	★★★★

Dementia/Alzheimer's

Alzheimer's Caregiver, The	Hodgson	3	1.14	14	★★★
Hidden Victims of Alzheimer's Disease, The	Zarit et al.	3	1.18	11	★★★
36-Hour Day, The	Mace & Rabins	3	1.55	49	★★★★★
When Your Loved One Has Alzheimer's	Carroll	3	0.86	7	♦

Divorce

Boys and Girls Book about Divorce, The	Gardner	1	1.39	212	★★★★★
Crazy Time	Trafford	3	1.44	16	★★★

Category and title	Author(s)	Study no.	Avg. rating	No. of raters	Guide rating
Divorce *(cont.)*					
Creative Divorce	Krantzler	1	0.66	88	★★★
Custody Revolution, The	Warshak	3	0.60	5	—
Dinosaurs Divorce	Brown & Brown	1	1.42	44	★★★★★
Divorce: The Best Resources to Help You Survive	Wemhoff	3	1.33	6	—
Dumped	Warren & Thompson	3	1.00	3	◆
Growing Up with Divorce	Kalter	1	1.00	33	★★★★
Helping Your Kids Cope with Divorce	Neuman & Romanowski	3	1.05	18	★★★
How It Feels When Parents Divorce	Krementz	1	1.09	70	★★★★
Mars and Venus Starting Over	Gray	3	0.09	22	★
Parents Book about Divorce, The	Gardner	1	1.88	8	◆
Second Chances	Wallerstein & Blakeslee	1	0.99	102	★★★
Eating Disorders					
Body Betrayed, The	Zerbe	3	1.11	9	◆
Dying to Be Thin	Sacker & Zimmer	3	1.24	21	★★★★
Fat Is a Family Affair	Hollis	1	0.88	41	★★★
Food for Thought	Hazelden Foundation	1	0.66	32	★★★
Healing the Hungry Self	Price	3	1.10	10	★★★
Hunger Within, The	Migliore & Ross	3	1.36	11	★★★
Love Hunger	Minirth et al.	1	0.13	31	★
Love-Powered Diet, The	Moran	1	−0.91	11	†
Overcoming Binge Eating	Fairburn	3	1.06	18	★★★
Twelve Steps & Twelve Traditions of Inner Eating	Billigmeier	1	0.22	9	—
12-Steps and 12 Traditions of Overeaters Anonymous, The	Overeaters Anonymous	3	1.00	14	★★★
When Food Is Love	Roth	1	0.66	32	★★★
Why Weight?	Roth	1	0.68	22	★★★
You Can't Quit Eating until You Know What's Eating You	LeBlanc	1	0.47	17	★★
Families and Stepfamilies					
Adult Children	Friel & Friel	1	0.52	49	★★★
Back to the Family	Guarendi	1	0.91	11	★★★
Blending Families	Shomberg	3	1.08	13	★★★
Bradshaw on the Family	Bradshaw	1	0.34	129	★★
Families	Patterson	1	1.78	12	★★★
Family Crucible, The	Napier & Whitaker	1	1.04	108	★★★★
Love in the Blended Family	Clubb	1	1.23	13	★★★
Old Loyalties, New Ties	Visher & Visher	1	1.28	42	★★★★★
Second Time Around, The	Janda & MacCormack	1	1.20	10	★★★
Shelter of Each Other, The	Pipher	3	1.43	14	★★★
Step by Step Parenting	Eckler	1	1.30	20	★★★★

Category and title	Author(s)	Study no.	Avg. rating	No. of raters	Guide rating
Stepfamilies	Bray & Kelly	3	1.71	7	♦
Step-Fathering	Rosin	1	1.10	21	★★★★
Strengthening Your Stepfamily	Einstein & Albert	1	1.10	10	★★★

Love and Intimacy

Art of Loving, The	Fromm	1	1.05	257	★★★★
Couples	Dym & Glenn	3	0.86	7	♦
Creating Love	Bradshaw	3	0.74	35	★★★
Dance of Intimacy, The	Lerner	1	1.23	145	★★★★
Do I Have to Give Up Me to Be Loved by You?	Paul & Paul	1	0.83	56	★★★
Going the Distance	Barbach & Geisinger	1	0.67	33	★★★
In the Meantime	Vanzant	3	1.50	8	♦
Love Cycle	Cutler	1	0.60	5	—
Love Is Never Enough	Beck	3	1.36	67	★★★★★
Love the Way You Want It	Sternberg	3	0.67	6	—
Loving Each Other	Buscaglia	1	0.31	94	★★
Mars and Venus in the Bedroom	Gray	3	−0.16	38	†
Men Who Can't Love	Carter	1	0.27	141	★★
Men Who Hate Women and the Women Who Love Them	Forward	1	0.29	141	★★
Obsessive Love	Forward	1	0.94	18	★★★
Return to Love, A	Williamson	3	0.60	15	★★★
Soul Mates	Moore	3	0.72	39	★★★
Triangle of Love, The	Sternberg	1	1.00	23	★★★★
What Every Woman Should Know about Men	Brothers	1	−0.94	48	†
What Smart Women Know	Carter & Sokol	1	0.09	11	★
When Someone You Love Is Someone You Hate	Arterburn & Stoop	1	0.10	10	★
Women Men Love, Women Men Leave	Cowan & Kinder	1	−0.17	29	†
Women Who Love Too Much	Norwood	1	0.64	194	★★★

Marriage

Divorce Busting	Weiner-Davis	3	1.04	24	★★★★
Getting the Love You Want	Hendrix	3	1.05	63	★★★★
Husbands and Wives	Kinder & Cowan	1	0.55	10	★★★
I Love You, Let's Work It Out	Viscott	3	0.90	10	★★★
Intimate Partners	Scarf	1	1.06	87	★★★★
Love for a Lifetime	Dobson	3	1.14	7	♦
We Love Each Other but . . .	Wachtel	3	1.40	5	♦
Why Marriages Succeed or Fail	Gottman	3	1.59	34	★★★★★

Men's Issues

Being a Man	Fanning & McKay	3	1.56	16	★★★
Fire in the Belly	Keen	1	0.61	86	★★★
Hazards of Being Male, The	Goldberg	1	0.81	63	★★★
Iron John	Bly	1	0.30	158	★★
Man Enough	Pittman	3	1.00	14	★★★

Category and title	Author(s)	Study no.	Avg. rating	No. of raters	Guide rating
Men's Issues *(cont.)*					
Measure of a Man, The	Shapiro	3	0.67	6	—
New Male, The	Goldberg	1	0.67	39	★★★
Real Boys	Pollack	3	1.48	25	★★★★
Seasons of a Man's Life	Levinson	1	1.05	222	★★★★
Ten Stupid Things Men Do to Mess Up Their Lives	Schlessinger	3	−0.50	22	†
What Men Really Want	Bakos	1	−0.12	25	†
Why Men Don't Get Enough Sex and Women Don't Get Enough Love	Kramer & Dunaway	1	0.10	20	★
Mood Disorders					
Cognitive Therapy and the Emotional Disorders	Beck	1	1.16	198	★★★★★
Control Your Depression	Lewinsohn et al.	3	1.28	36	★★★★★
Feeling Good	Burns	1	1.51	254	★★★★★
Feeling Good Handbook, The	Burns	1	1.38	116	★★★★★
Getting Un-Depressed	Emery	1	0.93	42	★★★
Good News about Depression, The	Gold	1	1.01	50	★
How to Cope with Depression	DePaulo & Ablow	1	0.65	20	★★★
How to Stubbornly Refuse to Make Yourself Miserable about Anything	Ellis	3	0.84	31	★★★
Listening to Prozac	Kramer	3	0.57	83	★★★
Mind over Mood	Greenberger & Padesky	3	1.43	61	★★★★★
Self-Help Guide to Managing Depression, A	Baker	3	1.13	8	—
When Feeling Bad Is Good	McGrath	3	1.04	27	★★★★
When Living Hurts	Yapko	3	1.15	27	★★★★
When the Blues Won't Go Away	Hirschfield	1	0.62	13	★★★
You Can Beat Depression	Preston	3	1.23	13	★★★
You Mean I Don't Have to Feel This Way?	Dowling	1	0.44	16	★★
Zoloft, Paxil, Luvox, & Prozac	Sullivan	3	0.17	6	—
Pregnancy					
Complete Book of Pregnancy and Childbirth, The	Kitzinger	1	1.41	39	★★★★★
Expectant Father, The	Brott & Ash	3	1.40	5	♦
From Here to Maternity	Marshall	1	0.80	10	★★★
Girlfriend's Guide to Pregnancy, The	Iovine	3	1.00	6	♦
Pregnancy after 35	McCauley	1	0.90	20	★★★
Pregnancy, Childbirth, and the Newborn	Simkin	1	0.83	6	—
Well Pregnancy Book, The	Samuels & Samuels	1	0.87	15	★★★
What to Eat When You're Expecting	Eisenberg et al.	1	1.00	16	★★★
What to Expect When You're Expecting	Eisenberg et al.	3	1.56	43	★★★★★
Will It Hurt the Baby?	Abrams	1	1.00	5	—

Category and title	Author(s)	Study no.	Avg. rating	No. of raters	Guide rating
Schizophrenia					
Coping with Schizophrenia	Mueser & Gingerich	3	1.22	9	◆
How to Cope with Mental Illness in Your Family	Marsh & Dickens	3	1.08	12	★★★
Surviving Schizophrenia	Torrey	3	1.25	40	★★★★★
Understanding Schizophrenia	Keefe & Harvey	3	1.17	6	◆
Self-Management and Self-Enhancement					
All I Really Needed to Know I Learned in Kindergarten	Fulghum	3	0.78	89	★★★
Awaken the Giant Within	Robbins	3	0.00	14	★
Changing for Good	Prochaska et al.	3	1.17	23	★★★★
Chicken Soup for the Soul	Canfield & Hansen	3	0.72	100	★★★
Do It! Let's Get Off Our Butts	McWilliams	1	−0.06	9	—
Don't Blame Mother	Caplan	1	1.00	20	★★★★
Don't Sweat the Small Stuff . . . and It's All Small Stuff	Carlson	3	1.06	95	★★★★
Emotional Intelligence	Goleman	3	0.97	118	★★★
Feel the Fear and Do It Anyway	Jeffers	1	1.24	25	★★★★
Gentle Roads to Survival	Auw	1	0.70	10	★★★
How to Live 365 Days a Year	Schindler	1	0.58	12	★★★
How to Stop Worrying and Start Living	Carnegie	1	0.15	65	★
I'm O.K, You're O.K.	Harris	1	0.60	318	★★★
Learned Optimism	Seligman	1	1.27	89	★★★★★
Life's Little Instruction Book	Brown	3	0.82	33	★★★
Making Life Right When It Feels All Wrong	Fensterheim	1	0.78	18	★★★
New Guide to Rational Living, A	Ellis & Harper	1	1.12	238	★★★★
Overcoming Procrastination	Ellis & Knaus	1	1.00	69	★★★★
Positive Addiction	Glasser	1	0.82	89	★★★
Positive Illusions	Taylor	1	1.23	13	★★★
Power of Optimism, The	McGinnis	1	0.27	11	★★
Power of Positive Thinking, The	Peale	1	0.22	153	★
Self-Defeating Behaviors	Cudney & Hardy	1	0.80	10	★★★
7 Habits of Highly Effective People, The	Covey	1	1.28	67	★★★★★
60-Second Shrink, The	Lazarus & Lazarus	3	0.97	30	★★★
Spontaneous Healing	Weil	3	1.10	41	★★★★
Staying Rational in an Irrational World	Bernard	1	0.91	71	★★★
Steps to the Top	Zigler	1	0.13	23	★
Success Is a Choice	Pitino & Reynolds	3	1.33	9	◆
Talking to Yourself	Butler	1	0.80	18	★★★
Tough Times Never Last but Tough People Do	Schuller	1	0.41	42	★★

Category and title	Author(s)	Study no.	Avg. rating	No. of raters	Guide rating
Self-Management and Self-Enhancement (*cont.*)					
Unlimited Power	Robbins	1	0.54	14	★★★
What to Say When You Talk to Yourself	Helmstetter	1	1.10	21	★★★★
What You Can Change and What you Can't	Seligman	3	1.27	59	★★★★★
Winner Within, The	Riley	3	0.43	7	—
You Can't Afford the Luxury of a Negative Thought	John-Rogers & McWilliams	1	0.44	6	—
Your Erroneous Zones	Dyer	1	0.37	169	★★
Your Maximum Mind	Benson	1	0.47	25	★★
Sexuality					
Becoming Orgasmic	Heiman & LoPiccolo	1	1.79	9	♦
Dr. Ruth's Guide to Erotic and Sensuous Pleasures	Westheimer & Lieberman	1	−0.42	47	†
Dr. Ruth's Guide to Good Sex	Westheimer	1	−0.66	65	†
Family Book About Sexuality, The	Calderone & Johnson	3	1.60	5	♦
For Each Other	Barbach	3	1.69	29	★★★★
For Yourself	Barbach	1	1.87	17	★★★
Illustrated Manual of Sexual Therapy	Kaplan	3	1.19	41	★★★★
Making Love: A Man's Guide	White	1	0.81	27	★★★
Making Love: A Woman's Guide	Davis	1	0.77	26	★★★
Male Sexuality	Zilbergeld	1	1.89	18	★★★
New Joy of Sex, The	Comfort	1	0.99	173	★★★
Permanent Partners	Berzon	1	1.64	5	♦
Seven Weeks to Better Sex	Renshaw	3	1.00	8	♦
Sexual Awareness	McCarthy & McCarthy	3	1.67	12	★★★
Soul of Sex, The	Moore	3	0.80	10	★★★
What Really Happens in Bed	Carter & Coopersmith	1	0.80	15	★★★
Spiritual and Existential Concerns					
Be (Happy) Attitudes, The	Schuller	1	0.23	21	★
Care of the Soul	Moore	3	0.87	62	★★★
Celestine Prophecy, The	Redfield	3	0.28	76	★★
Clear Body, Clear Mind	Hubbard	1	−1.62	62	†
Dianetics	Hubbard	1	−1.77	187	†
Finding Flow	Csikszentmihalyi	3	1.32	25	★★★★
Flow	Csikszentmihalyi	1	0.57	43	★★★
From Beginning to End	Fulghum	3	0.60	5	—
Further Along the Road Less Traveled	Peck	3	0.93	61	★★★
Illuminata	Williamson	3	1.13	8	♦
Man's Search for Meaning	Frankl	1	1.27	260	★★★★★
Peace, Love, and Healing	Siegel	1	1.13	66	★★★★
Road Less Traveled, The	Peck	1	1.03	285	★★★★
Scientology	Hubbard	1	−1.88	173	†
Search for Significance, The	McGee	3	1.11	9	♦
Seven Spiritual Laws of Success, The	Chopra	3	0.63	32	★★★

Category and title	Author(s)	Study no.	Avg. rating	No. of raters	Guide rating
Spiritual Healing	Grayson	3	1.20	5	—
Way of the Wizard, The	Chopra	3	−0.20	10	†
When All You Ever Wanted Isn't Enough	Kushner	1	1.20	72	★★★★
Stress Management and Relaxation					
Beyond Chaos	West	1	0.83	6	—
Beyond the Relaxation Response	Benson	1	1.22	135	★★★★
Cool Cats, Calm Kids	Willliams & Burke	3	0.83	6	—
Each Day a New Beginning	Hazelden Foundation	1	1.05	34	★★★★
Inner and Outer Peace through Mediation	Singh	3	1.60	5	◆
Male Stress Syndrome, The	Witkin-Lanoil	1	0.68	22	★★★
Minding the Body, Mending the Mind	Borysenko	3	1.21	48	★★★★
No Gimmick Guide to Managing Stress	Neidhart	1	0.88	8	—
Relaxation and Stress Reduction Workbook, The	Davis et al.	3	1.52	81	★★★★★
Relaxation Response, The	Benson	1	1.28	212	★★★★★
Staying on Top When Your World Is Upside Down	Cramer	1	1.50	8	—
Stress and Relaxation Handbook, The	Madders	3	1.36	47	★★★★★
Stresses	Curran	1	0.89	9	—
Touchstones	Hazelden Foundation	1	0.90	30	★★★
Wellness Book, The	Benson & Stuart	3	1.26	38	★★★★★
Wherever You Go, There You Are	Kabat-Zinn	3	1.45	53	★★★★★
Why Zebra's Don't Get Ulcers	Sapolsky	3	1.19	21	★★★★
Teenagers and Parenting					
All Grown Up and No Place to Go	Elkind	1	1.20	49	★★★★
Between Parent and Teenager	Ginott	1	1.34	181	★★★★★
Bringing Up Parents	Packer	3	1.25	8	◆
Positive Parenting Your Teens	Joslin & Decher	3	1.54	11	★★★
Preparing for Adolescence	Dobson	3	0.36	11	★★
Reviving Ophelia	Pipher	3	1.42	87	★★★★★
Surviving Adolescence	Dumont	1	0.95	21	★★★
Toughlove	York et al.	1	0.54	124	★★★
What Teenagers Want to Know about Sex	Boston Children's Hospital et al.	3	1.00	6	◆
When Living Hurts	Gordon	3	1.25	12	★★★
You and Your Adolescent	Sternberg & Levine	3	1.00	11	★★★
Weight Management					
Beverly Hills Diet, The	Mazel	1	−1.35	61	†
Carbohydrate Addict's Diet, The	Heller & Heller	1	−1.09	34	†
Diet Center Program, The	Ferguson	1	−0.83	35	†
Diet for a Small Planet	Lappe	1	0.44	78	★★

Category and title	Author(s)	Study no.	Avg. rating	No. of raters	Guide rating
Weight Management *(cont.)*					
Dr. Abravanel's Anti-Craving Weight-Loss Diet	Abravanel & King	1	−1.05	22	†
Dr. Atkins' Diet Revolution	Atkins	1	−0.97	58	†
Dr. Atkin's New Diet Revolution	Atkins	3	0.00	28	★
Eat More, Weigh Less	Ornish	3	0.92	25	★★★
Eight Weeks to Optimum Health	Weil	3	1.30	27	★★★★
Fat Is a Feminist Issue	Orbach	3	1.12	41	★★★★
5-Day Miracle Diet, The	Puhn	3	−1.20	15	†
LEARN Program for Weight Control, The	Brownell	3	1.58	12	★★★
Make the Connection	Greene & Winfrey	3	1.07	14	★★★
New Fit of Fat, The	Bailey	1	0.69	65	★★★
One Meal at a Time	Katahn	1	0.00	21	★
Pritkin Program for Diet and Exercise, The	Pritkin	1	0.02	80	★
Rotation Diet, The	Katahn	1	−0.62	47	†
Sugar Busters	Steward et al.	3	0.58	12	★★★
T-Factor Diet, The	Katahn	1	−0.22	41	†
35-Plus Diet for Women, The	Spodnik & Gibbons	1	−0.90	19	†
Zone, The	Sears	3	0.33	27	★★
Women's Issues					
Backlash	Faludi	1	0.87	47	★★★
Body Traps	Rodin	3	1.18	17	★★★
Chicken Soup for the Woman's Soul	Canfield et al.	3	1.00	25	★★★★
Juggling	Crosby	1	0.75	8	—
Life Preservers	Lerner	3	1.17	6	◆
Making It Work	Houston	1	1.00	6	—
My Mother/Myself	Friday	1	0.59	187	★★★
New Our Bodies, Ourselves, The	Boston Women's Health Book Collective	3	1.54	81	★★★★★
Seasons of a Woman's Life, The	Levinson & Levinson	3	1.20	25	★★★★
Second Shift, The	Hochschild	1	1.39	28	★★★★
Secrets about Men Every Woman Should Know	DeAngelis	1	−0.42	19	†
Silent Passage, The	Sheehy	3	0.96	67	★★★
Too Good for Her Own Good	Bepko & Krestan	1	1.26	16	★★★
We Are Our Mother's Daughters	Roberts	3	0.81	26	★★★
Women on Top	Friday	3	0.25	8	—
Women Who Run with the Wolves	Estes	3	0.95	58	★★★

Ratings of Autobiographies in the National Studies

Only those autobiographies rated five or more times in our national studies are included in this list. Some books appear on this list but were not included in the text because they were rated by fewer than eight mental health experts. Please consult Appendix A for details on the methodology of the national studies and the meaning of the guide ratings.

Category and title	Author(s)	Study no.	Avg. rating	No. of raters	Guide rating
Abuse					
Child Called "It," A	Pelzer	4	1.00	9	★★★
Daddy's Girl	Allen	4	0.92	25	★★★
Secret Life	Ryan	2	0.54	13	★★★
Sleepers	Carcaterra	4	0.78	9	★★★
Triumph Over Darkness	Wood	4	0.60	5	—
Addictive Disorders and Codependency					
Both Sides of Recovery	Harrison & Harrison	4	1.00	5	—
Codependent No More	Beattie	2	1.00	142	★★★★
Drinking: A Love Story	Knapp	2	1.00	16	★★★
Drinking Life, A	Hamill	2	1.07	29	★★★★
Getting Better: Inside AA	Robertson	2	1.10	28	★★★★
Note Found in a Bottle	Cheever	4	1.14	7	◆
Now You Know	Dukakis	2	0.60	32	★★★
Portraits of Recovery	Gaynor	4	1.00	6	—

Category and title	Author(s)	Study no.	Avg. rating	No. of raters	Guide rating
Adult Development and Aging					
Fountain of Age, The	Friedan	4	0.96	23	★★★
Getting Over Getting Older	Pogrebin	4	1.00	7	♦
Tuesdays with Morrie	Albom	4	1.58	59	★★★★★
Virtues of Aging, The	Carter	4	1.24	17	★★★★
Anxiety Disorders					
Afraid of Everything	Woods	2	0.89	9	★★★
Flock, The	Casey & Wilson	4	0.71	7	—
Memoirs of an Amnesiac	Levant	2	0.93	14	★★★
Mind of My Own, A	Sizemore	2	1.00	8	★★★★
Panic Attack Recovery Book, The	Swede & Jaffe	4	1.25	12	★★★
Phantom Illness	Cantor & Fallon	2	0.89	9	★★★
Sybil	Schreiber	4	0.32	91	★★
When Rabbit Howls	Chase	2	0.48	48	★★
Attention-Deficit/Hyperactivity Disorder					
ADHD Handbook for Families	Weingartner	4	1.15	13	★★★
Maybe You Know My Kid	Fowler	4	1.14	7	♦
Parenting a Child with ADHD	Boyles & Contadino	4	1.06	16	★★★★
Death and Grieving					
After the Death of a Child	Finkbeiner	4	1.30	10	★★★
Grief Observed, A	Lewis	4	1.58	36	★★★★★
Letting Go	Schwartz	4	1.14	7	♦
Motherless Daughter	Edleman	4	1.35	23	★★★★
Wheel of Life, The	Kübler-Ross & Gold	4	0.75	8	—
Dementia/Alzheimer's					
Alzheimer's, A Love Story	Davidson	4	1.14	7	♦
Diminished Mind, The	Tyler & Anifantakis	1	0.87	23	★★★
Elegy for Iris	Bayley	4	1.20	5	♦
Eating Disorders					
Am I Still Visible?	Heater	2	1.09	11	★★★
Diary of a Fat Housewife	Green	2	1.00	14	★★★
Good Enough	Bitter	4	0.86	7	♦
Inner Hunger	Apostolides	4	0.60	5	—
Starving for Attention	O'Neill	2	0.91	22	★★★
Wasted	Hornbacher	4	0.33	6	—
Mood Disorders					
Beast, The	Thompson	2	0.90	10	★★★
Bell Jar, The	Plath	4	0.86	87	★★★
Breakdown	Sutherland	2	0.62	8	★★★
Brilliant Madness, A	Duke & Hochman	2	1.08	48	★★★★

Category and title	Author(s)	Study no.	Avg. rating	No. of raters	Guide rating
Call Me Anna	Duke	2	0.85	39	★★★
Darkness Visible	Styron	2	1.34	71	★★★★★
Daughter of the Queen of Sheeba	Lyden	4	1.14	7	◆
Girl, Interrupted	Kaysen	2	1.22	41	★★★★
Leaves from Many Seasons	Mowrer	2	1.06	16	★★★★
Loony-Bin Trip, The	Millett	2	0.07	13	★
Pain	Anderson	2	0.93	14	★★★
Prozac Nation	Wurtzel	2	0.49	37	★★
Undercurrents	Manning	2	1.11	25	★★★★
Unquiet Mind, An	Jamison	2	1.39	49	★★★★★

Schizophrenia

Angel at My Table, An	Frame	2	0.70	10	★★★
Autobiography of a Schizophrenic Girl	Conroy	4	0.67	9	★★★
Beyond All Reason	Coate	2	0.75	12	★★★
Eden Express, The	Vonnegut	2	0.89	53	★★★
Father, Have I Kept My Promise?	Weisskopf-Joelson	2	0.88	8	★★★
Nobody's Child	Balter & Katz	2	0.90	29	★★★
Out of the Depths	Boisin	2	1.27	22	★★★★
Quiet Room, The	Schiller & Bennett	4	0.64	11	★★★
Too Much Anger, Too Many Tears	Gotkin & Gotkin	2	1.12	16	★★★★
Welcome, Silence	North	2	1.08	12	★★★
When the Music's Over	Gates & Hammond	2	0.88	8	★★★

Weight Management

Breaking Free from Compulsive Eating	Roth	4	1.59	22	★★★★
Feeding the Hungry Heart	Roth	4	1.35	37	★★★★★
You Can't Quit Until You Know What's Eating You	Leblanc	4	0.20	5	—

Women's Issues

Deborah, Golda, and Me	Pogrebin	4	1.09	11	★★★
Mothers: A Celebration	Stoddard	4	1.00	5	◆

Ratings of Movies in the National Studies

Only those movies rated five or more times in our national studies are included in this list. Some movies appear on this list but were not included in the text because they were rated by fewer than 10 mental health experts. Please consult Appendix A for details on the methodology of the national studies and the meaning of the guide ratings.

Category and title	Study no.	Avg. rating	No. of raters	Guide rating
Abuse				
Color Purple, The	5	1.24	245	★★★★
Mommie Dearest	5	0.34	149	★★
Prince of Tides, The	5	−0.02	245	†
Radio Flyer	5	1.00	41	★★★★
Sleeping with the Enemy	5	0.60	134	★★★
Thelma and Louise	5	0.40	229	★★
This Boy's Life	5	1.14	49	★★★★
What's Love Got to Do with It?	5	0.88	83	★★★
Addictive Disorders and Codependency				
Cat on a Hot Tin Roof	5	0.99	171	★★★
Clean and Sober	5	1.19	90	★★★★
Days of Wine and Roses	5	1.37	167	★★★★★
Drugstore Cowboy	5	0.75	76	★★★
Gambler, The	5	0.53	30	★★★
Jungle Fever	5	0.61	54	★★★
Leaving Las Vegas	5	0.88	154	★★★

Category and title	Study no.	Avg. rating	No. of raters	Guide rating
Mask	5	0.89	121	★★★
My Name is Bill W.	5	1.22	54	★★★★
Postcards from the Edge	5	0.68	108	★★★
When a Man Loves a Woman	5	1.03	80	★★★★
Adult Development and Aging				
Christmas Carol, A	5	0.89	170	★★★
Cocoon	5	0.92	247	★★★
Doctor, The	5	1.28	88	★★★★★
Field of Dreams	5	0.96	252	★★★
It's a Wonderful Life	5	1.22	246	★★★★
On Golden Pond	5	1.47	307	★★★★★
Trip to the Bountiful, The	5	1.42	124	★★★★★
Anxiety Disorders				
As Good as It Gets	5	1.16	267	★★★★
Born on the Fourth of July	5	0.97	148	★★★
Deer Hunter, The	5	0.76	175	★★★
Fearless	5	0.89	44	★★★
Full Metal Jacket	5	0.52	103	★★★
High Anxiety	5	−0.03	127	†
Sybil	5	0.79	159	★★★
What about Bob?	5	0.15	244	★
Child Development and Parenting				
Big	5	0.71	192	★★★
Little Man Tate	5	1.02	94	★★★★
Parenthood	5	0.69	115	★★★
Searching for Bobby Fischer	5	1.19	108	★★★★
Splendor in the Grass	5	0.71	82	★★★
Communication and People Skills				
Children of a Lesser God	5	1.26	182	★★★★★
Dead Poets Society	5	1.11	284	★★★★
He Said, She Said	5	0.44	57	★★
Death and Grieving				
Accidental Tourist, The	5	0.84	146	★★★
Ghost	5	0.37	209	★★
Lion King, The	5	0.62	176	★★★
My Girl	5	0.50	30	★★★
My Life	5	0.93	40	★★★
Ordinary People	5	1.49	281	★★★★★
River Runs through It, A	5	1.15	214	★★★★
Steel Magnolias	5	1.18	220	★★★★
Summer of '42, The	5	0.77	170	★★★
Dementia/Alzheimer's				
Do You Remember Love?	5	1.20	10	★★★
Memories of Me	5	0.90	10	★★★

Category and title	Study no.	Avg. rating	No. of raters	Guide rating
Divorce				
Bye Bye Love	5	0.53	17	★★★
First Wives' Club	5	0.19	196	★
Four Seasons, The	5	0.93	115	★★★
Good Mother, The	5	0.88	40	★★★
Kramer vs. Kramer	5	1.24	280	★★★★
Mrs. Doubtfire	5	0.57	266	★★★
Unmarried Woman, An	5	1.02	94	★★★★
War of the Roses, The	5	−0.05	203	†
Eating Disorders				
Best Little Girl in the World	5	1.19	31	★★★★
Eating	5	1.00	25	★★★★
For the Love of Nancy	5	0.64	11	★★★
Karen Carpenter Story, The	5	1.25	76	★★★★★
Families and Stepfamilies				
Father of the Bride, The	5	0.67	169	★★★
Fly away Home	5	1.15	62	★★★★
Joy Luck Club, The	5	1.43	196	★★★★★
Radio Flyer	5	1.02	43	★★★★
Rain Man	5	1.15	274	★★★★
Terms of Endearment	5	1.19	256	★★★★
What's Eating Gilbert Grape?	5	1.14	133	★★★★
Love and Intimacy				
Four Seasons, The	5	0.97	116	★★★
9½ Weeks	5	−0.67	127	†
Pretty in Pink	5	0.36	103	★★
Sleepless in Seattle	5	0.55	259	★★★
Way We Were, The	5	0.73	174	★★★
When Harry Met Sally	5	0.94	289	★★★
Men's Issues				
City Slickers	5	0.67	208	★★
Fields of Dreams	5	1.11	245	★★★★
I Never Sang for My Father	5	1.48	80	★★★★★
Nothing in Common	5	0.90	40	★★★
October Sky	5	1.31	48	★★★★★
Rape of Richard Beck, The	5	0.50	20	★★★
Tootsie	5	0.66	246	★★★
Mood Disorders				
'Night, Mother	5	1.10	42	★★★★
Slender Thread, The	5	0.94	16	★★★
Pregnancy				
Baby M.	5	0.00	13	★
Father of the Bride II	5	0.12	92	★
Nine Months	5	0.02	41	★
Steel Magnolias	5	0.77	168	★★★

Category and title	Study no.	Avg. rating	No. of raters	Guide rating
Schizophrenia				
Benny and Joon	5	0.97	93	★★★
Birdy	5	1.18	66	★★★★
Fisher King, The	5	1.02	150	★★★★
Mad Love	5	0.06	17	★
Shine	5	1.14	149	★★★★
Sexuality				
Boys in the Band, The	5	0.77	107	★★★
Carnal Knowledge	5	0.51	123	★★★
9½ Weeks	5	−0.22	112	†
Paris Is Burning	5	0.80	46	★★★
Torch Song Trilogy	5	1.22	81	★★★★
Teenagers and Parenting				
Breakfast Club, The	5	1.16	198	★★★★
Circle of Friends	5	1.11	71	★★★★
Dead Poets Society	5	1.23	275	★★★★
Good Will Hunting	5	1.03	275	★★★★
Little Women	5	1.10	156	★★★★
My Bodyguard	5	0.83	93	★★★
Pretty in Pink	5	0.63	102	★★★
Powder	5	0.66	47	★★★
St. Elmo's Fire	5	0.49	121	★★
Sixteen Candles	5	0.62	97	★★★
Stand by Me	5	1.35	185	★★★★★
Women's Issues				
Eating	5	1.00	26	★★★★
How to Make an American Quilt	5	1.02	102	★★★★
League of Their Own, A	5	1.18	190	★★★★
My Breast	5	0.70	10	★★★
Piano, The	5	0.88	235	★★★
Thelma and Louise	5	0.63	244	★★★

References

Ackerson, J., Scogin, F., McKendree-Smith, N., & Lyman, R. D. (1998). Cognitive bibliotherapy for mild and moderate adolescent depressive symptomatology. *Journal of Consulting and Clinical Psychology, 66,* 685–690.

Albom, M. (1997). *Tuesdays with Morrie.* New York: Doubleday.

Clifford, J. S., Norcross, J. C., & Sommer, R. (1999). Autobiographies of mental health clients: Psychologists' uses and recommendations. *Professional Psychology: Research and Practice, 30,* 56–59.

Cuijpers, P. (1997). Bibliotherapy in unipolar depression: A meta-analysis. *Journal of Behavior Therapy and Experimental Psychiatry, 28,* 139–147.

Cuijpers, P. (1998). A psychoeducational approach to the treatment of depression: A meta-analysis of Lewinsohn's "Coping with Depression" course. *Behavior Therapy, 29,* 521–533.

DiBlassio, J., Simonin, D., DeCarolis, A., Morse, L., Jean, J., Vassalotti, L., Franks, K., & Chambliss, C. (1999, April). *Assessing the quality of psychological healthcare sites available on the Internet.* Poster presented at the 70th annual meeting of the Eastern Psychological Association, Providence, RI.

Eisenberg, D. M., Davis, R. B., Ettner, S. L., Appel, S., Wilkey, S., Rompay, M. V., & Kessler, R. C. (1998). Trends in alternative medicine use in the United States, 1990–1997. *Journal of the American Medical Association, 280,* 1575–1589.

Gabbard, G. O., & Gabbard, K. (1999). *Psychiatry and the cinema* (2nd ed.). Washington, DC: American Psychiatric Press.

Gergen, K. (1991). *The saturated self.* New York: Basic Books.

Gould, R. A., & Clum, G. A. (1993). A meta-analysis of self-help treatment approaches. *Clinical Psychology Review, 13,* 169–186.

Grohol, J. M. (1999) *The insider's guide to mental health resources online.* New York: Guilford Press.

Hesley, J. W., & Hesley, J. G. (1998). *Rent two films and let's talk in the morning: Using popular movies in psychotherapy.* New York: Wiley.

Kurtzweil, P. L., Scogin, F., & Rosen, G. M. (1996). A test of the fail-safe N for self-help programs. *Professional Psychology: Research and Practice, 27,* 629–630.

Lawrence, S., & Giles, C. L. (1999). Accessibility of information on the web. *Nature, 400,* 107–109.

Lezak, M. D. (1995). *Neuropsychological assessment.* New York: Oxford University Press.

Marrs, R. W. (1995). A meta-analysis of bibliotherapy studies. *American Journal of Community Psychology, 23*, 843–870.

Morgenstern, J., Labouvie, E., McCrady, B. S., Kahler, C. W., & Frey, R. M. (1997). Affiliation with alcoholic anonymous after treatment: A study of its therapeutic effects and mechanisms of action. *Journal of Consulting and Clinical Psychology, 65*, 768–777.

Ouimette, P. C., Finney, J. W., & Moos, R. H. (1997). Twelve-step and cognitive-behavioral treatment for substance abuse: A comparison of treatment effectiveness. *Journal of Consulting and Clinical Psychology, 65*, 230–240.

Project MATCH Research Group. (1997). Matching alcoholism treatments to client heterogeneity: Project MATCH posttreatment drinking outcomes. *Journal of Studies on Alcohol, 58*, 7–29.

Rosen, G. M. (1987). Self-help treatment books and the commercialization of psychotherapy. *American Psychologist, 42*, 46–51.

Rosen, G. M. (1993). Self-help or hype? Comments on psychology's failure to advance self-care. *Professional Psychology: Research and Practice, 24*, 340–345.

Rosen, R. D. (1977). *Psychobabble.* New York: Atheneum.

Santrock, J. W., Minnett, A. M., & Campbell, B. D. (1994). *The authoritative guide to self-help books.* New York: Guilford Press.

Scogin, F. (1998). Bibliotherapy: A nontraditional intervention for depression. In P. E. Hartman-Stein et al. (Eds.), *Innovative behavioral healthcare for older adults: A guidebook for changing times* (pp. 129–144). San Francisco: Jossey-Bass.

Scogin, F., Bynum, J., & Calhoun, S. (1990). Efficacy of self-administered treatment programs: Meta-analytic review. *Professional Psychology: Research and Practice, 21*, 42–47.

Scogin, F., Floyd, M., Jamison, C., Ackerson, J., Landreville, P., & Bissonnette, L. (1996). Negative outcomes: What is the evidence on self-administered treatments? *Journal of Consulting and Clinical Psychology, 64*, 1086–1089.

Scogin, F., Hamblin, D., & Beutler, L. (1987). Bibliotherapy for depressed older adults: A self-help alternative. *Gerontologist, 27*, 383–387.

Seligman, M. E. P. (1995). The effectiveness of psychotherapy. *American Psychologist, 50*, 965–974.

Skow, J. (1999). Lost in cyberspace. *Time*, p. 61.

Solomon, G. (1995). *The motion picture prescription.* Santa Rosa, CA: Aslan.

Sommer, R., Clifford, J. S., & Norcross, J. C. (1998). A bibliography of mental patients' autobiographies: An update and classification system. *American Journal of Psychiatry, 155*, 1261–1264.

Tonigan, J. S., Toscoova, R., & Miller, W. R. (1995). Meta-analysis of the literature on alcoholic anonymous: Sample and study characteristics moderate findings. *Journal of Studies on Alcohol, 57*, 65–72.

van Lankveld, J. J. D. M. (1998). Bibliotherapy in the treatment of sexual dysfunctions: A meta-analysis. *Journal of Consulting and Clinical Psychology, 66*, 702–708.

Watson, A. L., & Sher, K. J. (1998). Resolution of alcohol problems without treatment: Methodological issues and future directions of natural recovery research. *Clinical Psychology: Science and Practice, 5*, 1–18.

Wedding, D., & Boyd, M. A. (1999). *Movies and mental illness: Using films to understand psychopathology.* New York: McGraw-Hill.

Weekes, C. (1996). Bibliotherapy. In C. G. Lindemann (Ed.), *Handbook of the treatment of the anxiety disorders* (2nd ed., pp. 375–384). Northvale, NJ: Jason Aronson.

Author and Title Index

Subject Index

Boldface indicates main text discussion; *t* indicates a table.